WI ☞ S0-BLV-261

DATE DUE

JUN 13			

Migrants to the Metropolis

Space, Place, and Society
John Rennie Short, *Series Editor*

OTHER TITLES IN SPACE, PLACE, AND SOCIETY

Alabaster Cities: Urban U.S. since 1950
John Rennie Short

Becoming a Geographer
Peter Gould

*The Boundless Self: Communication
in Physical and Virtual Spaces*
Paul C. Adams

Geography Inside Out
Richard Symanski

*Inventing Black-on-Black Violence: Discourse,
Space, and Representation*
David Wilson

New Worlds, New Geographies
John Rennie Short

*The Politics of Landscapes in Singapore:
Constructions of "Nation"*
Lily Kong and Brenda S. A. Yeoh

Tel Aviv: Mythography of a City
Maoz Azaryahu

Verandahs of Power: Colonialism and Space in Urban Africa
Garth Andrew Myers

*Women, Religion, and Space: Global Perspectives
on Gender and Faith*
Karen M. Morin and Jeanne Kay Guelke, eds.

Migrants
to the
Metropolis

The Rise of Immigrant Gateway Cities

Edited by MARIE PRICE and LISA BENTON-SHORT

SYRACUSE UNIVERSITY PRESS

Copyright © 2008 by Syracuse University Press
Syracuse, New York 13244-5160

First Edition 2008

08 09 10 11 12 13   6 5 4 3 2 1

The paper used in this publication meets the minimum requirements
of American National Standard for Information Sciences—Permanence
of Paper for Printed Library Materials, ANSI Z39.48–1984.∞™

For a listing of books published and distributed by Syracuse University Press,
visit our Web site at SyracuseUniversityPress.syr.edu.

ISBN-13: 978-0-8156-3161-3 (cloth)   ISBN-10: 0-8156-3161-8 (cloth)
ISBN-13: 978-0-8156-3186-6 (pbk.)   ISBN-10: 0-8156-3186-3 (pbk.)

Library of Congress Cataloging-in-Publication Data

Migrants to the metropolis : the rise of immigrant gateway cities / edited by Marie Price and
Lisa Benton-Short. — 1st ed.
p. cm. — (Space, place, and society)
Papers originally presented at a workshop held at George Washington University in January 2006.
Includes bibliographical references and index.
ISBN 978-0-8156-3161-3 (hardcover : alk. paper) — ISBN 978-0-8156-3186-6 (pbk : alk. paper)
1. Emigration and immigration—Congresses.   2. Emigration and immigration—Social aspects—
Congresses.   3. Cities and towns—Congresses.   I. Price, Marie.   II. Benton-Short, Lisa.
JV6201.M53 2008
307.76—dc22
2008011118

Manufactured in the United States of America

Contents

FIGURES | *vii*

TABLES | *ix*

ACKNOWLEDGMENTS | *xi*

CONTRIBUTORS | *xiii*

1. Migrants to the Metropolis: The Rise
   of Immigrant Gateway Cites, an Introduction
   LISA BENTON-SHORT and MARIE PRICE | *1*

2. Urban Immigrant Gateways in a Globalizing World
   MARIE PRICE and LISA BENTON-SHORT | *23*

PART ONE | Established Gateways

3. New York City: America's Classic Immigrant Gateway
   NANCY FONER | *51*

4. Sydney: The Globalization of an Established Immigrant Gateway
   GRAEME HUGO | *68*

5. DiverCity Toronto: Canada's Premier Gateway City
   LUCIA LO | *97*

6. The Non–"Global City" of Birmingham, UK: A Gateway Through Time
   CHERYL McEWAN, JANE POLLARD, and NICK HENRY | *128*

7. Amsterdam: A Multicultural Gateway?
   ANNEMARIE BODAAR | *150*

PART TWO | **Emerging Gateways**

8. Gateway Singapore: Immigration Policies, Differential (Non)Incorporation, and Identity Politics
   BRENDA S. A. YEOH and NATALIE YAP | *177*

9. Washington, D.C.: From Biracial City to Multiethnic Gateway
   ELIZABETH CHACKO | *203*

10. Dublin: An Emerging Gateway
    MARY GILMARTIN | *226*

11. Mean Streets: Johannesburg as an Emergent Gateway
    JONATHAN CRUSH | *255*

PART THREE | **Exceptional Gateways**

12. In the Margins of Riyadh: Indonesian Domestic Workers in Saudi Arabia
    RACHEL SILVEY | *283*

13. Immigrants and Natives in Tel Aviv: What's the Difference?
    DAVID BARTRAM | *301*

14. Keeping the Gateway Shut: Regulating Global City-ness in Seoul
    YEONG-HYUN KIM | *322*

15. São Paulo: Historic Immigrant Gateway to Contemporary Emigrant Outpost
    EMILY SKOP and SARAH ZELL | *345*

APPENDIX: Cities with More Than 100,000 Foreign-Born | *371*
REFERENCES | *377*
INDEX | *425*

Figures

1.1. World foreign-born, 1960–2005 | 3

1.2. Case-study cities | 7

2.1. Annual net-migration rates of selected countries, 2000–2005 | 24

2.2. Toronto foreign-born, 2001 | 29

2.3. Cities with 1 million or more foreign-born | 43

2.4. Cities with more than 100,000 foreign-born | 44

3.1. New York City foreign-born, 2000 | 58

4.1. Sydney: Growth of total and non-English-speaking overseas-born populations, 1911–2001 | 71

4.2. Sydney: Birthplace composition, 1947–2001 | 73

4.3. Sydney: Vietnam-born as a percentage of total population, 2001 | 79

4.4. Sydney: China-born as a percentage of total population, 2001 | 80

4.5. New South Wales: Permanent departures of Australia-born, 2004–2005 | 83

4.6. Sydney statistical division: Net internal and international migration, 1971–2000 | 85

4.7. Structural adjustment model of the relationship between internal and international migration | 93

5.1. Immigrant settlement patterns in the Toronto CMA, 2001 | 104

5.2. Settlement patterns of recent immigrants to Toronto, 1971 | 106

5.3. Settlement patterns of recent immigrants to Toronto, 2001 | 107

5.4. Dominant immigrant groups in the Toronto CMA, 2001 | 110

6.1. Foreign-born population of Birmingham, 2001 | 133

6.2. City of Birmingham | 138

6.3. The pagoda, Birmingham | 144

7.1. Composition of foreign-born in the Netherlands | 157

7.2. Distribution of foreign-born in Amsterdam, 2001 | 158

7.3. Ghanaians in the Bijlmermeer | 170

vii

9.1. Distribution of Korean foreign-born, 2000 | *206*

9.2. Distribution of Ethiopian foreign-born, 2000 | *207*

9.3. Washington, D.C., foreign-born country of origin, 2000 | *209*

9.4. Korean stores and signage in the Great World Plaza, Annandale, Virginia | *216*

9.5. Salome Ethiopian restaurant on U Street, Washington, D.C. | *221*

10.1. *Famine* (1997), by sculptor Rowan Gillespie | *227*

10.2. Nationality of immigrants to Ireland, 1995–2005 | *229*

10.3. Birthplace of foreign-born residents of Dublin, 2002 | *232*

10.4. Percentage of non-Irish households in Dublin, 2002 | *233*

10.5. Moore Street, Dublin, July 2006 | *234*

10.6. Abbey Street, Dublin, July 2006 | *235*

11.1. Gender breakdown of migration | *266*

12.1. Growth of the foreign-born in Saudi Arabia, 1960–2005 | *289*

12.2. Composition of the foreign-born in Riyadh, 1997 | *290*

13.1. Composition of Tel Aviv district population | *309*

13.2. Foreign workers in a Tel Aviv market | *316*

13.3. Foreign-worker neighborhoods in Tel Aviv–Yafo, 1998 | *317*

14.1. Greater Seoul | *325*

14.2. Foreign labor force in South Korea, 1994–2005 | *330*

14.3. Ethnic business center in Ansan, Outer Seoul | *340*

14.4. Immigrant populations in Seoul and Outer Seoul | *341*

15.1. Immigration to São Paulo, 1820–2000 | *351*

15.2. Foreign-born residents in São Paulo by country of birth, 2000 | *356*

15.3. A Japanese store specializing in imported goods | *357*

15.4. Immigrants in São Paulo as a percentage of each *Area de Ponderaçao*, 2000 | *358*

15.5. Numerous labor-broker offices recruit *Nikkeijin* through advertisements in Brazil's major newspapers | *362*

Tables

3.1. Foreign-born population of New York City, 1900–2000 | *52*

3.2. Top-fifteen source countries of the foreign-born, New York City, 2000 | *54*

4.1. Sydney: First- and second-generation immigrant populations, 1981–2001 | *72*

4.2. Representation and growth of major overseas birthplace groups, 1981, 1991, and 2001, in Sydney | *74*

4.3. Sydney statistical division: Internal migration by birthplace, 1996–2001 | *86*

4.4. Sydney statistical division: Industry by birthplace by year of arrival, 2001 | *92*

5.1. Origins of the Toronto CMA's immigrant population, 2001 | *101*

5.2. Toronto's visible minority population between 1981 and 2001 | *102*

5.3. Concentration of main immigrant groups, 2001 | *112*

5.4. Index of dissimilarity, 2001 | *114*

5.5. Percentage of employment and location quotients by industry and immigrant status, 2001 | *117*

6.1. Worldwide place of birth of Birmingham's population, 2001 | *139*

7.1. Ethnic composition of Amsterdam, first generation only, 2006 | *155*

7.2. Population of Southeast Amsterdam by ethnicity, 2000 | *167*

8.1. Changing proportion of citizens to foreign nonresidents in Singapore, 1947 to the present | *180*

8.2. Resident population by ethnic group and residential status, 2000 | *182*

8.3. Foreign workers in Singapore, 1970–2000 | *184*

8.4. Different eligibility schemes for employment-pass holders | *186*

9.1. Foreign-born population by region of origin, 2000 | *208*

10.1. Migration to and from Ireland, 1995–2005 | *228*

10.2. Resident nationalities in Ireland and Dublin, 2002 | *231*

10.3. Work permits issued in Ireland, 1999–2005 | *241*

10.4. Top-five countries receiving work permits in Ireland, 2002–2005 | *241*

10.5. Asylum applications in Ireland, January 1992–November 2005 | *243*

11.1. Region of birth of Johannesburg migrants, 2001 | *257*

11.2. Country of birth of Johannesburg migrants, 2001 | *258*

11.3. Legal immigration to South Africa, 1990–2004 | *259*

11.4. Work permits issued and renewed, 1990–2001 | *261*

11.5. Refugee applications in South Africa by country of origin,
1994–2004 | *263*

13.1. Foreign workers in Israel | *311*

14.1. Population in Seoul and Outer Seoul, 1949–2005 | *326*

14.2. Foreign labor force in Korea | *335*

14.3. Countries of origin of illegal migrant workers in Korea, 2002 | *336*

14.4. Documented foreign nationals in Seoul and Outer Seoul,
1970–2004 | *337*

14.5. Countries of origin of documented foreign nationals in Greater Seoul,
2004 | *342*

14.6. Gender in documented foreign nationals in Greater Seoul, 2004 | *342*

15.1. Immigration to São Paulo, by nationality, 1884–1923 | *349*

15.2. Number of foreign-born residents by country of birth in São Paulo,
2000 | *354*

Acknowledgments

This book would not have been possible without the generosity of the George Washington Center for the Study of Globalization, directed by Dr. John Forrer. A series of grants from the center provided initial support for our research on global cities and the immigrants who reside and work in them. In 2002 we received a small grant to begin collecting data at the urban scale on immigrant destinations around the world. That project led to the development of the globalization, urbanization, and migration Web site that posts data on more than 150 metropolitan areas around the world, as well as relevant tables, maps, and articles (http://www.gstudynet.org/gum). The Web site was developed through a collaboration with the Department of Geography and the George Washington Center for the Study of Globalization. The following graduate students at George Washington University assisted us in the research and data collection: Sapna Shaw, Jenny Brown, Devin Keithly, Patrick Ryan, and Kaitlin Yarnall.

Because of this research, we were convinced that the number and range of urban immigrant destinations were growing and a more detailed analysis was needed. In January 2006 a grant from the George Washington Center for the Study of Globalization allowed us to convene a dialogic workshop at George Washington University to bring together scholars and policy makers to explore how immigrants were transforming cities around the world. Most of the original papers in this collection were first presented and discussed at that workshop. In addition to the contributing authors, several individuals enthusiastically participated in the two-day event, providing commentary and critique of the various papers. Our thanks to John Forrer and Jennifer Brinkerhoff of George Washington University; Doris Meissner of the Migration Policy Institute; Mark Miller,

University of Delaware; Katharyne Mitchell, University of Washington; John Rennie Short of the University of Maryland–Baltimore County; and Audrey Singer of the Brookings Institution for their contributions. Patrick Ryan, a masters student in the Department of Geography, coordinated many of the administrative details of the workshop and continued to work with us throughout the manuscript production process. His time, commitment, and research skills were instrumental in our research, and we are deeply indebted to him.

Additional grants from the George Washington Center for the Study of Globalization supported the production of this manuscript. We are especially grateful to Nuala Cowan, manager of the George Washington Department of Geography Spatial Analysis Lab, for the many maps and figures she produced quickly, with humor and good spirits. During 2006 Marie Price was a visiting scholar at the Migration Policy Institute (MPI). While at MPI, many staff members and interns offered their expertise in helping us develop key themes in understanding the role of cities as central to the story of migration. Our thanks to Demetrios Papademetriou, Michael Fix, Doris Meissner, Kathleen Newland, Deborah Meyers, Kirin Kalia, and Jeanne Batalova at MPI. Two MPI interns, Esha Clearfield and Jennifer Smyers, did a superb job copyediting various drafts of these chapters.

Finally, any book requires a substantial amount of time, usually at the expense of family. We can't begin to thank the men in our lives for their unqualified love and support—John, Rob, Joe, and James.

Contributors

DAVID BARTRAM is a senior lecturer in sociology at the University of Leicester. His primary interests are in foreign workers in Israel, Finland, and Japan. His most recent book is *International Labor Migration: Foreign Workers and Public Policy*. He is currently writing about migration and happiness, reflecting on the natural assumption that people are better off for having succeeded in gaining entry to a wealthy country.

LISA BENTON-SHORT is an associate professor of geography at George Washington University. Her research focuses primarily on cities, and current research interests include cities and global change, urban migration, urban environmental issues, and urban public space. Her work has appeared in journals such as the *Annals of the Association of American Geographers, Urban Geography, International Journal of Urban and Regional Research, Society and Space,* and *GeoJournal.* Her books include *Cities and Nature* (with John Rennie Short), *Environmental Discourse and Practice* (coauthored with John Rennie Short), and *The Presidio: From Army Post to National Park.*

ANNEMARIE BODAAR is a PhD student at the Department of Geography at Ohio State University. She is also a policy advisor for the City of the Hague, where she is responsible for developing and monitoring citizenship policies. She is interested in questions of immigration and the city, specifically in the investigation of immigrant incorporation and urban policy, and questions of identity and place, public space and ethnicity, and multiculturalism. Her most recent article is "Multicultural Urban Space and the Cosmopolitan 'Other': The Contested Revitalization of Amsterdam's Bijlmermeer."

ELIZABETH CHACKO is an associate professor of geography and international affairs at George Washington University. Her research interests include the transformation of cities owing to the process of globalization and migration, using case studies from the United States and India. She has studied the creation and maintenance of ethnic space by new immigrant groups and identity formation and retention among recent immigrant populations such as the Ethiopian community in the United States. Elizabeth has published on these issues in various scholarly journals and is coauthor of the book *Contemporary World Regional Geography: Global Connections, Local Voices.*

JONATHAN CRUSH is a Queen's Research Chair and professor of global development studies at Queen's University and honorary professor in the Department of Environmental and Geographical Sciences at the University of Cape Town. He is the director of the Southern African Migration Project (http://www.queensu.ca/samp) and has published extensively in the migration and development field. He is currently coordinating a major international research project on migration, urban food security, and HIV/AIDS. He has written numerous articles and authored or edited several books, including *Power of Development, Transnationalism and New African Immigration to South Africa,* and *Destinations Unknown: Perspectives on the Brain Drain in Southern Africa.*

NANCY FONER is a distinguished professor of sociology at Hunter College and the Graduate Center of the City University of New York. She has thirteen books to her credit, including *From Ellis Island to JFK: New York's Two Great Waves of Immigration, Not Just Black and White: Historical and Contemporary Perspectives on Immigration, Race, and Ethnicity in the United States* (edited with George Fredrickson), and *In a New Land: A Comparative View of Immigration.*

MARY GILMARTIN is a lecturer in geography at the National University of Ireland, Maynooth. Her research focuses on issues of migration and citizenship in Ireland, and she has helped organize the Migration and Citizenship Research Initiative at the University College–Dublin.

NICK HENRY recently left his position as reader in urban and regional studies at Newcastle University in the United Kingdom to lead the regional economic development team in the Birmingham office of GHK Consulting. He undertakes research and policy evaluation of European, UK, and regional public policy. He is coauthor of *Motorsport Going Global: The Challenges Facing the World's Motorsport Industry.*

GRAEME HUGO is a professor of geography at the University of Adelaide in Australia. He is the author of numerous books, articles, and chapters in books. He is coauthor of *Worlds in Motion: Understanding International Migration at the End of the Millennium.* His research interests include immigration and urbanization in Australia and Asia.

YEONG-HYUN KIM is an associate professor of geography at Ohio University. Her research interests lie in urban and economic geography. Her most recent book is *Cities and Economies* (coauthored with John Rennie Short). She is currently studying ethnic Korean migrants returning from China to South Korea.

LUCIA LO is an associate professor of geography at York University in Canada. Her current research focuses on the impact of ethnocultural diversity on urban economies and immigrant economic incorporation, examining issues ranging from ethnic economies and ethnic consumer behavior to settlement patterns and human services provisions. She has also written extensively on Chinese immigrants in Toronto.

CHERYL McEWAN is a senior lecturer in human geography at Durham University in the United Kingdom. Recent research projects have examined issues of multiculturalism in Birmingham, UK, and gender, citizenship, culture, and "empowerment" in postapartheid South Africa. She is author of *Gender, Geography, and Empire* and coeditor (with Alison Blunt) of *Postcolonial Geographies.*

JANE POLLARD is a senior lecturer in the Centre for Urban and Regional Development Studies and the School of Geography, Politics, and Sociology at Newcastle University in the United Kingdom. Recent research projects have examined issues of muliticulturalism in Birmingham, the development of Islamic finance, and the financial architecture of clusters. She is coeditor of *Knowledge, Space, Economy.*

MARIE PRICE is an associate professor of geography and international affairs at George Washington University. A Latin American specialist, her research has explored human migration, regional development, and globalization. Her current research focuses on transnational migration and its impact on cities. She has written numerous articles in journals such as the *Annals of the Association of American Geographers, Geographical Review, Urban Geography, International Journal of Urban and Regional Research,* and *GeoJournal.* She is also coauthor of the textbooks *Diversity amid Globalization: World Regions, Environment, and Development,* now in its fourth edition, and *Globalization and Diversity: Geography of a Changing World,* now in its second edition. In 2006 she was a visiting scholar at the Migration Policy Institute in Washington, D.C.

RACHEL SILVEY is an associate professor in the Department of Geography and Program in Planning at the University of Toronto. Her work focuses on migration, Indonesia, feminist theory, critical development studies, and the politics of transnationalism. Her expertise is in the gender dimensions of migration and economic change in Indonesia, and her recent research focuses on the ways in which the gender politics of Indonesian migration to the Gulf states is inflected by Islam. Her work has been published in geography, migration, and gender studies journals, including the *Annals of the Association of American Geographers, Political Geography, Women's Studies International Forum,* and *World Development.*

EMILY SKOP is an assistant professor in the Department of Geography and Environmental Studies at the University of Colorado at Colorado Springs. She is an urban and population geographer with interests in international migration processes and patterns; the social and spatial constructions of racial, ethnic, and gender identities; and urbanization, segregation, and inequality in the contexts of the United States and Latin America. Her explorations of the migrant experience have been published in journals such as *International Migration Review; Geographical Review; Population, Space, and Place; Professional Geographer;* and *Yearbook of the Association of Pacific Coast Geographers.*

BRENDA S. A. YEOH is a professor of geography at National University of Singapore as well as research leader of the Asian Migration Research Cluster. Her research interests include the politics of space in colonial and postcolonial cities and gender, migration, and transnational communities. Her books include *Contesting Space: Power Relations and the Urban Built Environment in Colonial Singapore, Singapore: A Developmental City State* (with Martin Perry and Lily Kong), *Gender and Migration* (with Katie Willis), and *Migration and Health in Asia* (with Santosh Jatrana and Mike Toyota).

SARAH ZELL is a PhD student in human geography at the University of British Columbia. Her research interests include international migration patterns, transnationalism and the nation-state, return migration and diasporic identity, and labor recruitment and the migration industry, with specific focus on North America and Latin America.

Migrants to the Metropolis

1

Migrants to the Metropolis

The Rise of Immigrant Gateway Cites, an Introduction

LISA BENTON-SHORT and MARIE PRICE

New York Times journalist Thomas Friedman (2005) asserts that economic globalization has leveled the global playing field—having a flattening effect. Through technological advances, free trade, outsourcing, offshoring, and supply chaining, advantages such as location and relative and absolute distances seem to matter less now as far-flung places in the world are intricately connected to and compete with each other. Yet the metaphor of the "flat" earth ignores the sheer unevenness with which these changes are occurring. Rather than a flat surface, globalization has produced scores of plateaus and peaks—the global city regions—that rise above the surrounding terrain. The highest peaks are those cities that serve as the command and control centers of the global economy, such as London, New York, and Tokyo. It is the uneven impact of globalization that drives, in part, the global immigration patterns detailed in this book. As the metaphorical high ground, global cities are linked to each other by the flow of capital, technology, information, and trade. Yet such urban agglomerations also attract people in the search for employment, opportunity, and services. The world is now half urban, and it is this international movement of people, both between global immigrant cities and from the surrounding hinterlands to these cities, that inspired us to assemble this book.

By focusing on the movement of people to metropolitan areas, we hope to shift the scale of analysis away from borders and states and onto cities where immigrants tend to settle. All of the metropolises in this study are large, at least 1 million people, and most of these cities are homes to tens of thousands, if not millions, of immigrants. We call these cities immigrant gateways and assert that the number of these cities and the diversity of people within them are growing in response to the globalization of immigration. The immigrant gateways of the twenty-first century are not all alike, as this book demonstrates, but the movement of people to these cities creates similar changes and tensions in the socioeconomic, cultural, and political life of each city.

Globalization, the growth of cities, and the global movement of people are increasingly interrelated processes (Sassen 1988; Sassen 2002; Beaverstock et al. 2000). For most migration scholars, the state is the container of convenience. The United Nations, for example, collects and publishes state-level data estimating the world's migrant stock (United Nations, Department of Economic and Social Affairs, Population Division, 2006b). These data show an absolute growth in the number of immigrants, although proportionally they represent less than 3 percent of the global population (fig. 1.1). Yet the lived experience for both immigrants and residents alike unfolds at a much smaller scale, in neighborhoods, cities, and metropolitan areas. Most contemporary economic immigrants go to cities that are increasingly linked to the global economy (Ellis 2006; Castles and Miller 2003, 7–8; Waldinger 1996). For North America, Europe, the Middle East, and Australia, immigration is a quintessentially urban phenomenon.

Of course, immigration scholars do study cities, and there is a burgeoning literature on intercity migration, the mobility of transnational business elites, unskilled labor flows, and the role of cities in shaping policy and settlement patterns (Fan 2002; Ley and Tutchener 2001; Beaverstock and Smith 1996; Castells 1996; Light 2006). There are also hundreds of studies on individual cities such as Toronto, New York, Sydney, and Singapore (Anisef and Lanphier 2003; Foner 2000; Burnley 1998; Yeoh and Chang 2001); particular immigrant groups in cities, such as Ethiopians in Washington, D.C. (Chacko 2003), the Surinamese in Amsterdam (Duerloo and Musterd 2001), and the Vietnamese in Sydney (Wilson 1989); and global diasporas of particular ethnic groups (Sowell 1996; Nyiri and Saveliev 2003; Carney and Voeks 2003). Collectively, these writings provide important contributions to understanding the dynamics of globalization, cities, and migration,

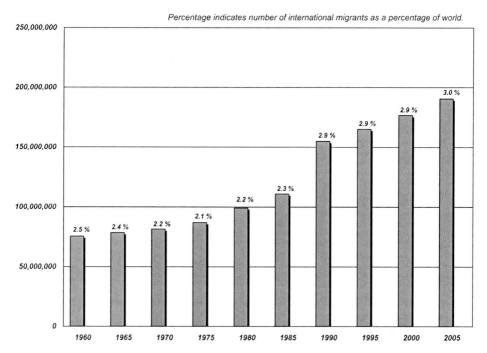

Fig. 1.1. World foreign-born, 1960–2005. *Source:* United Nations, 2005.

yet individually they focus on a narrow range of migrants or on a few select cities. A comprehensive picture of the world's urban immigrant destinations does not exist (Benton-Short, Price, and Friedman 2005).

In order to fill this gap, a dialogic workshop was convened at George Washington University in January 2006 to explore the relationship between global cities and immigration. From this workshop we selected thirteen cities from eight different world regions. The chapters examine ethnic composition, map patterns of settlement, and explore how these metropolitan areas benefit from, struggle with, and seek to manage large numbers of foreign-born people. Whereas many people are aware of established immigrant cities such as New York, Sydney, and Toronto, many scholars and policy makers would be hard pressed to identify the top twenty immigrant destinations in the world. How many would list Dubai, Riyadh, Hong Kong, Singapore, and Washington, D.C., as major immigrant gateways? How many would recognize cities such as Amsterdam, Frankfurt, and

Perth as places where more than one in four residents are foreign-born? In Chapter 2 our research on the global distribution of immigrants in cities will be laid out as a means to contextualize the gateway cities examined in the book, but for now the relationship between immigration and world cities deserves closer scrutiny.

IMMIGRATION AND WORLD CITIES

Cities are the command and control centers of globalization and the destinations for most immigrants. Initially, global-cities research privileged a few large cities such as London, Tokyo, New York, and Los Angeles (Sassen 1991; Beaverstock, Smith, and Taylor 1999; Dear 2002). Over time, however, the literature on global cities has geographically expanded (Sassen 2002), yet much of the analysis still focuses on a limited range of economic and technological factors. Moreover, as John Rennie Short has noted, the search for world city-ness has bent the research toward the top end of the urban hierarchy, limiting the discussion to a narrow range of world cities and world-city functions (2004, 295).

Although much of the literature regarding the impact of globalization on world cities disproportionately weighs economic power, there are signs that global-cities research is expanding beyond the focus on economic criteria. For example, Samers (2002) calls for an inclusion of a different set of networks, such as international labor migration and urban labor markets in global-cities analysis. *Foreign Policy*'s annual globalization index (of countries, alas, not cities) now considers four categories of criteria: economic integration (foreign direct investment, trade, and capital flows), political engagement (membership in international organizations, number of embassies, and international treaties ratified), technological connectivity (Internet users, Internet hosts, and secure servers), and personal contact (international travel and tourism, international telephone traffic, and cross-border transfers such as remittances). However, there is still much to be done to analyze the cultural, political, and social aspects of globalization, particularly with regards to the movement of people.

A survey of migration by the *Economist* concluded that "it is impossible to separate the globalization of trade and capital from the global movement of people" ("The Longest Journey" 2002, 3). Stephen Castles and Mark Miller have held that "while movements of people across borders have shaped states and societies since time immemorial, what is distinctive in recent years is their global scope, their centrality to domestic and international politics and their enormous economic and social consequences" (2003, 1). Migratory networks have developed, intensifying the links between areas of origin and destination. Saskia Sassen concurs, noting that people who travel and move help shape the material and spiritual cultures of places: migration, therefore, should be seen as as central a component to globalization as trade and finance (1999, xi). Interestingly, migration was identified as an important factor in the original formulation of the world-city hypothesis of John Friedmann, who observed that "world cities are points of destination for large numbers of both domestic and/or international migrants" (1986, 75). The relationship between globalization and immigration makes a strong case for studying immigration in a range of world cities.

With the globalization of migration, most countries host more than one category of migrant, receiving a diverse range of skilled and unskilled immigrants (Castles and Miller 2003). As a result, many of the immigrants in this study are not considered permanent settlers, but instead are temporary (albeit necessary) laborers. For example, in Singapore there are citizens, residents and nonresidents, all of whom may live in the city for years, if not their entire lives. In Dubai, the most immigrant-dependent city in the world, four out of five of the city's residents are guest workers, yet many of them have labored for years to build one of the fastest-growing cities in the Middle East. Employment in both highly specialized labor and low-skilled service jobs is characteristic of global cities. Different types of labor demands result in different sources of migrant streams, as several of the essays here will show. The demand for unskilled labor, for example, tends to generate a regional flow, whereas high-skilled labor draws from a more global distribution. This is true for Singapore, Seoul, Tel Aviv, São Paulo, and Dublin. Both skilled and unskilled migration affect host cities and countries alike.

By linking globalization and immigration in thirteen cities, this edited collection identifies many overlooked immigrant gateways—such as Birmingham, Tel Aviv, Riyadh, and Johannesburg—where globalization as a "bottom-up" process is transforming urban social, political, and cultural space. The cities discussed in this book are situated on a continuum of immigrant experiences and rates of migration. Some cities remain remarkably closed to foreign labor (such as Seoul), whereas others are dependent on immigrants for more than half their labor force (Riyadh). Collectively, these cities illuminate the dynamics of migration to key urban areas, thus adding significantly to our understanding of urban immigrant gateways and the human networks that create and maintain them. In this collection we organize the gateway cities into three working categories: established, emerging, and exceptional. The significance of these categories will be developed in the next section.

THE RISE OF IMMIGRANT GATEWAY CITIES

Gateway cities warrant closer attention in immigration debates because they are the crucibles for an immigrant-driven expression of globalization that has profound economic, cultural, and political dimensions. Immigrants can contribute to the hyperdiversity and cosmopolitanism that make gateway cities distinct. Yet the visible difference of immigrants, coupled with the desire by state and local actors to control them, also produces urban spaces that are highly segregated and socially stratified along a continuum of native-born citizen to illegal migrant (Sassen 1999). To understand how twenty-first-century immigrant gateways function, it is important to recognize a range of outcomes in which immigrants can be integrated into the social, political, and economic life of a city or excluded in such a way that their presence is relatively muted.

The term *gateway* is increasingly found in sociology, history, and geography literature in reference to major urban immigrant destinations. The meaning of this ubiquitous term is assumed rather than systematically developed or conceptualized. In this book, our definition of an urban immigrant gateway recognizes that these cities are not only settlement points for immigrants but also critical entry points that draw from a wide range of sending countries, facilitate cultural exchange, and are nodes for the collection and dispersion of goods, capital, and people. Yet these gateways are often socially and spatially segregated places. For many immigrants, these cities are not endpoints but turnstiles, with migrants moving into and out of them.

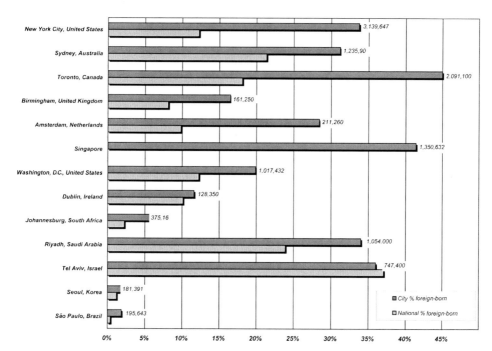

Fig. 1.2. Case-study cities. This graph compares the percentage of foreign-born in the case-study cities with the percentage of foreign-born at the national level. The absolute number of foreign-born is shown for each city. Adapted by the authors using various census data.

This book compares the experience of established immigrant cities such Toronto, Sydney, and New York with cities often ignored in either global-cities or immigration research, such as Tel Aviv, São Paulo, Riyadh, Seoul, and Singapore. Figure 1.2 compares the percentage of foreign-born in the thirteen cities with the percentage of foreign-born for that country as a whole. In every case (save Tel Aviv) the urban percentage of foreign-born far exceeds the national percentages. Seven cities in this study are places where more than one in five urban residents are foreign-born; five cities have more than 1 million foreign-born residents. At the other extreme, two global cities (Seoul and São Paulo) are metropolitan areas where less than 2 percent of the urban population is foreign-born. One of these cities is an immigrant destination in decline, whereas the other is just beginning to admit foreign labor.

ESTABLISHED GATEWAYS

Established gateways are those cities with large numbers of foreign-born and a percentage of foreign-born well above the national average for that country. These are well-known and studied immigrant destinations that have experienced significant levels of immigration for more than a century. The five established gateways in this collection are New York, Sydney, Toronto, Birmingham, and Amsterdam.

Because established gateways have a long history of receiving immigrants, the urban landscape has been continually reshaped by wave after wave of new migrants making their influence felt. Yet the volume and diversity of recent immigrant flows present challenges to local and national governments and service providers, unleashing new debates about multiculturalism, integration, and exclusion. In addition, whereas some immigrants continue to settle in traditional immigrant enclaves, others have chosen to settle in more dispersed or suburban locations. Thus, the spatial distribution of immigrants remains an important element to assess in both established and emerging gateways.

Nancy Foner's essay on New York discusses how established gateways result in an urban population with deep immigrant connections. Many New Yorkers trace their immigrant roots back one, two, three, or more generations. For this reason, she argues, New York is a particularly welcoming place for new immigrants. What is distinct about New York are the diversity and sheer numbers of immigrants (some 3 million in the city proper and more than 5 million in the metropolitan statistical area), making it the largest immigrant destination in the world. An established gateway with a continuous flow of immigrants, this city has layer upon layer of diversity in the landscape. The urban immigrant landscape is dynamic, which increases the level of acceptance of change in many neighborhoods. What was once an Irish immigrant enclave was transformed into a Russian one, and is now a Caribbean destination. Foner also explores how recent immigrants alter perceptions of race and ethnicity and influence social relations.

Graeme Hugo's essay draws on the enormous wealth of data on immigration to and emigration from Sydney. In addition to current trends, Hugo includes historical data that show the shifting composition of immigrants since the 1940s. Sydney is the preeminent gateway for international migrants to Australia, home to some 30 percent of the overseas-born population and 37 percent of those who have arrived in Australia since 2000. Intense and ongoing immigration has changed the spatial distribution of immigrants in Sydney into a more suburban ethnic mix rather than segregated ethnic enclaves in the urban core. Recent flows from Asia have dramatically changed the ethnic mix and increased the number of non-English-speaking Sydneysiders. Hugo also draws attention to the impact of nonpermanent migration, which has seen an exponential increase since the 1990s. Sydney is not just a city of reception; it also serves as an emigration gateway through which Australians leave the country. Hugo notes that Sydney has become an "escalator city," attracting young, skilled immigrants from elsewhere in Australia who then may leave for work abroad.

Lucia Lo's essay on Toronto highlights a city in which more than 44 percent of the inhabitants are foreign-born. During the past four decades, Toronto has become Canada's premier immigrant gateway, with more than 2 million foreign-born residents. Toronto is often touted as a model of multiculturalism and tolerance. Lo cautions, however, that the social and economic integration of immigrants in Toronto, particularly the large black population from the Caribbean and Africa, is poor. Although there has been considerable spatial integration of immigrants in this gateway city, their economic integration has been uneven. Lo's examination of the foreign-born and labor markets shows that many of Toronto's immigrants work in only a handful of industries, namely, construction, garment manufacturing, child care, accommodations, and food and beverage services. Many highly skilled immigrants, selected through Canada's point system, often are unable to find employment in their respective professions and work in low-skilled jobs instead.

Cheryl McEwan, Jane Pollard, and Nick Henry's essay on Birmingham presents an example of an established gateway that is often overlooked in world-cities research. They show that although Birmingham has experienced recent immigration, it was also an important immigrant gateway in the British imperial machine, attracting a variety of immigrants as early as the eighteenth and nineteenth centuries. The 1940s brought new patterns of migration from the Indian subcontinent. This historical analysis is important, they note, because the city's banking and industrial history still bear the imprint of older transnational flows of migrants. Today, Birmingham's ethnic diversity has been central to its economic redevelopment as a postindustrial city. For example, Birmingham produces and distributes halal baby food to the rest of the UK and into the European Union and has thus created a niche in the regional global economy by capitalizing on its immigrant diversity.

Amsterdam is another European city with a long history as an immigrant destination for a diverse range of immigrants. The essay by Annemarie Bodaar highlights the politics of scale when considering immigrant reception in a host society. For several decades the Dutch have fervently embraced multiculturalism and ethnic tolerance. But in the past few years, multiculturalism has been replaced by a more stringent integrationist approach aimed, particularly, at Muslim immigrants. The national discourse ignores practices and policies in ethnic neighborhoods such as Bijlmermeer, Amsterdam. There, ethnic differences are negotiated and new forms of living with diversity are being established. She concludes that cities and neighborhoods are the scale at which solutions to living with diversity will be found.

EMERGING GATEWAYS

The next section highlights emerging gateway cities. Emerging gateways are those cities with relatively recent immigrant flows, such as Singapore, Washington, D.C., Dublin, and Johannesburg. A common theme among these cities is that because mass immigration is relatively recent, these cities have wrestled with new ethnic communities, changes in the urban fabric, and questions of identity at both the urban and the national scale. The visible changes have often generated fierce debates about the appropriation of space from long-term residents by the newcomers. In addition, many of these emerging destinations lack the institutional services that are found in established gateways, and may be just beginning to establish organizations to assist in settlement and integration.

Brenda S. A. Yeoh and Natalie Yap's essay showcases Singapore's contemporary immigrant flows alongside its older colonial immigration heritage. They document how old migration streams were directly related to colonial politics and continue to be important sources of migrants today, notably coming from China and Malaysia. The Singaporean government has been keen to fashion the city-state as a selective immigrant gateway, primarily privileging transitional elites, while putting in place measures that prevent unskilled migrants from permanent settlement. Since the 1990s economic growth has generated a need for more unskilled labor, mostly from the Philippines and India, coming on temporary work permits. Yeoh and Yap note that the more recent arrivals have drawn attention to the ambiguous categories of citizen-noncitizen, resident-nonresident, noting that such categories are charged with identity politics.

Elizabeth Chacko explores migration trends in Washington, D.C. Immigration to metropolitan Washington has primarily occurred since the 1980s, transforming Washington from a "black and white" city to a multiethnic one. Immigrant trends in Washington, D.C., contradict the established Chicago model that assumes that immigrants first settle in inner-city ethnic enclaves, then with greater economic attainment move to the suburbs. Chacko notes that many immigrants in Washington first settle in the suburbs, with little ethnic clustering. There is, however, a marked geographic concentration of immigrant-owned businesses and services (but not residences), which she terms "sociocommerscapes." For example, Korean enterprises in suburban Annandale such as restaurants, karaoke bars, groceries, and video rental stores cater to a large, but dispersed, Korean clientele. Such spaces challenge the historical identity and ethnicity of what were once dominantly white suburbs. In contrast, Ethiopians have located their businesses in an economically depressed area of the District of Columbia. But this neighborhood has traditionally been the center of African American culture, and African Americans have resisted Ethiopians' efforts to have these new ethnic spaces designated as "Little Ethiopia."

Mary Gilmartin considers recent immigration in Dublin. Ironically, Ireland is consistently rated as among the most "globalized" countries in *Foreign Policy*'s annual globalization index. Although it is true that the intersection of capital and labor migration has redefined both Ireland and Dublin in particular, there remain few foreign-born in Dublin. On the surface, it could be argued that Dublin has been largely bypassed by immigrants; however, Gilmartin notes that since the 1990s, Dublin has been shifting from a city of net emigration to one of net immigration. The data show that there has been an increase in the number of migrants to Dublin, though many of these migrants are of Irish descent (that is, Americans who claim Irish ancestry) or British nationals. Yet there are signs that cultural diversity is increasing: there are now foreign-born from China, Nigeria, France, Poland, Romania, South Africa, and the Philippines, and their presence is visible in immigrant-run markets and pubs as well as food, beauty, and money-transfer services. Gilmartin notes that the shift from emigrant city to immigrant city has generated new debates about Irish citizenship and belonging. She examines the hidden or obscured landscapes of immigrants in Dublin, and the reactions to real and perceived immigrant-driven change that result from Dublin's new role as an emerging gateway. The essay concludes that Ireland's robust economic growth will likely create conditions for continued immigration to Ireland, and continued controversy and hostility toward the new migrant laborers.

The city of Johannesburg, once insular and isolated, has been redefined in the postapartheid global era. Jonathan Crush notes that although many predicted the end of apartheid would bring a flood of people into South Africa, this influx has not yet transpired, in part because the first postapartheid decade has been dominated by xenophobic and intolerant immigration policies. He notes that many of the prototypical features of a gateway city are emerging in Johannesburg; migration is on the rise. However, a distinguishing feature is the transience of the city's immigrant population. In Johannesburg many foreign-born residents are more "sojourners" than settlers, and they see the city as a turnstile to somewhere else. Some are escaping from war (Angola and the Democratic Republic of the Congo), and others from collapsing economies (Zimbabwe). Regardless, migration is helping to reshape the geography of the city. Skilled migrants go to the suburbs, unskilled migrants go to the townships, and refugees from Francophone and West Africa go to the inner city. The result is an uneven and contested spatial insertion of African immigrants into the city.

EXCEPTIONAL GATEWAYS

Our last section introduces cities that we call exceptional because they are often considered global cities but in regard to immigration they are exceptional because of their highly restrictive immigration policies or because they have been largely bypassed by the world's immigrants. We consider Riyadh, Tel Aviv, Seoul, and São Paulo in this section. One of the common themes shared by the first three case studies is the power of a strong central government to both regulate and restrict immigration through "temporary" labor systems that often work in opposition to long-term migration.

Rachel Silvey explores the connections between Indonesian female immigrants and the domestic labor they provide in Riyadh. The Kingdom of Saudi Arabia is one of the world's top immigrant destinations, home to more foreign-born people than Canada or the United Kingdom. Yet the policies of immigrant exclusion reduce the social and cultural impact of immigrants on the city's residents. As a result, Riyadh is an ethnically segregated city, and Saudi citizens are both socially and spatially distant from immigrants. Silvey notes that women, particularly Indonesians and Filipinas, constitute a significant part of the domestic labor force. These women reside in the homes of their employers and must conform to restrictive Saudi norms regarding female behavior, dress, and mobility. Consequently, they develop little knowledge of the city and remain politically excluded from and socially subordinated to the Saudis. In addition, the kingdom's immigration policy has been to encourage ethnically distinct temporary guest workers while simultaneously refusing immigrants the ability to apply for citizenship. Silvey concludes that Riyadh is a gateway of segregation rather than social incorporation.

David Bartram examines the position of Tel Aviv as an ambiguous gateway. Bartram begins by challenging migration scholars' vocabulary. What, he asks, is foreign-born? In Israel, the Jewish homeland, Jews are not "foreign," even if they were not born in Israel. Thus, Jews born outside of Israel are only "returning" to their homeland. His challenge of conventional terms reveals unexpected dimensions to identity politics among immigrants. Jewish immigrants are viewed as "compatriots" from the moment they arrive. They are granted instant citizenship, because in the mainstream Israeli perspective, being Jewish is a fundamental component of Israeli identity and citizenship. Bartram also notes that there are foreign-born in Tel Aviv and that recent immigration of large numbers of non-Jews has complicated debates about Israeli identity. Some recent immigrants are non-Jewish Russians who could not establish Jewish heritage. There are also noncitizen (non-Jewish) foreign workers, yet they are not considered immigrants either—they are temporary residents, who, it is assumed, will eventually return to their origin countries. These two groups—Russians and foreign workers—are challenging the nature of Israeli identify and citizenship while making Tel Aviv less of an exceptional gateway and more like an established one.

Yeong-Hyun Kim's essay explores the relative absence of labor migration and immigration in the global city of Seoul. Although Seoul has been recognized as a global city in terms of its economic power, it remains an exception to the common characteristics of global cities as hubs of cultural networks and diversity. Like the Singapore essay, this essay also shows the power of the state to effectively "shut the gate" to immigration. Kim notes that the Korean government has maintained highly restrictive policies on labor migration while simultaneously promoting Seoul as a "global city." In Seoul the foreign-born make up less than 1 percent of the population. On the surface it would appear that Seoul has been bypassed by immigrants. However, Kim documents that since the early 1990s Seoul has been receiving a small but growing number of migrant workers from developing countries in Asia, primarily China, Bangladesh, the Philippines, and Mongolia. Although Seoul is a long way off from being a multicultural, multiethnic society, the gate has been wedged open and change is occurring.

Emily Skop and Sarah Zell document the rise and fall of São Paulo from an immigrant destination to an emigrant outpost. In the last great age of migration (from the 1880s to the 1920s) São Paulo attracted more than 4 million immigrants, including Portuguese, Germans, Italians, Spanish, and Japanese. Whereas established gateways such as New York, Sydney, and London have continued to act as immigrant gateways throughout the late twentieth century and into the twenty-first century, other cities such as São Paulo no longer attract many immigrants. Skop and Zell note that since the 1960s, São Paulo has changed from a net importer to a net exporter of international migrants. Although there are some 400,000 foreign-born in São Paulo, this city functions primarily as a turnstile to the rest of the world, notably Japan, Europe, and the United States. Skop and Zell document the early-twentieth-century recruitment of Japanese to Brazil, and the more recent phenomenon of Brazilians of Japanese descent who return to work as unskilled labor in Japan as well as the largely undocumented flow of Brazilians to the United States. Skop and Zell conclude that we should not "write off" former immigrant gateways as "has-beens" because these cities remain part of migrant circuits.

TEN THEMES THAT UNITE AND DIVIDE GATEWAY CITIES

The examination of a diverse range of immigrant gateway cities invites comparison. Certainly, there is a tremendous difference between a metropolis such as New York, with more than 5 million foreign-born, and Seoul, home to 200,000 foreign-born residents. Yet even when comparing a quintessentially open city such as New York with a relatively closed one such as Seoul, it is possible to see similarities in how the foreign-born are described, distributed, and inserted into urban social and economic spaces. Based on a review of the urban immigration literature and the contributions of authors to this volume, we highlight ten themes that characterize gateway cities. Though each of these themes may not be applicable for all immigrant gateways, they are indicative of overall trends in the relationship between cities, immigration, and globalization.

1. The Hyperdiversity of Immigrant Gateways

At the dawn of the twentieth century, New York City was the premier gateway in the United States, yet nearly all the immigrants were European. The city was linguistically and ethnically diverse but not so racially. Now, at the dawn of the twenty-first century, many gateway cities are among the most racially and ethnically diverse places on the planet. Of the top-ten sending countries to metropolitan New York, only one is European, Italy (U.S. Census Bureau 2000). This hyperdiversity is characterized by cities where no one country of origin accounts for 25 percent or more of the immigrant stock and immigrants come from all regions of the world. London, for example, is one of the most hyperdiverse gateways. Its top sending country is India, which accounted for 8.9 percent of the city's foreign-born population in 2001. Together, thirteen more countries, including Bangladesh,

China, Germany, Ireland, Jamaica, Nigeria, South Africa, and the United States, account for half of the city's foreign-born population. Nearly every country in the world has an immigrant in London.

Not all immigrant gateways are hyperdiverse, but because of globalization the tendency is for immigrants to come from a broader range of sending counties and in the process create cities that are more racially and ethnically diverse. How native-born and newcomer cope with living in such increasingly diverse environments is one of the important themes explored in these essays.

2. The Episodic Nature of Gateway Cities

The population dynamics of immigrant flows in gateways are never static. Cities such as New York and Sydney have been continuous destinations for well over a century, though even in these celebrated examples annual and decadal flows vary considerably. Audrey Singer's study (2004) of immigration to U.S. cities examines a century of census data from 1900 to 2000. She develops a typology in which established gateways such as New York and Chicago continue to attract new arrivals, emerging immigrant gateways such as Atlanta and Washington, D.C., have formed, and older gateways such as Buffalo and Detroit have declined as immigrant destinations. She also notes that some gateway cities are reemerging as immigrant destinations after decades of decline, including Denver, Minneapolis, and Portland, Oregon.

In this collection, there are a mix of gateways: established, emerging, and exceptional. Gateways expand and contract owing to several factors. Some have to do with structural shifts in global, national, or regional economies. Others grow as immigrant destinations because of the power of immigrant social networks and the potential of the immigrant economy itself to absorb labor (Light 2006). And some rise and fall as a result of changes in national immigration policy or local responses to the foreign-born.

3. National Immigration Policies and Cities

Migration scholars Stephen Castles and Mark Miller contend that international migration's most lasting impact is on politics—at the local and national levels (2003, 255). In short, shifting national policies are extremely important in explaining the changing flows and composition of immigrants to cities around the world. Several essays in this book address the role of state-based immigration policy as it directly and indirectly shapes who enters the country and under what circumstances. Policy changes such as amendments to the 1965 Immigration and Nationality Act in the United States resulted in considerable increases in Asian and Latino immigrants to U.S. cities (Zolberg 2006). Similarly, the composition of immigrants to Australia radically changed with the ending of the "white" Australia policy (which made access to citizenship nearly impossible for nonwhite immigrants) and the formal acceptance of ethnic diversity in the Australian Citizenship Act of 1973 (Castles and Davidson 2000, 165–68). A dramatic shift in immigration trends resulted in the mid-1990s with the end of apartheid in South Africa. After decades of highly restrictive migration policies (both for the native-born blacks and African immigrants), Johannesburg and Cape Town are now emerging immigrant gateways, especially for Africans from neighboring states (Crush and McDonald 2002).

4. Expanding Categories of Entry

Many of the essays in this collection address the wide range of conditions upon which immigrants enter a country. The raw data on the number of foreign-born in a city say nothing about their classification and degree of permanency. In many countries around the world a caste-like system has developed that differentiates citizens, residents, nonresidents, temporary workers, trainees, students, guests, refugees, and undocumented or illegal immigrants. As countries compete for highly skilled labor and are compelled to control labor flows, particularly at the unskilled level, the number of entry categories has inflated along with an increase in the numbers of immigrants.

The rise of temporary workers is of particular interest in this collection. Several cities such as Singapore, Riyadh, Tel Aviv, and Seoul are explicit in admitting workers on a contract basis with no path to permanent residency or citizenship. Moreover, in established countries of immigration, such as the United States, the expansion of a guest-worker program over residency-based admission has been proposed by the George W. Bush administration as part of a larger immigration-reform effort. Viewing the foreign-born as "guests" rather than as future citizens has both economic and political benefits and costs. The impact is especially pronounced in cities where large numbers of noncitizen residents are concentrated. Thus, a significant percentage of urban residents in gateway cities are excluded from full political participation, discouraged from investing in their communities, and, in the case of the undocumented, fearful of expulsion.

5. Urban Immigration Policies

City governments and their residents have varying responses to the opportunities and problems resulting from new and diverse immigrant flows. Thus, cities are often the first to respond to new waves of immigrants and their needs by creating de facto immigration policies and institutions at the metropolitan level. Typically, urban planners and various nongovernmental associations respond to needs in housing, transportation, health care, and education. City officials can also make public space available for festivals and other events that display the cultural diversity of new residents or provide formal sites where immigrant day laborers can await employers. In some cases, urban governments can be proactive in formalizing the political status of noncitizen residents—for example, allowing noncitizens to vote in local elections or proactively arresting or detaining illegal immigrants. In the case of Los Angeles, growing intolerance toward immigrant poverty (reflected in overcrowded housing and more day-labor sites) has resulted in the heightened enforcement of existing industrial and housing regulations that, though not originally intended to restrict unwanted immigration, had the effect of doing so (Light 2006, 13).

The proactive role of urban actors and institutions in New York, Toronto, Birmingham, Amsterdam, and Dublin demonstrates that cities do become de facto policy makers in regards to immigrant social, economic, and spatial integration. Not all local policies seek to include or assist the foreign-born. In new destinations such as Johannesburg, xenophobia toward African newcomers has produced a climate in which the foreign-born fear deportation, violence, and arrest by local police.

6. *Issues of Identity*

In a globalizing world, most people have nested identities based on different scales of belonging. This point is especially true for immigrants, who often feel a dual or transnational identity based on their country of birth and their country of residence. Identity is further complicated by relocation to a new city in which one's particular ethnic or racial identity is forced to conform with the identity categories commonly used in that particular city. Thus, an immigrant from Latin America who perceives herself as white and European is likely to be reclassified as nonwhite and Hispanic in the United States.

For many of the contributing authors, questions of identity and belonging are essential parts of the immigrant urban experience. In the case of Singapore, which has a large ethnic Chinese population, newcomers from mainland China are easily differentiated from the native-born Chinese population and often discriminated against. In the case of Tel Aviv, Jewish newcomers are considered not immigrants or foreign-born but "returnees" who under Israeli law are entitled to settle and must be absorbed into the host society. Yet large numbers of Jews who arrived after 1990 from the former Soviet Union and Ethiopia are not so easily integrated into the dominant culture and thus challenge Israeli Jewish identity.

7. *Immigrants and Spatial Assimilation or Segregation*

Where immigrants reside or establish businesses has concrete spatial implications for a metropolitan area. As many of these essays show, emerging gateways may experience different settlement patterns than do established destinations such as New York or Toronto. In many cities, the majority of foreign-born are settling in the suburbs rather than the central city. The essays on Washington, D.C., Sydney, and Seoul confirm these patterns. This practice diverges from the historical pattern established during the last great wave of immigration in the early twentieth century when most immigrants settled in the inner city and may pose an interesting challenge to existing theories of immigrant spatial integration.

There are also profound examples of immigrant segregation, both imposed and chosen. In Toronto the majority of immigrants show very dispersed and decentralized settlement patterns, but a few country groups such as those groups from mainland China and Vietnam tend to self-segregate in relatively inexpensive housing in inner-city Chinatown. In Riyadh the majority of foreign laborers are segregated into company-provided worker housing, usually on the periphery of the city. In Johannesburg, Francophone and West African immigrants are clustered in the inner city, which is notorious for its dilapidated housing and high crime rates.

8. Gateways and New Socioeconomic Spaces

As the number and diversity of urban-bound immigrants increase, new social, cultural, and economic spaces are created. In cities such as Sydney, Toronto, Birmingham, and Washington, immigrant entrepreneurs have refashioned urban neighborhoods, introducing new industries, markets, restaurants, services, and commercial centers.

In Washington, D.C., though many immigrants are dispersed residentially, they have created ethnic commercial centers where coethnics congregate. The term *sociocommerscape* is used to define a dynamic landscape element in gateway cities. Sociocommerscapes are created by immigrant entrepreneurs, provide a visual expression of group presence and identity, and are often cited as an indicator of the cosmopolitan nature of a city. These same sociocommerscapes are not always welcomed by native residents, who worry about the changing ethnic representation of their neighborhoods and communities. In postindustrial Birmingham, South Asian, Chinese, and other immigrants have helped to transform a once declining urban economy into a more robust one that has grown because of the socioeconomic global networks of its foreign-born population. The example of Birmingham shows that through trade and immigration flows, a postindustrial city has become more thoroughly linked to the global economy.

9. Immigrants and Labor Markets

Perhaps the most researched aspect of the impact of immigrants on cities is the study of labor markets. In most of the cities in this book, immigrants constitute a higher percentage of the labor force than they do of the population as a whole. This fact is not surprising because most immigrants tend to be young and of working age. Moreover, there is a tendency for immigrant labor to be segmented into certain occupations.

Immigrants to Toronto have entered through a Canadian point system that tends to favor educated and skilled immigrants. The Toronto case reveals that immigrants of color are concentrated in particular sectors: manufacturing, accommodation, and food and beverage industries. They are underrepresented in government services, education, information, and cultural industries. The study of Riyadh shows a preference for hiring immigrant women to do domestic labor, particularly women from certain countries such as Indonesia and the Philippines. Migrant workers in Seoul are predominately found in manufacturing and entertainment; few opportunities exist for them elsewhere in the economy.

10. *Cities as Sites of Contestation*

Cities are not only destination points for immigrants. They are also the stages upon which the various impacts of immigrants are negotiated and contested. In every case study, the presence of ethnically distinct newcomers has produced reactions. In the extreme cases, xenophobia develops in which native-born residents blame immigrants for various social ills. In other cities, immigrant contributions to urban renewal and redevelopment simultaneously garner praise from local officials but disdain from residents, who may feel socially or economically threatened by immigrant success.

Because of the large numbers of immigrants, cities can also be sites of protest. In 2005 several French cities erupted as many immigrants and ethnic minorities (especially from North Africa) rioted in protest of their disenfranchisement from the dominant white French society. In the case of metropolitan Paris, immigrants tend to be highly concentrated in suburban housing projects that isolate them from many of the educational and employment opportunities found in the central city. In the fall of 2005, after a police incident involving ethnic youth, ethnic and immigrant North Africans took to the streets, burning cars and demanding better economic opportunities. A few months later, in the suburbs of Sydney, anti-Arab immigrant protests by white youths in a beach community attracted international attention.

And in the United States during the spring of 2006, there were scores of marches in cities across the country protesting a restrictive congressional bill that would had made undocumented immigrants felons, thus forcing mass deportations. The largest march was in Los Angeles, where more than 500,000 protesters (mostly immigrants from Mexico and Central America) peacefully rallied for recognition of their work and a path to citizenship (Balz and Fears 2006).

The cities explored in this collection will continue to be sites in which immigrants and native-born residents exchange and express their reactions to urban changes in a globalizing world. Inevitably, some of these expressions will be driven by racism and fear. However, immigrant gateways also have the potential to foster greater tolerance and understanding among ethnically and racially distinct peoples.

Collectively, gateway cities offer a vantage point from which to understand critical issues surrounding immigration, integration, and the globalized metropolitan areas to which immigrants are contributing. How residents and policy makers learn to navigate this diversity will shape local and national policy debates in the years ahead. In many ways the cities in this collection are unique in how they have experienced (or not experienced) significant and diverse immigration flows. At the same time, these cities share many common issues as they face the economic, political, and social consequences of migration.

The linking of immigration and cities is a view of globalization from below. This book is a first step in deepening the theoretical and empirical connections between a range of cities and the foreign-born that reside in them. The cities profiled here will enliven the conceptualization of urban immigrant gateways as vital cultural, political, and economic hubs in a global age. The flow of foreign labor to these localities is explained not by the "flattening" of the world but by the uneven distribution of material and human resources. Large cities attract a disproportionate number of the world's immigrants. By focusing on human migration at the metropolitan scale, it is possible to understand globalization as a bottom-up process, instigated, in part, by the agency of immigrants and the socioeconomic changes they summon.

2

Urban Immigrant Gateways in a Globalizing World

MARIE PRICE and LISA BENTON-SHORT

There is a constellation of urban immigrant gateways that links millions of immigrants to scores of cities around the world. As global migration patterns intensify and diversify, and as more immigrants move to cities, the established models of urban immigrant settlement and assimilation can no longer adequately explain new social, economic, and political spaces being created in a wide range of urban immigrant destinations. The aim of this chapter is threefold. First, the case is made for the value of studying large cities when examining immigration trends. Second, this chapter deepens conceptualizations of gateways in the twenty-first century, moving beyond the idea of gateways as simply places where immigrants settle. Finally, the last section maps out the major urban immigrant destinations in the world based on an analysis of census data from more than fifty countries.

"Migration today touches the lives of more people and looms larger in the politics and economics of more states than at any other time in the modern era," argues Demetrios Papademetriou, head of the Migration Policy Institute (2006, xv). All states are both senders and receivers of immigrants, but the intensity of these flows and rates of net migration vary greatly. Thus, countries such as the United States, Canada, and Saudi Arabia have high positive rates of net migration, whereas countries such as the Philippines, Mexico, and Pakistan have high negative rates of net migration (fig. 2.1). With the globalization of labor, both low-skilled and high-skilled workers are crossing state boundaries with the intention of living outside

23

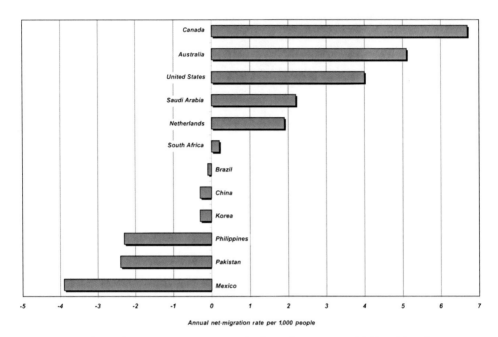

Fig. 2.1. Annual net-migration rates of selected countries, 2000–2005. *Source:* United Nations, 2006.

their country of birth for more than a year, and for our purposes are considered immigrants.

In cities around the world, but especially in western Europe, Australia, the Persian Gulf, and North America, immigrants play a fundamental role in the labor force and the social life of cities. For sending regions such as Africa, Asia, and Latin America, the remittances from laborers living in these cities are increasingly viewed as an essential component in household-livelihood strategies. By focusing on urban immigration and settlement in gateway cities it is possible to see how global processes become localized, from highly visible Chinese commercial districts to the enclaves of residential guest workers and the barely visible presence of foreign nannies in scattered suburban settings. By taking a global perspective, it becomes possible to distinguish new and emerging immigrant destinations, and how they are transforming the way people and places are linked.

Sociologists Mary Waters and Tomás Jimenez make the case that new gateways (at least in the U.S. context) may differ fundamentally from more established gateways and deserve closer examination. New gateways lack the institutional networks that accommodate the needs of newcomers because the cities previously lacked demand for such networks. Waters and Jimenez also highlight the "funds of knowledge" that experienced immigrants draw on when leaving established gateways to build and support communities in newer immigrant destinations. And, most important, they suggest that the lack of immigration history in emerging gateways means that the "place of immigrants in the class, racial, and ethnic hierarchies is less crystallized and immigrants may thus have more freedom to define their position" (2005, 117). For many cities around the world, one should not assume that the form and function of new urban immigrant destinations will necessarily replicate older patterns found in established gateways. In contrast to internal migrant flows, the growth in the number and percentage of the foreign-born in cities raises important questions about citizenship, identity, race, and the integration or exclusion of distinct groups of people. Although the vast majority of people in the world live in their county of birth, more and more cities in developed economies host large numbers of immigrants and rely on them to function. For North American and Australian cities the numbers are reminiscent of the early twentieth century, although the diversity of origin countries is far greater. For many European and Persian Gulf cities, both the scale and the diversity of the flows are relatively new phenomena. For all the major receiving countries, immigration has become one of the central political issues of our time and is likely to remain so, given the demographic and economic realities driving foreign labor flows (Castles and Miller 2003).

In many destination cities, there is also an inherent tension between the need for immigrant labor and the lack of desire for more settlers or new citizens. Many immigrants arrive in cities as part of temporary-worker programs. Cities in the Persian Gulf, Singapore, and East Asia (Japan, Korea, Hong Kong, and Taiwan) rely on contract-labor or worker-trainee programs that are designed to limit an immigrant's ability to politically or socially integrate into the host society. Yet, as has been shown time and time again, and despite the considerable efforts of state and local authorities, foreign labor is made up of real people with needs and reasons to form attachments to places and communities. It calls to mind Swiss playwright

Max Frisch's poignant observation, "Man hat Arbeitskräfte gerufen und es kommen Menschen" (We called for labor and people came instead). Regardless of status or intention, and even in locations where citizenship or permanency is aggressively denied, there is a tendency for immigrants to overstay or extend terms of entry, or simply to settle (legally or illegally). As their numbers increase, the foreign-born alter the socioeconomic fabric of the cities in which they stay.

WHY STUDY IMMIGRANT CITIES?

Immigration policy is the domain of national governments, and laws are created to determine under what status a foreign-born person may enter a country. Hence, there is a predisposition in migration research to compare countries and state-level data. Yet the localities that receive large numbers of immigrants are typically cities (Waldinger 1996; Pennix et al. 2004). What may be a workable policy at the national scale—say, allotting temporary-worker visas for low-skilled laborers—can become a local crisis when such workers need health care, housing, and education for their children. In a global age when capital and information freely cross borders, the movement of people is still highly regulated by the state, and policies can be altered dramatically in response to the needs of the labor market and sudden shifts in national security concerns. Moreover, Saskia Sassen makes the case that the very concept of citizenship is strained owing to large-scale immigration that calls into question nation-state membership (2006, 293).

The concept of the immigrant (or foreign-born) is a relatively modern one. Immigrants can exist only in a system of recognized territorial states that have the infrastructure to determine who are immigrants and the ability to enumerate them. The enumeration of immigrants varies greatly; states with long histories of immigrant settlement (Australia or Canada) tend to gather more data than states with limited experience with immigration (China or India). Today, most states collect data on the numbers of foreign-born residing in their borders, and the United Nations has provided comprehensive estimates of the foreign-born at the state level since the 1970s. Yet the same is not true for the enumeration of the foreign-born at the metropolitan or urban scale for cities around the world (Benton-Short, Price, and

Friedman 2005).[1] For countries that do track and make available these data, the trend is a higher proportion of immigrants in cities than in a country as a whole.

The United States, following 2005 estimates from the U.S. Census, is a nation in which 12.4 percent of its 300 million residents are foreign-born. In other words, approximately one in eight people residing in the United States was born in another country. Yet for the two largest metropolitan areas, New York City and Los Angeles, the percentage of foreign-born residents is far greater (27.9 percent and 34.7 percent, respectively, based on the 2005 new metropolitan statistical area (MSA) definitions that extend well into the suburbs). The foreign-born in these two dynamic metropolitan regions account for 27 percent of 35.7 million foreign-born in the country (U.S. Census, American Community Survey, 2005). In terms of absolute numbers, these cities are the largest immigrant destinations in the world, with a total of 9.5 million foreign-born. Yet scores of other metropolitan areas—from Seattle to Trenton, Las Vegas to Miami—have foreign-born populations that far exceed the U.S. national average. The same trend is evident in Canada, where 19 percent (or nearly one in five) of the population was foreign-born in 2001. Yet in metropolitan Toronto, a staggering 44 percent of the population was foreign-born, according to the 2001 Canadian census.

European cities also receive a disproportionate number of the region's immigrants. "In every European context, most immigrants live in cities. That is where the jobs, housing, schools, support services, religious and leisure facilities and their own social networks are concentrated" (Pennix et al. 2004, 1). Since the 1990s many European cities have experienced a steady rise in their foreign-born populations, both from flows within an enlarged European Union and arrivals from throughout the world. By 2000 several European cities, such as Amsterdam, Brussels, Frankfurt, Geneva, London, Munich, and Zurich, had populations of at least 20 percent or more foreign-born residents. Other major cities such as Athens, Berlin, Birmingham, Bonn, Cologne, Copenhagen, Dublin, Düsseldorf, Hamburg, Lyon, Marseilles, Paris, Rotterdam, Stockholm, and Vienna experienced steady increases in immigrants so that the foreign-born currently account for 10 to 20 percent

1. For detailed data on the foreign-born by city, see http://www.gstudynet.org/gum.

of their total populations. If one were to narrow the scale and look at particular neighborhoods, it would be possible to find locations where more than half the population is foreign-born. Thus, the consideration of scale is essential in examining how immigration is changing localities. Since metropolitan areas are the primary zones of contact between native- and foreign-born populations, it is vital to study the settlement patterns and integration processes at the urban scale, not just at the national level.

The questions of immigrant integration, assimilation, or exclusion become more pressing when one considers the diversity of destinations from which immigrants arrive. Many cities attract the majority of their immigrants from a narrow range of countries—thus, Mexicans dominate in Los Angeles and Houston, whereas Turks are the leading group in Berlin, Indians in Dubai, and Malaysians in Singapore. Yet many cities are extremely diverse. Figure 2.2 illustrates the internationalization of present-day Toronto. Such hyperdiverse cities are a product of the globalization of labor that has both economic and cultural implications. With more than 2 million foreign-born residents, no one group dominates Toronto's immigrant stock. Nine countries account for half of the foreign-born population, whereas the rest of the foreign-born come from nearly every country in the world, making Toronto one of the most hyperdiverse metropolitan areas in the world (Price and Benton-Short 2007; Anisef and Lanphier 2003).

Within these receiving areas there are considerable differences in how each of these groups organizes itself (spatially, socially, economically) as well as how local governments and service providers have structured their responses to large and diverse communities of immigrants. City governments and their residents have varying responses to the opportunities and issues resulting from new and diverse immigrant flows. Typically, urban planners and various nongovernmental associations respond to needs in housing, transportation, and education. For example, the city of Vienna, Austria, created a public housing complex in the 1990s called "Global Yard" that mixes native-born Viennese with foreign-born residents at a fifty-fifty ratio to encourage greater social integration. Resettlement centers are created and maintained by governmental and nongovernmental actors to deal with refugees and economic migrants. Cities can also make public space available for festivals and other events that display the cultural

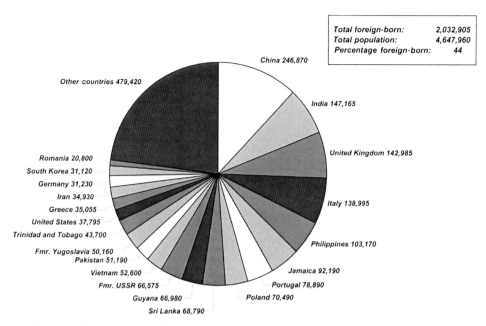

Fig. 2.2. Toronto foreign-born, 2001. *Source:* Statistics Canada, 2001.

diversity of residents. In some cases, urban governments can be proactive in formalizing the political status of its noncitizen residents, as was the case of Berliners in the 1990s with regards to the citizenship status of its immigrant-derived ethnic population (Ireland 2004). Or city officials can create administrative units that address the needs and concerns of the foreign-born (Friedmann and Lehrer 1997).

Ivan Light's recent monograph on Los Angeles makes the case that the actions of local officials and even proimmigrant groups can result in "deflecting" poor immigrants out of one city and into others. Light concludes that immigrant networks led to an oversupply of newcomers that depressed wages and raised housing costs in Los Angeles. Growing intolerance toward immigrant survival strategies and poverty (especially overcrowding and informal labor) resulted in the heightened enforcement of existing industrial and housing regulations that, though not originally intended to restrict unwanted immigration, had the effect of doing so (2006, 13). Certain industries, such as garment sweatshops, were shut down, owing to greater scrutiny by local officials. Enforcement of housing codes made it difficult for immigrants to find housing they could afford. Finally, the success of immigrant-rights groups in Los Angeles in raising the county's minimum wage seemed to have a negative effect on certain industries that left the metropolitan area for new cities or new countries where labor was cheaper. These local reactions served to deflect (or push) immigrants to other destinations in the United States. Light concludes, "Municipalities have long assumed practical responsibility for receiving and managing the overly numerous immigrants they receive as a result of the partly failed immigration policy and border enforcement of their national states. That part is well understood. But, contrary to the accepted wisdom, in so doing, cities also assume a de facto role in national immigration policy" (12).

As cities are the places where foreign-born and native-born residents are most likely to come into contact, cities are also crucial settings of both tolerance and intolerance of ethnic and cultural differences. City leaders and officials are not passive recipients of newcomers. Their policy decisions, as well as the activities of religious and nongovernmental organizations, play a critical role in how immigrants are incorporated into or excluded from the social and economic systems of gateway cities (Foley and Hoge 2007).

Partly in response to the need to share urban-based experiences, the International Metropolis Project held its first meeting in 1995 and is coordinated by secretariats in Ottawa, Canada, and Amsterdam, Netherlands—two immigrant gateway cities. Still active today, the lead nations in the project believe that urban policy is vital to the integration of the foreign-born into a host society. European countries and cities have been especially active in this international effort to foster dialogue among government officials, nongovernmental organizations, and academics in an effort to develop better immigration policy. "The underlying idea is that the members will work collaboratively on issues of immigration and integration, always with the goal of strengthening policy and thereby allowing societies to better manage the challenges and opportunities that immigration presents, especially to their cities" (Metropolis 2006, n.p.).

Gateway cities are culturally diverse and have complex histories of immigrant integration, assimilation, and exclusion. Each city's particular context varies considerably, and practices that work in one city may be ineffective or unworkable in another (Brettell 2003). The flow of immigrants to a particular city increases or declines over time because of internal factors, changes in national policies, and larger structural forces. Thus, the episodic, rather than continual, draw of gateways must be kept in mind. It is also a mistake to think of these destinations as sites of permanent settlement. A more accurate metaphor may be that of a turnstile, where immigrants enter for a period of time and then leave for other cities in the transnational network or return to their countries of birth. Therefore, in order to establish some common attributes shared by many gateway cities, it is important to deepen our conceptualization of gateways beyond the notion of a location where immigrants settle.

CONCEPTUALIZING THE TWENTY-FIRST-CENTURY GATEWAY

Increasingly, one finds the term *gateway* in reference to major urban immigrant destinations (Clark and Blue 2004; Ley and Murphy 2001; Skop and Menjívar 2001; Singer 2004; Goździak and Martin 2005). The meaning of this ubiquitous term is assumed rather than systematically developed or conceptualized. Consequently, the term can connote vastly different meanings, which leads to confusion rather than clarity. One of our purposes in this book is to expand the notion of "gateway" beyond merely places of entry and settlement and to see the gateway as a more dynamic arena of human movement. In the following section, six conceptualizations of gateways are developed: as critical entry points, nodes of collection and dispersion of goods and information, highly segregated settings, sites of global cultural exchange, turnstiles for other destinations, and urban immigrant destinations and settlements. Most contemporary urban immigrant gateways embody each of these definitions and are not simply locations where the foreign-born reside in large numbers. By articulating how urban immigrant gateways function as part of a global system of cities, it is possible to see why such gateways are creating new urban sociocultural spaces as well as global linkages.

Viewed historically, there have always been urban centers that have attracted ethnically and culturally diverse peoples long before the modern concepts of immigrants or even citizenship came into existence. Trading centers of great empires or colonial outposts were sites of diversity and, at times, highly segregated spaces following cultural, ethnic, and class divisions. It would be intriguing to explore the temporal depths of immigrant gateway formations, but it is not practical, given the global scale of this project and the data limitations. Consequently, this chapter and most of the chapters that follow focus on recent immigration since the 1970s.

Gateways as Critical Entry Points

At its most literal level, a gateway is a restricted passage that controls entry and exit, much as a garden gate delimits space yet allows passage through the yard to the front door. Taken this way, the world has millions of gateways. Perhaps the most obvious gateways are found along international borders; thus, El Paso, Texas, and San Isidro, California, are gateways into the United States from Mexico. Historically, New York City and particularly Ellis Island presented the popular image of an immigrant entry point in which millions of newcomers were processed before settling in New York or going on to other places. One might even consider major airports, such as John F. Kennedy in New York City or Heathrow in London as, in Nancy Foner's terms, the "new" Ellis Islands (2000; Waldinger 1996). These places are dynamic settings where millions of people, native-born and immigrants, are processed before continuing to their final destination.

International borders provide obvious points of entry, but there are other localities that become screening points in which immigrant access is granted or denied. For many authorized immigrants, the first gateway is a consular office in their home country, where it is determined if they will receive an entry visa—be it as a tourist, temporary worker, or immigrant. The international network of embassies and consulates, based in cities around the world, thus forms another important set of gateways that control access to national spaces. Yet these gateways are embedded in hundreds of different cities far from the actual intended destinations.

Gateway entry points, especially along international borders, imply a measure of control and restriction. The unimpeded flow of people and goods through these sites is critical to the global economy, yet these spaces are where the state also tries to exert its greatest authority. A sojourner can be turned away or detained even before meeting an immigration officer.

Airports, embassies, train stations, ports, and many border crossings are entry points that are now intensely scrutinized, with patrol officers, layers of fencing, video surveillance, close-circuit television, and biometric technology. These gateways project what Michel Foucault calls the panoptic "gaze" of the state, watching over who comes and who goes (1995). This level of control and surveillance appears to contradict claims that the authority of the state is increasingly becoming irrelevant in a global context. It is precisely these spaces where the state exerts its greatest control. Such gateways are not the "glorious mosaics" of cosmopolitanism that Jan Lin refers to in her work (1998). Although these critical entry points deserve greater study, these spaces are not where people live their lives. Rather, they are transitory spaces demanded by nations and controlled by states.

Gateways as Nodes of Collection and Dispersion

In the 1970s Andrew F. Burghardt, an economic geographer, hypothesized about the evolution of gateway cities. Burghardt defined gateway cities as critical nodes that serve large tributary areas in a frontier context, such as Winnipeg, Kansas City, Bratislava, and St. Louis. The essence of a gateway city is to serve as an "entrance to the hinterland" (1971). He saw gateways as contact zones between areas of differing production and concluded that "gateway cities develop in positions which possess the potentiality of controlling the flows of goods and people" (282). In Burghardt's research the flow of immigrants into gateway cities was never explicitly addressed, but his conceptualization of gateway cities emphasizes the ability of these cities to exert influence over a wide geographic area. The term *gateway cities*, therefore, entered the geographic literature to refer to those cities "that are necessary regional cities, in other words, prime locations that serve a larger market" (Taylor 2004, 91–92).

More recently, globalization scholars have employed the term *gateway* when discussing the role of cities with regard to social and economic networks and linkages. These economic gateways are the catalysts of neoliberal, transnational, post-Fordist capitalism: places where multinational corporations exert disproportionate influence and the voice of the state is relatively muted.

Peter J. Taylor (2004) uses the term *gateway* to refer to the connectivity of world-city networks through economic and political criteria. His leadership of the Globalization and World Cities Study Group and Network has helped to produce numerous quantitative urban studies that analyze a variety of economic measurements of both productivity and linkages within the global economy.[2] Their assemblage of world cities is dominated by western European, North American, and East Asian centers of production and finance. The principal criteria are economic: producer services, financial services, foreign direct investment, and corporate headquarters.

Extending the concept of world-city networks, Richard Grant and Jan Nijman (2002) have applied the gateway concept to cities in the developing world, such as Accra, Ghana, and Mumbai, India, to highlight the ways these cities are incorporated into the global economy. In the developing world, most gateways are port cities and may also have been colonial commercial centers. Through the liberalization of trade and increased foreign investment, these cities have become particularly exposed to political and economic change. Yet they are also the sites through which access to a larger region is facilitated. In this conceptualization of gateway, cities that receive foreign direct investment, experience foreign corporate activity, or process large sums of remittance are gateway cities for the flow of capital. The impact of these economic changes has created what Grant and Nijman term "global CBDs" (central business districts) that are located on the urban periphery, rather than in the traditional city center. Yet in their understanding of gateways, immigration plays little or no role. We draw on Grant and Nijman's recognition that gateways in the developing world are dynamic localities where new economic spaces are being forged, often far from the central cities.

Gateways as Socially and Spatially Segregated Spaces

In her seminal book *The Global City*, Saskia Sassen forges the link between globalization and urbanization literatures. In singling out particular cit-

---

2. To access the Globalization and World Cities Study Group and Network, see http://www.lboro.ac.uk/gawc/.

ies—New York, Tokyo, and London—as the command and control centers of the global economy, Sassen focuses on the economic role of these cities. Yet toward the end of her argument she emphasizes the heightened social polarization that occurs in global cities. This social and spatial polarization is linked to increased concentrations of immigrants and ethnic minorities in low-wage jobs and the informal economy, and their relative spatial segregation within the cities (1991, 245–319). Labor-market segmentation dictates which immigrants dominate certain sectors of the economy, often, though not always, being low-paid jobs with low status. Social and spatial polarization can often heighten interracial conflict.

Some of the most highly segregated gateways are in the Middle East, where immigrants typically arrive as contract guest workers and seldom receive permanent status or citizenship. In the case of Dubai in the United Arab Emirates, social and spatial segregation is achieved by the construction of a vast array of worker hostels at the edge of the city. Hundreds of buses move workers from their accommodations to job sites—typically in construction—and back to their quarters at the end of the day. Given the relatively low incomes of guest workers and residential distance from the urban core, foreign workers in Dubai are isolated socially and spatially. Most of their interaction is with other coethnics or immigrants.

Yet in other global cities, immigrants are also seen as vital agents of neighborhood renewal, especially in older areas of a city that perhaps would have a high proportion of abandoned residences and storefronts if not for the influx of immigrant residents and the "ethnic" or immigrant neighborhoods they create (ibid., 315). These ethnic places, according to Jan Lin, serve as "polyglot honeypots" in which both their commercial and their cultural functions are seen "alongside producer services as leading edges of globalization" (1998, 314).

Gateways as Sites of Global Cultural Exchange

Some globalization scholars have begun to integrate cultural dimensions into their conceptualization of gateways. The gap in the literature with regard to the relationship between the globalization of culture and global cities was first commented on in 1996 (Short et al. 1996, 709). John Rennie

Short has since called for using the term *gateway city* to refer to the fact that almost all cities can act as a gateway for the transmission of economic, political, and cultural globalization (Short et al. 2000). This definition is by far the broadest sense of the term *gateway* and one that could potentially include any city in the world to varying degrees.

For example, scholars have looked at the location of Olympics, World's Fairs, carnivals, and film festivals as efforts by city officials to achieve global recognition (Short 2004; Shoval 2002). Thus, when Seoul or Beijing hosts the Olympics or Cannes hosts its annual film festival, they receive the attention of the global community and presumably are elevated as prestigious places attractive for tourism and investment. One of the interesting aspects of achieving such status is that it is a collaboration of local entrepreneurs and officials—often, the state plays little role in the initial planning and competition stages.

In terms of cultural exchange, immigrant enclaves (such as Chinatown in San Francisco or Little Havana in Miami) are important conduits for goods and services that serve their coethnics and the broader community. In cases where residential enclaves do not form, immigrant entrepreneurs and city officials may promote diverse "ethnoscapes" or "ethnoburbs:— commercial or residential districts that function as transnational business centers, tourist sites, and hubs of immigrant social life (Appadurai 1990; Li 1998). For example, anthropologist Caroline Brettell (2005) discusses the role of the Richardson Heights shopping center in suburban Dallas as a key cultural locale for the area's widely dispersed Indian immigrants. Anchored by the Taj Mahal Grocery, Indians gather there to shop, eat, collect business cards, and organize service organizations. In Southern California's San Gabriel Valley, geographer Wei Li focuses on Chinese commercial centers in the suburbs of Monterey Park, Rosemead, and Alhambra. These ethnoburbs are suburban ethnic clusters of both residential areas and business districts. Li notes that "the local context of the ethnoburb is characterized by both vibrant ethnic economies, due to the presence of large numbers of ethnic people, and strong ties to the globalizing economy, revealing their role as outposts in the emerging international economic system" (1998, 482). These immigrant-led spaces also function as important economic generators in the urban economy and contribute to the sense of cultural diversity and cosmopolitanism (Short and Kim 1999, 89).

It is important to note that cities can become places of cultural exchange without the presence of a diverse population. Thus, a city may appear "cosmopolitan" without being home to a multicultural population. Tokyo has a very small percentage of foreign-born residents (about 2 percent), yet the urban milieu presents a global self-consciousness, perhaps because of the many transnational elites and firms that reside there. Even in the East Asian megacity of Beijing, the upcoming 2008 Summer Olympics are viewed as a strategic cultural and social event that demonstrates the city's global significance. Yet Beijing's aspirations for global stature are somewhat at odds with the striking homogeneity of its residents.

Gateways as Turnstiles

Cities receive immigrants, but they also produce them. Thus, it may also be appropriate to conceive of gateways as *turnstiles* where foreign laborers work for varying periods of time before returning to their countries of birth or moving on to other cities in the transnational network (Castles and Davidson 2000). The turnstile function is an engineered aspect of many cities in the Middle East that rely on large numbers of temporary workers. But even in cities where immigrants are given permanent residency or citizenship, the foreign-born may and do leave (Van Hook et al. 2006). Ironically, the United States, the largest immigrant destination in the world, has no systematic information on emigration from the United States, which would enable researchers to better document the turnstile function of gateways. Brenda S. A. Yeoh and Natalie Yap's essay on Singapore's immigrants (Chapter 8) explores the concept of turnstile functions, as does research by Emily Skop and Sarah Zell (Chapter 15), which looks at emigration flows from the former gateway city of São Paulo, Brazil.

The turnstile function of gateway cities is relevant for the native-born as well. Lisbon receives newcomers from Africa, eastern Europe, and South America, but it is also from Lisbon that many native-born Portuguese leave to work in other cities in Europe (Malheiros and Vala 2004). The same can be said for immigrant cities such as Kiev and Moscow in the former Soviet

Union, where the native-born often emigrate yet new immigrants are arriving from nontraditional destinations (Braichevska et al. 2004). Graeme Hugo makes a similar point when exploring Sydney's gateway functions (Chapter 4). Given the dynamics of immigration in a globalizing world, the gateway as turnstile may emerge as a more common pattern in the twenty-first century than the notion of the gateway as a final destination.

Gateways as Immigrant Destinations and Settlements

The term *gateway* is also used to designate a major metropolitan area where large numbers of immigrants have settled (Clark and Blue 2004; Ley and Murphy 2001; Skop and Menjívar 2001; Singer 2004; Goździak and Martin 2005). What makes contemporary gateways a significant object of study is that urban economies are increasingly reliant upon new and large flows of foreign labor for distinct segments of the labor market. At the same time, the discourse about citizenship has intensified as growing numbers of foreign-born peoples in urban areas challenge assumptions about identity and belonging.

In contemporary research cities such as London, Los Angeles, Miami, New York, San Francisco, Sydney, Toronto, and Vancouver are often labeled as gateways because they are home to many of the world's immigrants. Scholars examining North American and Australian cities are much more likely to apply the term *gateway* to these cities, whereas the term is less often used in the European context. The reluctance to conceive of European cities as gateways may be a reflection of the overall unwillingness of many European states to view themselves as countries of immigrant settlement, despite the high proportion of foreign-born residents within them (Pennix et al. 2004, 2).

In a comparative study of Vancouver and Sydney, David Ley and Peter Murphy argue for the need to study gateway cities. They assert that (1) all continents are implicated in the transfers of populations, (2) there is immense diversity in terms of immigrant status and country of origin, (3) the numbers of international migrants are at a high level, and (4) destinations are focused on large metropolitan centers, or gateway cities, in advanced societies (2001, 119).

The concentration of immigrants in just a few Canadian cities is especially striking. According to geographer David Ley (1999), 70 percent of Canada's immigrants are in three cities: Vancouver, Toronto, and Montreal. Canada's immigrant destinations have become decidedly more concentrated over time, focusing on three main cities, whereas in the United States there has been a greater dispersion of immigrants into new urban destinations, especially in the Southeast, with a decline in some former northeastern and midwestern immigrant destinations such as Philadelphia and Cleveland (Singer 2004).

Immigrants select urban destinations for a variety of reasons: family unification, job opportunities, educational opportunities, settlement among other coethnics, or participation in a resettlement program. Urban immigrant gateways are less tightly controlled spaces compared to discrete gateway entry points such as airports, ports, and border crossings. It is here where immigrant groups can create permanent or ephemeral spaces in which they assert their identity. Yet there is also tremendous variation in how different immigrant groups settle in a city: whether they are clustered or dispersed, found in the inner city or the suburbs, segmented into particular labor markets as skilled or unskilled laborers, or designated as temporary workers or permanent settlers. Before exploring the inner workings of particular gateway cities, an assessment of the number and diversity of immigrant gateway destinations will be presented.

MAPPING THE WORLD'S IMMIGRANT GATEWAYS

Our interest in urban immigrant gateways began in 2002 when we were awarded a grant from the George Washington Center for the Study of Globalization to find and map the world's major destination cities. Quickly, we discovered that these data were not readily found and that there was not a simple answer to this question: What are the world's top urban immigrant destinations? After four years of research we were able to gather data and build a Web site with information on the foreign-born in more than 150 cities (see http://www.gstudynet.org/gum). Such data, to our knowledge, had never been gathered before, and we have produced various research papers analyzing these data that develop an urban immigrant index and a preliminary typology (Benton-Short, Price, and Friedman 2005; Price and Benton-Short 2007).

The cities considered in this research are metropolitan areas of 1 million or more people characterized by both large numbers of foreign-born residents—at least 100,000—and an above-average percentage of foreign-born compared to state population averages.[3] Since many immigrants reside in suburbs and not just city centers, metropolitan-level data were sought whenever possible in preference to data for the official city limits. Admittedly, there are many smaller localities that can be important immigrant destinations (say, a university town or a specialized agroindustrial center). But given the focus of this research—to link the literatures about globalization, urbanization, and immigration—understanding what is happening in the world's largest and most connected metropolitan areas is a priority.

Gathering comparable urban-level data is difficult. The definition of *urban* varies, and metropolitan boundaries often change. For U.S. cities, the data used are the foreign-born estimates for MSA based on the 2005 American Community Survey data and the 2000 census data for the primary metropolitan statistical areas (PMSA).[4] The introduction of the MSA in 2003 produced many definitional and demographic changes for metropolitan areas in the United States so that direct comparisons between

---

3. A few cities of fewer than 1 million people are included in this analysis because they tend to be the urban cores of metropolitan areas of 1 million or more people (for example, Muscat and Amsterdam). In general, metropolitan-level data were selected over city-level data, but when the foreign-born was reported at only the city level, we used that level of geography. We have yet to find reliable urban-level data for the foreign-born in India, China, and most of Africa.

4. In 2003 the widely used U.S. metropolitan classification was reorganized by the Office of Management and Budget. The new classification system positions the metropolitan statistical area as the standard for comparing metropolitan areas in the United States (eliminating the older systems that included the MSA, PMSA, and consolidated MSA, CMSA). Under the new system, 81 of the nation's 102 largest metropolitan areas have undergone changes in territory and population. Consequently, direct comparisons between the foreign-born in metropolitan areas after 2000 must be made with care. Under the old system, the PMSA of New York and of Los Angeles was approximately 9.5 million each in 2000. With new MSA boundaries, the 2000 census data show New York with 18.3 million and Los Angeles with 12.4 million people (Frey et al. 2004).

2000 and 2005 foreign-born data are difficult. In general, how countries report urban-level data vary, and, as the U.S. case shows, definitions of metropolitan areas can suddenly change. Inconsistencies are a problem in any comparative international urban research, but such difficulties should not preclude research being undertaken and general trends noted (Short et al. 1996).

This analysis uses data on the foreign-born found in national censuses rather than relying on the yearly flow of immigrants reported by various government agencies. Flow data typically provide a breakdown of different immigrant categories (permanent settlers, guest workers, students, agricultural laborers, or asylum seekers) that are not always found when examining foreign-born-stock data and thus are valuable for immigration scholars (Bardsley and Storkey 2000). Yet flow data are inconsistently available from country to country and rarely report the flow of immigrants at the urban scale, which makes these data problematic given the objectives of this research.

There are considerable advantages in analyzing the urban foreign-born stock when doing comparative global research. The most obvious is the availability of the data. Many national censuses provide foreign-born data that can be extracted at the urban and metropolitan scale. Second, more often than not, individuals recorded in a census reflect a residential stock of foreign-born, whereas more transient flows of foreign-born tourists, students, and temporary workers are less likely to be counted in a census. These transient flows of people are important, but their relative impact on cities is less significant than groups of migrants who stay for longer periods of time or actually settle in the city. Third, census data on the foreign-born stock at the urban level can be used to produce a detailed spatial analysis of settlement patterns. Understanding the social-spatial dimensions of immigrant settlement in relationship to each other and the native-born is increasingly significant when trying to analyze questions of immigrant integration, assimilation, and differentiation.

There are limitations to using census-derived foreign-born data. First, censuses tend to be taken every ten years, and each country conducts its censuses at different cycles. (A few developed countries, such as Germany, no longer conduct a national census at all.) Thus, the data we have reflect a range of reporting years, mostly from 2000 to 2005. In general, the foreign-born counted in censuses usually represent a minimum documented figure for the foreign-born, whereas the actual number could be significantly higher, especially when a city receives a large number of undocumented immigrants. There are also different definitions of who constitute the foreign-born, although most states define the foreign-born as individuals born outside the territorial state. In the Netherlands, for example, the definition of foreign-born considers the children of immigrants to be "foreign-born" even if they were born in the host country (Hagendoorn, Veenman, and Vollebergh 2003). Yet in the Dutch case we were able to distinguish the children of immigrants born in the Netherlands and not include them in the total counts, so as to be consistent with other countries.

In cases of large circular immigrant flows, the foreign-born label can be misleading. Take, for example, the Mexican census, which counts anyone not born in Mexico as foreign-born. Many of the foreign-born in Mexico are from the United States. These "foreign-born" individuals could be the children of native-born Mexicans, speak Spanish, and be undistinguishable from the general population. Thus, their foreignness is determined strictly by their place of birth and does not take into account their cultural heritage. Despite these limitations, documenting the foreign-born found in census data is an important first step in a broader comparative analysis of the development of urban immigrant gateways.

In answer to the question of which cities are the world's top immigrant destinations, figure 2.3 shows there are nineteen cities with more than 1 million foreign-born residents. Combined, these metropolitan areas have 34.5 million foreign-born residents, which accounts for 18 percent of the world's foreign-born stock (United Nations, Department of Economic and Social Affairs, Population Division, 2006a). These few points on the globe are the destinations for one in five of the world's foreign-born. This selectivity of immigrant destinations underscores the significance of cities, especially a few large ones, as locations that are disproportionately impacted by immigration. Figure 2.3 also clearly demonstrates that immigration is a global phenomenon—nine high-destination cities are in North America, three are in Europe, three are in the Middle East, two are in Asia, and two are in Australia-Oceania. Several of these cities topped the 1 million mark

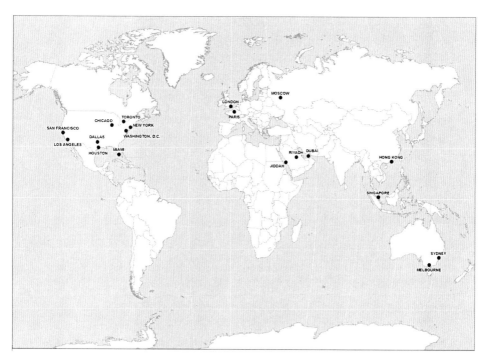

Fig. 2.3. Cities with 1 million or more foreign-born. *Source:* By the authors, using multiple national censuses.

only recently. In 2005 Dubai, Houston, Washington, D.C., Dallas–Fort Worth, and San Francisco were added.[5] Of these nineteen cities, six are featured in the chapters that follow (New York, Riyadh, Singapore, Sydney, Toronto, and Washington).

Latin American and African cities are absent from figure 2.3, although they are destinations for internal and international migrants. This point is reflective of the fact that most countries in these regions have a negative rate of net migration, with more emigrants leaving then immigrants arriving. Buenos Aires, a long-established immigrant destination, had fewer than 1 million foreign-born residents according to the 2001 Argentine census

5. The addition of San Francisco and Dallas–Forth Worth is, in part, a reflection of the new MSA boundaries for these areas. The San Francisco MSA includes Oakland and thus gives the metropolitan area 1.2 million foreign-born in 2005. The Dallas MSA includes Forth Worth and just topped 1 million in 2005.

(approximately 920,000 foreign-born), a decrease from earlier censuses. Other megacities in Latin America such as São Paolo, Rio de Janeiro, and Mexico City attract far fewer foreign-born residents, and if anything these localities tend to be sources for immigrants to other regions of the world, including North America, Europe, and Japan (Pellegrino 2004; Douglass and Roberts 2000). For many African countries, the data are simply not available on the urban scale, although the cases of Accra and Johannesburg will be discussed later. Even if the data were available, there is little evidence that these cities are attracting large numbers of foreign-born residents, with the exception of some South Africa cities (see Southern African Migration Project 2003).

Figure 2.4 maps cities with at least 100,000 foreign-born. In this figure the North American and European cities stand out as key immigrant destinations. The dominance of North America, a traditional region of

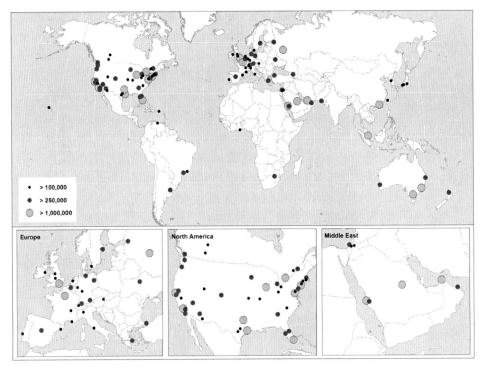

Fig. 2.4. Cities with more than 100,000 foreign-born. *Source:* By the authors, using multiple national censuses.

immigration, is not surprising, but the range of cities, especially in the United States, has expanded to include southeastern cities such as Atlanta and western cities outside of California and Texas, such as Seattle, Denver, and Las Vegas. The numbers of foreign-born in European cities continues to rise as a result of immigration from within Europe and outside of it. Figure 2.4 shows thirty European cities with more than 100,000 foreign-born. Since European metropolitan areas tend to be smaller than North American ones, the 100,000-person threshold often accounts for 10 percent or more of a city's total population.

All the western European states now have at least one major immigrant gateway, and states such as Germany, France and the United Kingdom have several. The numbers of foreign-born in Moscow, St. Petersburg, Kiev, and Tbilisi are also significant, but the numbers are more of a by-product of political change and reclassification of people after the breakup of the Soviet Union in 1991. Peoples that were once classified as citizens of the Soviet Union turned into "foreign-born" residents if their republic of birth was not their republic of residence. The cities of the former Soviet Union are destinations of new or "nontraditional" immigrants such as Afghans, Angolans, or Chinese, but their numbers are still relatively small (Braichevska et al. 2004).

The Middle East and Oceania (including Australia and New Zealand) also have many urban immigrant destinations. Oceania has Auckland, Brisbane, and Perth, whereas the Middle Eastern cities include Istanbul, Medina, Muscat, Karachi, Tel Aviv, and Jerusalem. The large number of immigrants in the Arab cities of the Persian Gulf is owing to established temporary-worker programs that result in thousands of laborers migrating to this region, especially from North Africa and South Asia. Seldom are these workers permitted to settle permanently in these cities, but they do account for a major proportion of the labor force and the population. The extreme case is Dubai, where more than 80 percent of the population is foreign-born, mostly from India, Pakistan, and Bangladesh. The Israeli case is also unique in that all Jews are legally permitted to immigrate to the Jewish homeland. In fact, the State of Israel classifies these arrivals not as immigrants but as returnees, as David Bartram discusses in Chapter 13. Given the relative newness of the State of Israel and the large influx of newcomers from the former Soviet Union and eastern Europe, more than one-third of the residents in Israel were not born there.

Finally, there are several cities in East Asia, Latin America, and Africa with more than 100,000 foreign-born residents, although the populations of these cities are so large that the percentage of foreign-born within them is quite low. Several important East Asian cities appear in figure 2.4, including Seoul, Nagoya, Tokyo, Osaka, and Taipei. These are major urban agglomerations with more than 5 million people and with foreign-born numbers ranging from 100,000 to 250,000, which is proportionally very low. At the same time, these countries and cities have seen a rapid increase in foreign-born workers since the 1990s. This increase is driven both by demographic shifts (the aging of the population) and by economic need. Yet in each of these countries and cities, newcomers are usually admitted on only a temporary basis (typically as worker trainees), with limited access to permanency and citizenship. With that point in mind, it is highly likely that the numbers of foreign-born workers will continue to increase in the region, especially from China, Indonesia, and the Philippines (Hugo 2006b). As an example, Yeong-Hyun Kim's research on Seoul (Chapter 14) demonstrates how suddenly the foreign-born population can increase, even in a global city that has been previously closed to immigrants.

In Latin America, in contrast, emigration from the region has become the norm (United Nations, Department of Economic and Social Affairs, Population Division, 2006a). In the early twentieth century, cities such as São Paulo and Buenos Aires attracted tens of thousands of immigrants. Likewise, the oil boom in Venezuela in the mid-twentieth century resulted in new immigrants from Europe (especially Italy, Portugal, and Spain), as well as from neighboring Colombia. These cities still have substantial foreign-born populations from Europe, South America, and Asia, but the absolute numbers of foreign-born, as well as the percentage of foreign-born compared to the overall city populations, are declining. Moreover, these cities are losing native-born and foreign-born residents to destinations in Europe, Japan, and the United States (Pellegrino 2004). It is quite possible that if the macroeconomic situation improves for the region, inflows of migrants, especially from poorer countries in South America, will result. Yet the historical sending countries for South America (Italy, Japan, Portugal, and

Spain) are unlikely to be contributing significant numbers of immigrants to the populations of these cities.

Finally, figure 2.4 shows only two African cities, Accra and Johannesburg. In general, the data for this region are poor, and certainly there is more interregional movement of people between countries than this map suggests. Moreover, many of the refugee populations in this region are probably not picked up in the urban data. South Africa, the most prosperous country in sub-Saharan Africa, is likely to continue to grow as an immigrant destination for African immigrants. At the same time, as Jonathan Crush explains in Chapter 11, South Africans are reluctant recipients of other Africans because of serious problems with unemployment and poverty among the native-born.

Mapping the world's current immigrant gateways is a snapshot approach to a far more complex immigration story. Given limitations, especially the lack of data for India and the urban foreign-born in China, there are major urban centers that are left out of this analysis. The Appendix lists more than one hundred cities with 100,000 or more foreign-born residents, data that provided the basis for figure 2.4. It also shows the percentage of the total population that is foreign-born in these cities, which ranges from a high of 83 percent to a low of 1 percent. Finally, the absolute and relative numbers do not begin to address the composition or distribution of the foreign-born within cities. For this reason, we turn to the thirteen case studies in this book for a deeper understanding of how immigrant gateway cities are an outgrowth of the globalization of migration.

PART ONE | Established Gateways

3

New York City

America's Classic Immigrant Gateway

NANCY FONER

New York is America's quintessential immigrant city—the major historical gateway for the country's new arrivals and a major receiving center today. It is fitting that the nation's two most powerful symbols of immigration— Ellis Island and the Statue of Liberty—stand in New York's harbor. Millions of southern and eastern European immigrants passed through Ellis Island's halls a hundred years ago, and many of them remained in New York. In 1910 one out of seven of the nation's immigrants lived in New York City—and 41 percent of the city's residents were foreign-born. Nearly a hundred years later, at the beginning of the twenty-first century—after four decades of massive immigration—the sheer size of the city's immigrant population is greater than ever before.

New York City is what Audrey Singer (2004) calls a continuous gateway. Since 1900, about 10 percent or more of the nation's foreign-born population have lived in New York City. And throughout the twentieth century around a fifth or more of the city's population was foreign-born; even at its lowest ebb, in 1970, after a lull in mass immigration lasting several decades, 18 percent of New Yorkers were born abroad. Since then, the figure has been steadily on the rise. For the past few decades, New York City has been in the midst of what, in absolute numbers, is the greatest wave of immigration in its history. The proportion of immigrants in the city's population—36 percent in 2000—may be below the 1910 figure, but the 2.9 million immigrant residents counted in the 2000 census represent an all-time high (see table 3.1). Although the focus of this chapter is New York City, it should be noted that the larger metropolitan area has also received huge numbers of immigrants in the past few decades. According to the 2000 U.S. Census, the Consolidated Metropolitan Statistical Area (CMSA), a large geographic unit that stretches into suburban New York, Connecticut, and New Jersey, is home to nearly 5.2 million immigrants—one in six of all foreign-born in the nation.

New York City is a unique mixture of past and present. Given its immigrant history and the enormous contemporary inflow, the vast majority of New Yorkers have a close immigrant connection. If they are not an immigrant themselves, they have a parent, grandparent, or great-grandparent who is. Moreover, the city's institutions and, one might say, New York's culture, style, or "way of doings things" are a product of dozens of decades of immigrant inflows (see Foner 2006).

If present-day New York City has been shaped by its immigrant past, it is also being remade by the latest arrivals. It is these recent transformations that are the focus of the chapter. I begin the analysis by providing basic

TABLE 3.1

FOREIGN-BORN POPULATION OF NEW YORK CITY, 1900–2000

Year	Total population (in thousands)	Foreign-born population (in thousands)	Percentage of foreign-born in New York City	Percentage of all U.S. foreign-born in New York City
1900	3,437.2	1,270.1	37.0	12.2
1910	4,766.9	1,944.4	40.8	14.3
1920	5,620.0	2,028.2	36.1	14.5
1930	6,930.4	2,358.7	34.0	16.5
1940	7,455.0	2,138.7	28.7	18.3
1950	7,892.0	1,860.9	23.6	17.8
1960	7,783.3	1,558.7	20.0	16.0
1970	7,894.9	1,437.1	18.2	14.9
1980	7,071.6	1,670.2	23.6	11.9
1990	7,322.6	2,082.9	28.4	10.5
2000	8,008.3	2,871.0	35.9	9.2

Sources: Foner 2000, 5; Singer 2004.

background about the new immigration to New York City. I then go on to explore ways that it is affecting the city's neighborhoods and institutions as well as adding new ingredients to the ethnic and racial stew—altering perceptions of race and ethnicity and influencing intergroup relations. In conclusion, I discuss how and why New York, with its distinctive immigrant history and immigrant flows, is a particularly welcoming place for the newcomers who are remaking the city once again.[1]

THE NEW IMMIGRATION: BACKGROUND

What stands out, perhaps above all, about contemporary New York City's immigrant population is its extraordinary diversity. In the past two great waves, immigrant groups, to use Nathan Glazer and Daniel Moynihan's apt analogy, came two by two—the Irish and Germans in the mid-nineteenth century, followed by the Russian Jews and Italians at the turn of the twentieth century (1970, 8).[2] Today, no two groups dominate New York that way, and most immigrants come not from Europe but from Latin America, the Caribbean, and Asia.

It is often said that virtually every country in the world is represented in New York City. What is remarkable is the large number from so many different countries. Between 1990 and 1996 alone, as many as twenty countries each sent more than 5,000 immigrants to the city (Kraly and Miyares 2001). In 2000, the top three groups—Dominicans, Chinese, and Jamaicans— were just under 30 percent of all the foreign-born. No other foreign country accounted for more than 5 percent, and there were substantial numbers of

1. For a comparison of immigration to New York in the last great wave a hundred years ago and in the contemporary period, including a discussion of immigrant skill levels; residential, occupational, and educational patterns; transnational ties; gender roles; and the construction of racial and ethnic identities, see Foner 2000 as well as Foner 2001 and 2005.

2. By 1855, the Irish-born made up 28 percent of the city and the German-born 16 percent, and they remained the dominant foreign-born groups until the end of the century. In 1890, the Irish-born and German-born and their children made up 52 percent of the population of New York and Brooklyn (Glazer and Moynihan 1970; Rosenwaike 1972). By 1920, after several decades of enormous Jewish and Italian immigration, foreign-born Jews and Italians and their children made up about 43 percent of the city's population.

West Indian, Latin American, Asian, and European nationalities (see table 3.2). The Caribbean presence is striking: in 2000, one out of three immigrant New Yorkers was Caribbean-born. There is, moreover, a huge native minority population of African Americans and Puerto Ricans. (As U.S. citizens by birth, island-born Puerto Ricans are not classified as immigrants when they move to New York.) The product of a massive migration from the South between World War I and the 1960s and from Puerto Rico after World War II, blacks and Hispanics of native stock (native-born to native parents) made up about a quarter of the city's population in the late 1990s.

The post-1965 immigration has replenished older groups and created new ethnic mixes. At the time of the 2000 census, more than a quarter of the city's 2.1 million non-Hispanic blacks were foreign-born, most of them West Indians. A substantial proportion of the newest arrivals hail from Europe. In 2000, the former Soviet Union (including Russia and the Ukraine) ranked

TABLE 3.2

TOP-FIFTEEN SOURCE COUNTRIES OF THE FOREIGN-BORN,
NEW YORK CITY, 2000

Country of birth	Number	Percentage
Dominican Republic	369,186	12.9
China	261,551	9.1
Jamaica	178,922	6.2
Guyana	130,647	4.6
Mexico	122,550	4.3
Ecuador	114,944	4.0
Haiti	95,580	3.3
Trinidad/Tobago	88,794	3.1
Colombia	84,404	2.9
Russia	81,408	2.8
Italy	72,481	2.5
Korea	70,990	2.5
Ukraine	69,727	2.4
India	68,263	2.4
Poland	65,999	2.3
Total foreign-born	2,871,032	100

Source: Lobo and Salvo 2004, 11, based on 2000 U.S. Census SF3.

fourth among the top sending countries to New York City, Poland was fifteenth, and altogether about one out of four of the city's non-Hispanic whites was foreign-born (see table 3.2). Put another way, only about half of New York City's non-Hispanic whites were native-born people with two native-born parents (Mollenkopf, Olson, and Ross 2001). New York City's white population is dominated by first-, second-, and third-generation Catholics (Irish and Italian) and Jews, and white Protestants are practically invisible, if still economically and socially powerful (Mollenkopf 1999, 419).

The incredible diversity of New York's immigrants is matched by the heterogeneity of their skills. New York's great variety of nationalities has ensured a mix of class and occupational origins, with high-skilled and low-skilled immigrants roughly equal in number in the New York metropolitan area (Waldinger and Lee 2001, 50, 52, 63). At the time of the 2000 census, nearly a quarter of foreign-born New Yorkers twenty-five years and older had a college degree, and the figure was slightly higher (27 percent) for those individuals who entered the United States in the 1990s; at the other end of the spectrum, 35 percent of the foreign-born twenty-five years and older had not graduated from high school (Lobo and Salvo 2004, 154, 169).

As elsewhere in the nation, New York City's immigrants are primarily of working age (79 percent were between the ages of eighteen and sixty-four in 2000), and women outnumber men in virtually all the major national-origin groups (ibid., 150). In 2000, the sex ratio for New York City's foreign born was 91, meaning that there were 91 males for every 100 females. This figure was almost the same as the sex ratio for the native-born, which was 89. In virtually all the major new immigrant groups, women outnumbered men, the exceptions being Mexicans, Ecuadorans, Indians, Pakistanis, Bangladeshis, and Greeks. Mexicans and Bangladeshis had the highest sex ratios: 154 males for every 100 females among Mexicans, 161 males for every 100 females among Bangladeshis (ibid.).

IMMIGRANT IMPACT: NEIGHBORHOODS AND LOCAL COMMUNITIES

If immigrants have brought about a dramatic demographic transformation of New York City, they have also been remaking it in other ways. There is, for a start, the residential landscape. New ethnic neighborhoods and ethnic conglomerations have cropped up in every borough. New York now boasts three Chinatowns, a little Odessa-by-the-Sea, a Caribbean Brooklyn, and a Dominican colony in Washington Heights.

As in the past, the new arrivals often gravitate to areas with kinfolk and friends, where they find comfort and security in an environment of familiar languages and institutions; at the same time, they are limited by the availability of affordable housing and by prejudice and sometimes outright discrimination by dominant groups. In some cases, this situation has led them to the same neighborhoods that Italians and Russian Jews inhabited a hundred years ago. In general, however, the new arrivals are branching out to new areas of settlement. Most are avoiding long-standing immigrant and minority neighborhoods to settle in places that, several decades ago, were the domain of middle- and lower-middle-class native white New Yorkers, many of whom subsequently left for the suburbs and the Sunbelt.

Many sections of the city have taken on a new cultural character. In Crown Heights, Flatbush, and East Flatbush in central Brooklyn—and, increasingly, in many bordering neighborhoods—West Indian beauty parlors, restaurants, record stores, and bakeries dot the landscape, and Haitian Creole and West Indian accents fill the air. "When I walk along . . . Nostrand Avenue," novelist Paule Marshall has written, "I have to remind myself that I'm in Brooklyn and not in the middle of a teeming outdoor market in St. George's, Grenada, or Kingston, Jamaica" (1987, n.p.). Several neighborhoods in the northeastern Bronx and southeastern Queens also now have a definite West Indian flavor. For West Indians, race is a primary factor determining where they live, placing severe constraints in their way. West Indians, like African Americans, are highly segregated from white New Yorkers. Real estate agents often steer them to black neighborhoods or withhold information on housing availability elsewhere. Those West Indians who have braved open hostility and branched out from Brooklyn and Queens West Indian areas to adjacent white communities find that their new neighborhoods become increasingly black. Antiblack prejudice tends to fuel a process of racial turnover as whites begin to leave and no new whites move in; at the same time, the growing number of black families makes the neighborhood seem more welcoming for West Indians (and

African Americans) looking for homes. The result is a pattern of segregation in which West Indian residential enclaves are located in largely black areas; the index of dissimilarity, which measures residential segregation (100 indicates total segregation), was 83 between West Indians and non-Hispanic whites in New York City in 1990 (see Crowder and Tedrow 2001).

Although no immigrant group is as segregated from non-Hispanic whites as West Indians, Dominicans come close (with a segregation index of 80 in cities in the New York CMSA in 1990). Dominicans have created a city within a city in northern Manhattan's Washington Heights. Upper Broadway, one journalist has written, "abounds with *bodegas, farmacias* . . . restaurants serving *pollo* and *platanos* and travel agents offering bargain [flights] to the Dominican Republic" (quoted in Foner 2000, 49). With the surge of Dominican immigration in the 1990s, Inwood and areas of the Bronx to the north and Hamilton Heights to the south of Washington Heights have also taken on an increasingly Dominican character; Corona, in Queens, has become the third-largest Dominican immigrant neighborhood in the city. In addition, Manhattan's expanding Chinatown has spilled over into adjacent districts—and what have been called satellite Chinatowns have developed in Flushing (Queens) and Sunset Park (Brooklyn). The Chinese, it should be noted, are much less segregated from whites than Dominicans and West Indians—with a segregation index of 58 calculated for cities in the New York CMSA in 1990 (Alba et al. 1999).

Immigrant settlement in New York today is not just about these—and the many other—ethnic enclaves. Polyethnic neighborhoods have emerged that are amalgams of newcomers from all parts of the world (fig. 3.1). The number 7 train that connects Times Square in Manhattan with Flushing in Queens has been dubbed the International Express, as it weaves through multiethnic neighborhoods in Queens that have no parallel in previous waves of immigration. Elmhurst is one of New York's most diverse immigrant areas, with large numbers of Chinese, Colombians, Ecuadorans, Mexicans, Koreans, Indians, Filipinos, Dominicans, Bangladeshis, and Peruvians (Lobo and Salvo 2004). Although Flushing is sometimes referred to as a new Chinatown in the making, it is in fact home to a growing number of Central and South Americans as well as Chinese, Indian, and Korean immigrants who join a still quite sizable native-born white population.

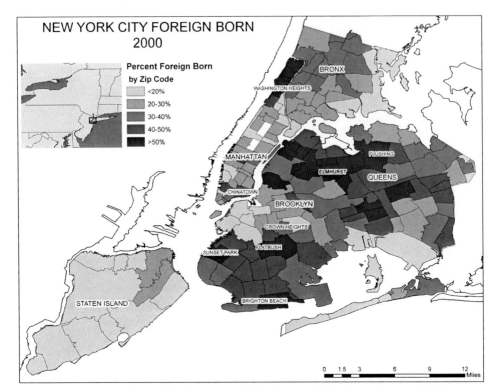

Fig. 3.1. New York City foreign-born, 2000. *Source:* U.S. Census Bureau 2001.

Astoria, formerly a predominantly immigrant Greek and Italian neighborhood in Queens, welcomed large numbers of Asians and Latin Americans
from different countries in the 1990s—becoming another ethnic stew.

There is no denying that many immigrants are forced into extremely
crowded and substandard housing conditions owing to their limited incomes
and limited access to publicly subsidized apartments.[3] In 2000, a quarter of
the city's foreign-born households were overcrowded (more than one person
per room in a housing unit) compared to 8 percent of native-born households, with the levels of overcrowding most acute among Mexicans (66
percent), Bangladeshis (61 percent), and Pakistanis (53 percent), all heavily

---

3. In February 2006, nearly 136,000 families were on the waiting list for public housing
in New York City; the vacancy rate of apartments available for occupancy was 0.79 percent
(New York City Housing Authority 2006).

male groups with high proportions in poverty (ibid.). At the same time, immigrants have played a critical role in revitalizing many neighborhoods that had fallen on hard times. In Brooklyn's Brighton Beach, Soviet Jews breathed fresh life into a fading community, filling apartments and developing a thriving commercial center, with nightclubs, restaurants, state-of-the-art electronics stores, and clothing boutiques selling European designer clothing (Orleck 2001). Another Brooklyn neighborhood, Sunset Park, was in the "throes of a long twilight" that began in the 1950s when the area was devastated by, among other things, a drastic cutback in jobs on its waterfront and in industry and the exodus of tens of thousands of white residents for the suburbs. It has been argued that in Sunset Park, as in many other city neighborhoods "outside the yuppie strongholds of Manhattan and other favored areas of Brooklyn and Queens," immigrants have been the leading factor in neighborhood revitalization: "Owing to their high employment rates and multiple wage earners, the new foreigners have injected large doses of new purchasing power into the rehabilitation of an aging housing stock and the resurrection of inert retail streets" (Winnick 1990, 62). In general, as a recent Department of City Planning report notes, "Immigrants . . . help sustain the housing stock in many of the city's neighborhoods. Overall, 48 percent of recently-occupied (between 1990 and 2002) housing units had a foreign-born householder, with this figure rising to over 70 percent in many neighborhoods in Brooklyn and Queens. Immigrant demand for housing is also influencing demand for new construction. . . . Many of these new units are in neighborhoods that had witnessed housing abandonment in the 1970s" (Lobo and Salvo 2004, 186).

IMMIGRANT IMPACT: RACE AND ETHNICITY

Clearly, a major impact of the new immigration is the way it has changed, and is changing, the racial and ethnic dynamics of New York City. More and more, in political and street-level discourse, New Yorkers think of a four-race framework of white, black, Hispanic, and Asian. The proportion of Asians and Hispanics is growing; the proportion of whites is on the decline. Between 1980 and 2000, non-Hispanic whites went from 52 to 35 percent of New York City's population, Hispanics from 20 to 27 percent,

Asians from 3 to 11 percent, and non-Hispanic blacks held fairly steady, 24 percent in 1980 and 26 percent in 2000.

Gone are the days when Hispanic meant Puerto Rican; in 2000, Puerto Ricans accounted for only a little more than a third of the city's Hispanic population, outnumbered by a combination of Dominicans, Mexicans, Ecuadorans, Colombians, and other Latin Americans. Asian no longer means Chinese but also Korean, Indian, and Filipino (to name the largest non-Chinese groups). The black population is being Caribbeanized—and a small but growing number of Africans is also adding new diversity. Altogether, by 2000 more than a quarter of the non-Hispanic black population was foreign-born (for a more detailed discussion of the changing construction of race and ethnicity in New York, see Foner 2005).[4]

The growing number of Caribbean and African blacks may well be "tweaking" monolithic notions of blackness, as Milton Vickerman (2001) has argued—making whites (and others) more sensitive to ethnic distinctions within the black population. Hispanic immigrants, for their part, often see themselves in terms of the relatively new Hispanic or Latino category—and are often identified as Hispanic or Latino by others—even if most prefer to be known in terms of their group of national origin (see Foner 2005, 23–28). Asians have undergone a contemporary metamorphosis. Once stigmatized as "aliens ineligible for citizenship," they are now often cast in the model minority stereotype, a view that flourishes in New York, with its large numbers of well-educated Asians and tiny population of Southeast Asians from Cambodia and Laos, who have low levels of education and high poverty rates. New York's Asians rank just below non-Hispanic whites in the city's ethnoracial hierarchy—and they generally meet with greater acceptance from middle-class white New Yorkers than other racial minorities.

The new racial and ethnic amalgam in New York is not only changing perceptions of race and ethnicity but also creating new divisions, alliances, and relationships. On the downside, tension and conflict between racial and ethnic groups persist, although in new forms and with the involvement

---

4. After a decade of heavy in-migration, nearly 70,000 Africans born in a sub-Saharan African country lived in New York City. There were also more than a half-million Afro-Caribbeans (that is, people of Afro-Caribbean ancestry) (Logan and Mollenkopf 2003).

of new groups. Residential segregation between whites and blacks continues at extraordinarily high levels, with serious implications, as I have mentioned, for hundreds of thousands of West Indian newcomers. Black and Latino immigrants often engage in distancing strategies to set themselves apart from, and to claim superiority to, African Americans and Puerto Ricans. For their part, native minorities often resent what they see as numerical, residential, economic, or political encroachment by immigrants. And there is a general tendency, out of preference but also on account of prejudice, for members of racial and ethnic groups to stick to their own kind in day-to-day interactions. This situation is true even in the city's polyethnic neighborhoods. In his study of a multiethnic Queens neighborhood with a mix of Latino and Asian immigrants, African Americans, and whites, Michael Jones-Correa speaks of communities that overlap but do not touch (1998, 32). In the 1990s, the city witnessed several black boycotts of Korean-owned stores, and tensions have been reported in many neighborhoods between long-term residents and new arrivals—Flushing being one example, where old-time whites often resent the influx and increasing dominance of Asian groups (Zhou 2001).

The fact is, however, that by and large peaceful coexistence among members of different racial and ethnic groups is the rule in New York, as it is in other established gateway cities. Nor is it just a case of tolerance and accommodation; genuine cooperation and coalition building also occur. Among other things, friendships develop in schools, colleges, playgrounds, and workplaces, and political alliances are formed on certain issues and in certain campaigns (see Sanjek 1998). Indeed, as a result of New York's immigrant history, ethnic politics is the lifeblood of New York City politics; no group "finds challenge unexpected or outrageous" (Glazer and Moynihan 1970, xxx), and ethnic politics has long been practiced as a shorthand method of coalition building (Marwell 2004, 243).

The increasing number of multihued neighborhoods that have emerged all over the city provides the basis for the creation of ties, particularly among Asians, whites, and Latinos. By 1990, only 8 percent of neighborhoods in the New York City region were all white, down from 29 percent twenty years earlier. Nearly half of the region's neighborhoods could be classified as white, Hispanic, and Asian or as white, black, Asian, and

Hispanic (Alba et al. 1995). Significant numbers of American-born Hispanics and Asians have non-Hispanic white spouses or partners (Liang and Ito 1999); an increasing number of marriages are taking place between Dominicans and Puerto Ricans (Itzigsohn and Dore-Cabral 2000, 241); and West Indian–African American unions are not unusual, especially among second-generation West Indians. All over the city, countless examples exist of amicable relations developing among immigrants from different countries, as well as between immigrants and the native-born, in work, school, and neighborhood contexts.

As for the second generation, a recent study shows that many describe themselves as "New Yorkers"—meaning people who "could come from immigrant groups, native minority groups, or be Italians, Irish, Jews, or the like" (Kasinitz, Mollenkopf, and Waters 2002, 1034). The cultural hybrids being created among the second generation have a particularly New York flavor, partly because they are being melded out of the interaction of such a remarkable number of groups—Asians, Latin Americans, Caribbeans, and Africans from many countries as well as native-born African Americans, Puerto Ricans, and non-Hispanic whites, the latter mostly Jewish, Italian, and Irish American.

Although the children of immigrants, like their parents, often feel the sting of disadvantage and discrimination, they "move in a world where being from 'somewhere else' is the norm" (Kasinitz, Mollenkopf, and Waters 2004a, 397). Because established minority and second-generation immigrant young people in New York dominate their age cohort—63 percent of New Yorkers under the age of eighteen are second- or 1.5-generation immigrants—they have a great deal of contact with each other in their neighborhoods and a variety of city institutions (Kasinitz, Mollenkopf, and Waters 2002, 1027; 2004b, 2).

In describing the vibrant inner-city youth culture emerging in New York, Kasinitz speaks of a "melting pot of urban youths, all 'of color' but from a variety of cultures." He writes of young people creating new forms of music (for example, Filipino and Indian hip-hop) that fuse Asian and African American forms and of fluid exchanges between African Americans and Jamaicans and other West Indians: "The New York youth sporting dreadlocks . . . is as likely to be African American as Jamaican, and the street slang of central Brooklyn youth owes as much to Kingston and Port of Spain as to the American South. . . . African-American young people dance to Jamaican dance hall music and imitate Jamaican patois, even as West Indian youngsters learn African American street slang. Puerto Ricans can meringue and Dominicans can play salsa and rap in two languages" (2000, 41).

IMMIGRANT IMPACT: DOMINANT FORMAL INSTITUTIONS

The city's nearly 3 million immigrants are, not surprisingly, having an impact on a wide range of dominant formal institutions in the city. Briefly consider three: schools, churches, and hospitals.

The surge of immigration has led to major increases in public school enrollment, which is now over the 1 million mark. With so many students and a limited budget, the public schools are squeezed for space. Although many immigrant students are doing remarkably well in school, there is no denying that they bring with them a host of special needs. Many have to overcome poor educational preparation in their home countries or, at the very least, unfamiliarity with subjects taught and the teaching methods (and discipline) used (see Foner 2000, Chapter 7). In addition to adjusting to new norms and customs in New York, many have a language problem to contend with. With the diverse mix of immigrants in New York City, it often means a dazzling array of languages. In one Queens elementary school, nearly 80 percent of the incoming students arrived speaking no English; among them, the children in the school spoke 36 languages (Hedges 2000). In the late 1990s, close to 80,000 students were enrolled in bilingual programs in the New York City public schools. The largest number (85 percent) were of Spanish-speaking background, followed by, in descending order, Chinese, Haitian Creole, Russian, Korean, Bengali, Polish, Arabic, French, Urdu, and Punjabi (Board of Education of the City of New York 1999). In response to the immigrant influx, the city has opened several new schools specifically designed for recent immigrant children with limited English proficiency. Higher up the educational ladder, the City University of New York (CUNY), the largest urban public university system in the nation, reflects the city's amazing ethnic and racial diversity. Its more than 200,000 undergraduate students represent 172 countries and speak

131 languages in addition to English. In 2006, 38 percent of CUNY's first-time freshmen were born outside the U.S. mainland.

New York's immigrants are also having an impact on the city's religious institutions. Many newcomers, of course, have formed their own churches and houses of worship. By the late 1990s, for example, Koreans had established more than five hundred Protestant congregations in the New York area (Min 2001), and Asian Indians had built many Hindu temples in Queens (Khandelwal 2002, 83–86). At the same time, large numbers of immigrants have been drawn to established Catholic and Protestant congregations. New York's Catholic Church has a growing Latino presence, and an increasing number of Catholic churches conduct masses in Spanish as well as other languages (Sanjek 1998, 67–68, 335–41). In the mid-1990s, fourteen Catholic churches in Brooklyn and Queens celebrated masses in French or Creole, and the thriving Haitian congregation at Saint Jerome's in Brooklyn drew an estimated 1,400 parishioners each Sunday (McAlister 1998, 144–45). Catholic churches in Washington Heights have emerged as Dominican congregations, holding mass in Spanish and inviting religious officials from the island to participate in church activities; elsewhere in the city, Mexican immigrants, whose numbers quadrupled between 1990 and 2000, have been "Mexicanizing" many Catholic churches (see Smith 2006).

The composition of the staff and patients in New York City's hospitals has changed as well. The nurses, aides, and orderlies are often West Indian or Filipino; patients, especially at municipal hospitals, are frequently non-English-speaking immigrants who bring with them their own set of cultural values regarding health and medical treatment—which, in the New York context, means a bewildering array of patterns. New York hospitals have begun to establish programs to address the need for better interpreter services, although what is available, in terms of language services and responsiveness to cross-cultural health care, is unfortunately still often inadequate.

CONCLUSION

New York City is a long-established, indeed a classic, immigrant gateway that has received successive waves of immigrant inflows throughout its history. It is, once again, being transformed by a massive inflow from abroad. In 2000, more than a third of its residents were foreign-born—more than 70 percent of the foreign-born, or about 2.1 million people, entered the United States in 1980 or later (Lobo and Salvo 2004, 16).

The new arrivals come to a city where being an immigrant—or the child or grandchild of an immigrant—is nothing unusual. The city has had a sizable share of immigrants throughout the twentieth century so that the current influx represents a gradual increase, not the kind of sudden growth spurt seen in many other U.S. cities, such as Las Vegas, Charlotte, and Washington, D.C. Many of the nearly 1 million Jewish New Yorkers—and hundreds of thousands of Italian Americans—have grandparents or great-grandparents who came from Europe at the turn of the twentieth century. New York's Irish Americans often trace their immigrant roots further back, to the mid-nineteenth century. Many black New Yorkers are descended from immigrants who arrived a hundred years ago from what was then the British Caribbean. And at the time of the last census, the city was home to around 830,000 Puerto Ricans, many of them island-born, though, technically speaking, they are not immigrants.

Ethnic diversity is the expectation in New York. Indeed, the incredible ethnic mix that results from the combination of the city's immigrant history and the current inflows can sometimes be confusing to the newest arrivals. Russian teenagers whom Annelise Orleck studied were confounded when they entered high school in Brooklyn, wanting to know where the Americans were: "It is . . . hard to know what we are supposed to be becoming. Everybody here is from someplace else" (1987, 295).

Earlier waves of immigrants left their stamp on New York—creating and molding institutions and, one could say, a New York culture that now greets the latest arrivals. In the past, Irish, Jewish, and Italian immigrants helped shape the city's political institutions, labor unions, schools, hospitals, and a host of other organizations. Now it is the new immigrants' turn to leave their mark—and they are doing so in a city that is accustomed to, and feels comfortable with, an immigrant presence. In 2000, Trinidadian-born Roger Toussaint—the leader of New York's Transport Worker's Union (TWU)—won the union presidency with support from a multiethnic and largely second-generation immigrant coalition, displacing African

American leaders, who had themselves displaced an Irish American leadership decades earlier:

> The New York press immediately began to draw parallels between Toussaint and Mike Quill, the colorful Irish onetime revolutionary who led the TWU in the mid-twentieth century. For New Yorkers facing a potentially crippling transit strike, this should not have been a comforting analogy, for Quill led some of the bitterest public employee strikes in the city's history. Yet the analogy is strangely comforting nevertheless: its subtext is that the accent may be new, but the story familiar. (Kasinitz, Mollenkopf, and Waters 2004a, 399)

Even during the three-day transit strike of December 2005, which was decidedly uncomfortable for New Yorkers and in which Toussaint came in for much public criticism, he was accepted and portrayed as a distinctly New York figure who symbolized the city's multicultural working class—and was repeatedly compared to Quill. "The closest approximation to Mr. Toussaint—who speaks softly with a lilting accent," according to one newspaper story, "was his most famous predecessor, 'Red' Mike Quill who was as garrulous as Mr. Toussaint is sober, but whose County Kerry accent was just as strong as Mr. Toussaint's West Indian one" (Schuerman and Smith 2005, 13; Chan and Santos 2005).

Apart from its immigrant history, New York is a relatively welcoming town for new arrivals because of the nature of the current influx (see Foner 2005). Each significant ethnoracial group in New York City—white, black, Hispanic, and Asian—includes a substantial proportion of recent immigrants, which has facilitated the "reproduction of an inclusive immigrant identity" (Keogan 2002, 228). So has the sheer diversity of the current immigrant flows, as well as the fact that the new immigrants include a large number of well-educated and highly skilled people. This situation, it should be noted, is a contrast to many suburban and outer-rim areas of the New York metropolitan area where, since the 1990s, formerly all- or nearly all-white communities have received large numbers of low-skilled and often undocumented Latino immigrants—and where tensions are frequently rife between established residents and newcomers. Two hate crimes on Long Island in Farmingville, a community about fifty miles from New York City, attracted national attention: in 2000, two Mexican day laborers were beaten nearly to death by two men from nearby towns, and three years later, four Farmingville teenagers burned down the house of a Mexican family, who barely escaped. Although these two crimes are extreme, they are indicative of a deep anti-immigrant and anti-Latino sentiment and reaction that have not occurred, or at least have been sharply curtailed and contained, in New York City.

There is a danger, of course, in overemphasizing the positives. New York City is not a racial or immigrant paradise. New Yorkers may boast that their city celebrates all cultures and welcomes everyone, but it remains a remarkably segregated place—particularly for blacks, who are segregated from whites at exceptionally high rates. Relations among different groups are far from tension-free. Between 2000 and 2004, the city's Hate Crimes Task Force investigated nearly 2,000 crimes—the vast majority of them antiethnic or antiracial crimes: the task force determined that 95 percent of the crimes were motivated by hate, including 20 percent involving physical attacks.[5]

Still, New York does have an openness to immigrants that stems from its particular history and contemporary features. If "Italians are yesterday's newcomers and today's establishment," it has been written, "then maybe Colombians are the new Italians and, potentially, tomorrow's establishment. New Yorkers, old and new, are happy to tell themselves this story. It may not be completely true, but the fact that they tell it, and believe it, is significant and may help them make it come true" (Kasinitz, Mollenkopf, and Waters 2004a, 398). As New York City welcomes new flows of immigrants and as a second and third generation come of age, this very New York story is bound to continue to exert an influence in a city that shows every sign of remaining, for some time to come, one of the world's major immigrant gateways.

5. Thirty-five percent of the hate crimes were anti-Semitic, 16 percent antigay, 12 percent anti-other, 11 percent antiblack, 10 percent antiethnic, 6 percent antireligious, 5 percent antiwhite, 3 percent anti-Hispanic, and 2 percent anti-Asian (McGinty 2005).

4

Sydney

The Globalization of an
Established Immigrant Gateway

GRAEME HUGO

Given the unprecedented increase in the scale and significance of international migration since the early 1990s, the role of world cities as major elements in global migration systems has been neglected. Moreover, in the literature on world cities, immigration as a formative element has been neglected in favor of a focus on economic processes (Benton-Short, Price, and Friedman 2005). It is clear, however, that there are complex and significant relationships between the increase in international migration, on the one hand, and the emergence of world cities, on the other. This chapter focuses on this complex relationship through examining the case of Sydney, Australia. This case study is pertinent since Australia is one of the world's nations most influenced by migration. Currently, some 23.6 percent of Australia's population is foreign-born, and another fifth are Australia-born with at least one parent who is foreign-born. Moreover, in mid-2004, some 590,566 persons (equivalent to 3 percent of the population) were foreigners in Australia on a temporary basis, while Australia has a diaspora equivalent to around 5 percent of its national population (around 1 million persons). Sydney plays a pivotal role in the Australian migration as the preeminent gateway for international migrants (Ley and Murphy 2001). In 2001 the Sydney Statistical Division was home to 21.1 percent of the national population (3,997,321 persons), but also 30 percent of the overseas-born population (1,233,537 persons) and 37.3 percent (215,908 persons) of those individuals who had arrived in Australia in the previous five years.

This chapter begins with a brief discussion of Sydney's development as a global city before examining the significance of migration in its growth. In their examination of global immigrant cities Lisa Benton-Short, Marie Price, and Samantha Friedman (2005) focus on the numbers, percentage, and diversity of foreign-born in world cities, and these elements are investigated for Sydney. However, it is argued that the migration element in global city development has a number of additional important dimensions, as is demonstrated in the Sydney case. The next section of the chapter makes some brief remarks on the changing spatial distribution of immigrants in Sydney. This pattern of settlement is related to the changing profile of immigrants to Sydney tending toward a bimodal distribution, with highly skilled migrants playing a key role in the higher-end jobs in the financial, managerial, technological, and producer service activities that characterize global cities, while unskilled migrants are significant in the increasingly unregulated lower-income service jobs that also characterize these cities. Finally, the role of policy, national and regional, in shaping contemporary and future migration to Sydney is examined.

This chapter is based largely on secondary data on migrant stocks and flows for Australia but also on surveys of migrants to and from Sydney. Australia has some of the most comprehensive and accurate data on migration in the world (Hugo 2004, 17–22). First, with respect to flows, the Department of Immigration and Multicultural and Indigenous Affairs maintains a Movements Data Base (MDB) that includes key characteristics on all persons leaving and arriving in Australia, classified into permanent, long-term, and short-term movers. From the perspective of the present study, a limitation of this source is that the MDB does not identify the origin or destination of movers at a lower level of geographical detail than the state. Stock data are drawn from the quinquennial censuses that cover the total population and include a suite of questions relating to immigrants (birthplace, birthplace of parents, year of arrival in Australia, citizenship, ancestry, language spoken at home, and religion).

SYDNEY AS AN IMMIGRANT GATEWAY AND GLOBAL CITY

The Globalization and World Cities study group's roster of world cities ranks Sydney as one of the ten "beta"-level such cities (Beaverstock, Smith, and Taylor 1999, 2000), whereas Peter Hall ranks it as "sub-global" (1995, 22). For much of Australia's post-European settlement history, Sydney and Melbourne have competed to be Australia's preeminent city, but in the era of globalization Sydney has developed as Australia's primary link with the global economy. It is the nation's main international air and communications gateway, the primary location of transnational company command-and-control functions and associated producer services, the center for most international financial transactions, and the location of more corporate headquarters than any other center (Searle 1996; O'Connor 1991; O'Connor, Stimson, and Daly 2001).

Related to Sydney's increasing global role, international migration has increased in significance. Figure 4.1 shows the growth of Sydney's population. Between 1947 and 2001 the overseas-born grew more than five times faster than the Australia-born residents (545 percent compared with 90 percent). The growth of those individuals born in countries where English is not the main language has been even more striking.

Although Sydney gained large numbers of immigrants during the "long boom" period of the first two postwar decades, and saw its overseas-born population more than double between 1947 and 1961, the impact was less than what occurred in Melbourne so that its share of the national overseas-born population fell during the 1950s. However, in the past two decades Sydney has reasserted itself as the major focus of immigrant settlement in Australia so that at the 2001 census it had 30 percent of the nation's overseas-born. There was, however, a continuous increase in the proportion that the overseas-born made up of Sydney's total population, from around a tenth in 1947 to a fifth in 1961, a quarter in 1981, and a third in 2001. Moreover, the proportion of the overseas-born who had been in Australia less than five years and resided in Sydney was 37.3 percent in 2001.

The significant impact of immigration on recent population growth in Sydney can be appreciated from table 4.1, which shows the growth of

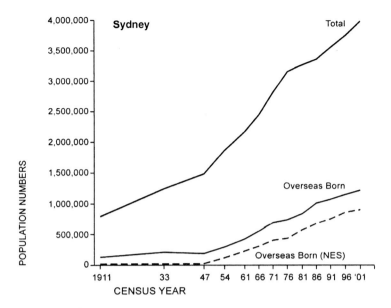

Fig. 4.1. Sydney: Growth of total and non-English-speaking overseas-born populations, 1911–2001. *Source:* Australian Bureau of Statistics, Censuses.

the first- and second-generation immigrant population in Sydney between 1981 and 2001. Half of the metropolitan area's population is either an immigrant or the child of an immigrant. The share of Sydney's population that is either immigrant or the second generation increased from 49.8 percent in 1981 to 52.2 percent in 2001.

In examining the impact of this immigration on the ethnic composition of Sydney, it is important to appreciate that postwar immigration to Australia has occurred in a series of waves, each characterized by a different mix of birthplace groups as Australia's immigration policy and the national and global economic, political, and demographic situation have changed. The UK- and Ireland-born have been the largest single birthplace group in the immigration intake most years, and they have remained a constant element in the postwar immigration streams, although their share of the total intake has declined significantly (from 78.7 percent in 1947 to 15.4 percent in 2004–2005). However, the mix of other (mainly

TABLE 4.1

SYDNEY: FIRST- AND SECOND-GENERATION IMMIGRANT
POPULATIONS, 1981–2001

| | 1981 | | 2001 | | Percentage change 1981 |
	No.	%	No.	%	to 2001
Total population	3,205,000	100.0	3,997,321	100.0	+16.7
Overseas-born	882,503	27.5	1,233,500	30.9	+30.2
Australia-born with overseas-born parents	772,870	22.3	1,245,500	21.3	+8.2

Sources: Australian Bureau of Statistics, Censuses, 1981 and 2001.
Note: Total population includes overseas visitors.

non-English-speaking) birthplace groups in the incoming stream has
undergone significant change, with different groups dominating successive waves over the postwar period. Eastern European refugees formed the
first of these waves in the late 1940s and early 1950s and were followed
by a substantial influx of Dutch- and German-origin settlers in the early
1950s, who in turn were followed in the mid- and late 1950s by Italians,
Greeks, Yugoslavs, and Lebanese. In the most recent flows, ethnic Chinese
have been the most significant group.

Accordingly, there has been a substantial shift in the ethnic structure
of Sydney during the postwar period. Figure 4.2 shows changes in the
proportions of the overseas-born population who originated from various
regions of the world, at various postwar censuses. It is clear that the shifts
have been substantial. Most striking is the consistent pattern of decline in
the proportion from the UK and Eire (Ireland) over the period (78.7 to 15.4
percent). Also, the spectacular increase of Asian origin immigrants since
1971 is especially apparent, increasing from 3.2 to 33.8 percent of overseas-born Sydneysiders. Overall, then, the rapid increase in the overseas-
born population in Sydney has been accompanied by an equally striking
increase in ethnic diversity among them.

Sydney attracts immigrants from every world region, but the ethnic
diversity becomes more complex when the flows from individual nations

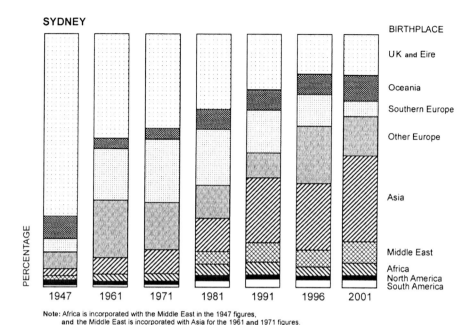

Fig. 4.2. Sydney: Birthplace composition, 1947–2001. *Sources:* Australian Bureau of Statistics, Censuses 1947 to 2001.

are considered. It is difficult to depict this diversity adequately here, but in 2001 there were more than twenty separate birthplace groups with more than 1,000 representatives in Sydney, and there are many other smaller but viable communities (for example, see Burnley 1996, 1999, 2004). Recent changes in the sizes of the largest overseas-born groups are shown in table 4.2. Substantial change has occurred since the 1980s, with the Asian presence becoming especially pronounced. In Sydney the ten largest overseas-born groups in 1981 did not include a single Asian origin group, but by 2001 the Chinese, Vietnamese, Filipinos, Hong Kong–born, and Indians were in the ten largest groups. The Asian-born groups all have more than doubled in numbers, whereas most of the European-origin groups actually declined, as death and return migration reduced their numbers.

In sum, there can be no doubt that ethnic diversity in Sydney's population has increased exponentially since 1980. This fact is understated by the data on birthplace, since the numbers of overseas-born from countries where English is not the main language increased from 509,902 in 1981 to

TABLE 4.2

REPRESENTATION AND GROWTH OF MAJOR OVERSEAS BIRTHPLACE
GROUPS, 1981, 1991, AND 2001, IN SYDNEY

	1981	1991	2001	Percentage of national total	Percentage change, 1981–2001
United Kingdom[a]	234,598	208,605	183,991	17.8	-21.6
China (excl. SARs and Taiwan Province)[b]	13,162	41,741	82,029	57.5	523.2
New Zealand	53,025	62,529	81,963	23.0	54.6
Vietnam	15,385	47,492	61,423	39.7	299.2
Lebanon	36,010	49,937	52,008	72.9	44.4
Italy	62,682	56,887	48,900	22.4	-22.0
Philippines	7,734	33,410	47,090	45.3	508.9
Hong Kong (SAR of China)[b]	7,964	29,673	36,039	53.7	352.5
India	10,182	17,851	34,503	36.1	238.9
Greece	43,628	40,531	33,688	28.9	-22.8
Korea, Republic of (South)[c]	3,099	15,044	26,928	69.2	768.9
Fiji	5,022	16,972	25,368	57.3	405.1
South Africa	9,012	16,112	25,190	31.7	179.5
Indonesia[d]	4,973	13,174	19,719	41.8	296.5
Germany	24,097	21,418	19,711	18.2	-18.2
Malaysia	8,076	17,501	18,996	24.1	135.2
Egypt	14,862	16,194	16,506	49.4	11.1
Yugoslavia, Federal Republic of[e]	NA	NA	15,935	28.8	NA
Sri Lanka	3,261	9,595	15,744	29.4	382.8

Sources: Australian Bureau of Statistics, Censuses, 1981, 1991, and 2001.
[a]Includes England, Scotland, Wales, Northern Island, Channel Islands, Isle of Man, and United Kingdom nfd.
[b]SAR is an abbreviation for "special administrative region." SARs comprise Hong Kong (SAR of China) and Macau (SAR of China).
[c]In 1981, it included the Democratic People's Republic of Korea.
[d]In 1981 and 1991, it included East Timor.
[e]In 1981 and 1991, it formed part of the former Yugoslavia.

907,337 in 2001—an increase of 77.9 percent compared with one of 0.9 percent among those from mainly English-speaking (MES) countries.

NONPERMANENT MIGRATION

There can be no question that Sydney's development as a world city and as Australia's preeminent gateway city easily fulfills all of the criteria laid down by Lisa Benton-Short, Marie Price, and Samantha Friedman (2005) for cities to be regarded as "global immigrant cities." These factors include a high percentage of the national foreign-born population (30 percent), a substantial number of foreign-born residents (1.23 million), a substantial percentage of the foreign-born not being from a neighboring country (87 percent), and no single group representing more than 25 percent of the foreign-born (the largest group, the UK-born, represents 14.9 percent, and the largest non-English-speaking [NES] group is the China-born, who constitute 6.7 percent of the total foreign-born). Indeed, in their classification of ninety world cities according to an immigrant index, Sydney is in the "alpha" category and is overall ranked sixth (Melbourne is eighth; the other cities in the category are New York, Toronto, Dubai, Los Angeles, London, Miami, Amsterdam, and Vancouver).

However, it is argued here that the elements of the size and diversity of the foreign-born population included in the immigrant index reflect only a small part of the role of international migration in world cities. There are at least three other important migration elements in global cities that are of significance and will be addressed in the case of Sydney. The first is that world cities are the focus of increasingly significant nonpermanent migration, or circulation of transnationals into countries. Second, they are also the main gateway for emigrants leaving the country. Third, there are some important relationships between international and internal migration in world cities.

With respect to nonpermanent migration, I have argued elsewhere (Hugo 1999) that there has been a profound change in population movement to and from Australia in recent years that amounts to a paradigm shift. The most important element is the reversal of Australian government policy that prior to the mid-1990s eschewed acceptance of temporary migrant workers in favor of an overwhelming emphasis on settlement migration. As a result, there has been an exponential increase in the numbers of entrants granted temporary residence with the right to work in Australia. In 2003–2004 there were 496,037 foreigners granted temporary residence with the right to work in Australia, while the number granted permanent residence was 148,884 (Department of Immigration and Multicultural and Indigenous Affairs 2005). The important points to make here are that temporary residents with the right to work in Australia are disproportionately concentrated in the high-skill groups. Indeed, the main temporary-visa categories are restricted to high-skill groups (Hugo 2006c). Second, they are also disproportionately concentrated in major metropolitan areas, especially Sydney (Khoo et al. 2003).

One of the major categories of temporary migrants is "Long-Stay Temporary Business Entrants" (visa category 457). Some 51 percent of all people in this category arriving in 2001–2003 went to Sydney, and 83.6 percent went to Australia's five largest cities (ibid.). Even among "working holiday makers," who are likely to be involved in both sightseeing and work outside of the major cities, some 42 percent reported working in Sydney (Harding and Webster 2002). Students are spread across the nation but are also concentrated in capital cities. Hence, although there are some minor exceptions, such as temporary migrant doctors who are channeled to nonmetropolitan locations, the bulk of temporary labor migration is directed to Australia's largest cities, especially Sydney.

The important point here is that census data traditionally used to assess immigration in gateway cities significantly understate the impact of nonpermanent international migration on world cities like Sydney. Sydney has a crucial gateway function not only for permanent settlers, but also for large numbers of temporary migrants who circulate between it and other world cities. Moreover, this group includes many transnationals who move from one world city to another owing to job transfers or as they change jobs within global labor markets. With high-level skills and income, they represent a significant presence in the world city at any single point in time and play an important role in its economic growth and labor market. They need to be added to the list of migration features that characterize and influence world cities.

CHANGING PATTERNS OF IMMIGRANT SETTLEMENT IN SYDNEY

The distribution of immigrants in Sydney, especially the degree of spatial concentration, and its implications have been an issue of considerable debate among social scientists in Australia. On the one hand are commentators (Blainey 1993, 1994; Healy and Birrell 2003) who argue that the development of immigrant concentrations in particular suburbs jeopardizes social harmony and cohesiveness in Australian society. On the other hand are commentators (Viviani, Coughlan, and Rowland 1993; Jupp 1993) who stress the positive roles played by ethnic concentrations in assisting immigrant economic and social adjustment. A distinctive characteristic of Sydney compared to some other world cities, however, is that although there are suburbs with high proportions of foreign-born residents, these concentrations are not dominated by a single birthplace group. Ian Burnley (2004) makes a detailed analysis of ethnic diversity at the district level of spatial desegregation. He found that even among the most "segregated" population, the Vietnam-born, there was only one district in which there was more than half the population born in Vietnam and nine in which 40–49 percent were. Moreover, 56 percent of the Vietnam-born lived in districts where they made up less than 5 percent of the resident population. For other concentrated groups the relevant percentages were 61 percent for the Lebanon-born and 86 percent for the China-born. Indeed, Burnley demonstrates that birthplace diversity is more evident in areas of in-migrant concentration than elsewhere in the city.

I have also noted (Hugo 2004) that more recent immigrant arrivals to Sydney have a greater degree of spatial dispersal than earlier generations of arrivals. This factor is a function of the increasing bifurcation in both global migration and Australian immigration between skilled migration (both permanent and temporary), whereby Australia has increasingly targeted its immigration program at highly educated, highly skilled, higher-income groups (Hawthorne 2005), and unskilled migration, largely through the refugee-humanitarian and family-reunion components of the Australian immigration program. This latter group has significantly lower skills, educational, and income levels, and many face significant linguistic, cultural, educational, and economic barriers to successful adjustment to the labor and housing markets.

There are clearly differences between the two groups in their capacity to exercise choice about where to live upon arrival in Sydney and the constellation of forces that shape where they settle. Those immigrants in the second category are much more constrained with regards to where they can afford to live in Sydney and the desire and need to reside among coethnics who will support them in adjusting to life in Australia. The reality is that the balance between the numbers in the former and latter groups settling in Sydney has moved in favor of skilled migrants since the mid-1990s, though it has been argued that the unskilled group is more likely to settle in Sydney and Melbourne than in other parts of the nation.

The differing patterns of settlement are evident when the spatial distribution of two birthplace groups—the Vietnamese and the Chinese—are compared. Figure 4.3 shows the distribution of Vietnamese in Sydney in 2001. They are one of the most concentrated groups, with 40.6 percent living in SLA-Fairfield, which has 4.6 percent of the total Sydney population. The Vietnamese have predominantly arrived in Australia under the refugee-humanitarian and family parts of the migration program and experienced difficulties in achieving success in the labor market. The China-born, on the other hand, are much less concentrated, as is evident in figure 4.4. Moreover, there is a spread between the higher-status as well as lower-status suburbs, reflecting the larger proportion of the group who enter Australia under the skilled component of the immigration program.

There have been two major interpretations of those spatial patterns. First, Ernest Healy and Bob Birrell argue that "not only is the city's population growing it is also bifurcating. . . . [T]here are now two Sydneys—one increasingly dominated by low to moderate income non English-speaking migrant communities in the west and south-west and the other comprised of established, inner, affluent areas and predominantly English-speaking 'aspirational' areas in the metropolitan periphery" (2003, 65).

Other commentators argue that Sydney is *not* characterized by ghettos or polarized ethnic enclaves but is rather an exemplar of ethnic mix (Poulsen, Johnston, and Forrest 2002). They argue that it is inappropriate to regard all non-English-speaking groups as a single group because doing

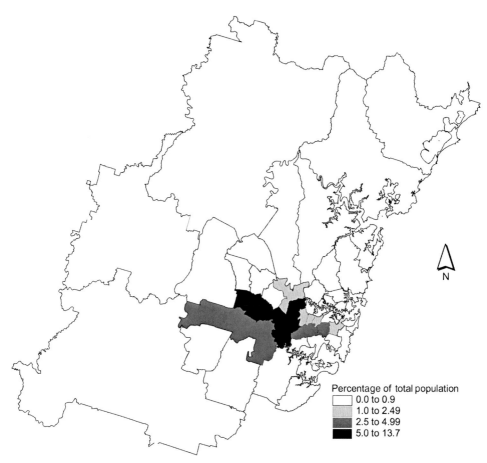

Fig. 4.3. Sydney: Vietnam-born as a percentage of total population, 2001. *Sources:* Australian Bureau of Statistics 2001.

so ignores the differences between individual groups, and state that it is necessary to separate more recent and longer-standing migrants as well as incorporate consideration of not just the first-generation migrants included in birthplace data but the second generation as well. A more nuanced analysis of changing patterns of ethnic distribution in Sydney that considers these issues concludes:

> The primary feature of Sydney's ethnic population to emerge from this study is one of residential mixing not of segregation or bifurcation. . . . Sydney appears to be moving towards being a city in which most of the

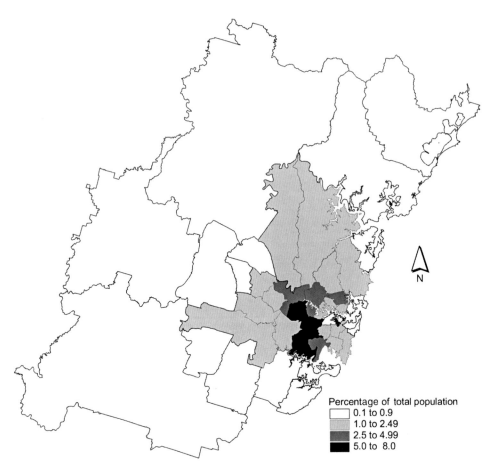

Fig. 4.4. Sydney: China-born as a percentage of total population, 2001. *Source:* Australian Bureau of Statistics 2001.

population will live in areas that are classified as either non-isolated host communities, associated assimilation—pluralism communities or mixed enclaves—a hybrid city (to use a term popular with post modern theorists) in which the ongoing processes of hybridization are clearly reflected in the city's geography. (Poulsen, Johnston, and Forrest 2002, 375)

As Sydney's foreign-born population has grown, the overall pattern of settlement reflects a greater ethnic mix—in both high- and low-socioeconomic areas. The metropolitan area has not, in contrast to other gateway cities, seen an expansion in ethnically isolated enclaves, which is not to say that there are not significant divisions within Sydney; rather, as Ian Burnley has expressed it:

> Overall, the experience of major immigrant concentrations in Sydney is different from that in American and European cities. While there are serious societal issues in these concentrations, notably low incomes and unemployment, the ethnic composition of disadvantaged communities is not the central issue. . . . [T]he issue now is not the distributional aspect of ethnically or racially distinct "subgroups" but the conditions of life of racialized minorities, and more importantly, the dominant cultural forms which result in racialization. Hence Sydney is becoming an increasingly ethnically diverse city. However the increase in the proportion of the city's population who are first or second generation immigrants is not only a function of increased levels of immigration into the city. It is also a function of increasing outmovement of Australian-born. (1999, 1313)

MIGRATION OUT OF THE GATEWAY CITY

It is important to characterize the gateway city not just as a destination for immigrants but also as an important node in a system of international mobility involving a large amount of coming and going, both permanent and temporary. This mobility was made apparent in an earlier section, which showed that Sydney is Australia's premier destination not only for permanent settlers but also for temporary residents and visitors who at any single point in time make up a significant proportion of the metropolitan population. In the case of Sydney, it is both a gateway into Australia and a significant gateway through which Australians leave the country.

Australia is not only a country of immigrants; it is estimated that there are around 900,000 Australians living in foreign countries (Hugo, Rudd, and Harris 2003). Australia is one of the few nations that collects detailed information on all departures from the country, so its information about emigration is of high quality. These data provide some indication of an "escalator" effect (Fielding 1992; Champion 2004), whereby there are three stages, or conditions, that an escalator region (ER) or city plays in relation to individual internal migrants:

STAGE 1: The ER attracts many young people with potential in the
early stages of their working lives—in other words, they step on the escalator by moving to the ER.

STAGE 2: The ER provides the context where these immigrants achieve
accelerated upward social mobility as they progress in their working life—
that is, they move up the escalator by living and working in the ER.

STAGE 3: The ER then loses many of these people who step off the
escalator and move to a higher-order city or region, building on the economic and social capital they have accumulated while in the ER.

This model appears to have considerable applicability in the Sydney case.
First, with respect to stage 1, it is apparent that internal migration to Sydney is a common choice for young adults (Hugo 2006a). The average age
of in-migrants to Sydney is slightly younger (28.9 years) than the age of
immigrants (29.7 years). Indeed, there is an internal net-migration gain
of persons ages 15–24 in Sydney but net-migration losses in other age
groups, so other than in the young-adult age group there are more internal
migrants moving out of rather than into Sydney. Internal migration into
Sydney is also selective of the "brightest and the best" in that young age
group, with young immigrants disproportionately having high incomes,
high levels of educational attainment, and concentration in managerial
and professional occupations.

Moreover, there is some evidence that Sydney is also the "launching
point" for many young Australians to move to overseas destinations, predominantly to higher-order world cities. The first piece of evidence to support this argument is the Movement Data Base's statistics on departures
from Australia. The departure card asks only the *state* of residence of persons leaving Australia permanently, but it is possible to separate out the
Australia-born in this group of emigrants. The state of New South Wales
(NSW), in which Sydney is located (63 percent of the NSW population
live in Sydney), stands out as a disproportionately large origin of Australia-born emigrants: some 38.9 percent of the emigrants left from NSW,
though it has only 32.6 percent of all Australian residents. The age-sex
profile of Australia-born emigrants leaving NSW is quite different from the
profile of internal migrants to Sydney, with the peak migration being in the

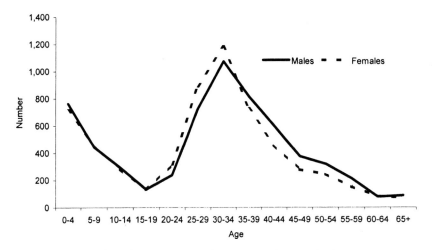

Fig. 4.5. New South Wales: Permanent departures of Australia-born, 2004–2005. *Source:* Department of Immigration and Multicultural and Indigenous Affairs, unpublished tables.

30–34 age group compared with the 15–24 age group (fig. 4.5). This point would appear consistent with the escalator hypothesis that migrants move into the ER city soon after they complete their education, spend several years gaining experience, and then subsequently "reemigrate upward." The median age of Australia-born permanent departures from NSW in 2004–2005 was 36.9 years, compared with 28.9 for internal migrants in 1996–2001, which would also support the escalator hypothesis.

Another piece of evidence that Sydney operates as an escalator region, attracting young skilled immigrants from elsewhere in Australia, many of whom subsequently emigrate to higher-order world cities, is a survey undertaken of some 2,072 Australians residing in foreign countries in 2002 (Hugo, Rudd, and Harris 2003). Of the respondents, 1,886 (91 percent) indicated they had graduated from an Australian university. The survey found that 565 of these respondents (30 percent) departed Australia from New South Wales, but only 293 (51.8 percent) had actually attended a university in NSW. Hence, there is a clear pattern of young Australians recently graduated from universities outside NSW to move to NSW and subsequently move overseas. It should be pointed out in this context that the great majority of

Australian undergraduates attend a university in the state in which they grew up. The survey also clearly demonstrates that the emigration from Sydney was predominantly from the young, highly skilled, higher-income groups.

It would seem, then, that Sydney operates as a migration gateway outward as well as a gateway for incoming immigrants from other parts of the world. This outward gateway function has two elements. First, many of the newcomers to Sydney from foreign countries are only temporarily in Australia as transnationals and eventually leave. There is, however, another escalator function, whereby Sydney funnels skilled young people from all around Australia to live and work there, many of whom eventually emigrate from Australia to higher-order world cities. The second type of out-migration from gateway cities is of course especially characteristic of second- and lower-order world cities, which act as conduits to the most dominant global cities, especially New York and London. There may also be some type of "hierarchical cascade effect" whereby "beta" world cities like Sydney attract substantial numbers of immigrants from cities in less developed countries, but in turn also experience a loss of natives to higher-order global cities.

THE RELATIONSHIP BETWEEN INTERNAL
AND INTERNATIONAL MIGRATION

Although the concern here is predominantly with international migration and the gateway city, it is clear from the previous section that there are important linkages between internal and international migration. Like many other world cities, Sydney has for an extended period experienced substantial net internal migration *losses* while at the same time recording net international migration gains. With respect to the native-born and other permanent resident populations, Sydney has experienced a net internal migration loss since 1976. It was at a lower level in 1996–2001 than in earlier years, partly associated with the massive amount of development in Sydney with the preparation for the 2000 Olympic Games.

The apparent relationship between substantial net gains from international migration and net losses from internal migration in Sydney has frequently been remarked upon (McKay and Whitelaw 1978; New South

Wales Department of Urban Affairs and Planning 1995; Hugo 1992; Bell 1995). Indeed, if one graphs the annual levels of net internal and international migration for Sydney, as in figure 4.6, one profile presents a mirror image of the other, suggesting a strongly negative association, as has been demonstrated statistically (for example, see Flood et al. 1991, 7; Bell and Cooper 1995, 102). The patterns depicted in figure 4.6 raise the issue as to whether there is a connection between internal and international migration and the suggestion in the literature (for example, Frey 1993) that there is a

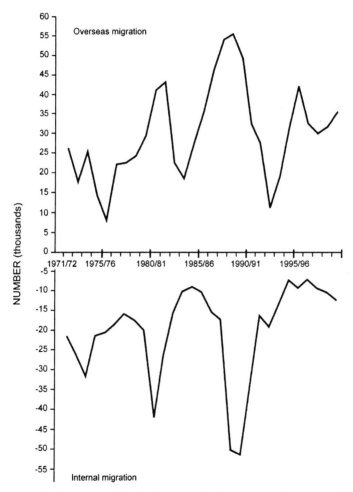

Fig. 4.6. Sydney statistical division: Net internal and international migration, 1971–2000. *Source:* Planning New South Wales.

causal linkage between high immigration levels and net internal migration losses. It is to this issue, in the Sydney context, that we now turn.

The first explanation was developed by John McKay and Jim Whitelaw (1978, 66), Chris Maher and John McKay (1986), and Wendy Jarvie (1989) and involved the idea of Sydney operating as a "switching point." This concept sees Sydney as the initial settling point of immigrants who are then subsequently recycled down the urban hierarchy within Australia. This argument views large cities as "halfway houses" that allow newly arrived migrants to adjust to life in Australia in the partially familiar environment of an ethnic enclave. It is expected that later they will move on when they have adjusted to Australian society and economy. The hypothesis is in fact the reverse of the escalator hypothesis considered earlier. There is some support for this theory in the Australian context from analyses of the internal migration of the overseas-born population (Bell and Hugo 2000). For example, table 4.3 shows that there was a net-migration loss of overseas-born persons through internal migration in 1996–2001, but it is apparent that the loss is overwhelmingly of migrants from mainly English-speaking-country origins, although those immigrants from non-English-speaking origins make up the majority of the overseas-born in Sydney. Analyses of internal migration of the overseas-born in Australia conclude

TABLE 4.3

SYDNEY STATISTICAL DIVISION: INTERNAL MIGRATION
BY BIRTHPLACE, 1996–2001

Birthplace	Immigrants		Outmigrants		Net migration	
	No.	%	No.	%	No.	%
Australia	138,915	80.5	183,754	80.1	-44,839	79.0
Foreign	33,637	19.5	45,588	19.9	-11,951	21.0
English-speaking country	13,785	8.0	24,094	10.5	-10,309	18.2
Non-English-speaking country	19,852	11.5	21,494	9.4	-1,642	2.8
Total	172,552	100.0	229,342	100.0	-56,790	100.0

Source: Australian Bureau of Statistics, 2001 Census, unpublished data.

that the overseas-born leaving Sydney are by no means a random cross-section of all Australian migrants (ibid.). They are almost all long-established immigrants. Indeed, some 92.5 percent of all immigrants moving into nonmetropolitan NSW between 1986 and 1991 had been in Australia longer than ten years. This figure compares with some 61.2 percent of Sydney's and 68.1 percent of the national overseas-born population having been in Australia for longer than ten years in 1991. Hence, the movement of overseas-born out of Sydney is highly selective of long-established immigrants. Second, it is clear that the movement is dominated by immigrants originating in mainly English-speaking-origin countries. Immigrants from mainly non-English-speaking countries made up only 24.7 percent of the internal migration gain of the overseas-born in nonmetropolitan areas, but they made up 58.4 percent of all Australian overseas-born and 69.9 of overseas-born residents of Sydney.

Indeed, there is evidence that some NES-origin communities in Sydney have not only provided anchors for settlement of newly arrived overseas immigrants of the same background but also attracted people of the same background who initially settled elsewhere in Australia but subsequently were drawn to the larger and more viable communities in Sydney. Ian Burnley (1989), for example, has shown that this movement was the case with the Vietnam-born, who often had little choice in where they initially settled because they arrived under the refugee part of the immigration program and were hence allocated to a hostel in a city where space was available. The attraction of a large, diversified community such as the one in Sydney, with the possibility of obtaining a job with a Vietnamese employer and access to services run by Vietnamese, has led to a great deal of secondary migration to Sydney.

It would thus appear that there is limited support for a "switching point" explanation of the relationship between internal and international migration in Sydney. This argument would run along the lines that with extended residence in Australia, the overseas-born converge toward the Australia-born in their demographic, economic, and social characteristics. This demographic convergence has been shown to be the case with other characteristics, such as fertility (Young 1991; Ware 1975). The argument that there is some convergence between overseas and Australia-born in

their patterns of internal migration as part of a wider process of adjustment to living in Australia is also supported by the fact that it is mainly
MES-origin immigrants who are involved in the counterurbanization process. MES-origin immigrants are more similar to the Australia-born than
NES-origin migrants (Wooden et al. 1994). It is apparent that proficiency
in English as well as other cultural elements facilitate more rapid adjustment to Australian society.

A second hypothesis, put forward by William Frey (1993) in the
United States, where a pattern similar to Sydney's is observed in Los
Angeles, is that net internal migration losses are owing to international
migrants "pushing out" long-standing residents through bidding down
wages, placing pressure on services, increasing costs of living in metropolitan areas, and creating a new "white flight." The data presented above
indicate that there can be no doubt that the Australia-born are disproportionately represented in the internal migration out of Sydney and that
the overseas-born component of that outflow disproportionately involves
migrants from the United Kingdom, Ireland, South Africa, New Zealand,
Canada, and the United States, while migrants from non-English-speaking origins are underrepresented.

Frey argues that the "white flight" out of the U.S. high-immigration
cities may also be partly a function of a "possible race and ethnic prejudice factor, which has long been known to effect local moves across neighborhoods and between cities and suburbs, when earlier immigrant waves
entered cities. It is conceivable that the increased multi-ethnic presence
that now encompasses entire metropolitan areas, and most neighborhoods
within them, could precipitate some of the metropolitan-wide out-migration in high immigration metros" (1996, 7). There is little direct evidence,
though, that such a push factor operates in the Sydney context. Indeed,
some might argue that the significant overseas-born component in the internal out-migration from Sydney would negate the Frey argument. However,
in this context it should be noted that although this out-movement most
certainly involves overseas-born persons, these people are overwhelmingly
from MES origins; when they involve NES groups, they are mainly drawn
from earlier waves of European immigration, not the new waves in which
groups from Asia and the Pacific dominate. Hence, ethnically, the incoming

immigration streams and international migrant streams moving to other Australian destinations are quite different.

How far is there a "white flight" from Sydney? Ian Burnley and Peter Murphy interviewed a sample of more than 250 migrants from Sydney to coastal New South Wales in 2000 and asked whether respondents thought migration out of Sydney was because there were "fewer immigrants" in the nonmetropolitan region. Around a quarter of the respondents considered this factor important. In a similarly sized sample in perimetropolitan areas outside of Sydney, 16 percent indicated it was an element in movement. The authors conclude, "Overall most movers did not consider the immigration factor as being fundamental, but clearly there were significant numbers who did" (2004, 149). Hence, there is some support for white flight being one of the elements in the internal migration flow out of Sydney.

The "push factors" operating on former residents of Sydney moving elsewhere in Australia may also be associated with the pressures that have built up in Sydney as a result of its continued growth within a relatively constrained physical situation (National Population Council 1991). These pressures have included the fact that Sydney has by far the highest housing costs in Australia and, as a result, one of the lowest rates of home ownership among Australia's cities. It also has the highest cost of living of the major cities in Australia and the longest average commuting times, there are signs of significant environmental strain in Sydney with respect especially to water and air pollution, and the city's infrastructure is under severe strain (ibid.). Some have blamed immigrants for these negative aspects that have increased the financial costs of living in Sydney and, to some extent, reduced the area's urban amenities (for example, Birrell 1990, 1991). It has been suggested that immigration is the direct cause of these negative externalities. In 1995, for example, the then newly elected premier of NSW called for a reduction of the immigration intake to reduce the economic, environmental, and infrastructural pressures developing in Sydney, and he continued to do so right up to his retirement in 2005 (Withers 2004). This position brought to the surface a debate that has continued for many years, with other commentators claiming that the blame for Sydney's difficulties hardly lies with newly arrived immigrants and has more to do with the inadequate planning for urban development and insufficient spending on infrastructure (Nieuwenhuysen 1995).

The relationship between immigration and housing in gateway cities is complex and significant. Burnley and Murphy (1994) have demonstrated a strong relationship between housing prices and immigration levels. However, Ley and Murphy (2001, 146) demonstrate that the relationship becomes more complex when there is a geographically disaggregated analysis. For example, the price increases are most marked in central areas. Certainly, Sydney has by far the highest cost of housing in Australia, and fieldwork indicates that some middle-aged out-migrants from Sydney are people who have used the capital gains earned by selling their Sydney homes to semiretire to nonmetropolitan locations. One area where little is known is the impact on the housing market of large numbers of temporary migrants. There can be little doubt that they have inflated the price of rental housing, especially in more central areas. However, the extent to which this price increase has pushed people out of Sydney is not known.

It has been claimed that high levels of immigration to Sydney have been responsible for the large increases in housing prices in the city. Indeed, it is clear that migrants coming to Australia under the "Business Migration Scheme" often have invested substantially in real estate (Shen 1996). J. Flood and colleagues (1991) have suggested that the pressure on housing prices created by immigrants may have been a factor precipitating long-established Sydney residents to move elsewhere. However, other studies (Burnley and Murphy 1994) have concluded that the soaring housing costs are just as much a reflection of poor planning and environmental restrictions on the expansion of Sydney. Burnley and Murphy (1994) have shown that much of the net internal migration loss in Sydney has been recorded from areas that have been the least affected by inflation in housing prices.

A third explanation sees the relationship between international and internal migration in Sydney as a function of the structural change in the city's economy as a result of its development as a world city (Hugo 1996). The argument here runs that the types of employment opportunities available in Sydney have undergone substantial change over the past two decades, which has meant that the match between the skills and experience of the longer-established population in the city and the job opportunities now available has become less close over that period. Accordingly, people with qualifications, skills, and experience inappropriate to the current labor market have tended to migrate out of the city. On the other hand, international migrants may be either better qualified or more willing than long-standing residents to take up opportunities in contemporary Sydney.

Some indications of the extent to which this situation has developed is evident in the changes in the labor force that have occurred in the Australia-born and overseas-born groups in Sydney. There was a greater increase in the number of persons employed in Sydney over the 1981–2001 period among the overseas-born (23.3 percent) than was the case among the Australia-born (16.8 percent). Hence, the overseas-born share of the labor force is increasing faster even than its share of the total population of Sydney. Overseas-born workers made up 33.0 percent of Sydney's labor force in 1981, 35.9 in 1991, and 36.2 in 2001. The impact of structural change is evident in the substantial loss of jobs in the manufacturing and utilities sectors for both Australia-born and overseas-born and in transportation and administration among the former. On the other hand, the most important gains were in construction, trade, financial services, property, and service industries. These gains are especially pronounced in relative terms among the overseas-born. The heaviest net losses of jobs among the Australia-born in Sydney have been in the unskilled, blue-collar, and clerical areas. It would thus appear that although structural change has impinged on both Australia-born and overseas-born groups, it has fallen especially hard on the former. On the other hand, the overseas-born have been more able to take up opportunities opened up by the development of tertiary and quaternary sectors of Sydney's economy (table 4.4). This fact is reflected in the occupational profile of overseas workers who have been resident for less than five years and are more concentrated in the areas of property and business, trade, accommodations, restaurants, finances, and insurance than is the case for the Australia-born or long-standing migrants (Hugo 2004).

Overall, it would appear that there is little evidence of incoming international migrants displacing Australia-born and long-standing overseas-born residents of Sydney from their jobs and pushing them to migrate elsewhere.

TABLE 4.4

SYDNEY STATISTICAL DIVISION: INDUSTRY BY BIRTHPLACE
BY YEAR OF ARRIVAL, 2001

| | Overseas-born | | | | Australia-born | |
| | Arrived 1996–2001 | | Arrived before 1996 | | | |
Industry	No.	%	No.	%	No.	%
Agriculture	200	0.2	2,600	0.5	7,500	0.7
Mining	100	0.1	300	0.1	1,500	0.1
Manufacturing	13,800	14.1	81,800	16.3	113,800	10.2
Electricity, gas,						
and water supply	200	0.2	2,900	0.6	8,700	0.8
Construction	6,500	6.6	34,700	6.9	78,300	7.0
Wholesale trade	7,100	7.3	35,400	7.1	63,200	5.7
Retail trade	13,600	13.9	61,500	12.3	159,800	14.3
Accommodation,						
cafés, and restaurants	7,500	7.7	27,100	5.4	47,900	4.3
Transport and storage	3,700	3.8	25,600	5.1	57,300	5.1
Communication services	2,600	2.7	14,300	2.9	26,400	2.4
Finance and insurance	7,900	8.1	30,000	6.0	69,100	6.2
Property and business						
services	18,600	19.0	72,500	14.5	166,700	14.9
Government						
administration						
and defense	1,800	1.8	15,400	3.1	43,800	3.9
Education	3,500	3.6	23,900	4.8	81,900	7.3
Health and						
community services	6,300	6.4	49,700	9.9	104,800	9.4
Cultural and						
recreational services	1,600	1.6	10,500	2.1	38,700	3.5
Personal and other						
services	2,900	3.0	12,700	2.5	48,200	4.3
Total	97,900	100.0	500,900	100.0	1,117,600	100.0

Source: Australian Bureau of Statistics, 2001 Census, One Percent Sample.

Certainly, job displacement is occurring, but not because of immigration; rather, it is a result of the processes of structural change, mechanization, and computerization of many blue-collar and clerical jobs; movement of manufacturing offshore; reduction of protective tariffs for Australian manufacturing; and deregulation of the labor market.

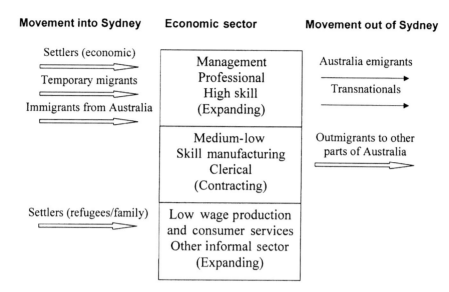

Fig. 4.7. Structural adjustment model of the relationship between internal and international migration.

Figure 4.7 is a diagrammatic representation of the structural adjustment explanation of the relationship between internal and international migration in Sydney. The upper and lower segments of the economy in the diagram are expanding while the middle sector is contracting, and migration is one of the elements involved in the expansion and contraction. It is also evident from a national internal migration study that environmental and lifestyle considerations are more important among internal migrants leaving Sydney than economic factors (Hugo et al. 2005). Moreover, many of the out-migrants from Sydney are able to sell their Sydney homes for substantially more than what they have to pay for equivalent or better housing at their new destinations.

SOCIAL AND POLITICAL REACTIONS TO IMMIGRATION

Australia and Sydney in particular have had a long history of immigration, and there has been a general acceptance of the beneficial impacts of immigration. Opinion polls show an increasing proportion of the population supporting the idea that immigration is a good thing for Australia. In

2004, some 66.1 percent agreed that Australian immigration levels were either about right or too low (Betts 2005). But there are also some in the community who oppose immigration, as was evident in the temporary rise in the mid-1990s of the anti-immigration One Nation political party (Jupp 2002). There have been, however, few incidents of violence such as the clash between Lebanese and other youth in the Sydney suburb of Cronulla in 2005 (Barclay and West 2006).

Immigration policy in Australia is totally within the federal government's ambit, but it has been shown that states and territories are becoming more significant players in both immigration and settlement (Hugo 2005). The issue of increasing concentration of Australia's immigrant intake in Sydney has seen some commentators (most notably the premier of New South Wales for the decade after 1995) argue that it has exerted pressure on the city's housing, infrastructure, and environment. Former premier Robert Carr repeatedly called for limitations on immigration to Sydney, as he saw the population growth they engendered as a cause of the city's economic, social, environmental, and infrastructural problems. Others have attacked this view as scapegoating and argued that the problems being experienced by Sydney are more a function of inadequate urban planning and resource allocation (Withers and Powell 2003; Nieuwenhuysen 1995). Undoubtedly, Premier Carr's views were a significant factor in the introduction of the "State Specific and Regional Migration Schemes" designed to divert immigrants away from Sydney, which in 2004–2005 accounted for 15.1 percent of the Australian immigrant intake (growing from 2.3 percent in the year of introduction, 1997–1998). These schemes include a range of settler categories that involve immigrants agreeing to settle for their first three years in Australia in "regional areas." The latter exclude the key current areas of settlement, including the Sydney metropolitan area. However, it would seem that Premier Carr's successor is not maintaining the vociferous opposition to migration. Other issues related to immigration that have attracted controversy in recent years include the debate about ethnic concentrations, which were discussed earlier in the chapter. Similarly, the periodic involvement of immigrants in crime is an issue that attracts public attention.

CONCLUSION

In classifying immigrant gateway cities (Singer 2004), Sydney is an "established" or "continuous" gateway in that for most of more than two centuries it has been either the main or the second most significant portal through which immigrants have entered, and settled in, Australia. However, this role must be seen as dynamic rather than static, as it has changed dramatically over this period. In the era of globalization Sydney has reasserted its dominance as Australia's most significant immigrant gateway after a quarter century when more immigrants settled in Melbourne. This chapter has argued that the role of immigration in the development of world cities is a complex one. World cities like Sydney are characterized by an increasing numerical and proportionate presence of immigrant settlers, and they play an important role in the economic, social, and cultural life of the city and in the elaboration of its crucial international linkages and networks. Sydney undoubtedly is the premier gateway for immigrants settling in Australia. But there are also other important and related migrations shaping Sydney and its role as a world city. In particular, temporary transnational migrants are important players in the world city's economy. However, it has also been argued that the world city not only is a gateway to settlers and temporary immigrants but also operates as an outward gateway for Australians seeking to live and work in higher-order cities. Finally, it has been shown that there are significant links between international migration in Sydney, or any world city, and internal migration linkages with the rest of the country.

Immigrant settlement in Sydney takes a distinctive form, with concentrations consisting of a diverse range of ethnic groups rather than a "ghetto" of a single group. The increasing significance of highly skilled migrants among the settlers has meant than immigrants are settling across the full gamut of socioeconomic areas and housing markets. As a result, the proportion of areas in which there is increasing diversity has expanded. Immigrants are well represented in both the most disadvantaged parts of Sydney and the better-off parts of the city.

(Im)Migration is a key process in the development of global cities, and will continue to be as the numbers and diversity of immigrants continue to grow. Immigration is the major engine of population growth, and immigrants are crucial to several sectors in the economy, shaping the cultural and social life of the city and developing vital transnational networks that link the city with the rest of the world. Yet our understanding of the dynamics of immigration in shaping world cities and its effects remains limited. A barrier to this search for understanding is a failure to recognize that the world city is an important and appropriate unit for analyzing the effects of both immigration and internal migration.

5

DiverCity Toronto

Canada's Premier Gateway City

LUCIA LO

As North American immigrant gateways go, Toronto is often overshadowed by the dominance of New York City. Yet Toronto's percentage of foreign-born residents far exceeds New York City's, and, by some measures, Toronto is more diverse than the metropolis to its south. Although some prefer to think of Toronto as a beta version of the globalopolis (Beaverstock, Smith, and Taylor 1999), Toronto outpaces most global cities as a region that trumpets multiculturalism and mutual respect among diverse cultures. Toronto is Canada's premier immigrant gateway. Thus, it is befitting to ask how well Toronto's immigrant population of more than 2 million people has integrated into such a racially and ethically diverse gateway. By integration, I refer to the process of creating long- and short-term arrangements between an immigrant group and a host society to fulfill the settlement needs and interests of immigrants, and to introduce newcomers to existing norms held by the wider community. Raymond Breton (1992) argues that there are three aspects of integration: first, the political and economic context that moderates the conditions of integration; second, the inclination of immigrants toward integration or segregation; and finally, the processes

This work was completed when the author was the economics domain leader of CERIS, the Joint Toronto Centre of Excellence for Research on Immigration and Settlement. The research was funded by the CERIS domain leader grant. The research assistance provided by Alexander Lovell is deeply appreciated.

by which agents of resettlement (both immigrant and native-born) engage with the local institutional setting.

The Canadian government officially endorses multiculturalism as a policy that celebrates diversity while treating all people equally, regardless of race or ethnicity. Multiculturalism is especially relevant to the question of immigrant integration because in theory immigrants are treated equally, free to live where they like, and have similar employment opportunities and income-generating capabilities as the native-born. How true is this supposition? Many would argue that this situation is hardly the case owing to the presence of institutional racism. Institutional policies and practices embedded within a set of cultural codes and understandings can consciously or unconsciously create barriers for professional and business developments of immigrants. For example, in Ontario, the home province of Toronto, only 35 percent of immigrants with professional backgrounds who require licensing, certification, or registration are working at the same status level in their field of expertise or a related field within four years of their arrival (Government of Ontario 2002). It is widely believed that "systemic barriers within the credentialing, experience recognition and employment processes . . . as well as barriers within the regulatory processes for individuals pursuing professional licensing and registration, amongst others, are responsible for this" (Afroza, Chakrawarti, and Rasheed 2006, 4). The same argument, referring to Canadian banking institutions, has also been suggested as an explanation as to why Caribbean and Somali immigrants in Toronto face more challenges than others in their entrepreneurial pursuits (Teixeira, Lo, and Truelove 2007).

Using the most recent data available at the time of writing (the 2001 Canadian Census), this chapter examines the social, spatial, and economic integration of immigrants in Toronto. It seeks to address the question posed above and identify experiences of exclusion in an immigrant gateway that is characterized by pluralism and globalness. This work begins with the premise that although racism has traditionally appeared to be a less prominent issue in Canada than in Australia, Great Britain, or the United States, immigrant complaints of discrimination do exist (Head 1975; Henry 1989, 1994; Darden 2004). This chapter explains how diversity is managed or incorporated into Toronto, and if it actually strengthens Toronto's position as a global city. Specifically, this work examines the spatial dimensions of urban immigrant settlement, and the achievements of immigrants in the general labor markets, paying particular attention to the presence of residential segregation and labor-market segmentation.

TORONTO AS A HYPERDIVERSE GATEWAY

Demographically, Canada presents a varied and rich cultural mosaic. The 2001 census lists more than 200 ethnic groups. According to Statistics Canada (2003), as of 2001, 5.4 million people, or 18.4 percent of the total population, were born outside the country. Internally, this figure was the highest proportion since 1931, when foreign-born people made up 22.2 percent of the population. This proportion is much higher than the 11 percent figure of the foreign-born in the United States in 2000. The increase has been great since the late 1980s, when the annual intake averaged about 1 percent of Canada's total population, proportionally higher than both the Untied States and Australia (where 22 percent of the population are foreign-born). In the 1990s, 2.2 million immigrants arrived in Canada, compared to the 1.3 million in each of the previous three decades. It reflects the increasing importance of immigration to the growth of the overall population as fertility rates decline.

Nearly 90 percent of Canada's immigrants settle in the provinces of British Columbia, Ontario, and Quebec. Not surprisingly, more than three-fourths of all Canadian immigrants are found in the three largest metropolises: Montreal, Toronto, and Vancouver. Of particular significance is that 44 percent of all immigrants in Canada reside in the Toronto Census Metropolitan Area (CMA).

In 2001, the Toronto CMA was home to more than 4.65 million people, including 2,032,905 immigrants from 169 countries, making Toronto the most multicultural region of Canada, and one of the largest immigrant destinations in the world. The CMA's proportion of immigrants, at 44 percent, was more than twice as high as Canada's national average of 18 percent, and is higher than Miami's 40 percent, Sydney's 31 percent, Los Angeles's 31 percent, and New York City's 24 percent (Statistics Canada 2003, 28).

On average, between 50,000 and 100,000 immigrants arrive in Toronto annually (Citizenship and Immigration Canada, various years). Prior to 1961, more than 90 percent of all Canadian immigrants came from Europe, whereas only 3 percent were born in Asia. During the 1990s, only 17 percent came from Europe and 63 percent from Asia (Statistics Canada 2003). The 1990s was a period of especially high immigrant growth: 792,000 immigrants arrived to make up 17 percent of the CMA's population. Of these immigrants, 11 percent came from China, 10 percent from India, and 7 percent each from the Philippines and Hong Kong. Other top countries of origin included Sri Lanka, Pakistan, Jamaica, Iran, Poland, and Guyana.

As the major destination city for new immigrants to Canada, Toronto has a large black population arriving from both the Caribbean and Africa, which distinguishes it from the other Canadian gateway cities. Since blacks generally report higher levels of perceived discrimination than other minorities (Breton et al. 1990; Dion 2001), Toronto is a critical "test case" to examine ethnic segregation and compare it with gateway cities in Europe and the United States.

Table 5.1 shows the top places of birth of Toronto's immigrants. Immigrants from 14 countries made up 31 percent of the CMA's total population. The largest source countries were India, the United Kingdom, Italy, China, Hong Kong, and the Philippines; each sent more than 100,000 immigrants to Toronto. Jamaica, Portugal, Poland, Sri Lanka, Guyana, Vietnam, and Pakistan sent between 50,000 to 100,000. Thus, in Toronto, South Asians, Chinese, Caribbeans, British, Italians, Filipinos, Portuguese, Polish, and Vietnamese are the largest immigrant groups. The picture is complex when place of birth and ethnicity are considered together. Although people of British origin accounted for almost 12 percent of the total population, immigrants from the United Kingdom stood at 3.4 percent of the total population. Similarly, ethnic Italians accounted for 9.5 percent of the total population, but Italian immigrants were about 3.3 percent. The percentage of ethnic Chinese and ethnic South Asians (including Indians, Pakistanis, Sri Lankans, and Bangladeshis) was slightly behind the number of the British, yet their immigrant proportions (more than 6 percent) were nearly twice the British figure. Because of these differences between old and new countries of origin, Toronto's ethnic composition is changing rapidly. In terms of ethnic origin (single response only), British and Italians retained the top two ranks until 2001, when ethnic Italians (9.5 percent) were replaced by ethnic Chinese (11.6 percent) as the second-largest ethnic group in Toronto,

TABLE 5.1

ORIGINS OF THE TORONTO CMA'S IMMIGRANT POPULATION, 2001

Place of birth	Number of immigrants	Percentage of all immigrants	Percentage of total population
India	147,165	7.2	3.5
United Kingdom	142,985	7.0	3.4
Italy	138,995	6.8	3.3
Mainland China	136,130	6.7	3.2
Hong Kong	110,730	5.4	2.6
Philippines	103,173	5.1	2.4
Jamaica	92,195	4.5	2.2
Portugal	78,895	3.9	1.9
Poland	70,495	3.5	1.7
Sri Lanka	68,790	3.4	1.6
Guyana	66,980	3.3	1.6
Vietnam	52,600	2.6	1.2
Pakistan	51,190	2.5	1.2
Trinidad/Tobago	43,705	2.1	1.0
Greece	35,055	1.7	0.8
Iran	34,925	1.7	0.8
Germany	31,230	1.5	0.7
Korea	31,080	1.5	0.7
Russia	23,205	1.1	0.5
Ukraine	22,390	1.1	0.5
Yugoslavia	21,115	1.0	0.5
Romania	20,805	1.0	0.5
Taiwan	14,760	0.7	0.3
Hungary	14,580	0.7	0.3
Croatia	13,310	0.7	0.3
South Africa	12,830	0.6	0.3
Egypt	12,445	0.6	0.3
Bangladesh	11,885	0.6	0.3
Afghanistan	11,660	0.6	0.3
Lebanon	10,585	0.5	0.2
Iraq	11,075	0.5	0.3
Tanzania	9,560	0.5	0.2
El Salvador	9,075	0.4	0.2
Kenya	8,890	0.4	0.2
Ireland	8,140	0.4	0.2

Source: Statistics Canada, 2001 Census.

followed closely by Indians (8.6 percent), and more distantly by Portuguese, Filipinos, Jamaicans, and Poles (between 2.6 and 4 percent).

Immigrants who arrived after the 1970s have dramatically altered the ethnic landscapes of Toronto. As table 5.2 indicates, Toronto's colored (visible minority, in official terms) population has increased fourfold since 1981, from 13.6 percent of the CMA total to 36.8 percent in 2001. The metropolitan area's visible minorities include 10 percent South Asians, 9 percent Chinese, 7 percent blacks, 3 percent Filipinos, 2 percent each of Arabs–West Asians and Latin Americans, and 1 percent each of Southeast Asians and Koreans. They speak more than a hundred tongues and are highly differentiated by class, religion, language, and culture. Among Toronto's immigrant population there were as many Muslims and Hindus combined (16 percent) as Protestants (15 percent) in 2001 (Citizenship and Immigration Canada 2005, 10). As a result of the points system intended to attract skilled immigrants, recent arrivals mostly have an urban middle-class background and are generally more educated than their predecessors. For example, in 2001, 38 percent of those individuals who immigrated between 1996 and 2001 held a university degree, compared with 18 percent of those individuals who arrived before 1986 (ibid., 16). Given this background, it is not surprising that the City of Toronto adopted the motto "Diversity, Our Strength" in 1998.

TABLE 5.2
TORONTO'S VISIBLE MINORITY POPULATION BETWEEN 1981 AND 2001

	Total population	Visible Minorities Number	Percentage of total population
1981	2,975,495	404,790	13.6
1986	3,399,680	586,500	17.3
1991	3,868,875	997,500	25.8
1996	4,232,905	1,338,095	31.5
2001	4,647,955	1,712,530	36.8

Source: Hou and Picot 2003.

IMMIGRANT SETTLEMENT: SHIFTING "GATEWAYS"
WITHIN THE GATEWAY

Toronto's immigrant population is concentrated in the urbanized part of the Census Metropolitan Area but, as expected, is not evenly distributed. Figure 5.1 shows the residential pattern of Toronto's immigrants in 2001. Affluent neighborhoods in the heart of Toronto and along the prestigious waterfront areas, as well as the urban fringe, have a smaller proportion of immigrants, especially immigrants of color.

In the early 1900s, Toronto was an extension of Great Britain, with a predominantly British character (Lemon 1985). Immigrants of non-British origins were relegated to the immigrant corridor of the city—now part of the inner core of the restructured city. The traditional reception areas in the corridor have been the first homes to generations of newcomers of various ethnicities—Chinese, Greek, Italian, Jewish, Polish, and Portuguese. Upon upward mobility, many first-generation immigrants or their children or both subsequently move to other parts of the city. So common is this passage that the reception areas along this corridor can be considered the smaller gateways within the larger gateway city.

These gateways or reception areas are, however, changing. During the past three decades, the region's immigrant settlement pattern noticeably changed. Immigrant groups such as the Chinese, Greeks, Italians, and Portuguese who arrived prior to the 1970s tended to settle in the traditional immigrant gateways in the inner city. These gateways are compact sociospatial units where a large number of immigrants from the same ethnic background live and where most of their cultural and religious institutions, businesses, and services are located. The spatial assimilation model predicts that with upward mobility, these groups would move to the suburbs and become spatially integrated with the dominant society. In the case of Toronto, these groups more often than not have resegregated. The newer groups that came after the 1970s do not necessarily follow this assimilation path. Many circumvent the traditional inner-city gateways and settle directly in the suburbs. More often, the affluent immigrants settle in the outer suburbs and the more disadvantaged ones in the inner

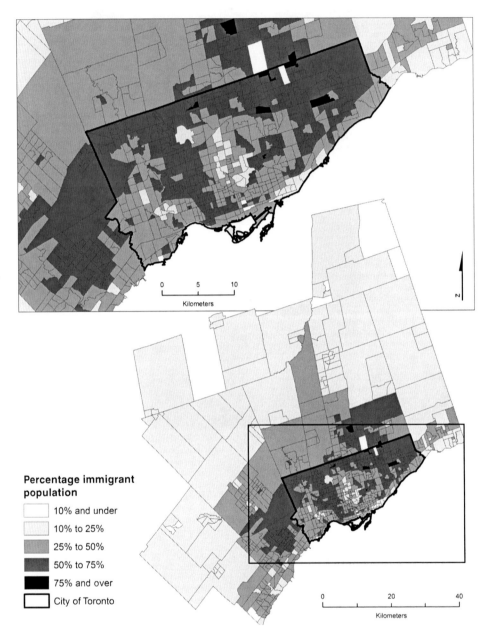

Fig. 5.1. Immigrant settlement patterns in the Toronto CMA, 2001. *Source:* Statistics Canada 2001.

suburbs. The overall pattern of immigrant settlement is characterized by increasing segregation.

Using census data, it is possible to chronicle the settlement patterns of recent immigrants over the past three decades. Recent immigrants are defined by Statistics Canada as those individuals who arrived in Canada within five years of the census day. To illustrate the changing trend, figures 5.2 and 5.3 contain location quotients that highlight where the new arrivals settled in 1971 and 2001. In 1971, the majority settled in the traditional inner-city gateways, forming an uneven V shape on both sides of the core of Toronto. Suburbanization of immigrant settlement began as some new arrivals joined more established families and friends who had already moved out to the inner suburbs of Toronto. The suburbanization of newcomers became obvious in 1981. The settlement of recent arrivals became more dispersed, forming a dotted circle around the most affluent neighborhoods of the city. Although the traditional immigrant corridor remained, suburban settlements took place both along the railroad lines of the west side (where some of the most undesirable neighborhoods are found) and in the new subdivisions of Scarborough in the northeastern part of the city. Since 1991, the declining role of the inner city as an immigrant destination and the increasing importance of the suburbs as new areas of settlement were apparent. In 1971, recent immigrants made up 47 percent of the immigrant population in traditional immigrant neighborhoods (here defined as those census tracts whose share of recent immigrants is at least twice as much as the CMA share). By 2001, the share of the foreign-born in these same tracts had dropped to 23 percent. The former gateways have begun undergoing gentrification; housing prices have become too expensive for those new immigrants arriving with few resources.

From 1900 to 1970, the traditional immigrant neighborhoods (gateways) were home to mostly Chinese, Greeks, Italians, Jews, and Portuguese. With the exception of the Greeks, these groups had their enclaves very close to one another. Over time, especially since the 1950s, these communities expanded and dispersed to single-family dwellings found in the suburbs. For most groups, "home ownership was a major goal and the move to the suburbs was both an expression of upward economic mobility and a way of showing that mobility" (Murdie and Teixeira 2003, 152). However, in the

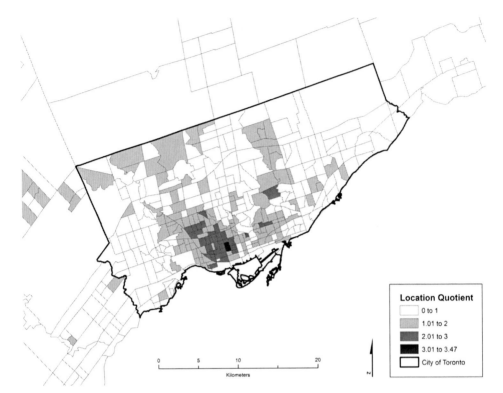

Fig. 5.2. Settlement patterns of recent immigrants to Toronto, 1971. *Source:* Statistics Canada 1971.

process of moving out, some groups became more spatially integrated and others resegregated. Resettlement also took different directions. Noticeably, the Italians moved in a northwestern direction, the Portuguese in a western direction, and the Chinese mostly in a northeastern direction. The degree of resegregation varies. It was highest among the Chinese and lowest among the Greeks. Resettlement took two major forms: the corridor expansion of the Italians was accompanied by little retention of their original inner-city residential neighborhoods, and the suburban relocation of the Chinese, Greeks, and Portuguese was accompanied by the retention of a relatively strong residential and commercial presence in the inner city.

Since 1970, Asia has become the largest source of immigrants to Canada. The Asians are a highly differentiated group, including refugees from Vietnam and Sri Lanka; highly skilled immigrants from mainland China,

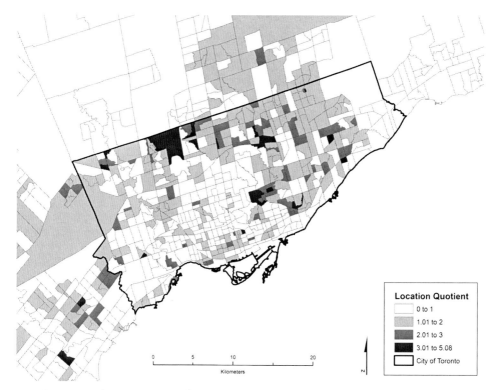

Fig. 5.3. Settlement patterns of recent immigrants to Toronto, 2001. *Source:* Statistics Canada 2001.

India, and Korea; wealthy Chinese immigrants from Hong Kong and Taiwan; and live-in domestic workers from the Philippines. Their presence has altered both the ethnic makeup and the residential and commercial landscapes of Toronto. Their different immigration statuses have influenced where they have settled. For example, Chinese from Hong Kong and Taiwan have settled directly in the suburbs, whereas those immigrants from China and Vietnam typically sought the inner-city Chinatowns where relatively inexpensive rental housing was still available (Lo and Wang 1997). Unlike the Chinese, Indians in particular and South Asians in general did not have preexisting inner-city ethnic enclaves to receive and assist them during their initial settlement. Hence, they settled mostly in the suburbs, the well-to-do in the outer suburbs of Brampton close to the Italians and the less affluent in cheap rental housing in Etobicoke. The Filipinos, Koreans, and Vietnamese did not form residential enclaves, although a few pockets of concentration can be discerned.

A similar pattern of dispersed and decentralized settlements holds true for the remaining immigrant groups from the Caribbean, Africa, and Latin America. The Caribbean community has been around since the 1950s. This community is a highly varied group originating from many countries (Jamaica, Guyana, and Trinidad and Tobago) and ethnic backgrounds (African Caribbean, Chinese, and South Asian). As a group, they have not formed ethnic enclaves, although pockets of concentration are evident in both the inner city and the suburbs (Ley and Smith 1997; Murdie 1996; Ray 1998). Most of these concentrations are in public housing provided by the Toronto Community Housing Corporation (Murdie and Teixeira 2003).

African immigrants and refugees from Somalia and Ghana tend to locate in the older suburbs of Etobicoke and North York and concentrate in a few high-rise apartment buildings. This pattern of settlement is the result of several factors: the availability of low-cost private rental housing offering multibedroom configurations, the lack of resources on the part of the refugees, a highly structured social network in the housing search process, and opportunities for employment in manufacturing firms that are increasingly located in the suburbs of Toronto (Opoku-Dapaah 1995; Owusu 1999).

In sum, the residential geographies of immigrant groups arriving since the 1970s have been very diffuse. Whereas the larger and more privileged groups such as the Chinese and Indians moved to the suburbs, smaller groups such as the Ghanaians, Iranians, Pakistanis, Somalis, and Sri Lankans, who have not yet had the population numbers or settlement history to build institutionally complete neighborhoods with their own cultural, religious, and business organizations, tend to reside in highly segregated multiethnic areas of concentration dispersed throughout Toronto in areas often associated with poorly maintained private rental complexes and public housing developments (Murdie and Teixeira 2003).

Of course, the growth of Toronto's immigrant population and the resulting changes in the city's ethnic geography did not take place in a vacuum. They reflect the major demographic, social, and economic trends that have transformed the region, including population growth fueled by both immigration and internal in-migration, the development of Toronto as Canada's most important financial and business center, and the growth of the service sector in Canada's economy. For immigrants who arrived after 1970, their economic status—often associated with race—and the structure of Toronto's housing market influenced their residential location. Between 1961 and 2001, the population of the Toronto CMA more than doubled, producing a substantial demand for the construction of new and expensive homes on the suburban fringe, some within financial reach of more affluent immigrant groups. In the central city, executive jobs in the financial sector remained as manufacturing activities and routine office functions decentralized to the suburbs. Gentrification of the central city, much encouraged by city planning policies since the 1970s, has tended to displace low-income households to the inner suburbs that were mostly built between 1945 and the 1970s. The inner suburbs, where a considerable amount of public and low-cost private rental housing was built in the 1960s and 1970s, offered rental opportunities for many newcomers.

RESIDENTIAL SEGREGATION AND ETHNIC ENCLAVES

In 2001, 2 million immigrants called Toronto home. Of the immigrants from the top twenty sending countries in Toronto, 26.6 percent were from Europe, 34.4 percent from Asia, 9.9 percent from the Caribbean, and 1.7 from the Middle East. This section examines the spatial integration of these immigrant groups by identifying their degree of residential concentration or segregation and the social distance among different groups.

Immigrant Concentration

It is often believed that an immigrant group is spatially integrated if its members do not form residential enclaves, commonly defined as a particular demographic constituting 30 percent or more of a neighborhood's total population. In this chapter, accordingly, if an immigrant group dominates the immigrant population in an area, it indicates an emerging enclave formation. There are only six immigrant groups in Toronto with dominant residential enclaves (that is, when 50 percent or more of immigrants in a

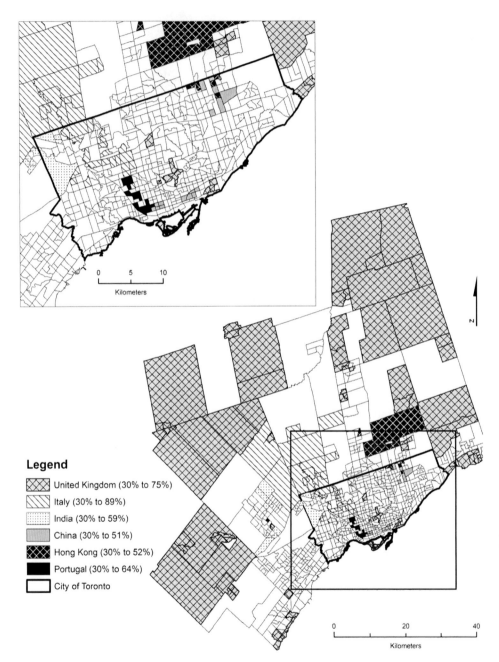

Legend

- United Kingdom (30% to 75%)
- Italy (30% to 89%)
- India (30% to 59%)
- China (30% to 51%)
- Hong Kong (30% to 52%)
- Portugal (30% to 64%)
- City of Toronto

Fig. 5.4. Dominant immigrant groups in the Toronto CMA, 2001. *Source:* Statistics Canada 2001.

neighborhood belong to a particular ethnic group). As depicted in figure 5.4, they are those immigrants from China, Hong Kong, India, Italy, Portugal, and the United Kingdom, all large immigrant groups. Chinese and Italians, followed by Indians and Portuguese, have the largest number of residential enclaves. Whereas the Chinese presence is still felt in the traditional immigrant reception areas, both Chinese and Italian enclaves are found in both the inner and the outer suburbs of Toronto, the Italians in the west and the Chinese in the east. The Portuguese and Indian enclaves are respectively found in the inner city and the suburbs.

Another, perhaps less scale-dependent, indicator is the percentage of census tracts within a region that contains half of an immigrant group's population (Qadeer 2003). Considering the cumulative sum of the most concentrated neighborhoods, this concentration index represents the proportion of census tracts one would need to access to find half the population. The lower the score, the more concentrated the immigrant group in the metropolitan area. Table 5.3 shows the scores for the main immigrant groups against their group's size by order of concentration. Thirty-five immigrant groups accounted for 82 percent of Toronto's immigrants and 40 percent of its total population. This method shows that British, Chinese, Indians, and Italians are not the most concentrated immigrant groups. In fact, immigrants from Britain are the least concentrated, as one would have to visit a quarter of the census tracts in the CMA to find 50 percent of the British immigrants, whereas less than 5 percent of the tracts need to be visited to locate 50 percent of the Afghans, Bangladeshis, Hong Kong Chinese, Iraqis, and Russians. Of the twenty most concentrated groups by this measure, only six have signs of visible enclaves: Hong Kong Chinese, Indians, Italians, mainland Chinese, Portuguese, and Russians. In this way, segregation and the formation of enclaves are two separate things. Larger groups are more likely to form enclaves, whereas segregation is unrelated to group size.

Regardless of their absolute numbers, most immigrants tend to settle among their coethnics. Among the thirty-five groups shown in Table 5.3, some panregional or panethnic neighborhoods exist. I and Shuguang Wang (1997) have shown both convergence and divergence in the spatial distribution of four Chinese subgroups—immigrants from China, Hong Kong,

TABLE 5.3

CONCENTRATION OF MAIN IMMIGRANT GROUPS, 2001

Place of birth	Number in Toronto CMA	Percentage of total immigrant population	Percentage of total population	Percentage of tracts with 50 percent of group's population
United Kingdom	142,985	7.0	3.4	25.4
Korea	31,080	1.5	0.7	18.5
Trinidad/Tobago	43,705	2.1	1.0	18.2
Philippines	103,173	5.1	2.4	14.9
Jamaica	92,195	4.5	2.2	14.6
Ireland	8,140	0.4	0.2	14.5
Hungary	14,580	0.7	0.3	14.1
Guyana	66,980	3.3	1.6	12.2
Poland	70,495	3.5	1.7	11.6
Yugoslavia	21,115	1.0	0.5	11.6
Greece	35,055	1.7	0.8	11.0
Pakistan	51,190	2.5	1.2	10.4
Egypt	12,445	0.6	0.3	10.2
Vietnam	52,600	2.6	1.2	9.8
Croatia	13,310	0.7	0.3	9.7
Kenya	8,890	0.4	0.2	9.7
Romania	20,805	1.0	0.5	9.6
India	147,165	7.2	3.5	9.5
China (PR)	136,130	6.7	3.2	8.7
Italy	138,995	6.8	3.3	8.3
South Africa	12,830	0.6	0.3	8.2
Lebanon	10,585	0.5	0.2	7.9
El Salvador	9,075	0.4	0.2	6.8
Iran	34,925	1.7	0.8	6.5
Sri Lanka	68,790	3.4	1.6	6.3
Tanzania	9,560	0.5	0.2	6.3
Portugal	78,895	3.9	1.9	5.7
Ukraine	22,390	1.1	0.5	5.5
Taiwan	14,760	0.7	0.3	5.4
Afghanistan	11,660	0.6	0.3	5.0
Hong Kong	110,730	5.4	2.6	4.9
Iraq	11,075	0.5	0.3	4.0
Russian	23,205	1.1	0.5	3.9
Bangladesh	11,885	0.6	0.3	2.8

Source: Statistics Canada, 2001 Census.

Taiwan, and Vietnam who claim Chinese ethnicity—that made up 84 percent of the total Chinese immigrant population in the Toronto CMA in 1991
and nearly 90 percent in 2001. Convergence is explained by cultural similarity, and divergence is related to differences in economic status and exposure
to Western culture. The same pattern may apply to South Asians and Caribbeans and Africans, although the divergence explanation can vary.

It is interesting to note that although the black population (Caribbean
and African) in Toronto is comparable in size to the Chinese population
and South Asians, they do not form dominant enclaves. The most plausible
explanation is that the black community in Toronto came from diverse origins, consisting of immigrants and refugees from various Caribbean islands
and African countries, many having been British colonies in times past.
In a sense it is a community of communities. As native English speakers
familiar with the "Anglo" culture, some black immigrants may feel less
need to stay spatially close to each other. Additionally, the fact that Canada
does not have a history of slavery, such as the United States, may make a
difference in Canadian urban settlement patterns. Blacks in Toronto are,
however, one of the most disadvantaged groups in terms of socioeconomic
indicators. It is very important, then, that their pattern of dispersed settlement may be explained by their dependence on public housing, which is
scattered throughout the city.

Immigrant Social Distance

Segregation can also be measured by the dissimilarity index. This index
measures how close two groups live together. It compares two groups
with the sum of the differences in their proportional representation in
each census tract. An index of less than 30 indicates low segregation from
other groups, between 30 and 60 denotes moderate segregation, and anything above 60 is considered high segregation (Massey and Denton 1993).
One criterion for convergence is the absence of heavy segregation among
groups. Table 5.4 reports the index for selected ethnic groups. Generally speaking, Toronto's immigrant groups are marked by only moderate
separation. The Russians, mostly of Jewish origin, appear most separated
from the other groups, whereas Filipinos, working largely as domestic

TABLE 5.4
INDEX OF DISSIMILARITY, 2001

	Chinese	South Asian	Black	Italian	Portuguese	Polish	Filipino	Vietnamese	Korean	Latin American	West Asian	Russian
British	31.3	26.2	32.5	28.3	27.8	24.1	24.7	33.4	27.1	33.0	31.1	30.9
Chinese		25.5	34.9	33.9	33.3	32.9	26.0	31.8	25.3	35.5	29.6	33.0
South Asian			20.2	27.9	27.6	27.0	17.6	27.3	28.5	28.8	25.6	34.1
Black				26.3	32.0	32.1	25.7	30.3	34.4	31.0	32.6	38.9

Source: Statistics Canada, 2001 Census.

caregivers, and South Asians, composed of different religious and national groups, are the least segregated. The color of one's skin appears to be one factor behind social separation. As table 5.4 demonstrates, people of British origin tend to live closer to the other white or fair-skinned ethnic groups such as the Italians, Poles, and Portuguese. Chinese reside closer to other Asians (for example, Koreans, Filipinos, and South Asians) and most distant from blacks. Besides the British, Chinese, and Russians, blacks are also more distant from the Polish and Portuguese than from Filipinos, Italians, and South Asians. It appears that even in multiethnic Toronto, one's race and, to a lesser extent, cultural similarities influence where one is likely to reside.

IMMIGRANT LABOR MARKET

The immigrants who arrived after 1970 are substantially different from their predecessors. They are more diverse in terms of their fluency in English, formal qualifications, and educational attainment (Citizenship and Immigration Canada 2005). Their economic experiences are equally varied, some easily integrated into the Toronto economy, whereas others struggled to be included. This section outlines the current state of knowledge about the labor-market experiences and socioeconomic outcomes of immigrants based on their period of entry, age, gender, and ethnoracial background.

Immigrant Status and Industry of Employment

As reported for both 1996 and 2001 (Ornstein 2006; Preston, Lo, and Wang 2003), many of Toronto's immigrants work in a handful of specific industries, namely, construction, garment manufacturing, and child care, often earning low wages and experiencing job insecurity. The goods-producing sectors of manufacturing and construction and specific consumer services, including accommodations, food, beverages, and personal services, are also major sources of employment for immigrants (Preston and Giles 1997; Mata 1996; Richmond 1992). However, patterns of industrial concentration vary depending on immigrants' gender and race or ethnicity.

Immigrant men and women often work in different industries, with immigrant women more likely to suffer from precarious and poorly paid employment. Ethnoracial background affects immigrants' industrial division of labor such that immigrants of color are overrepresented in the least-desirable industries, such as manufacturing, accommodation, and food and beverage services (Hiebert 1999; Mata 1996; Preston and Giles 1997; Preston and Cox 1999; Reitz 1998; Ornstein 2006).

In 2001, immigrants accounted for 48.4 percent of Toronto's employed workforce. Table 5.5 compares the participation of immigrants and the Canadian-born in major industries. Location quotients have helped identify the industries in which immigrants from each ethnoracial group are over- and underrepresented. Many differences are evident. The location quotients exceed 1 (which indicates overrepresentation) in six out of sixteen industries. They indicate that immigrant employment is concentrated in manufacturing; accommodation, food, and beverage services; other service industries; administrative and support and waste services; health and social services; and construction. In particular, immigrants are twice as likely to work in manufacturing, a declining industry in today's knowledge-based economy. They are also overrepresented in accommodation, food, and beverage and other service industries. In total, one-third of the immigrant force is employed in these old and declining industries shunned by the Canadian-born. They are underrepresented in the new and desirable industries: arts, entertainment, and recreation; government and educational services; and information and cultural industries. Earlier studies (for example, Preston, Lo, and Wang 2003) have shown that many immigrant women work in service industries, particularly other services, health and educational services, and financial, insurance, and real estate services, whereas immigrant men are more likely to work in construction, manufacturing, regulated utilities, and wholesale trade. Employment in accommodation, food, and beverage services is an exception to this pattern of gender differences. In 1996, among the Canadian-born, women and men had almost equal shares of employment in those industries, yet the relationship was reversed for immigrant workers (ibid.). Immigrants settle for jobs in the accommodation, food, and beverages sector because entry costs are

TABLE 5.5

PERCENTAGE OF EMPLOYMENT AND LOCATION QUOTIENTS
BY INDUSTRY AND IMMIGRANT STATUS, 2001

Industry	Percentage Canadian	Percentage immigrant	Location quotient
Manufacturing	11.1	20.6	1.85
Construction	4.8	5.0	1.05
Utilities	0.7	0.5	0.78
Wholesale	6.4	5.7	0.90
Retail	11.8	9.9	0.84
FIRE (finance, insurance, real estate)	9.5	9.1	0.95
Information and cultural industries	4.9	3.1	0.64
Professional, scientific, and technical industries	10.7	8.8	0.82
Management of companies	0.2	0.2	0.77
Administrative and support and waste services	4.5	5.1	1.14
Government	4.2	2.5	0.59
Education	7.0	4.3	0.61
Health and social services	7.2	7.9	1.09
Arts, entertainment, and recreation	2.6	1.1	0.42
Accommodation, food, and beverage	5.0	6.3	1.26
Other services	3.8	4.9	1.27
N	1,290,125	1,208,940	

Source: Statistics Canada, 2001 Census.

low, skill requirements are minimal, and other job opportunities are not available to them (Waldinger 1997).

Table 5.5 highlights the importance of jobs in manufacturing and accommodation, food, and beverage sectors for immigrant workers. Only a small proportion of immigrants work in the educational, government, and business service sectors where, traditionally, employment has been well paid and secure. The continued reliance of immigrants on manufacturing and hospitality jobs as a major source of employment renders them vulnerable to layoffs and unemployment. In particular, the manufacturing sector has experienced an overall decline since 1981, and employment in the hospitality sector is often unstable and subject to economic fluctuations that leave immigrants vulnerable.

Ethnoracial Backgrounds and Labor Divisions

Comparing the ethnoracial background of immigrant groups with their insertion in the labor market shows clear patterns of labor-market segmentation. Immigrants from western and northern Europe (including Britain and France) are similarly represented as the native-born population in all but three industries—utilities, retail trade, and accommodation, food, and beverage—in which they are underrepresented. Southern and eastern Europeans such as those immigrants from Italy, Portugal, and Poland dominate the manufacturing and construction industries. The southern Europeans' dominance in construction is especially notable. East Asians, especially Chinese, are overrepresented in manufacturing and accommodation, food, and beverage, but they are also well represented in the financial, insurance, and real estate and professional, scientific, and technical areas, showing a bifurcation in their industrial-occupational skills. South and Southeast Asians are overrepresented in manufacturing. The South Asians are also strong in transportation; administrative, support, and waste services; and accommodation, food, and beverage services. The major industries of employment for people from the Caribbean are very similar to the South Asians', with the exception that Caribbeans are also highly represented in health and social services. Many Caribbean women are known to work as nurses and orderlies in Toronto's hospitals. Immigrants from Africa, South Asia, and the Middle East have similar employment characteristics—they are overrepresented in manufacturing; retail; administrative, support, and waste services; and accommodation, food, and beverage services.

Generally speaking, Toronto's labor market is marked by a persistent concentration of immigrants of color in manufacturing and the accommodation, food, and beverage industries. Immigrants are offered few employment opportunities in government services, regulated utilities, the education field, and information and cultural industries. An industrial division of labor occurs in Toronto: Caribbeans, Southeast Asians, Americans, and Africans in health and social services; blacks (both from Africa and from the Caribbean), Latin Americans, and South Asians in administrative support and waste services; South Asians and Caribbeans in transportation and warehousing; North Africans and West Asians in retail; Americans, British, East Asians, and East Europeans in professional, scientific, and technical services; Chinese and other East Asians in financial, insurance, and real estate services; and British, western, and northern Europeans in government and education services.

Visible-Minority Status and Occupational Segmentation

Visible minorities, or immigrants of color, are especially vulnerable in Toronto's labor market. The evidence is clear when immigrant groups are compared to the British along occupation lines. First, people of western and northern European ethnicity are the most similar to the British in all occupational classes. Second, immigrants of eastern and southern European origins are underrepresented in management and professional jobs but are equally represented as the British in all other jobs. Third, visible minorities are, generally speaking, heavily concentrated in semiskilled and unskilled manual occupations and experience much fewer opportunities as managers and professionals. The only exceptions are Chinese, Japanese, and Korean men. The Chinese are known to have a bifurcated presence in the labor force (Lo and Wang 2004): many of the Chinese who arrived in the 1960s and 1970s have Canadian university degrees, whereas the Chinese who came in the 1990s, though highly educated, had difficulty getting their credentials and foreign work experience recognized and therefore worked in lower-status jobs. With the Japanese, few immigrated after World War II; the ones in management were likely to be born or educated in Canada. Unlike the Chinese and Japanese, a high proportion of Koreans are self-employed, thereby automatically assuming management titles. Among other visible-minority groups, the Vietnamese, who came largely as refugees, are the most overrepresented in semiskilled and unskilled occupations, followed by Filipinos and other Southeast Asians, South Asians, and Caribbeans. Last, visible-minority women are more likely than visible-minority men to work in the lowest rungs of the occupational ladder. For example, whereas Vietnamese men are three times more likely as British men to work as semiskilled manual workers and twice as likely to be employed as unskilled manual labor, Vietnamese women are, respectively, eleven times and seven times as likely as their British counterparts to be in semiskilled manual and unskilled manual jobs. The precarious nature of immigrant women's work in the Toronto labor market is especially troubling.

IMMIGRANT ECONOMIC ACHIEVEMENT

The low-status jobs of many immigrants in the Toronto labor market are reflected in their varied levels of economic attainment. This section explores the economic achievement of ethnoracial groups through an examination of unemployment rates and median employment income.

Unemployment Rates

Both immigrant men and women experience higher rates of unemployment than their Canadian-born counterparts (5.8 percent versus 4.9 percent for men and 7.7 percent versus 5.2 percent for women). In particular, there is a linear progression such that recent immigrants have higher rates of unemployment; for example, the rate for men who immigrated in the 1970s is 3.7 percent, whereas the rate for men who came in the 1990s is 8.6 percent. The most recent cohorts, who arrived between 1996 and 2001, experienced double-digit unemployment rates. Unemployment for immigrant men (10.3 percent) is twice the rate of Canadian-born men, and immigrant women have three times the rate of unemployment (15.3 percent) when compared to native-born women.

Visible-minority immigrant groups fare worse than white immigrants. With no exceptions, those immigrants who were born outside of western Europe and North America suffer from higher levels of unemployment. Of the latter two groups, only immigrants from France have unemployment rates higher than the Canadian-born. There are few French immigrants in Toronto; thus, their higher unemployment rates may be language related. The unemployment rates of immigrants from Asia, Africa, and Latin America are much higher than what is experienced by the Canadian-born and western European immigrants. Among all immigrant groups, except

the French, female unemployment rates are higher than male unemployment rates. The differential is especially high for women from South Asia,
the Middle East, and Africa. In addition, there is a wide range of female
unemployment rates, from 4 percent to 12.1 percent. These results are consistent with previous evidence that immigrants in general, and immigrant
women in particular, are at a disadvantage in competing for jobs in the
Toronto labor market (Preston and Cox 1999).

Employment Income

The employment income of immigrants is again closely related to their
period of arrival and their visible-minority status. As with unemployment
rates, those immigrants who arrived prior to the 1971 are more likely to
attain income parity with the Canadian-born, whereas those individuals
who came in the 1990s earn only a fraction of what their Canadian counterparts earn.

The median employment income of visible-minority immigrants was
$25,077 in 2001, three-quarters of what an average non-visible-minority
immigrant made. Except for immigrants from Japan, all visible-minority
groups earned less than the average native-born Torontonian. Employment
income is also gendered, with immigrant women earning 30 percent less
than their male counterparts. The gender differential is greatest among
Japanese and Arabs, likely owing to their cultural practices of not being
particularly concerned about women's careers. The gender income differential is smallest among Filipinos, blacks, and Caribbeans. Immigrant
women from these groups in fact have higher incomes than the average
metropolitan resident.

In terms of income generation, immigrant men from Britain, northern
Europe, and Germany are the top earners, and immigrant men from Korea
and the Middle East earn the least. The rank ordering of their female counterparts is different: female immigrants from France and Britain are at the
top, whereas women from the Middle East, Korea, Latin America, and
Vietnam are at the bottom.

In sum, poverty, low education, and unemployment exist in every ethnoracial group. However, these problems are spread very unevenly across

groups. Racial inequality exists, with the most socioeconomically disadvantaged being Africans, Jamaicans, Tamils, Sri Lankans, Pakistanis, Bangladeshis, Vietnamese, Iranians, and Latin Americans. What can explain the variation in immigrants' economic status? The literature attributes it to three major factors. First, duration of residence alters an immigrant's employment and economic status. Although concentrated initially in the least-desirable jobs, with the passage of time, immigrants are expected to achieve parity in wages and in the industrial division of employment (DeVoretz 1995; Ley 1999). Hence, older immigrant groups are doing better than recent groups. Second, the qualifications and educational levels of immigrants have changed as Canadian immigration policy has refined the points system to select more highly skilled immigrants. Among independent immigrants who have arrived since 1980, the ability to speak one of Canada's official languages has increased (Badets and Howaston-Lee 1999; Citizenship and Immigration Canada 2005). At the same time, more business migrants who are less likely to be highly educated and who often have limited fluency in either official language have been admitted under the entrepreneurial and investor programs (Ley 1999; Reitz 1998). Third, more selective immigration policies coincide with a shift in the origins of many immigrants. Asian, African, Caribbean, and Latin American countries have replaced European countries as the main sources of immigrants. As visible minorities, these non-European immigrants are more vulnerable to discrimination in the labor market (Reitz 1998).

INTEGRATION PROBLEMS IN CANADA'S DIVERCITY CAPITAL

How well do immigrants integrate in a racially and ethically pluralist Toronto that celebrates multiculturalism and adopts the motto "Diversity, Our Strength"?

The evidence presented indicates that the social and economic geographies of Toronto's immigrants are segmented. On the social side, most immigrant groups, irrespective of their size and history of settlement, to a certain extent, tend to segregate spatially and socially. On the one hand, segregation happens in the immigrant enclaves of the urban core, as well as in suburban localities. Whereas the larger British, Chinese, and Indian groups establish more enclaves, the smaller Bangladeshi, Iraqi, and Russian communities are highly concentrated in a few neighborhoods. On the other hand, Toronto's ethnic landscape is marked by a moderate degree of separation among its immigrant groups. With the British living closer to the Italians, Poles, and Portuguese; the Chinese to the Koreans, Filipinos, and South Asians; and the blacks more distant from the Polish and Portuguese than from Filipinos and South Asians, skin color, in association with cultural similarities, appears to influence intergroup social distances.

Like elsewhere, the phenomenon of spatial segregation and social separation cannot be easily explained. It involves a complex array of choices and constraints, ranging from a group's history of settlement in Toronto, its socioeconomic status and wealth position on arrival, the availability of public and private housing, the structure of Toronto's housing market, and the process of racialization. Apart from the obvious draw of cultural similarity and social networks, immigrant concentration by and large is affected by the nature of Toronto's housing and real estate markets. The latter is particularly influenced by the process of economic globalization, which tends to fill the downtown core with corporate headquarters and a professional class of workers with an appetite for cultural and other creative activities (Florida 2002). This trend adds to the pace of gentrification, turning once undesirable "immigrant or ethnic" neighborhoods into high-demand areas.

Currently in Toronto, race has not impacted residential segregation as much as it has in the United States. Blacks in Toronto have a lower degree of segregation than other racialized groups, in part because of their diverse origins and the dispersal of public and social housing in the region. Despite the presence of pockets of poverty, Toronto does not have the levels of concentrated urban poverty seen in the United States. Yet trend analyses have identified troubling signs that Toronto is moving in the direction of ethnic segregation and poverty concentration (Heisz and McLeod 2004; Hou and Picot 2003; Ornstein 2006; Picot and Hou 2003; United Way of Greater Toronto and the Canadian Council on Social Development 2004). Whereas poverty-stricken neighborhoods of the past comprised mainly the Canadian-born, today's poor neighborhoods, intensifying in the inner suburbs as opposed to the city core, are multiethnic, comprising predominantly newcomers and visible minorities (United Way of Greater Toronto and the Canadian Council on Social Development 2004).

With respect to the economic integration of Toronto's immigrants, the picture is likewise disturbing. Similar to what others have found in cities with heavy in-migration flows, the immigrant workforce concentrates in declining industries such as manufacturing, hospitality, and support services. Jobs in these sectors are often precarious. Only a small proportion of immigrants work in traditionally well-paid and secure educational, government, and business service sectors. There is a racialized industrial division of labor, with British and Europeans more likely to be employed in government, educational, professional, and technical services; East Asians in financial, insurance, and real estate services; South Asians and Caribbeans in transportation and warehousing; and Caribbeans, Africans, and Latin Americans in administrative and health support services and waste services.

With regard to occupations, racial inequality continues even after controlling for education and age. A progression of color again takes place. The darker one's skin, the more likely one ends up in a semiskilled or unskilled job. It has been reported elsewhere that it now takes recent arrivals to Toronto, compared with their earlier cohorts, a much longer time to attain economic parity.

It is distressing to see this picture taking place at the same time that Toronto's immigrant population is generally becoming more educated. Immigrants suffer from institutionalized labor devaluation because their foreign credentials and foreign work experience are not recognized. At the same time, Canada's point system encourages highly skilled immigrants but ignores lesser-skilled immigrants who might be better suited for low-skill jobs. Global cities are places of contradictions. They house the wealthiest as well as the poorest. They attract both financial and human capital. They rely on foreign capital inflows to propel their economies. They rely on large numbers of immigrants to keep themselves operational, but immigrant skills and contributions often go unrecognized. Toronto is no exception. Its cultural diversity makes the region a vibrant and exciting place to live in, yet that same diversity has helped produce a bifurcated labor pool with visible-minority immigrants serving subordinate roles. While light-skinned immigrants enjoy stable and well-paid jobs in the upper rung of the occupational ladder, dark-skinned migrants suffer from underemployment and unemployment. As Manuel Castells has stated, "Immigrant workers do not exist because there are 'arduous and badly paid' jobs to be done, but, rather, arduous and badly paid jobs exist because immigrant workers are present or can be sent for to do them" (1975, 54). Language and cultural diversity gives Toronto important tools to compete in the global economy. It is indeed ironic that immigrant poverty amid city prosperity helps strengthen Toronto's global presence in the world economy.

Toronto's strength is its diversity. Although this strength in diversity is much celebrated by political and economic interests, the bearers of diversity—the immigrants—are increasingly excluded from the larger Toronto society and economy. Spatial segregation and social exclusion have created "hot spot" neighborhoods characterized by a high level of immigrants and visible minorities, low income, and high unemployment. Although large-scale ghettos characteristic of some U.S. cities are not observable in Toronto, the history in the United States tells us that the concentration of neighborhood poverty is an early warning sign of neighborhood decline and possible ghettoization.

CONCLUSION

Distressed neighborhoods pose a significant threat to a city's economic competitiveness. As the largest metropolitan area in Canada, Toronto produces 20 percent of the country's gross domestic product and is home to 40 percent of its corporate headquarters (Drummond et al. 2002). The phenomenon of increasing segregation and alienation among some of its neighborhoods has not escaped the attention of public, private, and voluntary sectors. With an interest in maintaining the region's vibrancy and economic competitiveness in the global economy and its commitment to multiculturalism, the Toronto City Summit Alliance, a multisector coalition of civic leaders, was formed in 2002. In April 2003, it released a report, *Enough Talk,* that called on then prime minister Paul Martin and the premier of Ontario, Dalton McQuinty, to implement a new fiscal deal for municipalities and to immediately address the need for new physical infrastructure—

more affordable housing, improved access to postsecondary education, quicker economic integration of newcomers in the Toronto area, and new social infrastructure in the city's poorest neighborhoods. An outcome of this coalition is the Strong Neighborhood Task Force, a joint initiative of the United Way of Greater Toronto (Toronto's largest community funder) and the City of Toronto, with support from both the federal and provincial governments. Driven by a vision of inclusion, opportunity, and community cohesion, the task force called for an action plan to revitalize Toronto's at-risk neighborhoods (Strong Neighborhood Task Force 2005). With its strategy of addressing gaps in services and facilities in nine vulnerable neighborhoods, the task force urges all three levels of government to invest in the social infrastructure, increase the supply of affordable housing, and address systemic issues affecting these (and likely other) neighborhoods. The issues include the antiquated income security program and employment barriers facing new immigrants. To kick off this strategy, the United Way of Canada has committed $9.5 million to social investment in Toronto (Porter 2005). As an initiative of the Toronto City Summit Alliance, the Toronto Region Immigrant Employment Council was established to improve immigrants' access to employment. The goal is to find and implement local solutions that lead to more effective and efficient labor-market integration of immigrants in the Toronto region. The council includes private- and public-sector employers and representatives from colleges and universities, community organizations, assessment-service providers, organized labor, occupational regulatory bodies, foundations, and all three levels of government. Its work since 2003 has included providing paid internship opportunities, formalizing a mentoring program, and creating a Web site to showcase organizations that excel at bringing immigrants into their workforce and to lay out strategies that others can learn from and replicate.

At the provincial level the government of Ontario has been responding to the employment needs of immigrants. In 2003, several universities and community colleges established the program College Integrating Immigrants to Employment. The Ontario government funds the program, which aims to help immigrants with international professional training obtain licenses or certification to work. The program offers internationally trained nurses, optometrists, and social workers programs, occupation-specific language training, job shadowing, mentoring, work placement, and assistance in dealing with professional entities.

Recently (June 2006 and February 2007), the Ontario government legislated the Fair Access to Regulated Professions Act, the first of its kind in Canada, requiring Ontario's thirty-four regulated professions to ensure their licensing processes are fair, clear, open, and completed within a reasonable amount of time. This act is Ontario's latest step in helping newcomers succeed. Among others, initiatives include launching an internship program in the public sector for internationally trained professionals, doubling training and assessment positions for internationally trained doctors, creating a Web site for newcomers with up-to-date information on everything from Ontario communities to working in professions and trades, and negotiating with the federal government for increased funding for language training and settlement programs, which have been consistently called for by various researchers (Preston, Lo, and Wang 2003; Lo and Wang 2004). "We're making sure the skills and talents of thousands of internationally trained professionals are a brain gain for Ontario, not a brain waste. We're demonstrating our commitment to breaking down the barriers for so many talented newcomers who chose Ontario," said Mike Colle, Ontario's citizenship and immigration minister during a press release announcing the proposed legislation (Ontario Ministry of Citizenship and Immigration 2006). The billboard beside him read, "When newcomers succeed Ontario succeeds."

The programs aimed at reducing social exclusion have been moving slowly. Nonetheless, the latest initiatives are to be commended. It is hoped that data from the 2011 census will reveal a multicultural and inclusive Toronto.

6

The Non–"Global City"
of Birmingham, UK

A Gateway Through Time

CHERYL McEWAN, JANE POLLARD, and NICK HENRY

Recent years have witnessed numerous critiques of the concept of global cities—those cities that constitute the "command and control" centers of the global economy (Sassen 1994)—from a variety of different perspectives. Several writers have sought to question the biases inherent in classifications and categorizations of cities. John Rennie Short and colleagues, for example, argue that there is an "elitist bias" to globalization discourses, that globalization is "written from the metropolitan centre," and that the focus on "world cities" has neglected the cause and effects of globalization for cities further down the urban hierarchy (2000, 317). In a similar vein, Jennifer Robinson (2002a) argues that the focus on global and world cities is both hierarchical and Western-centric. She also points out that the desire within urban theory to understand cities across a wide range of different contexts leads either to implying the possibility of universal theories that are relevant everywhere or to accepting the incommensurability of different kinds of cities: "Neither of these is satisfactory, of course: but the current situation, where an urban theory framed in a western context parades as universally relevant knowledge while ignoring the urban experiences of most of the world, is also

We would like to thank Geoff Dowling (formerly of the School of Geography, University of Birmingham) for producing figure 6.3.

unacceptable" (2002b, 571). Definitions and understandings of global and world cities are further limited by being narrowly economistic, failing to situate contemporary urbanization within historical contexts and trajectories (see, for example, Smith 2001) and ignoring cultural and political practices (see, for example, Ley 2004). And, as Robinson argues, understandings of contemporary urbanization based on such categorizations as "global," "world," and "third world city" impose substantial limitations on "imagining or planning the futures of cities around the world" (2002a, 531).

To counter these problems, there is a need to shift away from the drive toward classification and toward a more cosmopolitan urban theory. This need is what Robinson (2002a) has in mind in her call for approaches that are more inclusive in their geographical reach and concerned with the diverse dynamics of "ordinary cities." It may also be what Short and colleagues (2000) intend in their proposed use of the term *gateway cities* to emphasize the fact that almost any city can act as an entryway for the transmission of economic, political, and cultural globalization. Similarly, David Ley suggests a means for countering the economistic tendencies and related suppression of political and cultural domains by opening up "globe talk" (2004, 162) and acknowledging the agency and everyday lived experiences that constitute cosmopolitan, transnational city spaces. For Ley, the privileging of "a view from above" (ibid., 154) has meant that the voices of dwellers in global cities have, too often, been absent in accounts of these cities. Finally, in a recent treatise on transnational urbanism, Michael Smith argues for the need to "historicize the Global City" (2001, 61–63). He asserts that a historical perspective reveals "globalization" not as a recent, all-encompassing system of economic power but rather as a historically specific, variant, and contested set of economic and social practices (see also Held et al. 1999). In turn, "The urban future . . . is far less predictable but far more interesting than the grand narrative of global capital steam-rolling and swallowing local political elites and pushing powerless people around. . . . Rather than viewing global cities as central expressions of the global accumulation of capital, all cities can then be viewed in the fullness of their particular linkages with the worlds outside their boundaries" (Smith 2001, 71).

These concerns about straitjacket definitions of global cities have informed our research on Birmingham, the UK's second-largest metropole.

Alternative views point toward the benefits in attending to the diversity of urban experiences; propose alternative urban theories based on difference, "ordinariness," and connectedness of cities; and broaden the scope of analysis beyond the economic. Drawing on such approaches, we have argued elsewhere that, in contrast to economistic classifications that would have Birmingham nowhere near global-city status, it is in fact a place intrinsically constituted by forms of cultural and economic globalization that draw on the city's residents, their histories, and their social and cultural networks (Henry, McEwan, and Pollard 2002; McEwan, Pollard, and Henry 2005). And we have argued that rather than perpetuate a polarizing and exclusionary city "boosterism" in pursuit of global-city status, city authorities would be better served by acknowledging the flows of people, cultures, commodities, and knowledges that already position the city in global networks.

In this chapter, we seek to exemplify these arguments by exploring Birmingham as a long-established "urban immigrant gateway." Its status as such has been built largely within UK, European, and Commonwealth contexts, and it is only recently that it has received attention in North American contexts (see Sandercock 2003). We begin by examining briefly the nature of gateway cities in the UK. We then consider Birmingham as a gateway city, using census and other data to demonstrate that it is an established gateway. Exploring Birmingham as a gateway city through time, we argue, following Ley (2004) and Smith (2001), that current patterns have their roots in specific urban and migratory histories that are, in turn, related to much older patterns of globalization. This historical context provides a basis for understanding Birmingham as a contemporary gateway city, the sociocultural impact of immigrants, and their role in shaping the contemporary urban economy (see Benton-Short, Price, and Friedman 2005). Finally, we reflect on what this means for the gateway-city concept, particularly in the UK context.

GATEWAY TOWNS AND CITIES IN THE UK

Gateway cities are defined as cities with large numbers of foreign-born residents, where the percentage of the foreign-born population exceeds the national average. The foreign-born population of the UK as a whole has long exceeded the global average of 3 percent. According to the Office of National Statistics, one in twelve people in 2001, or 8.3 percent (4.9 million) of the total population of the UK, was born overseas. This figure is almost double the proportion in 1951 (4.2 percent). Between 1991 and 2001, the overseas-born population increased more than it did in any of the preceding postwar decades, with a 1.6 percentage point increase over the decade to 2001. This rise compares with previous decade-to-decade increases between 1951 and 1991 that were all less than 1 percent. These figures have undoubtedly increased since the 2001 census. Most recent available figures, for example, report that net international migration to England and Wales totaled 217,000 (made up of 542,000 in-migrants and 325,000 out-migrants). Inflows and outflows have been steadily increasing since the mid-1990s with a sharp increase in inflows since 2004, owing mainly to increased freedom of movement within the European Union (EU) for citizens from eight central and eastern European countries following accession in May 2004 (Gask 2006). The years 2003 and 2004 witnessed a sixfold increase in in-migration of EU citizens, which has undoubtedly increased the overseas-born population.

Compared with the UK-born population, the overseas-born population has a much more diverse mix of ethnic groups. Whereas 96 percent of the UK-born population identified as white in 2001, only just over half (53 percent, or 2.6 million) of the overseas-born population identified as white. The next largest ethnic groups for people born overseas were Indian (570,000), Pakistani (336,000), black African (322,000), and black Caribbean (238,000). Other ethnic groups with significant representation among the UK overseas-born population are Chinese (176,000 were born overseas) and Bangladeshi (152,000) (UK Office of National Statistics 2001). Furthermore, 75 percent of the overseas-born population is of working age, as compared with 60 percent of the UK-born population (ibid.).

The non-native-born population tends to be strongly attracted to London and the South East region (indeed, London is the only region that is above the national average of 8.3 percent). In London 25 percent of the city's total population is foreign-born (representing 1.7 million people). In certain districts, such as Wembley in North London, more than half of the population (52 percent) was born abroad. The West Midlands region, in which Birmingham is located, has the highest rates of foreign-born residency outside of London and the South East.

There are more than forty towns and cities that exceed 8.3 percent foreign-born in the UK. Urban areas as diverse as Brighton, Cambridge, Coventry, Manchester, Oxford, and Slough aptly demonstrate the point made by John R. Short and colleagues that "almost any city can act as a gateway" (2000, 318). In the UK, it is clear that foreign-born populations are overwhelmingly concentrated in urban centers, since regional averages are all (except London) below the national average. Furthermore, we might speculate that the key determining factors to the clustering of high rates of foreign-born populations are: proximity to London as the UK's only recognized "global" city, proximity to international airports and the burgeoning service economy associated with this (for example, Slough, Luton), the role of universities and spin-off science parks (such as Oxford or Cambridge) in the contemporary "knowledge economy," and the historical (imperial) role of commercial and industrial centers, especially in towns and cities in the Northwest and East and West Midlands. The latter is of significance in understanding Birmingham's role as a gateway city.

GATEWAY BIRMINGHAM

In 2001, the total foreign-born population of Birmingham was 16.5 percent, almost exactly double the UK average, with 13.4 percent of the total population originating from outside the EU (compared with an average for England and Wales of 6.6 percent) and 3.1 percent from other EU countries (compared with an average for England and Wales of 2.3 percent). As figure 6.1 illustrates, Birmingham mirrors the national trend as a recipient of immigrants largely from the Indian subcontinent and Ireland.

Although the 2001 census contains the most up-to-date official statistics, midyear estimates from the Birmingham City Council suggest that whereas Birmingham's population was generally falling between 1981 and 2002, since then it has started to increase. The latest estimate (2005) shows Birmingham's population to have risen to just over 1 million: 0.9 percent (8,800) greater than it was in 2004, with a projected annual

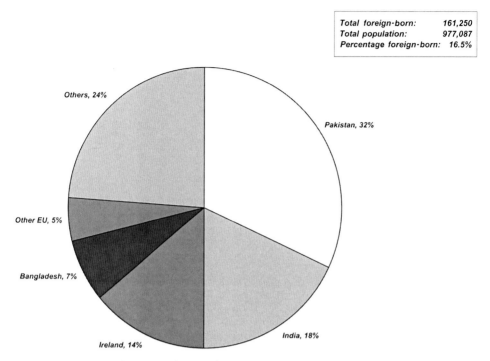

Fig. 6.1. Foreign-born population of Birmingham, 2001. *Source:* Office of National Statistics 2001.

increase of between 4,000 and 5,500 people until 2028. According to the Birmingham City Council, the increase is associated with high levels of international migration, more births, and fewer deaths, which implies that Birmingham's foreign-born population is increasing in total numbers and, perhaps, proportionately.[1]

Not surprisingly, Birmingham ranks first of thirty-four districts within the West Midlands region in terms of the percentage of population born overseas. Therefore, on the basis of the 2001 census data and on the criteria outlined in this book, Birmingham is a gateway city. The point that we wish to make is that this phenomenon is not new, nor is it a consequence wholly of contemporary globalization. Rather, Birmingham is a long-established

1. Information accessed from http://www.birmingham.gov.uk/GenerateContent?CONTENT_ITEM_ID=26205&CONTENT_ITEM_TYPE=0&MENU_ID=12672.

urban immigrant gateway, and, unlike London, patterns of immigration today mirror almost precisely the same patterns in evidence throughout the twentieth century. We can demonstrate this point clearly by exploring the history of migration to Birmingham and how it is related to current trends, particularly regarding the origins of its foreign-born population.

BIRMINGHAM: A GATEWAY CITY THROUGH TIME

Birmingham was an important political and economic cog in the British imperial machine. It was home to Joseph Chamberlain's nineteenth-century populist imperial policies.[2] Birmingham was thus also home to a local political and commercial caucus that advocated imperialism abroad. During the eighteenth and nineteenth centuries, British colonial expansion and the slave trade encouraged a demand for guns and other apparatus of colonialism, which Birmingham's metal industries were well equipped to satisfy (Rex and Tomlinson 1979, 98). The wealth of one of today's largest employers and landowners in the city, Cadbury's, was based on slavery and cocoa extraction on plantations in West Africa. Countless other small manufacturers depended on overseas markets in the empire for their success. At this time, Birmingham was known as the "city of a thousand trades," and the city morphology itself was shaped by colonial industries, with a gun quarter, an assay house, and a jewelry quarter (Mason 1998). The jewelry quarter is still the largest concentration of dedicated jewelers in Europe, and one-third of the jewelry manufactured in the UK is made within one mile of the Birmingham city center. Until 2003, coins for circulation were manufactured in the jewelry quarter at the Birmingham Mint, the oldest independent mint in the world, which continues to produce commemorative coins and medals.

The position of Birmingham in transnational imperial networks and activities provided the initial impetus for in-migration of decolonized peoples to the city. Prior to this catalyst, however, there were significant flows of in-migration to the city. Irish migrants, for example, have a written

2. Chamberlain was mayor of Birmingham in the 1870s, later assuming two British government cabinet positions, first as president of the Board of Trade in the 1880s and second as colonial secretary in the 1890s.

record of their existence in Birmingham since the 1600s. Waves of people came over from Ireland desperate to escape the famine and the poverty of the country in the mid-1800s. Another influx arrived in the 1950s, seeking to escape unemployment. Many were manual laborers who helped build the roads and buildings in the 1960s reconstruction (much of Birmingham had been destroyed by bombs during World War II). Irish people initially lived in the poorer parts of the city (Deritend, Digbeth, and Sparkbrook), but as their fortunes improved they moved out of the inner city to the suburbs of Erdington and Hall Green.

The Italian presence in Birmingham probably started as early as the 1700s. Early immigrants were artists and craftsmen. In 1918, Thomas Fattorini—a firm of medalists and badge makers—migrated to the city and are still trading today. The Italian community became established in the latter half of the 1800s, made up primarily of street sellers and musicians. As with Irish immigrants, most settled in cheap but cramped accommodations in Digbeth; the area between Jennens Row, Fazeley Street, and New Canal Street became known as "Little Italy." Street entertainers and hawkers had a ready audience at the nearby Bull Ring Market; others ran boardinghouses, confectioners' shops, cafes, and fish and chip shops. In the 1891 census, nine ice cream makers and vendors were listed as living in two Digbeth streets (Birmingham Government Web Site n.p.; Chinn 1994; Birmingham City Council 2001d, 2001e).

Birmingham has also long been a center for refugees. Jewish people fleeing from religious discrimination in the eighteenth and nineteenth centuries settled in the city. Throughout the twentieth century, war and political upheaval resulted in in-migration: Serbs and Belgians during World War I; Basques escaping the Spanish civil war in the 1930s; and Jews, Greeks, Polish Catholics, and Serbs fleeing Nazi and Communist persecution during the 1940s and 1950s. The Polish community, in particular, arrived in significant numbers and established the Polish Community Centre in Digbeth in 1958 (Chinn 1994; Slater 1996). Significantly, the arrival of the first nonwhite residents in Birmingham also predated the Second World War, the majority of whom traveled from the Caribbean and Indian subcontinent, with smaller numbers of Yemeni and Chinese migrants. Colonial links in Southeast Asia provided a legacy of in-migration dating back to the early twentieth century. The earliest Chinese emigrants to Birmingham were recruited from the villages of the New Territories of Hong Kong to serve as sailors aboard freighters. Ties with these communities provided the base for second-wave emigration after 1945, with economic migrants from Hong Kong seeking to exploit the opportunities that were opening up in the UK catering business (Birmingham City Council 2001e).

In the 1940s, patterns of migration from the Indian subcontinent remained highly specific, made up of Bengalis from Sylhet in East Pakistan (now Bangladesh), Punjabis from the Campbellpur district of the North-West Frontier Province of West Pakistan, and Kashmiris from the Mirpur district of Azad Kashmir (officially in India). Mirpur and Sylhet were sources of cheap labor on British steamships in the early twentieth century. These former seamen began to settle in postwar Birmingham in response to the shortage of labor, the displacement caused in the early days of the Kashmir dispute, and the flooding of villages for hydroelectricity schemes within their home region. The Campbellpur district of Pakistan was the area in which the British North-West Frontier Army recruited its bearers, cooks, batmen, and caterers. Thus, early links were formed between Britain and these areas (Rex and Moore 1967, 115; Birmingham City Council 2001a).

Other in-migrants at this time were Gujaratis and Punjabis from East Africa and India. They came to Birmingham partly as a result of a long history of migration, an aspect of the story of British imperialism (many of them were already part of a diaspora that had worked on the British railways in Uganda and Kenya), and partly because of Birmingham's booming post–World War II economy. Colonial links to the plantation economies of the West Indies also provided the basis for postwar emigration to what was perceived by decolonized peoples to be the mother country (Rex and Moore 1967, 100–101; Birmingham City Council 2001b). West Indians had been subject to British cultural imperialism for centuries and had much less of a cultural barrier to cross than other migrants. Birmingham was a primary recipient of New Commonwealth immigrants because of its significant manufacturing base (especially labor-intensive automobile and automobile-components industries) and its demand for manual laborers in postwar rebuilding. As Michael Samers (1999) argues, in Europe, migration during the postwar period was seen as satisfying acute labor shortages (though in most cases complementing native workers), boosting capital accumulation, and reducing inflationary pressures. However, migrant laborers also provided the "spatial vent" for a growing crisis within the manufacturing sector, enabling producers to reduce labor costs in situ through a system of racialized Fordism (a mass-production system that relied on comparatively large numbers of relatively unskilled, low-paid, and, increasingly, migrant workers). This shift in the division of labor, which was facilitated by colonial links to overseas territories, undoubtedly shaped postwar patterns of migration to Birmingham.

The 1950s witnessed the first wave of numerically substantial in-migration, first from the West Indies and later from the Indian subcontinent. The 1961 census showed these population groups to be highly concentrated around the middle ring of Victorian and Edwardian bye-law housing—the high-density, grid-iron streets of terraced public housing familiar in industrial cities in the UK that were meant to improve conditions in slum areas. The Soho and Handsworth wards to the northwest of the city center, for example, contained 27 percent of the West Indian population; the Aston, Market Hall, Sparkbrook, and Balsall Heath wards to the east and southeast contained nearly 35 percent of the Asian population (see fig. 6.2). The majority of the "New Commonwealth" immigrants were men ages twenty to thirty-five who were primarily economic migrants (Slater 1996, 141–42). Between 1961 and 1966, the black and Asian population of the city doubled, with Birmingham becoming the largest center of influx outside London. This trend continued into the 1970s, still following mainly traditional migration routes but also supplemented by Asians migrating from East Africa as a result of political upheavals in Uganda in 1972. By 1981 a number of wards had "New Commonwealth" populations of more than 50 percent (Handsworth, Soho, Sparkbrook, Sparkhill), but patterns showed dispersal into more affluent housing areas such as Moseley and Edgbaston, with 25 percent "New Commonwealth" occupancy.

In summary, Birmingham has long been a gateway city for urban international migrants, with patterns of migration that date back to the end of the nineteenth century and continue to the present day. In what follows, we explore how this historical legacy continues to shape patterns of migration into the city and examine some of the consequences.

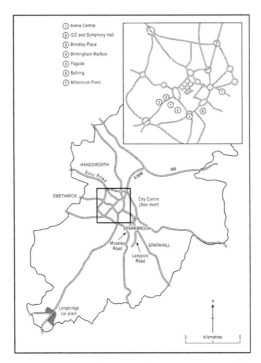

Fig. 6.2. City of Birmingham. *Source:* By the authors.

BIRMINGHAM: THE CONTEMPORARY GATEWAY CITY

Table 6.1 provides a breakdown of the birthplace of residents living in Birmingham in 2001. Just over 9 percent of Birmingham's residents were born in Asia, compared with under 4 percent in the West Midlands and just over 3 percent in England. More specifically, 4 percent were born in Pakistan, 2 percent in India, and 1 percent in Bangladesh. Birmingham's residents include 25,000 people born in the Republic of Ireland. This figure is more than 2 percent of residents compared with under 1 percent in England overall. Almost 20,000 persons living in Birmingham, 2 percent of all residents, originated from the Caribbean and West Indies. Just over 14,000 came from Jamaica. A sizable number of Birmingham residents, nearly 10,400, were born in South Africa and East Africa.

TABLE 6.1

WORLDWIDE PLACE OF BIRTH OF BIRMINGHAM'S POPULATION, 2001

	Number	Percentage
All people	977,087	100.0
Europe	849,890	87.0
United Kingdom	816,054	83.5
England	791,040	81.0
Rest of UK	25,014	2.6
Republic of Ireland	22,828	2.3
Channel Islands and IoM	245	0.0
Other Western Europe	7,555	0.8
Eastern Europe	3,208	0.3
Africa	13,606	1.4
North Africa	1,089	0.1
Central and western Africa	2,140	0.2
South and eastern Africa	10,368	1.1
Asia	89,235	9.1
Middle East	5,199	0.5
Far East	7,344	0.8
South Asia	76,692	7.8
Bangladesh	10,785	1.1
India	23,194	2.4
Pakistan	41,724	4.3
Rest of South Asia	989	0.1
North America	21,210	2.2
Canada, USA, and other NA	1,675	0.2
Caribbean and West Indies	19,535	2.0
Jamaica	14,207	1.5
Other Caribbean and WI	5,328	0.5
South America	552	0.1
Oceania	973	0.1
Other	1,621	0.2

Source: Office of National Statistics, 2001 Census of Population.

The dispersal of immigrants described previously continues to the present time, but the geography of black and South Asian residence has been remarkably stable over the past sixty years. The 1991 census demonstrates a strong correlation in the areas of residence between Birmingham's overseas-born population and its nonwhite population, and between the overseas-born population and residency of Asians and Afro-Caribbeans. The initial zones of residence in the central city are still apparent despite some dispersal, in contrast to the Irish community, which is now dispersed throughout the city. The reasons for these patterns are in part structural, relating to restrictions on access to council housing until the 1970s, which prevented suburbanization of the immigrant communities. However, cultural reasons, such as the desire for house ownership on the part of South Asians and proximity to mosques, are also significant. So too are economic reasons, which led to the concentration of deprivation—low income, high unemployment, poor housing, and reduced access to health, educational, and other service provisions—in the inner-city areas (Slater 1996). Equally, although there are high proportions of foreign-born in these locations today, these are also now communities of black British and Asian British people, a high proportion of whom are under the age of twenty-five.

What both the 1991 and 2001 censuses reveal, then, is that dominant contemporary patterns of migration follow long-established trends in terms of origin and residency on arrival. This trend is not only the case for nonwhite migrants but also applies to patterns of migration from Europe. For example, as economic decline hit Ireland in the 1980s, young Irish people again migrated to find employment in the catering and service sectors.[3] But what do these long-established and enduring migration patterns mean for Birmingham today?

Our argument is that if we look beyond the traditional "global city" imaginaries and think of Birmingham as a long-established urban gateway,

3. Although there are no available statistics on Birmingham's foreign-born population since the 2001 census, we might speculate that since 2004 a greater proportion of overseas migrants have originated in the EU accession countries. We might also speculate that many of them will be Polish, since Birmingham has an established Polish community.

different accounts of social, cultural, and economic life in the city can be revealed. In terms of ethnicity, Birmingham's economic position is constructed through and interwoven with its numerous minority ethnic economic networks, some more visible than others. Birmingham's "overseas Chinese" population, for example, is prominent in property development within the city. The areas of Sparkbrook and Sparkhill include Pakistani banks, and the city is home to the first branch of the new Islamic Bank of Britain to be located outside London. In the United States, so-called ethnobanks, owned and run by minority ethnic employees, have played an important role in funneling capital to minority ethnic small businesses and more generally meeting unmet banking needs that have arisen through "redlining" and discrimination by "mainstream" financial institutions (Li et al. 2002). The UK, however, is renowned for having a banking system that is both highly centralized and internationalized. In April 2004, there were 256 overseas banks (and 48 branches) in the UK. In terms of their geography, these banks are, not surprisingly, centered in London (78 percent). Birmingham, however, is one of the top destinations for overseas banks (together with Manchester) outside London.

Birmingham's banking history, like its industrial history, bears the imprint of its colonial past and its transnational flows of immigrants. The first overseas bank to establish in Birmingham was the Bank of Ireland (UK registered in 1901), followed by the Bank of India and Bank of Baroda (India). More recent institutions to open branches in Birmingham include the Bank of China, the Bank of Tokyo–Mitsubishi, Sonali Bank (Bangladesh), and Habib Allied International Bank (Pakistan). The Islamic Bank of Britain will be the first "pure" Islamic bank in the UK to offer sharia-compliant financial products. Sharia law prohibits *riba* (interest) and investments in certain kinds of businesses—for example, firms that produce alcohol or engage in gambling or prostitution.

The formation of Britain's first Irish Business Association in the city is another example of how some of Birmingham's economic networks are identified primarily by their ethnicity (Griffin 1998). Although "white" business groups do not usually identify themselves in ethnicized terms, the Irish business community in Birmingham is constructing an ethnic identity based on "minority white" experiences. It is explicit about Irishness and economic advantage, and includes any business of Irish origin or with trading or cultural links with Ireland.

The production of particular commodities has also become associated with (minority) ethnicity within the city—for example, ethnic foods and particular musical styles, such as bhangra (popularized for white audiences in the film *Bend It Like Beckham* but long established as a popular hybrid musical form in Birmingham and London). Birmingham's multicultural and transnational economic activities extend across a range of economic operations and products. The Sparkhill area is the center for the South Asian jewelry quarter and the retailing of clothing, saris, and other textiles. Perhaps less well known is the Greek-Cypriot fish-frying network that, as early as 1989, constituted 25 percent of Birmingham's three hundred fish-and-chip shops (Stewart 1989). Today, the city's halal butchers number more than fifty; Birmingham's National Halal Center is growing through demand from non-Muslims and is exporting goods such as halal baby food throughout Europe.

More widely celebrated is the success of the "Birmingham *balti*"—a range of spicy vegetable and meat dishes tailored to the English palate and first served by Kashmiri restaurateurs in Birmingham in the 1970s. *Baltis* are unheard of in the Indian subcontinent and differ from curries by being cooked very quickly in a flat-bottomed iron wok (or *balti*). The *balti* is thus a hybrid product combining British and Asian tastes and styles of cooking and identified with a particular set of migrants to, and residents of, Birmingham and its region. These migrants have redefined traditional dishes so that they combine their ethnic roots with living in a specific Western city, a globalization parable if ever there was one. Birmingham and the West Midlands region are now world famous for the production and consumption of the *balti*, which has also been "exported" to other cities in the UK. Furthermore, the city council has been active in promoting the idea of a "*balti* quarter" that will focus on the so-called "*balti* triangle" of Sparkbrook and Sparkhill, an area housing some fifty restaurants. The details, including the name of the development, are still being finalized, but colorful Asian gateways, carved elephants, and a minaret are among the suggestions. This idea is undoubtedly evidence of the city council seizing on ethnicity as a marketing opportunity, as it did with the Chinese quarter (below), but it is also likely to help the local restaurateurs, and signals a recognition of the importance of acknowledging diversity in the city's future.

This kind of engagement with diversity is demonstrated by the creation of the Birmingham City Council's Chinese quarter. In 1998, the residents of Birmingham received a gift of a pagoda from Chinese businessman Wing Yip. The pagoda, shipped from China, serves as a gateway to the quarter. The idea of Birmingham's Chinese quarter is clearly fused with the traditional route of early Hong Kong Chinese migrants into the catering industry during the 1950s and 1960s. Yet as this transnational community expands its economic horizons into areas such as property development, so Birmingham is experiencing new forms of investment and new forms of global linkage. Along with Wing Yip's supermarket and branches of the Bank of China and the Bank of East Asia, the pagoda advertises the presence and importance of the Chinese community in Birmingham (Dean 1997; see fig. 6.3).

Although data are scarce, some figures (which use the limited, rigid framework of census ethnic descriptions) suggest that up to 33 percent of Birmingham's business activity occurs within minority ethnic-owned enterprises ("Birmingham" 1998). This business activity includes food manufacturing, the music business, and property development (McEwan, Pollard, and Henry 2005). The possibilities for continued development are myriad. For example, Eastern Foods has launched a range of halal Chinese meals for British Muslims who otherwise cannot eat in Chinese restaurants ("Menu Master" 2000). Another example is the 1993 establishment of the Birmingham/Mirpur Friendship Association (around 90,000 people in Birmingham originate from the Kashmiri district of Mirpur). The Chambers of Commerce in both cities are now incorporated in this association and are currently in active collaboration to develop and extend commercial links between the two cities. Furthermore, the recognition of this particular migratory path has seen "fusion housing"—highly flexible panel-and-frame concrete structures—proposed by community architects Shillam and Smith for development in Birmingham's predominantly Kashmiri-populated districts of Saltley and Small Heath (Glancey 1999). And the Birmingham Chamber of Commerce has been involved in a recruitment exercise in Mumbai to bring Indian information technology specialists to

Fig. 6.3. The pagoda, Birmingham, gift of Mr. Wing Yip. Photo by Geoff Dowling.

the city to fill a skills gap within the local (and national) economy, which has the potential to position Birmingham within global IT networks (*BBC Midlands Today,* September 7, 2000).

The range of "ethnic" economic activity illustrated above derives from the ever changing but historically circumscribed migratory paths of the residents of Birmingham. The roots of Birmingham's economy are derived from its centrality within a (European) colonial past. A key question to ask of these illustrations is to what extent the city's economic future might draw on its postcolonialism and multiculturalism (Jacobs 1996; Fincher and Jacobs 1998; Sandercock 1998, 2003). Our argument is that this diversity is increasingly being recognized as a strength and, indeed, as a route to economic development (Henry 1998; Henry and Passmore 1999; Henry, McEwan, and Pollard 2002). In attempting to re-vision Birmingham's contemporary economic place in the world, we have developed an account based on the distinctiveness of an economy rooted (and routed) in transnational networks—in other words, a distinctiveness drawn from the city's multicultural population and their particular linkages with worlds beyond the city's boundaries (see also Scott 2001). The intention is, therefore, to signal a rather different understanding of "global" as it relates to economic advantage, transnationalism (in the form of cross-border connections; see Vertovec 1999, 2001), and ethnic diversity within cities in general, and Birmingham in particular. This different understanding of the global has important policy implications, not simply in terms of economic representations of the city but also in terms of developing the possibilities of such transnational networks and engaging with the constraints that they face.

The city and its governance, however, are not without problems. Ethnicity has been fetishized somewhat within city boosterism, which, as Rajinder K. Dudrah (2000) argues, masks overt references to race and belonging. Notions of space in the city become marked out through palatable differences for white consumers. "Ethnic" areas of settlement in the inner cities become fashionable (Chinese quarters, *balti* quarters, sari shops, African and Caribbean bakeries, and so on) but at the same time are continually ghettoized as areas where some of the ills of racialized urban living continue to flourish. In the 1980s, these ills emanated in riots in Birmingham, primarily in response to high levels of deprivation among Afro-Caribbean communities in areas such as Handsworth. In some versions of the city as it has been represented in urban policy since the 1980s, multiculturalism is conceived, at best, as a display of "other" cultures and artifacts on the periphery of white British culture and not as a serious politics of dialogue and engagement with diversity and difference (Hesse

1993, 1999; Modood and Werbner 1997). Like any large urban center, there are still problems, as evidenced by recent riots (in 2005) between black and Asian young men.[4] However, it is significant that more recently the Birmingham City Council has recognized the need to revisit its strategic vision to focus on "place making" as well as "place marketing" in an attempt to link immigrant and poor neighborhoods with the downtown economy (Sandercock 2003).

THE SIGNIFICANCE OF GATEWAY STATUS

Birmingham has received little attention as a "global city"; indeed, it fails to register in the rankings of global-city theorists. Yet it clearly has been global, it is still global, and its place in the global economy is evolving in new ways that are often related to multiculturalism, its status as a postcolonial city, and the transnationalism of many of its residents. Birmingham has long been a destination for overseas investment through its historical (colonial) links and postcolonial and other migratory paths that position it within global networks. The city was and is globalized through particular circuits: as the "workshop of the world" (Bryson, Daniels, and Henry 1996), it was positioned centrally as a nodal point in global circuits of commodities from the nineteenth century onward; as the "city of a thousand trades," it was a key center in circuits of production, particularly around skilled manufacturing trades and engineering; and as a gateway city, it has been and remains one of Europe's major nodes in circuits of people and immigrants. However, Birmingham is bypassed in the key circuit that defines world or global cities today—whereas in the past it was a command-and-control center in global commerce, it is no longer a major center for flows of international finance. Thus, although Birmingham is not a global city in terms of international finance or knowledge production, it has long been globalized through trade and its position as a key center in migration flows, dating back to the beginning of the twentieth century.

---

4. There are many debates about whether this riot was racial or simply related to business competition and criminality, fueled by gender and generational issues (see Vulliami 2005).

Birmingham today is positioned within complex global networks through flows of people, commodities, remittances, cultures, and so on associated with this past. We could say the same thing about many towns and cities in the UK, since many are immigrant gateway cities. In demonstrating that a multiplicity of towns and cities are connected to processes of globalization through the movements of people, the gateway-city concept is a useful corrective to the limitations of the "global"- or "world"-city thesis. However, we wish to argue that it provides only a starting point in understanding contemporary patterns of international migration and urbanization. We have suggested that provincial UK towns and cities, and the migration patterns that continue to shape them, reflect a long history of particular forms of industrialization linked explicitly to British colonialism. Despite widespread deindustrialization since the 1980s, migrant flows are still overwhelmingly from the former colonies (in particular, Pakistan, India, Bangladesh, and Ireland). These spatial and temporal contexts, we argue, are crucial to any understanding of the concept of gateway cities in the UK. In particular, we argue that a more contextualized, cosmopolitan, and relational approach is vital in understanding contemporary migration patterns to cities like Birmingham and the socioeconomic outcomes of these patterns.

Thinking of Birmingham as a "gateway" facilitates a more *relational* way of understanding the city, as a place that can be conceived in terms of "the articulation of social relations" (Massey 1994, 120) produced by its diverse population. These relations are both located within Birmingham and stretched beyond it, tying the city to wider relations, places, and processes (ibid.; see also Amin 2004). This conceptualization, we argue, is important politically because it facilitates the exploration of the conditions under which these networks may either have the potential for advancing social well-being or, alternatively, (re)generating exploitation and exclusion.

CONCLUSION

Our research on Birmingham has highlighted the significance of understanding connections between the local and the global and in uncovering forms of agency that are usually ignored in traditional economic narra-tives of global cities in general and Birmingham's regeneration in particu-lar. Thus, if we take seriously the arguments of Smith (2001) and Ley (2004), Birmingham is a distinctive global city, but this distinctiveness is not based on its recent and very substantial development of prestigious urban-regeneration projects or even its marketing slogan as "The Meeting Place of Europe." Rather, its global distinctiveness is, in part, based on its residents' diasporic and transnational (economic) roots, which extend across Europe into Asia and the Pacific Rim. There are, of course, still questions about the possibilities of creating competitive advantage that is less exclusionary and translates into material gain for working-class and minority ethnic communities.

Such questions are of critical importance to a multicultural and postco-lonial city like Birmingham, still struggling against the social and economic effects of the restructuring of its manufacturing industries. However, of sig-nificance is the fact that the city's multiculturalism and its position within postcolonial and transnational economic networks are rapidly being recog-nized in policy circles as a crucial element of continued economic develop-ment. The precise contribution of these networks to the city's economic base is still a matter of conjecture, but diversity can clearly be mobilized "as a source of both social cohesion and urban economic competitiveness" (Amin 1997, 134). Far from being a postindustrial city whose glories as "the workshop of the world" have long since faded, Birmingham is a city now constituted through transnational networks and flows.

This chapter has demonstrated the importance of understanding gate-way cities as constituted through (relations structured in) time and space. Evidence in the UK supports the contention that, in this specific context at least, the gateway city can be ordinary—the UK has long had urban gateways, and in fairly "ordinary" places (see J. Robinson 2005). Their ordinariness is also their diversity, multiplicity, and connectivity (Massey 1994), which is too often neglected or ignored in popular and planning discourses. A relational and cosmopolitan approach to understanding cities like Birmingham ought to contribute to the creative imagining of possible city futures. In its proposition that almost any city can be a gateway, in distinguishing cities in the developed and developing worlds that receive large numbers of immigrants, and in acknowledging the social, cultural, and economic contributions that these immigrants make, the urban immigrant gateway concept is useful in encouraging us to attend to the diversity of urban experiences when theorizing about cities. It also helps in bringing cities like Birmingham, often overlooked in other urban hierarchies, to the forefront of analysis.

7

Amsterdam

A Multicultural Gateway?

ANNEMARIE BODAAR

On November 2, 2004, ethnic relations in Amsterdam and the Netherlands were put to the test when a young Muslim man murdered Theo van Gogh, a famous but controversial Dutch filmmaker. Van Gogh—cycling to his office—was shot several times and then stabbed to death in front of a large crowd. The murderer was a radical Muslim, who claimed his religious beliefs compelled him to commit this crime. Several months prior to the murder, Van Gogh had codirected the documentary *Submission,* which addressed the repression and physical abuse of Muslim women.[1] The content of the documentary formed the main motive for Mohammed B. to murder Van Gogh. The country was left in shock, and many feared—because the murderer was a Muslim—acts of retaliation aimed at Muslims would occur.

The violent murder not only shocked people in Amsterdam and the Netherlands but also made global headlines. While America was in the

---

1. Van Gogh coproduced the documentary with Ayaan Hirsi Ali, a politician and refugee from Somalia. It was Hirsi Ali's idea to produce a documentary on the suppression and abuse of Muslim women. The documentary is very controversial, as it is based on very extreme examples of abuse. For example, it portrays a woman whose body is tattooed with verses of the Koran by her husband, as a form of punishment. Many people, particularly Muslims, were very offended by the documentary. They condemn the examples chosen by Van Gogh and Hirsi Ali. Following the release of the documentary, both Van Gogh and Hirsi Ali received death threats, but Van Gogh never really thought he was in danger.

midst of the presidential elections, the murder of Van Gogh headlined on CNN, National Public Radio, and various, even local, newspapers. Many reporters wondered: how could such a gruesome murder happen in Amsterdam, a city internationally praised for and depicted as a laboratory of tolerance and cosmopolitan culture (for example, Hannerz 2000)? The murder cast doubt on the image of Amsterdam as a tolerant city and on the power of policy to counter extremism and soothe interethnic tensions. According to Susan Ruddick (1996) the place where a violent act occurs is of great importance for determining whether an event stays local or becomes the site for national or even international debates about a particular issue, in this case immigrant integration. It also matters who is killed in determining whether an assault in public space becomes the focus of extended debate and reports in the media and spurs public outrage and concern. Had the victim not been Theo van Gogh but a lesser-known local resident, and had the murder occurred in one of the neighborhoods with a high concentration of immigrants, then it probably would not have received national, let alone international, attention. It would certainly not have sparked a debate about the perceived lack of integration of (Muslim) immigrants in the Netherlands and Dutch cities in particular.

In order to prevent riots in the neighborhoods with high concentrations of Muslim immigrants, the mayors of Amsterdam, Rotterdam, and The Hague immediately increased police surveillance in these neighborhoods. Although a few mosques, churches, and Muslim schools were burned and a number of instances of racial violence were reported from several cities and towns, Amsterdam remained calm in the weeks that followed the murder. In fact, the place of the murder became a site for the active negotiation of immigrant integration, multiethnic relations, and a multicultural society. Neighborhood residents, visitors, and others engaged in fierce but nonviolent debates at this site. On the night following the murder, friends of Van Gogh organized a wake at Dam Square—the central square of the city—where approximately 20,000 people gathered to show their anger and disapproval of the murder and to express their support for a multicultural society and the disapproval of any form of fundamentalism. The mayor of Amsterdam, Job Cohen, the minister of immigrant integration, and other key persons spoke at the wake, with the goal of keeping a highly diverse society together at both the urban and the national level.[2] The Muslim community also joined in to condemn the murder. The wake, therefore, became a key moment of solidarity and dialogue between individuals and ethnic groups within a national context of anti-immigrant sentiments, particularly aimed at the Muslim minority.

Living with diversity has now become one of the key challenges in established gateway cities like Amsterdam, characterized by growing transnational flows and clashes between different population groups. Gateway cities, within an increasingly globalized world, function as the main entrance points for immigrants (see Benton-Short, Price, and Friedman 2005). Therefore, immigration is foremost an urban phenomenon, and ethnic and cultural difference "the new urban condition" (Sandercock 1998, 2003). Ongoing immigration has created new struggles over both economic space (that is, jobs) and belonging in the neighborhood, the city, and the nation, as newcomers arrive and become embedded in the city. When newcomers claim and transform urban space to incorporate new or alternative sociospatial practices, these changes may clash with older meanings of that space as conceived by long-term residents. This clash in the perceived meanings of urban spaces can produce tensions between national and multicultural visions of the city. Despite this reality of today's multicultural cities, studies and policy reports have tended to emphasize the national scale as the site for the development and implementation of immigration and integration policies. Work at the national scale, however, ignores the role of cities in the incorporation of immigrants. In the past decades, scholarly discussions have focused on issues of citizenship, rights, and ethnic identity. These debates have been mainly concerned with how national governments acknowledge and accommodate ethnic diversity (for example, Kymlicka 1995, 2003; Parekh 2000; Taylor 1992). Recently, a number of authors have suggested that cities are becoming increasingly important as sites for

2. *Time* magazine (the European edition) awarded Job Cohen as one of the heroes of 2004. Cohen received this recognition for his role in maintaining the social coherence in Amsterdam after Van Gogh's murder. Cohen called on Amsterdammers to come together and express their anger, but more important he emphasized dialogue to overcome differences in this multicultural city (see http://www.time.com/time/europe/hero2005/cohen.html).

managing and negotiating ethnic diversity, as well as for the generation and contestation of ethnic and cultural identities (Amin 2002, 2003; Amin and Thrift 2002; Body-Gendrot 2002; Isin 2002; Isin and Siemiatycki 2002; Sandercock 1998, 2003).

The purpose of this chapter is to explore why a backlash against multiculturalism at the state level is accompanied by "actually existing multiculturalism" in urban neighborhoods. Cities are the entry points for immigrants and the sites for immigrant incorporation and interethnic interaction. Urban neighborhoods, in particular, are the sites were policies aimed at immigrant integration are being implemented and negotiated. Ethnic minorities play an active role in (re)shaping neighborhood space, thereby challenging not only policies but also the dominant state discourses on immigrant integration. The first section gives an overview of Amsterdam as an established urban immigrant gateway. The next section discusses the debate that has recently revolved around the crisis of multiculturalism and the rise of novel approaches to immigrant integration and interethnic relations. Once known as a tolerant nation that embraced multiculturalism, the Netherlands has become more stringent in its integration policy. Multiculturalism is no longer enthusiastically accepted, yet a new ideology on how to tackle the integration of ethnic minorities in the Netherlands has yet to emerge at the national level. The third section focuses on a multiethnic neighborhood in Amsterdam as the site where difference is negotiated and new forms of living with diversity are established that in turn might affect urban and national integration policies. This section draws on fieldwork that took place between September 2003 and August 2004. The chapter concludes by discussing the implications of, on the one hand, a backlash against multiculturalism and, on the other hand, the ongoing practice of multiculturalism in the neighborhoods of Amsterdam.

AMSTERDAM AS AN ESTABLISHED IMMIGRANT GATEWAY

Amsterdam is an established immigrant gateway. Not only does the city have a large number of foreign-born residents (28.2 percent) that far exceeds the national average of 9.8 percent, but it also has a long history of immigration. Although the origin and size of flows have changed since the 1960s, immigration to Amsterdam dates back to the sixteenth century: Jews, Huguenots, and Frisians settled here, followed by German, Polish, and Russian Jews. People from the former Dutch Indies arrived in the 1950s. From the 1960s onward, guest workers and other settlers from southern Europe, Morocco, Turkey, Surinam, and the Dutch Antilles settled in the city. Amsterdam appealed to these migrants because of its culture as a trade center as well as the availability of work. Even so, compared to other cities labeled as "global cities" (for example, New York, London, and Tokyo), Amsterdam is a very small city in terms of population, with only 743,079 inhabitants in the city proper (table 7.1).

In the early 1970s the recruitment of foreign labor ceased when the Dutch economy showed its first signs of decline. Following the first oil crisis, industries closed down or moved their operations abroad. Foreign laborers especially were hit hard by the loss of jobs owing to industrial restructuring. The Dutch state had always expected that guest workers would return to their home countries once their labor was no longer needed, but quite the contrary occurred. Many guest workers ended up staying in the Netherlands.[3] Once granted permanent resident status, many moved their families to the Netherlands—through family-reunification programs—and there continues to be a significant immigration of brides from Turkey and Morocco, often through prearranged marriages (Central Bureau of Statistics 2005).

From 1975 into the mid-1980s, a second wave of immigration occurred, mainly from Surinam and the Netherland Antilles and Aruba.[4] A large number of these immigrants ended up in Amsterdam. Since then,

3. It was possible for them to stay because many guest workers had been living in the Netherlands for more than five years. They had arrived on one-year contracts, but because employers tended to renew their contracts, they became eligible for permanent residency in the Netherlands.

4. Migration from Surinam occurred in two waves. The first wave of migration occurred soon after the independence of Surinam. A second wave of migration from Surinam followed in the early 1980s, when it was decided that the Surinamese could no longer claim Dutch citizenship. Inhabitants of the Netherlands Antilles and Aruba have Dutch citizenship and are therefore free to settle in the Netherlands. Many of them immigrate to the Netherlands for educational reasons or in search of jobs, as job opportunities are limited on the islands.

TABLE 7.1

ETHNIC COMPOSITION OF AMSTERDAM, FIRST GENERATION ONLY, 2006

Country of origin	Absolute	Percentage
Total population of Amsterdam	743,079	100
Total first generation	209,657	28.2
Surinam	41,552	5.6
Morocco	34,868	4.7
Turkey	21,801	2.9
Indonesia	8,349	1.1
Netherlands Antilles and Aruba	7,192	1.0
Germany	6,677	0.9
Ghana	6,662	0.9
United Kingdom	6,479	0.9
United States	4,545	0.6
Yugoslavia (former)	3,773	0.5
Egypt	3,456	0.5
Pakistan	3,297	0.4
Soviet Union (former)	2,639	0.4
France	2,636	0.4
Italy	2,627	0.4
China	2,467	0.3
India	2,344	0.3
Spain	2,344	0.3
Portugal	2,223	0.3
Afghanistan	2,014	0.3
Iran	1,896	0.3
Iraq	1,873	0.3
Belgium	1,789	0.2
Poland	1,708	0.2
Japan	1,438	0.2
Dominican Republic	1,371	0.2
Brazil	1,363	0.2
Hong Kong	1,344	0.2
Philippines	1,256	0.2
Ethiopia	1,166	0.2
Australia	1,021	0.1
Colombia	949	0.1
South-Africa	887	0.1
Canada	795	0.1

(Continued)

TABLE 7.1 *(continued)*

Somalia	651	0.1
Austria	594	0.1
Greece	583	0.1
Hungary	552	0.1
Cape Verde	335	0.05
Vietnam	267	0.04
Other Africa	5,545	0.7
Other Europe	5,097	0.7
Other Asia	4,769	0.6
Other America	4,062	0.5
Other Oceania	401	0.05

Source: CBS 2006.

the source and destination regions of migrants to Amsterdam have multiplied, and immigration is now more global in scope than at any time in the past (Castles and Miller 1993). Currently, the city of Amsterdam counts more than 170 nationalities, and ethnic and cultural diversity has become part of the everyday reality and streetscape of the city. But although immigrant origin is becoming increasingly diverse, immigrants from Surinam, Morocco, Turkey, the Netherlands Antilles and Aruba, and Ghana are the most numerous in Amsterdam (fig. 7.1).

From 1992 until 2006, the total number of foreign-born residents in Amsterdam increased from approximately 180,000 to 210,000. From 1996 until 1998, the number of foreign-born residents in Amsterdam declined slightly. This decrease could be the outcome of the suburbanization of immigrants owing to large-scale urban-renewal operations in neighborhoods with large concentrations of immigrants as well as the tightening of immigration policy in the Netherlands in the mid-1990s. In 2005 the Central Bureau of Statistics reported that for the first time in decades, emigration exceeded immigration on the national scale. New immigration policies and integration requirements have caused the Netherlands to become less attractive as an immigration destination.

Initially, immigrants to Amsterdam concentrated in the old working-class neighborhoods east and west of the city center. Today, the distribution of immigrants in the city has changed. The areas of concentration of the

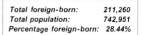

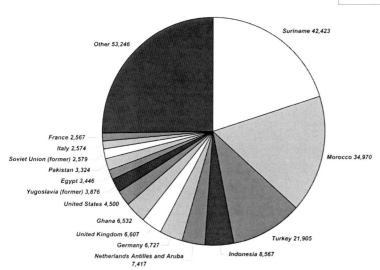

Fig. 7.1. Composition of foreign-born in the Netherlands.

1980s still have relatively high percentages of minorities, with some of these areas having increased further and at the same time expanding to include peripheral city districts (Social and Cultural Planning Office of the Netherlands 1995, 62). In Amsterdam, immigrants have increasingly moved westward, where larger, but relatively inexpensive, housing is available.

The city districts in Amsterdam with the largest concentration of foreign-born residents are Bos en Lommer (on the west side of the city, bordering De Baarsjes) and district Zuidoost. In Zuidoost 45.7 percent of the residents are foreign-born, whereas in Bos en Lommer 40.4 percent are foreign-born. The areas of the city from the center to the south have lower percentages of foreign-born residents in their population (less than 30 percent). The historical city center and areas to the south have traditionally been the wealthier parts of Amsterdam (fig. 7.2).

Figure 7.2 illustrates that immigrants are relatively dispersed throughout the city with the exception of a few districts. Moroccan and Turkish immigrants are concentrated in neighborhoods east and west of the city center, particularly in the nineteenth-century neighborhoods and the postwar

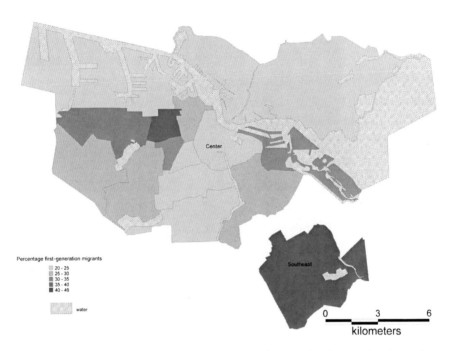

Fig. 7.2. Distribution of foreign-born in Amsterdam, 2001. *Source:* By the author.

neighborhoods west of the city center. District Zuidoost, on the other hand, has a large concentration of Surinamese, Antillean, and African migrants.

It is important to think about the implications of comparing statistical information across cities. Different countries and cities use different measures and terms for policy purposes. For example, in the Netherlands the impact of immigration on cities is usually not measured in terms of the number and distribution of the foreign-born. Instead, in Dutch statistics and language an important distinction is made between *allochtonen* (foreigner) and *autochtonen* (native). This distinction has been central to the selection of the empirical case study—Bijlmermeer (a neighborhood in district Zuidoost) (see again fig. 7.2)—that will be discussed in this chapter. In official statistics, *allochtonen* refers to those persons who are born abroad or of whom at least one parent is born abroad. Therefore, *allochtonen* makes no distinction between first-generation immigrants (a person born abroad) and second-generation (one or both parents are born abroad, but the child is born in the Netherlands). In Amsterdam, close to 48 percent are *allochtonen*. *Autochtonen*, on the other hand, refers to those persons of whom both parents are born in the Netherlands.

The term *allochtonen* is often used to refer to "ethnic minorities," a policy term not used in official statistics of the Central Bureau of Statistics. Policy makers use the term to refer to persons who are not only *allochtonen* but also have a weak socioeconomic position. The term *ethnic minorities,* the way it is used in the debate, is similar to the statistical category of "non-Western *allochtonen*." Official statistics distinguish between "Western" and "non-Western" *allochtonen,* where "non-Western *allochtonen*" refers to all persons born in a non-Western nation or those individuals who have parents born in a non-Western nation.[5] This category includes migrants from Africa, Asia, Latin America, and Turkey. "Western *allochtonen*," on the other hand, includes migrants from Europe, Indonesia, Japan, North America, and Oceania.[6] The main distinguishing feature between the two categories regards migrants' socioeconomic and sociocultural position, where "non-Western *allochtonen*" tend to occupy lower socioeconomic and sociocultural positions. The debate about ethnic minorities is almost always framed in terms of "integration." It should be no surprise, therefore, that integration policy is specifically targeted at "non-Western *allochtonen*" or "ethnic minorities" and not at "Western *allochtonen*." The need for integration policy is never questioned. Instead, the debate focuses on the question of what exactly this goal entails and how it can best be achieved. In the post-9/11 context the integration of Muslim immigrants has appeared as a new focus of integration policy.

5. Although this categorization may appear to be evidence of cultural racism, it is not intended to be. Rather, this distinction is made because Western *allochtonen* generally perform well in Dutch society and do not need additional government support. On the other hand, a large share of non-Western *allochtonen* do not perform well, and many are socioeconomically marginalized, lack education, are unemployed, or are illiterate. This category of non-Western *allochtonen* is used to address some of these problems, although it is acknowledged that doing so may cause stigmatization.

6. In the Netherlands statistics, Japan is considered a "Western" nation in terms of its high level of economic development. Migrants from Indonesia are counted as "Western" because they are considered to have successfully integrated into Dutch society and are no longer perceived as a group targeted for integration policies.

Statistical data on only the first generation are used in this chapter for the purposes of comparability with other immigrant gateways. However, the selection of the case study discussed in this chapter is based on the statistical category *allochtonen*. Because policy in the Netherlands is targeted at first- and second-generation immigrants, one selection criteria is that the percentage of *allochtonen* has to exceed the city average. District Zuidoost has the highest concentration of *allochtonen* in Amsterdam. Seventy-one percent of residents of this district are *allochtonen*. Zuidoost is also the district in Amsterdam with the highest concentration of foreign-born residents.

In 2005, 9.8 percent of the Dutch population was foreign-born. Currently, 13 percent of all foreign-born residents in the Netherlands live in Amsterdam. The nonimmigrant population in the city has declined because of ongoing suburbanization of families with children, while at the same time there is a growing diversity of ethnic groups. New immigrants increasingly arrive from the so-called non-Western nations. The increasing share of immigrants in the cities' population, as well as the increasing diversity of origins of immigrants, poses a series of questions for public officials as to how to manage difference, and complicates earlier efforts toward multiculturalism, which focused on groups rather than individuals as the starting points for policy development.

This section has provided a quantitative overview of Amsterdam as an established immigrant gateway. These numbers do not tell much about the relationships between host and immigrant populations, tensions in Dutch society, or how living with diversity is negotiated in the everyday life of urban neighborhoods. These ideas will be discussed in the next sections of this chapter.

CHANGING GOVERNMENTAL REGIMES: THE TRANSITION
FROM MULTICULTURALISM TO INTEGRATION

Until a few years ago, multiculturalism was widely applied as a suitable model for accommodating ethnic diversity, and it contributed to the development of an urban infrastructure of institutions concerned with the support of minority groups. As such, the multicultural label has come to entail, enable, and legitimate a whole series of policies and other forms of intervention aimed at managing diversity in cities. In recent years state programs of multiculturalism have been increasingly perceived as failing (Brubaker 2003; Joppke and Morawska 2003; Mitchell 2004). Katharyne Mitchell (2004) even observes a trend in the Western world whereby state-sponsored programs of multiculturalism, which were first introduced in the 1970s, are increasingly discarded to be replaced by assimilationist strategies. Although programs of multiculturalism actively facilitated and promoted pluralism in the public sphere, new programs of assimilation, characterized by a renewed focus on the core values of society—values believed to be lost owing to multicultural programs—now render expressions of difference a matter of the private sphere (Brubaker 2003). Increasingly, states have transferred power and responsibility to local scales, of the community or of the individual. In an increasingly global world, individuals have to take more responsibility for their own actions and for their success in life. As Mitchell contends, "The current discourse of state-sponsored multiculturalism as failing is intertwined with ongoing geopolitical efforts to shift the responsibility for controlling and facilitating immigrant integration from the institutions of the state to the local level" (2004, 645).

The Netherlands has not been an exception to this trend (Entzinger 2003). It has probably experienced the most marked shift away from multiculturalism. As a consequence, city officials also need to develop new ways to accommodate difference within a new overarching national policy framework. In Amsterdam (and the Netherlands), its immigrant gateway status has not yet become part of its identity and a source of local pride, as it has in cities such as New York or Chicago (Singer 2004). Although immigration to the Netherlands dates back to the sixteenth century, national policies aimed at immigrants (and their integration) did not exist until the 1980s. However, cities—where most immigrants settled—started developing various tactics and strategies to regulate the relationship between newcomers and natives practically as soon as immigrants arrived (Uitermark, Rossi, and van Houtem 2005). Therefore, cities have a much longer experience with immigrant integration policy than the Dutch state. Nevertheless, the importance of the local scale for immigrant incorporation declined when, in the 1980s, the Dutch state officially recognized the permanent character of immigration: guest workers would probably stay, and a new stream of immigrants would arrive from all corners of the world to settle.

The first official national policy toward immigrants was formulated in 1983, in a policy called Minderhedennota (Minority Memorandum). Immigrants were now considered "ethnic minorities" instead of guest workers or foreigners (Rath 1991), thus recognizing that immigrants needed special care and assistance to improve their socioeconomic position in Dutch society. Ethnic minorities were allowed to retain their own culture and to manage their own institutions, because it was expected that doing so would facilitate their comfort within Dutch society. This minority policy was a first step toward multiculturalism in the Netherlands, as it recognized the presence of distinct ethnic groups in the Netherlands that needed care based on group characteristics.[7] The Dutch state officially recognized the existence of a "multicultural society" (Scientific Council for Government Policy 2001) and took the ideal of multiculturalism as the guiding principle for the development of social policy.

Over time the multicultural model lost the support of Dutch society because of the perceived lack of integration of ethnic minorities into mainstream society. Minderhedenbeleid was replaced by a new Integratiebeleid (Integration Policy) in 1994. In the new model less emphasis was put on promoting and facilitating multiculturalism. Instead, more emphasis was put on the need to integrate through increased participation in education and the workforce (Entzinger 2003, 72). Under this model not only was it believed that ethnic minorities should be given a chance to integrate, but it was also expected that immigrants would take advantage of the opportunities provided to them. In fact, according to this policy a multicultural society involves peaceful coexistence—it is "the responsibility of individuals,

---

7. The choice for multiculturalism as a model for dealing with ethnic diversity should be understood in the context of the Dutch history of pillarization. Pillarization is a model that developed in the Netherlands in the early twentieth century and involves the state-supported autonomy of religious or ethnic groups. Each pillar developed its own institutions (schools, neighborhoods, political parties, social clubs, and so on), which explains why the new minority policy stressed representation of ethnic groups through consultative bodies and self-organizations.

businesses, and social institutions to create a place for all residents" (Ministry of Big Cities and Integration Policy 2002)—equal rights and opportunities for immigrants in social spheres, and encouragement of active participation of ethnic minority groups in local politics and decision making. And, finally, recognizing the growing diversity of immigrants, ethnic minorities were increasingly viewed as individuals rather than as groups.

By the mid-1990s, immigrants were increasingly held responsible for their successful integration into Dutch society. But it was not until 2003 that the newly elected Dutch government officially backed away from the ideal of multiculturalism for the development of a new social policy:

> From day one this cabinet has started a major shift in integration policy. This shift has been worked out in a response of the cabinet on the report of the Parliamentary Commission Blok.[8] The renewed integration policy of the cabinet contains a break with multiculturalism. The cabinet emphasizes the need to maintain the coherence of society without aiming at forcing assimilation of minorities. (Tweede Kamer der Staten-Generaal 2005, 30-304; Jaarnota Integratiebeleid 2005, vergaderjaar 2005–2006)

Although the policy stated that assimilation of minorities would not be forced, a series of programs have been introduced that have a strong assimilationist agenda. An example of these policies is the proposed language-testing centers in sending countries where migrants first have to prove their proficiency in the Dutch language before moving to the Netherlands. Other examples are the relocation of the Office of Integration from the Home Office to the Department of Justice following the elections of 2002 and mandatory integration programs for immigrants.

The recent policy shift in the Netherlands can be understood to be the result of two key paradoxes that characterize Dutch efforts to construct a

8. Soon after the initiation of the new cabinet in September 2002, a parliamentary commission was installed to investigate the success or failure of state integration policy from the 1970s until 2002. Immigrant integration—led by Pim Fortuyn—appeared as the number-one political priority in the national elections of 2002. The first action of the newly elected government was an evaluation of past integration policy in order to formulate a new integration policy for the future.

multicultural state. First, though multicultural policies aim for social inclusion, there is evidence that cities where these policies have been implemented have simultaneously experienced increased social exclusion and spatial segregation. Second, multicultural policies are framed in terms of equal rights, full acceptance, and integration into Dutch society. A growing section of the Dutch population is uncomfortable with the presence of ethnic minorities, especially Muslims, in urban spaces. Recently, fears created by the terrorist acts of September 11, 2001, in the United States have resulted in a political backlash against immigrants in the Netherlands. Some politicians have used this reaction to their advantage. Pim Fortuyn, a charismatic politician, was projected to win the national elections with a political program that entailed the forced assimilation of immigrants and a stop on further immigration. He was assassinated two weeks before the elections by a Dutch animal rights activist. Despite his death, immigrant integration continues to be a matter for public debate. Under the "mask" of tolerance, questioning the integration of immigrants had been taboo. In fact, it would have been perceived as an act of discrimination. Multiculturalism has now become the new taboo. The ascendancy of Fortuyn's political vision sped up a process of "toughening" views toward ethnic minorities and their place in Dutch society (see Prins and Slijper 2002). Communities and individuals themselves are held responsible for their integration into Dutch society. This trend corresponds with the findings of Katharyne Mitchell, who argues that "those who choose *not* to assimilate are represented as individuals unwilling to participate in civic life who can, as a result, be excluded from society without incurring damage to the core ideals of a universalist liberal project" (2004, 645). Immigrant integration in the Netherlands thus increasingly places responsibility for successful incorporation into society in the hands of the immigrants themselves. Hence, failure becomes increasingly conceptualized in terms of individual characteristics, rather than the outcomes of institutionalized racism, segregation, or marginalization in the host society.

Furthermore, integration has become spatialized. The problem of integration is associated with certain urban neighborhoods, particularly neighborhoods with large immigrant populations like the Bijlmermeer, a neighborhood in the southeastern district of Amsterdam suffering from dilapidated buildings, drugs, crime, and the socioeconomic marginalization

of a large proportion of its residents. The same can be said of neighborhoods on the western periphery of the city. In order to avoid further
downgrading of these neighborhoods, urban renewal, geared toward
attracting the middle and upper classes to disadvantaged neighborhoods
and the dispersal of low-income groups across the city, is seen as a solution.
Marketing diversity can be seen as one strategy to attract new groups,
thereby turning the problem (immigrants) into an asset (diversity) (Bodaar
2006, 177).

URBAN VERSUS STATE POLICIES

Since the late 1980s—when a national policy framework for managing
immigrant integration was put in place—policies in Amsterdam mirrored
policies on the national level. Specific policies were introduced to counter
discrimination, support minority organizations from different nationalities, and involve the latter in the process of policy formation (Uitermark,
Rossi, and van Houtem 2005, 629). For example, under the policy of
Minderhedennota, the local government established advisory councils
for different minority groups. Also, many migrant organizations received
subsidies. However, with the development of a new discourse on ethnic
diversity—which focuses more on the responsibility of the individual for
integrating into Dutch society—Amsterdam also restructured the institutions that support ethnic diversity. The minority councils, for example,
were abolished. At the same time, the negotiations between minority organizations, political parties, and civil servants resulted in the replacement
of minority policy with diversity policy in 1998. Four goals are stated in
the policy: adjust policies and services to the diversity of the population
of the city, reflect the diversity of the population in the composition and
organization of the city, stimulate participation of all Amsterdammers and
actively address and prevent negative stereotyping and exclusion, and create a broad societal coalition that focuses on the positive employment of
diversity (Gemeente Amsterdam 2003, 5). The policy recognizes that there
is a value in each culture by stating that *everybody* can make a contribution
to the city (ibid., 3). It emphasizes the contribution of every person as an
individual instead of as a group, and recognizes that individuals can take

on multiple identities. Whereas at the state level diversity is framed negatively in terms of "fear," in Amsterdam diversity is perceived as contributing to the attractiveness of the city.

Another policy instrument, funded by the state but implemented by cities, is urban renewal. Urban renewal policy is aimed at the revitalization of disadvantaged neighborhoods through social mixing. In theory, a more affluent population is attracted to the neighborhood because inexpensive, dilapidated housing is replaced by more expensive housing. It is expected that the presence of affluent households will benefit the less-well-off households in the neighborhood in terms of educational achievement, employment, and social networks. In this context it is important to know that most neighborhoods that qualify as disadvantaged are those neighborhoods where immigrants are concentrated. As Justus Uitermark illustrates, Dutch urban renewal policy represents an attempt to facilitate the social management of disadvantaged neighborhoods and to mitigate the social effects of the problematic integration of ethnic minorities (2003, 531). Southeastern Amsterdam is the district of the city with the largest foreign-born population, and is currently subject to large-scale urban renewal involving both physical renewal of the urban fabric as well as social and economic renewal, through projects aimed directly and indirectly at immigrants.

LIVING APART TOGETHER IN THE MULTICULTURAL CITY:
LITTLE AFRICA IN THE BIJLMERMEER

The Bijlmermeer is an important gateway for immigrants to the Netherlands and one of Europe's leading examples of a high-rise estate. It is located in the southeast of Amsterdam. The district's population is approximately 82,000, of which 46,000 live in the Bijlmermeer (Dienst Onderzoek en Statistiek 2004). According to official statistics, more than 55 percent of the population of the Bijlmermeer is foreign-born. However, in reality the foreign-born population exceeds this number, owing to the presence of an unknown number of illegal immigrants in the neighborhood. The Surinamese are the largest ethnic group in the neighborhood, but there are also significant Ghanaian and Antillean populations, as well as immigrants who have origins elsewhere in the world (see table 7.2).

TABLE 7.2

POPULATION OF SOUTHEAST AMSTERDAM BY ETHNICITY, 2000

	Surinam	Antilles	Turkey	Morocco	South Europe	Ghana	Other nonindustrial countries	Industrial countries	Dutch
Amsterdam	10	2	5	8	2	1	9	10	55
Southeast	31	6	1	2	2	7	13	5	33
Bijlmer-Centre[a]	40	9	2	2	2	10	16	3	16
Bijlmer-East	33	8	1	2	2	10	16	4	24

Source: Aalbers et al. 2003, 87.

Note: Figures are percentages.

[a] In official statistics, the Bijlmermeer is split up into two separate neighborhoods. For the purposes of this chapter, I take both neighborhoods together.

Together, they make up a highly diverse multicultural population of 130 different nationalities.

The Bijlmermeer was built between the late 1960s and mid-1970s as a middle-class neighborhood of uniform high-rise blocks with large open spaces between them. By the time the first apartments entered the housing market, they had to compete with new single-family homes in the suburbs. Middle-class families preferred the single-family housing to the high-rise blocks, leaving the new flats empty. To avoid vacancies, the apartments were rented for less money. At the same time, many migrants left the former colony of Dutch Guiana (now Surinam) and migrated to the Netherlands; they settled in the affordable Bijlmermeer neighborhood. Immigrants from Surinam and the Netherlands Antilles were soon followed by other immigrants, causing the Bijlmermeer to become the "gateway" for many newcomers, both legal and illegal, from all over the world (Bodaar 2006, 179).

Over the years, the neighborhood has become associated with various social problems, such as high crime rates, poverty, illegal immigration, social isolation, and a negative image. In this respect, the experience of the Bijlmermeer is not very different from other large housing estates in Europe that have experienced similar problems of deprivation (Aalbers et al. 2003; Helleman and Wassenberg 2004; Wacquant 1993). A major problem is the socioeconomic marginalization of the residents. In the 1980s and 1990s the residents of the Bijlmermeer were increasingly isolated from opportunities in the urban economy. A lack of skills and experience and alienation from the political system excluded many residents from Dutch society. High unemployment, debt problems, and other social issues led to the further deterioration of the neighborhood. The Bijlmermeer became a district of low-income, unemployed, ethnically diverse, and increasingly nonwhite residents (Blair and Hulsbergen 1993).

In 1992 the state, the city of Amsterdam, the southeastern district council, and various housing corporations decided to take on a large-scale urban renewal effort in the Bijlmermeer. This operation involved the demolition of more than 13,000 homes (approximately 50 percent of all high-rise blocks) between 1992 and 2010. The high-rise blocks are being replaced with 15,000 homes (single-family houses and four-story blocks). Before the renewal operation, 92 percent of all housing was in the public rental sector; after the renewal operation, this figure should be reduced to 55 percent (Kwekke-boom 2002), reflecting the ambition of the city to attract middle-class residents to the neighborhood and to allow current residents of the Bijlmermeer to own housing in the neighborhood. Besides funds for the renewal of the built environment, there are also funds available from the European Union and the Dutch Big Cities Policy Program for socioeconomic renewal.

As this policy was being implemented in the 1990s, the Bijlmermeer experienced a rapid increase of African immigrants. Most of them first arrived there because of the availability of cheap housing, the presence of other Africans, and the presence of an informal economy through which many resources for survival were provided. According to official statistics there are currently 2,000 Ghanaians living in the southeastern district (of which the Bijlmermeer is part). But because many Ghanaians arrive illegally, their numbers are certainly greater than official statistics indicate.

The presence of the Africans in the neighborhood is visible in the urban landscape of the Bijlmermeer (fig. 7.3). The church plays a key role in the lives of many Ghanaian and Nigerian migrants. Because of the presence of Ghanaian immigrants from many different tribes, they have established more than one hundred churches. Furthermore, immigrants, responding to the demand from the growing African community, began to open small businesses where they sell African products (such as dried fish, yams, and so on) or provide services for Africans (for example, hairdressers and money-transfer businesses). On Saturdays there is a big market that appeals to Africans from other places in Belgium, Germany, and the Netherlands. A young Ghanaian man, John, told me that he decided to move to Bijlmermeer because of this presence of Ghanaian churches and the availability of African food: "It was very far for us to come to church, because we come to church at Bijlmermeer. Where we were living was very far from here and so we decided to move here . . . and African food you can also get here. It's convenient."

The church also plays a key role as a support network for (illegal) immigrants, especially for those individuals who are excluded from access to social benefits in the Netherlands. At the church, funds are raised for families in need: for example, to pay for medical bills, a funeral, or a return to Africa. Also, the church has an important social function: it is through

Fig. 7.3. Ghanaians in the Bijlmermeer. Copyright © Rob Crandall/www
.robcrandall.com

churches that new relationships are started and friendships created. Church networks have an economic function as well, connecting new migrants to job opportunities. The church provides an important support network for Africans in Amsterdam.

By the end of the 1990s the Bijlmermeer had become the center of the Ghanaian community in northwestern Europe. Ghanaians from all over the Netherlands, and even from Italy, Germany and other European countries travel to the Bijlmermeer for celebrations, shopping, and other festivities. On a Saturday many can be found at the market, because it "is so African." As one woman, Diana, told me, "Anyone who come from Ghana or from anywhere he wants to come to Bijlmermeer because that is where most of us live, and so maybe someone who can help you and so it is a well-known place."

Even though the Surinamese and the Dutch population in the neighborhood outnumber the Ghanaians, the Ghanaians speak of their residential community as "Little Africa," a place where Ghanaians from the same region of origin tend to cluster together and where they can live relatively isolated from the larger Dutch society. As Marcus told me, "To be very honest, we only know of Holland when we got outside the city here. The Bijlmermeer is our stronghold. For us this is Africa, the Bijlmermeer is Africa, it is our town, it's our city, it's our home."

Many foreign-born Ghanaians indicate that they are not interested in integrating into Dutch society, although they do recognize that their children will become Dutch. In many ways, through their spatial practices they have negotiated their presence in the Bijlmermeer. They insist that as a community they are not confused with other "black" migrants in the neighborhood, whom they hold responsible for the community's deprivation. John said to me, "The Ghanaians, we don't like violence. We are different people, but our people are different people than the black people we meet here, we are better ones. . . . Surinamese, Antilleans, Curacao, Nigerians have also come to be part of them. That is very sad. And also, if you don't know the Ghanaians are very hard workers."

The Ghanaian community has been active in negotiating urban renewal plans for the neighborhood. In order to avoid the displacement of Ghanaians and the breaking down of the existing ethnic infrastructure (both legal and illegal), some Ghanaians have taken positions in the district council through which they gain a voice in the urban renewal plans. Through their efforts, for example, they have managed to negotiate new locations for churches that were subject to demolition. Also, they have received funds for educational projects to prepare the unemployed members of their community for the labor market by teaching them computer skills. Thus, within a national framework that is geared toward immigrant integration into Dutch society, multiculturalism still continues to exist locally, where immigrants can still function within the bounds of their ethnic group.

Despite the active negotiation of their presence in the Bijlmermeer, urban renewal is actually reducing the opportunities for illegal migrants. The rebuilt neighborhood is less suitable for informal economic activities and for providing shelter for illegal immigrants, which used to be the practice, according to Daniel:

> In our community we help one another. We have a welfare funds, we have many houses, so even when we don't have houses, when a brother as visitor comes, we call ourselves brothers and sisters and we really mean that. So if I have a house like this and three people come to have a place to stay, well it is my responsibility to take care of them for maybe three or four weeks, and then our neighbor says okay, and that will give them another month, and so we do, and then this person is looking for a black job, we are not ashamed. And we find black jobs for our people. I prefer to give them a black job than for them to become drug pushers and drug addicts.

The anonymity of the high-rise blocks has disappeared with the building of four-story and single-family housing. Also, through increased police surveillance and control, it is increasingly difficult to hide illegal residents. This decrease in illegal residents has implications for a number of Ghanaian churches, because once illegal immigrants begin to disappear from the neighborhood, the churches experience a significant reduction in attendance.

CONCLUSION

This chapter has discussed a number of recent events in the Netherlands that have resulted in a reevaluation and adjustment of policies aimed at immigrant integration. Ethnic diversity poses a series of new challenges for governments and particularly for cities, as immigrants tend to concentrate in cities. Increasingly, the state provides guidelines and funds for immigrant integration, whereas local solutions manage the living-with-diversity issues. Hence, the outcomes of immigrant integration will be different in different cities. Whereas, on the one hand, the state promotes an assimilationist stance toward immigrant integration, locally, a multicultural strategy is used to find ad hoc solutions for dealing with immigrant integration. Local policies do not contradict state models, but within the bounds of state policy cities develop their own directions based on local experiences.

In the Netherlands, ethnic diversity is negotiated locally, in neighborhoods and public spaces where different groups confront each other. Southeastern Amsterdam is now the most multicultural urban district in the country, a place where multiculturalism is still thriving despite a national context that demands the assimilation of immigrants. There, the district council includes immigrants, and different ethnic groups have their own religious organizations and institutions, some of which are housed in shared public facilities. In the Bijlmermeer, a multiethnic neighborhood in Amsterdam, the Ghanaian community has created a relatively self-sufficient community. The Ghanaians clearly distinguish themselves from the other ethnic groups in the neighborhood. Although the Dutch state strongly encourages immigrant integration, the Ghanaian residents themselves are not aware of these policies and live their lives mainly within the bounds of the Ghanaian community.

PART TWO | Emerging Gateways

8

Gateway Singapore

Immigration Policies, Differential (Non)Incorporation, and Identity Politics

BRENDA S. A. YEOH and NATALIE YAP

Within the world-city hierarchy, Singapore is often ranked in the second tier, among those cities aspiring for "superleague" status.[1] As Beng Huat Chua (1998, 995) points out, Singapore "eminently qualifies for a place in the collection of cities which are discursively grouped under [the term *world cities*]" as having been, since its "birth" during the modern age of mercantile capitalism, intensely part of global service capitalism. Indeed, three decades after becoming an independent nation, Singapore—the "child" of imperial and labor diasporas in the days of empire[2]—is once

---

1. The first half of this paper is adapted from Yeoh 2006. The case study on identity politics among PRC Chinese in Singapore is primarily based on Natalie Yap's work for her master's thesis. This paper is written in memory of the third anniversary of her passing away and in an attempt to fulfill her desire to share her work with a wider audience.

2. The history and fortunes of Singapore are closely intertwined with migrants and migration. Singapore's colonial history began in 1819 with the setting up of a trading post on the island (then known as Temasek) by the British, who were looking to dominate trade in the East Indies. Singapore's rapidly expanding economy, coupled with a liberal open-door policy on immigration, drew large numbers of immigrants from China, India, and the Malay archipelago at the turn of the twentieth century. Many came as manual laborers and played an integral role in shoring up the development of the port and city of Singapore. From a fishing village of a few hundred people in the early nineteenth century, the population size crossed the half-million mark by the census of 1931. The period of free immigration,

again a convergence point for both new and renewed migration streams. If "diaspora" (where constant harking back to a material or imaginary ancestral homeland is a key signature) captured the essence of large numbers of sojourners in Singapore engaged in "experimental migration" in the pre-independence days (Wang 2003, 3), then "transnational migration," with its emphasis on multiple, sometimes circular, journeys and diverse social and economic networks linking "host" and "home" in more ambivalent and flexible ways, is a more appropriate term to describe the mobility of people in a rapidly globalizing world.

The years after the Second World War hailed the end of more than a century of British colonialism in Singapore. In 1959, Singapore attained self-government, and in 1963 became part of the Federation of Malaya, along with Sabah and Sarawak. During these years, migration policies had to be adjusted and laws tightened, reflecting a country coming to terms with various stages of independence. When Singapore joined the Malayan Federation in 1963, Singapore citizens were not automatically granted Malaysian citizenship (Chew and Chew 1995). Such factors, as well as conflicts over racial issues, led to the separation of Singapore from Malaysia in 1965, when it became an independent, sovereign nation. Within Singapore, the 1957 Singapore Citizenship Act had conferred automatic citizenship on everyone born in Singapore. Those individuals born in Malaysia or to citizens of the United Kingdom and its colonies could become citizens if they had a minimum of two years of residence (later increased to a minimum of eight years), whereas all "aliens"—those individuals born in China—with at least eight years of residence (later increased to ten years) could apply for citizenship. Dual citizenship was prohibited in 1960.

---

which lasted more than a century, came to an end with the passing of the 1928 Immigration Restriction Ordinance. In 1932, the Aliens Ordinance introduced a fixed quota for "alien" immigrations. Prior to World War II, the dominant component of population growth was immigrants, as natural increase was negative prior to 1921, partly because the gross imbalance in Singapore's sex ratio in the nineteenth and early twentieth centuries depressed crude birthrates and also because of high crude mortality rates. A large proportion of Singapore's population today is composed of the descendants of these early immigrants.

By 1970, the total share of the nonresident population[3] in Singapore had dwindled to 2.9 percent of a population of more than 2 million as the newly independent city-state buckled down to the task of nation building, which included mechanisms to define fixed categories in order to incorporate citizens of the nation, on the one hand, and exclude others as noncitizens, or "aliens," on the other. As Anthony Marx (2002) has argued, the process of nation building depends on the exclusion of certain constituents from the geobody of the nation, rather than the inclusion of an across-the-board national community. The drawing of unambiguous citizen-noncitizen lines to divide the population—negotiable in that fulfilling residency requirements provides a means of crossing the divide—fixes the body of the nation and embeds an exclusive form of nationalism in a defined territory.

The first decade of the country's independence was devoted to planning and infrastructural provision, as Singapore began constructing its economic foundations by raising the country's living standards and economic competitiveness through welcoming foreign companies and investors. In the first few years of independence, strict controls were imposed on the importation of foreign workers (Chan and Abdullah 1999), but these rules were relaxed as industrialization went into full swing, characterized by high export-led growth. Relaxed immigration policies resulted in large numbers of unskilled foreign labor in the manufacturing, construction, and domestic-services sectors from "nontraditional" (that is, non-Malaysian) sources, such as India, Bangladesh, Sri Lanka, the Philippines, and Thailand (Hui 1997).

In Singapore the 1970s began with full employment, and except for the period after the 1973 world oil crisis, the economy boomed. At the end of the decade, a moderate wage-increase policy was adopted by the National Wages Council. The 1960s and 1970s therefore ended with an excess of labor demand over domestic supply and high export-led growth. The 1980s were less rosy, characterized rather by fluctuations

---

3. The resident population includes Singapore citizens and permanent residents, whereas the nonresident population refers to those individuals on short-term stays such as on an employment pass or a work permit.

TABLE 8.1

CHANGING PROPORTION OF CITIZENS TO FOREIGN NONRESIDENTS IN SINGAPORE, 1947 TO THE PRESENT

Census year	1947[a]		1957		1970		1980		1990		2000	
	No.	%	No.	%	No.	%	No.	%	No.	%	No.	%
Total	940,824	100	1,445,929	100	2,074,507	100	2,413,945	100	3,016,379	100	4,017,733	100
Total resident population (born in Singapore and Malaysia)	571,331	60.7	1,055,184	73.0	2,013,563	97.0	2,282,125	94.5	2,705,115	89.7	3,263,209	81.2
Citizens	—	—	—		1,874,778	90.4	2,194,280	90.9	2,595,243	86.0	2,973,091	74.0
Permanent residents					138,785	6.7	87,845	3.6	109,872	3.6	290,118	7.2
Others (excluding nonlocally domiciled services personnel) / Total nonresident population[b]	369,493	39.3	390,745	27.0	60,944	2.9	131,820	5.5	311,264	10.3	754,524	18.8

Sources: Compiled from del Tufo 1949; Arumainathan 1970; and Singapore Department of Statistics 2001.

[a]Singapore attained independence in 1965, the year when the term *citizenship* first began to be invoked, drawing a clear boundary between Singaporeans and foreigners. Prior to independence, the census classified the resident population according to place of birth. The numbers of people born in Singapore and Malaysia will be used as a proxy for citizens here. "Others" therefore denotes the numbers born outside of Singapore and Malaysia. "Nonlocally domiciled services personnel" refer to the officers and foreigners working for the British administrative service, as well as other temporary workers, and their families.

[b]"Total nonresident population" refers to individuals who hold passes for short-term stays in Singapore, including the Employment Pass, Work Permit, Dependant's Pass, and Long-term Social Visit Pass. This category excludes tourists and "transients."

in employment opportunities induced by the world economic recession in 1985. Economic restructuring led the transition from a production and manufacturing emphasis to higher skills and growth in the service and financial sectors, and finally toward high technology-related areas. This restructuring resulted in the doubling of the short-term foreign population between 1970 and 1980, a trend that continued to be reflected in the following decadal census in 1990 (table 8.1). Fueled by such changes, the period from the 1990s to the present saw the rise of foreign labor, both unskilled and skilled, in all sectors of the economy.

As revealed in the 2000 population census, increased transnational migration streams have expanded the nonresident population to 18.8 percent in a population of more than 4 million. Between 1990 and 2000, the nonresident population grew much more rapidly (9.3 percent per annum) than the resident population (1.8 percent per annum). Two years later, despite a drop of 3.3 percent in the number of foreigners as a result of the economic downturn, the total foreign population stood at a sizable 785,400 out of 4 million total (*Straits Times,* December 23, 2002). The latest figures from the General Household Survey (2005) reveal a nonresident population of 797,900 (out of a total population of 4,351,400).[4] Among the resident population (3,553,500), about 12.4 percent are permanent residents (PRs) rather than Singapore citizens. Between 1990 and 2000, PRs grew much faster (10 percent increase per annum) than Singapore citizens, which increased at 1.3 percent per annum. The corresponding rates for 2000–2005 were an increase of 8.7 percent per annum among PRs compared to a modest 0.9 percent per annum among Singaporeans. Despite the increasing share of PRs among the resident population, the ethnic composition of the Singapore resident population remained relatively stable (table 8.2). It is also interesting to note that about 18.3 percent (596,108) of the resident population base were born outside Singapore, mainly in Malaysia (306,998, or 9.4 percent); China, Hong Kong, and Taiwan (163,503, or 5 percent); South Asia, including India, Bangladesh, Pakistan, and Sri Lanka

---

4. Singapore Department of Statistics (2006), http://www.singstat.gov.sg/keystats/annual/ghs/r1/chap1.pdf.

TABLE 8.2
RESIDENT POPULATION BY ETHNIC GROUP AND RESIDENTIAL STATUS, 2000

	Total	Chinese		Malays		Indians		Others	
	3,263,209	2,505,379	76.8%	453,633	13.9%	257,79	17.9%	46,406	1.4%
Singapore citizens (91.1%)	2,973,091	2,284,617	76.8%	441,737	14.9%	214,642	7.2%	32,095	1.1%
Permanent residents (8.9%)	290,118	220,762	76.1%	11,896	4.1%	43,149	14.9%	14,311	4.9%

Source: Singapore Department of Statistics 2001.

(61,308, or 1.9 percent); Indonesia (32,785, or 1 percent); and other Asian countries (15,137, or 0.5 percent).[5]

In the context of Singapore, Neil M. Coe and Philip F. Kelly argue that "the state plays a *necessary* role in shaping both the real and discursive contours of the labor regime" (2002, 347). Indeed, the increasing share of the nonresident population at the millennial turn is a direct consequence of the city-state's policies to attract and rely on "foreign manpower," as made clear in the vision and aims of the Ministry of Manpower: "Singapore has always leveraged on foreign manpower at all levels to enhance our economic growth. The employment of foreign manpower is [a] deliberate strategy to enable us to grow beyond what our indigenous resources can produce. As we transit to a knowledge economy, we need to ensure that our manpower augmentation policies remain relevant and effective."[6] The "deliberate" and "strategic" reliance on "foreign manpower" is part and parcel of the dominant neoliberal discourse of globalization as "an inevitable and virtuous growth dynamic" central to the nation-state's economic prosperity plans, along with the deregulation of various economic sectors and the aggressive pursuit of foreign inward investments (Coe and Kelly 2002, 348). As elsewhere, the size of the transmigrant worker population grows in tandem with neoliberal restructuring processes designed to render labor more "flexible" in relation to capital. As a result, the workforce was rapidly reconfigured to include a significantly large foreign component: foreigners currently constitute approximately 30 percent of Singapore's total employment, giving Singapore the dubious distinction of having the highest proportion of foreign workers in Asia (*Straits Times*, August 31, 1997). As seen in table 8.3, the most rapid increase occurred between 1990 and 2000 when Singapore's nonresident workforce increased from 248,000 to 612,200.[7] The two main flows of transnational foreigners attracted to

5. Singapore Department of Statistics (2001), http://www.singstat.gov.sg/keystats/c2000/topline13.pdf.

6. Ministry of Manpower Web site, Manpower 21, http://www.gov.sg/mom/m21/strat3.htm.

7. In fact, between 1990 and 2000, the foreign workforce in Singapore grew much more rapidly than the resident workforce (9.4 percent compared to 1.4 percent).

TABLE 8.3

FOREIGN WORKERS IN SINGAPORE, 1970–2000

Year	Total labor force	Number of foreign workers	Percentage of foreign workers
1970	650,892	20,828	3.2
1980	1,077,090	119,483	7.4
1990	1,537,000	248,000	16.1
2000	2,094,800	612,200	29.2

Sources: For 1970 and 1980: Rahman 1999, 7. For 1990 and 2000: Singapore Department of Statistics 2001, 43.

Singapore are skilled professional and managerial workers in high-end positions and low-skilled contract labor. The former—higher-skilled and better-educated foreigners holding employment passes—have increased rapidly as a result of intensive recruitment and broader eligibility criteria. In 1997, employment pass holders numbered about 55,000, constituting about 12 percent of the total foreign workforce; this number doubled to 110,000 by 2000 (Hui 2000, 7).[8] Far greater numbers, more than half a million people in 2000, are work-permit holders engaged in unskilled or semiskilled jobs. A third transnational flow is the arrival of international students. Singapore fashions itself as an English-speaking educational hub for the region. The rest of the chapter will discuss each of these three transnational flows in turn before giving attention to a specific case study of identity negotiations among Chinese transmigrants in Singapore.

UNSKILLED FOREIGN WORKERS

In terms of unskilled foreign workers, the numbers in 1997 stood at about 470,000; they included approximately 80,000 Filipinos, 70,000 Thais, 20,000 Sri Lankans, and 300,000 Malaysians, Indians, People's Republic

---

8. According to Weng-Tat Hui (2000, 7), a significant number of these employment-pass holders became permanent residents: between 1980 and 1999, an estimated total of about 326,000 have been granted permanent-resident status in Singapore.

of China (PRC) Chinese, and Indonesians (*Sunday Times*, August 31, 1997).[9] These laborers are concentrated in the construction industry (about 200,000), domestic maid services (about 140,000), and the remainder in service, manufacturing, and marine industries (*Straits Times*, May 20, 1999). The high demand for these categories of workers reflects not only the low wages (well below the national norm) accepted by immigrants, but also the reluctance of Singaporeans—even during times of economic recession—to fill jobs that require manual labor or shift work in sectors such as manufacturing, construction, marine industries, personal services, and domestic service (*Straits Times*, June 30 1998; July 5 and 7, 2001; February 7, 2003). The demand for these workers is likely to continue, or even increase, as the socioeconomic and educational levels of Singaporeans rise over time, and "fussy Singaporeans . . . [will] not take jobs in less 'glamorous' areas," in the words of then deputy prime minister Lee Hsien Loong (cited in the *Straits Times*, February 7, 2003).

The reliance on temporary contract labor is a result of policy decisions based on opposition to long-term immigration and a preference for a transient workforce, subject to repatriation during periods of economic downturn. State policy has remained firmly committed to ensuring that unskilled and low-skilled foreign workers are managed as a temporary and controlled phenomenon through a series of measures, including the work-permit system, the dependency ceiling (which regulates the proportion of foreign to local workers), and the foreign-worker levy. Together, these measures act to "dampen cyclical domestic labor shortages without imposing on Singapore unbearable, long-term social and political costs" (cited in Wong 2000, 163).

As a control measure, short-term work permits (or "R Passes," usually of one- or two-year duration) are required for all foreign workers earning S$1,800 or less per month (in accordance with the Employment of Foreign Workers Act).[10] The system works to ensure the status of these unskilled and low-skilled workers as a short-term labor pool that is easily

9. Unfortunately, more recent figures providing the nationality breakdown of foreign workers in Singapore are unavailable.

10. Ministry of Manpower Web site, http://www.gov.sg/mom/fta/wp/wp3b.htm.

TABLE 8.4

DIFFERENT ELIGIBILITY SCHEMES FOR EMPLOYMENT-PASS HOLDERS

Type of pass	Pass	Eligibility	Eligible for dependent's pass?[a]	Eligible for long-term social visit pass?[b]
P[c]	P1	For foreigners whose basic monthly salary is more than S$7,000	Yes	Yes
	P2	For foreigners whose basic monthly salary is more than S$3,500 and up to S$7,000	Yes	Yes
Q	Q1	For foreigners whose basic monthly salary is more than S$2,500 and who possess acceptable degrees, professional qualifications, or specialist skills	Yes	No
S		A new category of work pass that replaces the Q2 Pass went into effect on July 1, 2004. For foreigners whose monthly basic salary is at least S$1,800. S Pass applicants will be assessed on a points system, taking into account multiple criteria including salary, education qualifications, skills, job type, and work experience. A levy of S$50 per month will apply, and there will be a 5 percent cap on the number of S Pass holders in each company based on the company's number of local workers and work permit holders.	Yes (if monthly basic salary is equal to or more than S$2,500)	No
R[d]		Work pass issued to a skilled[e] or an unskilled foreigner with a monthly basic salary of not more than SGD$1,800 to work in Singapore	No	No

Source: Adapted from Ministry of Manpower, http://www.mom.gov.sg.

[a] Dependent's passes are issued to the children (under twenty-one years of age) and spouses of employment-pass holders, entitling them to come to live in Singapore with the employment-pass holder.

[b] The long-term social visit pass accords long-term visit entitlements to parents, parents-in-law, stepchildren, spouse (common law), handicapped children, and unmarried daughters above the age of twenty-one.

[c] P Passes are for foreigners who hold acceptable degrees, professional qualifications, or specialist skills and are seeking professional, administrative, executive, or managerial jobs.

[d] R Pass holders are subject to a security bond, and a medical examination is required for current two-year work permit holders.

[e] A skilled foreign worker is one who possesses at least a SPM (Sijil Pelajaran Malaysia, or the Malaysian Certificate of Education) qualification or its equivalent, or an NTC-3 (Practical) (National Technical Certificate Grade 3) Trade Certificate (also known as ITEs, or Institute of Technical Education Skills Evaluation Certificate, Level 1, from July 2002) that is relevant to his or her occupation.

repatriated, especially in times of economic recession. For example, after Singapore entered a period of economic recession in 1997, 7,000 foreign workers had their work permits canceled in the first five months of 1998 as compared to about 6,000 cancellations for the whole of 1997 (Rahman 1999, 7). Work-permit holders enjoy few privileges and face restrictions such as noneligibility for the dependent's pass, which would allow them to bring their spouses and children with them (table 8.4). They are allowed to work only for the employer and in the occupation as reflected in the work permit and cannot legally gain access to the local labor market.[11] In addition, they cannot marry Singaporeans or permanent residents, and are subject to regular medical examinations, which includes a general physical checkup, a chest X-ray (to detect active tuberculosis infection), and a test for HIV/AIDS (*Business Times*, February 19, 2000).[12] These controls are draconian at best.

Female work-permit holders (that is, foreign domestic workers) who are found to be pregnant on medical screenings are repatriated without exception. The termination of employment also results in the immediate termination of the work permit, and the worker must leave Singapore within seven days (Wong 1997, 151). The number of work-permit holders that employers are allowed to employ is also subject to a dependency ceiling,[13] a quota that is tied to the number of local workers the company employs.[14]

---

11. Though it is illegal, some contract workers have ventured to moonlight on the side for additional income.

12. According to the Ministry of Manpower, "During a foreign worker's employment in Singapore, the employer is generally responsible for . . . arranging for the worker to be certified medically fit and free from contagious diseases and drug addiction by a Singapore-registered doctor when requested by the Controller of Work Permits" (http://www.mom.gov .sg/MOM/WPD/Procedures/2410_ WP_General_Guide_1Oct03.pdf).

13. The dependency ceiling varies by sector. For example, in the service industry, 30 percent of the workforce is permitted to be foreign, whereas in the construction industry, four foreign workers are allowed for every full-time local worker (http://www.mom.gov.sg/ MOM/WPD/Procedures/2414_WP_Guide_Construction_Sector(1_Oct_03).pdf). According to the Ministry of Manpower, the government varies the quota on work-permit rules by sector depending on where locals are less or more willing to work because it "has to balance the needs of both employers and citizens in implementing the foreign-worker policy" (*Straits Times*, January 30, 2002).

14. Ministry of Manpower Web site, http://www.gov.sg/mom/fta/wp/wp3b.htm.

188 | Brenda S. A. Yeoh and Natalie Yap

The other key measure, the monthly foreign-worker levy to be paid by the employer to the government, works to control the demand for contract migrant workers, as well as to ensure that their wages "reflect labor market conditions and not simply the marginal cost of hiring foreign workers" (Low 1995, 753). Levy rates—currently ranging from S$30 for workers considered "skilled" to much higher rates of S$240–470 for unskilled workers (with rates varying by economic sector)—are structured in such a way as to encourage the employment of skilled foreign labor and are periodically adjusted with shifts in the economic cycle to protect jobs for local workers (Straits Times, July 12, 2001). Adding to the cost of employing foreign workers, employers of work-permit holders are also required to post a S$5,000 security bond for each (non-Malaysian) worker. In addition, all employers of foreign domestic workers must take out personal accident insurance of at least S$10,000 for each, since foreign domestic workers are not entitled to claim worker's compensation.[15]

Although the duration of a work permit is usually two years, it may work out to be shorter in practice, as the work permit is also subject to the validity of the worker's passport (one month before its expiration), the banker's and insurance guarantee (two months before its expiration), and the worker's employment period, whichever is shorter.[16]

SKILLED FOREIGN WORKERS

The other burgeoning sector of foreign labor—professional and managerial workers—is usually referred to as "foreign talent" in both government and public discourse. Traditionally, the expatriate community of skilled professionals comprised Westerners from countries such as the United States (5,600), Britain (6,600), France (1,600), and Australia (3,300), as well as Japan (10,200) and South Korea (1,400) (Business Times, June 15, 1998). In 2000, skilled workers and professionals accounted for about 80,000 of the total number of foreigners, the numbers bolstered by policies

15. Ibid., http://www4.fov.sg/mom/wpeaw/wcfile/wc2.htm.
16. See http://www.mom.gov.sg/MOM/WPD/Procedures/2504_WP_General_Guide_13Dec03.pdf.

to target nontraditional source countries such as China and India. Given the aspirations of the natural resource-scarce, labor-short city-state to become a major player in a globalized world, Singapore's main economic strategy is premised on the development of a highly skilled human resource base as the "key success factor" in confronting a global future. Besides investing heavily in information technology and human capital to meet global competition, the state has emphasized the strategy of developing Singapore into a "brains service node," "an oasis of talent," and ultimately, the "talent capital" of the new economy, "where local and foreign talent combine their strengths, ideas and creativity to drive the economy and rise above global competition" (B. Lee 2000, 70).

In this formulation for a global future, major initiatives have been launched to "welcome the infusion of knowledge which foreign talent will bring," in the words of former prime minister Goh Chok Tong in 1997. In other words, skilled foreign labor, managed through generally liberal immigration policies, capitalizes on savings in human capital investments and allows for "technology transfers" (Hui 1998, 208). As such, Singapore, it is argued, must make strategic forays amid "the global war for talent" and augment its talent pool in order to "maintain the momentum to keep abreast in the global competition for wealth creation" (B. Lee 2000, 71). To secure its place in "a global network of cities of excellence," Singapore must reconfigure itself as a "cosmopolitan center, able to attract, retain and absorb talent from all over the world" (K. Lee 2000, 14). Various programs aimed at attracting "foreign talent" include company grants to ease the additional costs of employing skilled labor and recruitment missions by government agencies, and permanent residency possibilities have been implemented to boost the professional workforce (Hui 1997). In a similar vein, recent policies aimed at reimaging Singapore as a culturally vibrant "renaissance city" or a "global city for the arts" are at least partially driven by attempting to animate the city in order to attract and retain foreign talent.

Employment passes for skilled foreign labor comprise P Passes and Q Passes (see table 8.4).[17] P Passes are intended for the highly skilled and

17. A new category of "personalized" employment passes tied to the person rather than the employer was introduced in January 2007, allowing foreigners the flexibility to

generally issued to foreigners who hold university degrees and seek professional, administrative, executive, or managerial jobs (with salaries above S$3,500) or who are entrepreneurs or investors. Q Passes are issued to those individuals with a lower salary range (S$2,500 to S$3,500) and have evidence of "acceptable" degrees, professional qualifications, or specialty skills (*Straits Times,* November 9, 2001). Holders of P and Q Passes may work in any sector of the economy, are not subject to levies, and may bring family members with them. In 2004, S Passes were introduced as a new category for middle-level skilled foreigners such as technicians. All skilled foreigners may apply to become permanent residents or citizens. PRs are accorded most of the rights and duties of citizens, including eligibility for government-sponsored housing and mandatory national service (military service) for young male adults. They, however, may not vote in general elections. For foreigners to obtain full Singapore citizenship, they must be at least twenty-one years of age and have been Singapore PRs for at least two to six years immediately prior to the date of application. According to Singapore Immigration and Registration, citizenship applicants must also be "of good character," have the intention of residing permanently in Singapore, and be able to support themselves and their dependents financially.

FOREIGN STUDENTS

Although Singapore has long attracted foreign students from neighboring countries (especially from neighboring Malaysia and Indonesia), it has only been since 1997 that there have been specific efforts led by the Economic Development Board to develop Singapore into "a world-class education hub internationally renowned for its intellectual capital and creative energy" to capitalize on the US$2.2 trillion global market in education (*South China Morning Post,* September 16, 2003). The official tagline of "Singapore: The Global Schoolhouse" promotes Singapore as an educational destination that is "global in institutional composition and global in student mix."

---

change jobs or stay on in Singapore upon quitting a job. Applicants must earn a minimum of S$30,000 per annum and must have worked at least two years on a P Pass or five years on a Q1 Pass.

This program emphasizes that Singapore offers the best of both worlds, as the city "has coupled diverse Asian school systems with Western-styled education practices in our creation of a truly global education hub, where students have the best institutions in the world within reach."[18]

Additionally, the Singapore Tourism Board has established the Education Services Strategic Tourism Unit to spearhead the overall brand building and overseas marketing of "Singapore Education." Its Web site (available in Chinese, Indonesian, Vietnamese, Korean, Thai, and Japanese—an indication of its targeted markets in Asia) extols the many virtues of studying in Singapore, not least among which is Singapore's "bilingual policy (English with Malay/Mandarin/Tamil) and a broad-based curriculum where innovation and entrepreneurship command a premium" (quoted in Huang and Yeoh 2005, 385–86).

Recognizing that the demand for international higher education is predicted to quadruple from around 1.8 million students in 2002 to 7.2 million by 2025, Singapore is positioning itself to seize this window of opportunity by capitalizing on its strengths, including its English-speaking environment, its high standards in education, as well as its "squeaky-clean, nanny-state reputation [that] could prove an advantage because parents overseas would see it as a safe place for their children" (*Straits Times*, December 29, 2005). A government economic review panel recommended a target of 150,000 foreign students by 2012 (more than doubling the 2005 figure of 66,000), estimating that this increase would not only create 22,000 jobs but also raise the education sector's contribution to the gross domestic product from the current 1.9 percent (S\$3 billion) to 5 percent. In working toward Singapore's "Global Schoolhouse" aspirations, state agencies have designated the central Bugis and Bras Basah area as an "arts and learning hub," encouraged the setting up of private schools, wooed reputable universities to set up branch campuses or programs (in partnership with local universities) in Singapore, and set up the Singapore Education Services Center as a one-stop information and service center for foreigners wishing to study in Singapore. There are also plans to diversify the educational landscape by

18. Singapore Economic and Development Board Web site, http://www.edb.gov.sg/edb/ sg/en_uk/index/industry_sectors/education_services.html.

bringing in specialty institutions and preparatory schools. Given the fore-cast that Asian students will dominate the increasing global demand for international higher education, the main targeted markets include China and India, as well as neighboring Southeast Asian countries.

NEGOTIATING IDENTITY: PRC CHINESE IN SINGAPORE

As immigrant gateways, globalizing cities such as Singapore are places where the social, cultural, and economic fabric is woven out of a high den-sity of transnational relationships involving not only migrants and movers of different skill levels (as illustrated by the complex system of passes for foreign "manpower" and foreign students described previously) but also different sociopolitical characteristics combining ethnicity, nationality, gender, and class. Transnational practices and networks constitute a pow-erful force in reshaping the physical and sociocultural aspects of these cit-ies, opening up (and shutting down) different bases for hybridized forms of identity and mobilization. The rest of the chapter will illustrate the nature of identity negotiations among one major group of transmigrants in Sin-gapore—newly arrived transnational elites from the People's Republic of China[19]—as an illustration of the variegated nature of identity politics ani-mating metropolitan cultures in an emerging immigrant gateway.[20]

Four decades after the first efforts to create a nation out of diasporic fragments including a large Chinese presence, the introduction of "new" PRC Chinese transmigrants into the nation's social fabric, this time under

19. In the late 1990s, in order to augment the pool of foreign talent, attention was focused on drawing skilled-labor migrants from "nontraditional" sources of expatriates such as Asia. In particular, there have been substantial increases in the presence of skilled PRC Chinese professionals in research institutes, university laboratories, and the manufacturing and information technology industries. Official statistics on the number of PRC Chinese in Singapore are unavailable, but it is clear that they are one of the largest groups of skilled professionals in Singapore, along with Malaysian, Indian, and Japanese professionals.

20. The material used in this section of the paper is based primarily on sixty semistruc-tured interviews conducted in 2000 with PRC Chinese professionals and managers who were in Singapore as employment-pass holders. Pseudonyms have been used throughout the paper for reasons of maintaining anonymity.

the rubric of "foreign talent," adds yet another layer of complexity to the Singapore story. This unusual setting where the "new" Chinese diaspora is added into a social milieu dominated by once diasporic, now settled Chinese Singaporeans provides an interesting crucible for examining the negotiation of Chinese identities and Chineseness. As Ien Ang explains, "Central to the diasporic paradigm is the theoretical axiom that Chineseness is not a category with a fixed content—be it racial, cultural, or geographical—but operates as an open and indeterminate signifier whose meanings are constantly renegotiated and rearticulated in different sections of the Chinese diaspora" (1998, 225).

Unlike in Western contexts such as Australia (Kee 1995), Britain (Parker 1998; Tam 1998), and the United States (Wang 1991) where Chineseness is negotiated vis-à-vis predominantly non-Chinese cultures, Chinese transmigrants in Singapore are constantly defining their identities against a Chinese-dominated, albeit multiracial, setting, which requires contending with a finer racial mesh of difference as well as sameness.

The Chinese transmigrants interviewed find the notion of having to confront issues of "Chineseness" to be an unusual turn of events after leaving China, because, by and large, Chinese identity for them has been a much taken-for-granted fact in China, where life is strongly centered on the "Chinese" world. In China, they consider themselves to be of the Han population group as opposed to other ethnic minorities of China (see Dikotter 1996, 599). They identify themselves as *zhongguoren*, literally meaning the "people of the middle kingdom," which could also be interpreted in the modern context to mean "Chinese nationals." The Chinese transmigrants in turn view Singaporean Chinese as *huaren*, or "Chinese overseas." Chinese identity is not only very much tied to ethnicity but also strongly associated with and differentiated by nationality. As *zhongguoren*, the interviewees identify the Chinese in Singapore as *xinjiapo huaren* (Singaporean Chinese) and differentiate between at least two groups of Singaporean Chinese: the more "traditional Chinese" as compared to the more "cosmopolitan Chinese." Although the interviewees can identify—to some extent—with Singaporean Chinese because of common descent and a facility with Mandarin, they still consider themselves different from both groups. Indeed, interviewees suggest that the two distinct environments of

China and Singapore have produced major differences between the Singaporean Chinese and the PRC Chinese. The interviewees find themselves differentiated from the more "traditional" Singaporean Chinese because they do not share traditional Chinese practices that were largely eradicated during the Cultural Revolution in China but remain preserved in Singapore. For example, Chensheng (a research associate in his thirties) and Xiaocheng (a research officer in his twenties) point out that the religious practice of lighting joss sticks as a form of worship to the gods or ancestors is largely absent in China, as is the celebration of the Hungry Ghost Festival (where the gates of hell are opened for the hungry ghosts to feast in the earthly realm) marked by the Chinese in Singapore. Similarly, the interviewees find themselves unable to identify with the more "cosmopolitan Singaporean Chinese" as they are too "Westernized."

Chineseness thus takes on different hues in gateway Singapore. As Kian Woon Kwok (1998) notes, when the question of "Chineseness" is no longer taken for granted, one has to deal with the question of selfhood and cope with the "politics of difference," particularly crucial in a context where identities are also "imposed" by others. A crisis of identity may be triggered when people-in-diaspora are removed "from the familiarity of the home-nation" and when "self is rapidly reduced to the immigrant 'other'" (Yeoh and Huang 2000, 424). Being "guests" in Singaporean society, the interviewees are compelled to reformulate their identities in the context of the way their "hosts" regard them. Such politics of difference are heightened when Singaporeans differentiate themselves from PRC Chinese transmigrants using superior-inferior dualisms. For example, many interviewees feel that they are cast in the position of the "inferior other" as a result of social prejudices and barriers erected against them by the host society. Interviewees feel that they were perceived by the host society as "backward," "undeveloped," and "poor," as experienced by Xiaoling, a research assistant in her thirties: "On the whole, I feel that Singaporeans have an impression of China that is very outdated. . . . I get the feeling that they think we are living in poverty. . . . They ask if I knew how to use the air-conditioner. I could not understand. I already have air-conditioning at home in China; how is it possible that I do not know how to switch it on? They still do not have an accurate knowledge of us."

Stereotypical lenses used by the locals draw on technological and economic variables as means to distance themselves from PRC Chinese. Such labeling extends to the use of physical attributes, as exemplified in the rather derogatory incident encountered by a friend of Shirley, an analyst programmer in her thirties, who was identified as a PRC Chinese because of her "yellow teeth": "I heard from my friend. She says she went to the supermarket. When she was at the counter she paid the money. The lady who collect the things and put in the baggage asked her whether she is from China. She says yes. She [the staff] said, 'I look at your teeth. Your teeth are yellow. You Chinese people never wash your teeth.' [My friend] was quite angry."

Members of the host society tend to define Chinese transmigrants as being out of place in a "developed society" such as Singapore. Very often, the interviewees try to cope with such situations that belittle them as the "backward other" by resorting to anger and reducing the incidents to being the outcome of ignorance. At other times, they reaffirm their identities by asserting that they are equally well informed with regard to technology and are not economically impoverished. Xiaoyuan, for example, actively seeks to resist the image of the "backward other" by demonstrating his knowledge of video cameras ("I bought one in Germany before. . . . [I] was trying to tell the difference between those here and in Germany") and the availability of this "technologically advanced good" in China: "If you have a chance to visit China, you would realize that video cameras are available there. . . . This time 'round when I returned to China, I went specifically to see whether this item was available. . . . I saw this item at about the same price during my trip back. There isn't a huge difference in price."

Evidently, the interviewees feel that Singaporeans often see China as an undeveloped country "locked" in a time just before their grandparents emigrated to Singapore rather than one that has undergone rapid modernization. By emphasizing China's rapid development, interviewees attempt to take over the process of (re)drawing the boundaries between self and other. In fact, the demeaning attitudes of Singaporeans toward PRC Chinese as "other" may also be drawn upon and reversed in the politics of identity. As Shirley exclaims, "Actually I don't care about this [Singaporeans using physical attributes to label PRC Chinese]. [If] you have a broad mind, then you will be more tolerant. If anyone is not good to me, I think he is lower than me because . . . he is too narrow-minded. So I don't mind." By implying that they "do not care or mind" such "othering," interviewees refuse to be defined by the host society and in fact put themselves above the "narrow-minded Singaporeans." In doing so, they appear to suggest that PRC Chinese are in fact magnanimous and broad-minded compared to Singaporeans, and hence have every reason to be proud of their own identities.

Thus, the interviewees' identities are simultaneously defined by the fluid interplay of the "self" and "host," demonstrating Stuart Hall's view that "diaspora identities are those which are constantly producing and reproducing themselves anew, through transformation and difference" (1990, 235). In this context, where both difference and sameness have to be negotiated, a major identity issue that interviewees are constantly confronted with relates to the adoption of permanent residency or conversion of citizenship. As Filomeno Aguilar Jr. has argued, transmigrants "may decide to change their citizenship for unabashedly instrumental reasons, such as to facilitate international travel to access entitlements in their new country" (1999, 326). One of the most crucial reasons for obtaining foreign citizenship lies in the ease of travel conferred by such status as compared to being holders of a PRC Chinese passport. Possessing a PRC Chinese passport means complicated and troublesome travel procedures involving the high costs of securing visas, time-consuming paperwork, and often unpleasant encounters with immigration departments and officers. Haijie, a financial source analyst in her thirties, who has recently become a new Singapore citizen, explains why she opted for a Singapore passport: "The only aim is to have freedom to travel. It is easier to get in and out. . . . For Singaporeans like you [the interviewer], you are not able to understand what it is like to have your feet tied." The significance placed on gaining benefits and advantages is not only peculiar to getting foreign citizenship but observed in the interviewees' attempts to acquire permanent-resident status as well. As Xiaofeng Liu observes, "To obtain foreign residence has thus become an important form of power accumulation in post reform China" (1997, 107). Most of the interviewees in Singapore would seek permanent-resident status in Singapore even if they already have permanent residency or foreign citizenship elsewhere. Usually, the interviewees enter Singapore either on student passes or employment passes in the Q1 or P categories. A continuum seems apparent in that having permanent-resident status is perceived to be better than being on an employment pass, which is still better than a student pass. With a student pass, the interviewees are not allowed to work in Singapore. Thus, many students seek to convert to an employment pass. Although an employment pass permits one to work, it is difficult to change jobs. One is also not entitled to contributions to the Central Provident Fund.[21] Having permanent-resident status means that one can switch jobs more easily. One is also entitled to certain government subsidies and other privileges, such as the purchase of a Housing Development Board resale flat.

The intention of applying for permanent residency and citizenship is hence often motivated by the privileges they confer. For example, permanent-resident status comes with the freedom to change one's job without being tied to an employer. This point is well encapsulated by Xuting, a purchasing manager in her thirties, who is already a Singapore citizen:

> You must apply for PR in Singapore; otherwise you cannot buy flats. You cannot even buy secondhand ones. . . . Furthermore, if you don't like your employer, you can change a job. If not, you will have to apply for employment pass every time you change your job. . . . I applied for citizenship because I had a consideration. Singapore is a very small country. You must at least go to Malaysia. If you do not have a Singapore passport it is very difficult. To be honest, when I use Singapore's PR to apply for Malaysian visa, they told me I am a Singapore PR but not a Malaysian PR. "Your PR [means] nothing to us. You are still a Chinese passport holder. We still treat you as a Chinese passport holder." In that case, applying for a visa is very troublesome. . . . Like my husband, his company wants to send him to Batam [in Indonesia]. It was very troublesome for him. . . . He was hesitating whether he wanted to take up the citizenship. In the end, he took it. For me, taking it is good because it is convenient. So we applied for it.

21. The contributions are made by both employers and employees toward the common fund for the purpose of pension, medical insurance and hospitalization, and other government-approved expenses (for example, the repayment of housing mortgage loans).

It would appear that foreign citizenship and permanent-resident status are often acquired for utilitarian purposes, affirming Liu's argument that "the significance of obtaining permanent foreign residence and foreign citizenship lies in the very possibility for individuals to travel freely. In other words, obtaining foreign residence does not necessarily mean settling down in any single place, but rather acquiring greater flexibility in traveling and accumulating power" (1997, 108). Chenjing, a male in his midthirties who works as a research fellow in a university, puts it simply: "We get foreign passports for the sake of convenience." Nevertheless, this practical attitude does not imply the absence of identity negotiations relating to specific places, particularly in situations such as Singapore where dual citizenship is not allowed. Indeed, citizenship conversion or adoption of permanent residency has effects on, and at the same time draws on, one's sense of belonging to a place. It may be suggested that a person's attachment to a place could be strengthened when one has a formal identification with the "imagined community" in question (Anderson 1983). By extension, when an interviewee acquires citizenship or permanent-resident status, it may suggest that the interviewee potentially has a sense of attachment to this "foreign country" and wishes to settle down there ultimately. In other words, citizenship acquisition may signify the ideal destination or end of one's transnational sojourns.

However, this characterization does not appear to be entirely true for the interviewees. Securing foreign citizenship or permanent-resident status does not mean a "conversion" to having a strong sense of affiliation and commitment to the new "home nation." On the contrary, in most cases, the interviewees' identity and loyalty toward mainland China appear almost unchanged. Gu, a Chinese teacher in her thirties, reveals her feelings of indifference as a holder of a Singapore passport: "Although I have changed my passport, I actually do not feel that I identify with Singapore. For me, I have lived here for only five to six years. I lived in China for thirty years. It is different. After all, I still feel that I am like a Chinese national."

The interviewees "assume the citizenship of their country of residence for practical reasons without renouncing their cultural attachment to their nation of birth." Instead, they see their nationality and identities oriented toward China in "primordial" and "essentialist" terms (Aguilar 1999, 326). What is clear is that the interviewees hold on to their identity as *zhongguoren* regardless of whether they have changed their citizenship. Yangkun, an academic in his early forties, does not believe in "renouncing" his identity as a PRC Chinese even though he is now a Dutch citizen: "I still regard myself as Chinese. . . . [T]he fact doesn't change [that] I am Chinese. Even if I change to a different passport, this fact doesn't change."

Nonetheless, in the course of pursuing transmigratory trajectories, the interviewees' connections to various countries through citizenship and permanent residency necessitate the process of negotiating "Chineseness," thus coming to terms with "diasporic identities" (Brah 1996). Inasmuch as the interviewees have a strong sense of identification with China, their diasporic identities are also situational. The interviewees who have acquired citizenship or permanent-resident status strategically manipulate such identities to suit their complex situations. Lihong, a visiting research fellow in her thirties who holds U.S. citizenship, exemplifies how the nature of diasporic identities varies according to the circumstances: "I think I tend to be very situational. . . . [I]f I am with a bunch of Chinese visitors to the U.S., I would [feel a sense of] affiliation but . . . also distinction. I am not exactly the same as they are, the perspective, the experience, and so forth. But if I were with a bunch of Americans, I would feel very different, yeah, I am Chinese. It depends on situation."

Therefore, for many Chinese interviewees, transnational identities are fluid and malleable. One could be simultaneously a Chinese by ethnicity and Chinese national or Chinese American or Chinese Singaporean and/or a permanent resident of another country. In short, one could be a person of hybrid identities. This phenomenon affirms Nina Glick Schiller, Linda Basch, and Cristina Blanc-Szanton's argument that "within their complex web of social relations, transmigrants draw upon and create fluid and multiple identities grounded both in their society of origin and in the host societies. While some migrants identify more with one society than the other, the majority seem to maintain several identities that link them simultaneously to more than one nation" (1992a, 11).

Acquiring "foreign identities" does not, however, necessarily translate into the intention of staying in the country in question at the journey's end. Interviewees' "emotional home" tends to be strongly associated with China. The interviewees themselves are aware of these contradictions and contentions that may provoke hostile reactions in the country of sojourn. Chenjing explains the paradox of being a Singapore permanent resident who is leaving for Australia to take another job: "Many Singaporeans think that many Chinese nationals who come are given passports or permanent residence status. But they do not identify with Singapore. They are not loyal. That is a big problem. . . . What you hear [from Singaporeans] is that they [the Chinese nationals] treat Singapore as a stepping-stone. They want to go to the United States." Ironically, this statement suggests that acquiring citizenship and permanent residency is meant for furthering transnational journeys and not for settling down. They also have limited influence over the identities of the interviewees. Acquiring citizenship and permanent residency actually entails greater mobility in an increasingly globalized world.

CONCLUSION

Globalizing cities such as Singapore are probably better understood as "transnational turnstiles." In the case of Singapore, the concept of a "transnational turnstile" will have to be further qualified, depending primarily on the skill levels of transmigrants. For transnational unskilled workers, the turnstile is a structural condition that regulates their presence in the city. Use-and-discard state measures have been put in place to prevent them from gaining any significant foothold in Singapore society as sociopolitical subjects. In this case, the turnstile turns systematically and continually.

In contrast, for transnational elites with talents and skills that the city-state wishes to root and retain, the state attempts to slow down the turnstile as much as possible. The state is keen to fashion Singapore as an immigrant gateway that is able to attract international talent to supplement its small base of local talent in order to remain globally competitive. There are signs that efforts in this direction are bearing fruit: in 2005 there were 12,900 new citizens, compared to the annual figure of 6,000–7,000 in the previous four years. These figures are significant when put alongside the average figure of 800 Singaporeans giving up their citizenship each year. The Hua Yuan Association, a nongovernmental organization established in 2001 with the aim of assisting recent Chinese immigrants in adapting to and blending into Singapore society, has also seen increased membership over the years.[22]

The case study of skilled PRC transmigrants, however, indicates that international talent is highly mobile: even PR status and Singapore citizenship will not guarantee their integration into the fabric of society; ironically, accumulating such status may actually confer a higher degree of potential mobility, as the new status allows former PRC transmigrants to gain entry to other immigrant gateways around the world with greater ease. Living mobile, transnational lives requiring the negotiation of a range of gateways with no definite end in sight has become part and parcel of a way of life in a globalizing world.

Given the mobility and ambivalence of transnational lives, reshaping "turnstiles" into significant "immigrant gateways" will depend not only on formal mechanisms of awarding PR and citizenship status but also on the management of identity politics in the city. Immigrant gateways are animated by everyday identity politics dependent on a complex web of identifications with and pragmatic opportunities in "home" and "host." As Avtar Brah has argued, "The identity of the diasporic imagined community . . . is constituted within the crucible of the materiality of everyday life; in the everyday stories we tell ourselves individually and collectively" (1996, 183). Indeed, the negotiation of multiple identities should be understood neither as markers of transition nor as signs of pathology, but as "lasting and intelligible responses to the varied pressures they face" (Rouse 1995, 354). How comfortably the PRC transnational elites are able to negotiate their identities vis-à-vis similar yet different Singaporean Chinese in everyday lived realities will have a significant bearing on whether Singapore becomes "home" or simply part of an unending sojourn. As we have argued here, much of the host-migrant identity politics in Singapore at this time is confrontational and ridden with derogatory undertones;

22. The Hua Yuan Association Website, http://www.myhuayuan.org, reports a current membership of 2,300 members.

more has to be done to foster identity politics of a creative nature that will capitalize on sameness and difference in positive ways. In sum, how identity politics is managed in the city, and how the process eventually plays out in both material and ideological ways, will have an impact on Singapore's aspirations to become a significant immigrant gateway—a magnet for talent—in Asia.

9

Washington, D.C.

From Biracial City to Multiethnic Gateway

ELIZABETH CHACKO

Washington, D.C., named the capital of the United States in 1800, is widely recognized as the seat of the U.S. government and as the site for the headquarters of numerous national and international institutions with global reach. However, émigrés to Washington were insignificant in both number and diversity until the 1980s, largely because the city lacked the significant industrial and commercial bases that attracted immigrants to traditional destinations such as New York, Chicago, and Boston during the immigration surges of the late nineteenth and early twentieth centuries (Melder 1997). Foreign-born in the Washington metropolitan area did not top 5 percent of its total population until well into the 1970s.

During the past quarter century, however, Greater Washington has witnessed a tremendous increase in immigrant inflows from across the globe, prompting its classification as an emerging gateway (Singer 2004).[1] People from nearly two hundred countries have made their home in the city of Washington, D.C., and its suburbs, substantially altering the demographic makeup of the area, and transforming its sociocultural, economic, and political landscapes. Indeed, the traditional demographic characterization of Washington as a black-and-white city has given way to the image of a

---

1. Unless otherwise stated, the definition of metropolitan Washington is the same as the Washington primary metropolitan statistical area (PMSA) in U.S. Bureau of the Census 2000.

multiethnic city (Manning 1998). Immigrant populations are increasingly visible in economic areas that range from low-end construction work to high-end service-sector occupations and have also changed the cultural presentation of the metropolis in multiple ways. Among the changes wrought in both urban and suburban locales is the emergence and solidification of new ethnic spaces. Although the majority of new arrivals live in ethnically diverse neighborhoods that are sorted out by socioeconomic status rather than national origins (Price et al. 2005), in a few instances, even in multiracial and multiethnic areas, new immigrant groups are attempting to fashion distinctively ethnic places in the Washington metropolitan area.

In this chapter, I use the twin lenses of *place meaning* and *place memory* to examine the formation of new ethnic spaces and the manner in which they are viewed, experienced, and contested in an emerging immigrant gateway. John Agnew defines place as "a meaningful location" (1987, 7). It is through our experience of place as a locale in which people and the environment interact that we construct place meaning. Yi-Fu Tuan refers to place as "an archive of fond memories and splendid achievements that inspire the present" (1977, 154). Though not all recollections of place need be warm, our memories of experienced place inform place meaning and vice versa. Meanings and memories are embodied and retained in both the built environment, with its material and symbolic expressions, as well as in the people who live and work in the metropolis's neighborhoods. Unlike in the traditional immigrant gateways with their mélange of successive ethnic spaces, the construction and contestation of ethnic space is more readily observable in the emerging gateway. In the established gateway, succeeding waves of immigrant groups have been instrumental in continually changing the urban landscape. In contrast, neighborhoods and places in an emerging gateway are likely to have more long-standing landmarks and identities that are of significance to its nonimmigrant residents. New immigrants' efforts to "claim" city space are more likely to be challenged and be a contentious issue.

I examine how localities have been reconfigured and local subjects (both native and immigrant) repositioned as immigrant populations transform neighborhoods in the central city and in suburban Washington into ethnic enclaves. I focus on the spatial manifestations of the Ethiopian and

Korean populations in the PMSA, and their commercial enterprises in the neighborhoods of the U Street corridor in northwest Washington, D.C., and Annandale, Virginia, respectively. These two immigrant communities were chosen as case studies because of their prominence among newcomers from Africa and Asia in the metropolitan area and on account of their efforts and varying degrees of success in creating ethnic enclaves in urban and suburban Washington.

THE WASHINGTON METROPOLITAN REGION:
AN EMERGING IMMIGRANT GATEWAY

Audrey Singer (2004) has classified the Washington metropolitan area as an emerging gateway based on the very low percentages of foreign-born in the area until 1970, accompanied by a post-1980 expansion in the city's nonnative population. The trajectory of Washington's progression as an emerging immigrant city can be charted from the relative share of its foreign-born population over the past three decades. In 1970, the metropolitan area's foreign-born population accounted for slightly more than 4 percent of its total population, rising to 8 percent by 1980 and nearly reaching 12 percent in 1990 (U.S. Bureau of the Census 1999). Almost half (48 percent) of the population growth in Greater Washington in the decade of the 1990s can be attributed to immigration. According to the 2000 census, 17 percent of the metropolitan area's total population was foreign-born. By the mid-2000s, the region had more than 1 million foreign-born, accounting for 18.5 percent of the population (U.S. Bureau of the Census, American Community Survey, 2005).

Between 1970 and 2000, the foreign-born population of the central city more than doubled, even as the proportion of immigrants in the District of Columbia fell from more than 25 percent to approximately 9 percent. Much of the population flow into the district can be attributed to a rise in its immigrant population; the city's total population has been steadily declining over the past thirty years. Population growth in suburban Washington, on the other hand, was explosive over the same time period. The immigrants' share in the total suburban population more than quadrupled, from 77,500 (less than 2 percent of the population) in 1970 to 670,000

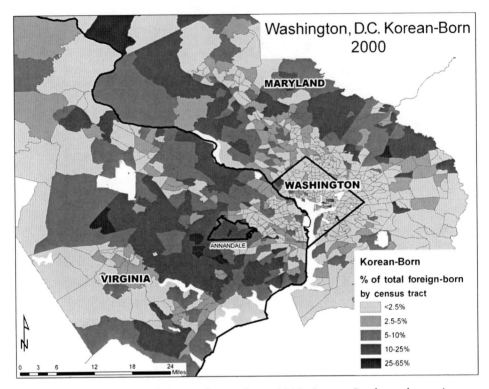

Fig. 9.1. Distribution of Korean foreign-born, 2000. *Source:* By the author, using U.S. Census data.

(9 percent of the population) in 2000. Most of this growth took place in the suburban areas closest to the city: Montgomery and Prince George's County in Maryland and Arlington County, Fairfax County, Fairfax City, and the cities of Falls Church and Alexandria in Virginia. Immigrants continue to settle in suburban Washington in large numbers, increasing in density in the inner suburbs and making noticeable inroads into the outer suburbs.

According to the 2000 U.S. Census, metropolitan Washington is home to some 832,000 foreign-born, whereas census estimates for 2005 show the immigrant population has continued to grow to more than 1 million foreign-born residents (U.S. Bureau of the Census, American Community Survey, 2005). Proportionally, Washington's immigrant population is currently on par with both older immigrant magnets such as Chicago and newer cities of immigrant settlement such as Dallas. Census figures for

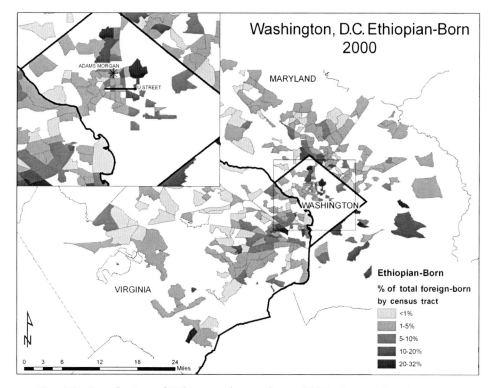

Fig. 9.2. Distribution of Ethiopian foreign-born, 2000. *Source:* By the author, using U.S. Census data.

2000 rank Washington as the seventh-largest metropolitan area of immigrant settlement in the United States. The status of the region as an immigrant metropolis is also substantiated by data from the U.S. Immigration and Naturalization Service, which positioned it as the fifth most popular immigrant destination in the United States during the 2000 fiscal year.

THE ETHNIC COMPOSITION OF WASHINGTON'S FOREIGN-BORN

A distinctive feature of Greater Washington is the remarkable diversity of its foreign-born population. The trickle of immigrants to the area in the 1970s grew to a steady stream by the 1990s, with increased flows from Asian, Latin American, and African countries (table 9.1). Although the greatest proportional increase (91 percent) in its immigrant population

TABLE 9.1

FOREIGN-BORN POPULATION BY REGION OF ORIGIN, 2000

Region of origin	Foreign-born population in the Washington metropolitan area	
	Total	Percentage
Latin America	321,078	38.59
Asia	301,192	36.20
Europe	100,993	12.14
Africa	93,271	11.21
Canada	12,26	11.47
Oceania	3,207	0.39

Source: U.S. Bureau of the Census 2000.

took place in the 1980s, Greater Washington witnessed the largest absolute growth in its foreign-born between 1990 and 2000, when this population nearly doubled from 490,000 to 832,000, an increase of 70 percent. The 1990s saw more immigrants enter the United States than at any time since peak immigration flows during the early 1900s. Washington's remarkable growth is thus in keeping with a broad trend across the country, a development that has led the U.S. Bureau of the Census (2004) to predict that whites will no longer be in the majority in the country after 2050.

Washington has become an important East Coast portal and destination for immigrants who settle in the metropolis as direct arrivals and through processes of secondary migration (Singer 2003). As table 9.1 reflects, these immigrants hail from all over the world; 39 percent are from Latin America, 36 percent from Asia, 12 percent from Europe, and 11 percent from Africa. Both Canada and Oceania account for less than 2 percent of the immigrant population. Among the Latin American foreign-born, the largest national group is from the Central American country of El Salvador, whose tumultuous history, including civil war in the early 1980s and a series of natural disasters in the late 1990s, instigated large-scale emigration of its citizens to the United States. The 2000 census reported 104,960 native Salvadorans, accounting for 12.62 percent of all foreign-born living in the region. Other Latin American countries such as Mexico (37,223), Peru (20,304), Guatemala (20,015), and Bolivia (19,558) are also among the top-ten countries of origin for immigrants to the metropolis, but, with the exception of Mexico, each contributes less than 2.5 percent to the region's total foreign-born population (U.S. Bureau of the Census 2000) (fig. 9.3).

Asians, who make up 36 percent of the metropolitan area's foreign-born, are the second-largest group. Unlike the case of Latin America, no one country dominates within this set. The 2000 census snapshot indicates that Korean foreign-born (45,835 persons), who constitute 5.51 percent of all foreign-born, are only slightly ahead of Asian Indians (45,610 persons, accounting for 5.48 percent of nonnatives). Similarly, China (5.07 percent of all foreign-born), Vietnam (4.47 percent of foreign-born), and the Philippines (3.81 percent of foreign-born) are all significant Asian countries of immigrant origin.

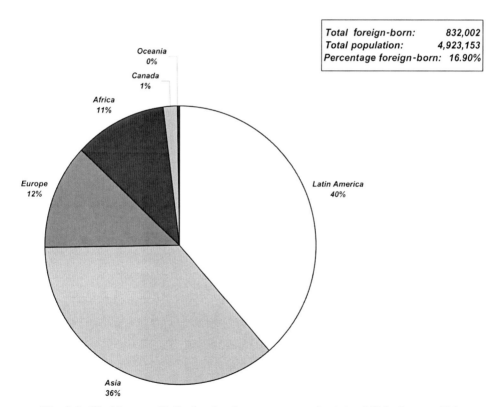

Fig. 9.3. Washington, D.C., foreign-born country of origin, 2000. *Source:* U.S. Census data.

Washington has had a long history of Chinese settlement; Chinese residents were first recorded in the District of Columbia in 1851, and by the late 1880s a small Chinatown had developed. Since then, the residential and commercial cluster of Chinese immigrants forming the city's Chinatown was relocated to make room for federal buildings, finally finding a home at the intersection of H and Seventh streets, N.W. (Chow 1996). Although remnants of the old Chinese community may still be found in this last location, Chinese immigrants, predominantly from the People's Republic of China, now live largely in suburban Washington.

The flow of immigrants from Southeast Asia was set into motion by the resettling of refugees from Vietnam, Cambodia, and Laos in the aftermath of the Vietnam War in Greater Washington, particularly in northern Virginia. Vietnamese continue to be the top Southeast Asian group in the metropolis. Other Asian states such as Pakistan and Iran are also represented in the top twenty sending countries (U.S. Bureau of the Census 2000).

Immigrants from Europe form the next-largest group, with the United Kingdom (2.27 percent) and Germany (2.08 percent) being the most prominent among sending countries. Both these nationality groups have had a long association with immigration to the United States and to Washington, D.C., in particular. German immigrants constituted approximately 30 percent of the city's foreign-born population in 1850, whereas the English, Scots, and Irish have been among its early settlers (Singer and Brown 2001).

Voluntary African immigration to the Washington metropolitan area is a recent phenomenon. Between 1990 and 2000, the African immigrant population in the Washington metropolitan area witnessed a 148 percent rise, compared to a 134 percent increase in the United States during the same period. With some 93,271 African foreign-born, the Washington PMSA is second only to the New York PMSA (which has 99,126 foreign-born Africans) in the size of its African population. Africans in the Washington metropolitan area, however, are a substantial percentage of the foreign-born population (11 percent), compared to 3 percent in the New York PMSA. Major sending countries from Africa to Greater Washington are Ethiopia (1.8 percent of all foreign-born), Nigeria (1.64 percent), Ghana (1.33 percent), and Sierra Leone (1 percent), although Somalia, Egypt, Liberia,

Morocco, Sudan, and Cameroon are growing source areas as well (U.S. Bureau of the Census 2000).

THE RESIDENTIAL PATTERNS OF WASHINGTON'S
IMMIGRANTS: KOREANS AND ETHIOPIANS

Heterolocalism, a nationwide trend of residential dispersion of immigrant groups that are linked by ethnic organizations and institutions rather than spatial proximity (Zelinsky and Lee 1998), is evident in metropolitan Washington. Because of the scattering of ethnic and nationality groups in Washington's urban and suburban settings, there is less evidence of the ethnic clustering that gave rise to late-nineteenth- and early-twentieth-century enclaves.

In keeping with an overall trend of residential dispersion of the foreign-born, Greater Washington also has the distinction among U.S. cities of drawing relatively few immigrants to its central city; émigrés favor suburbs in the neighboring states of Virginia and Maryland over the nation's capital. Thus, in 2000 only 12.9 percent of the population of the District of Columbia was foreign-born, compared to 16.9 percent for the entire PMSA. In surrounding suburbs in Arlington County, Virginia, the city of Alexandria in Virginia, and Montgomery County in Maryland, immigrants composed at least a quarter of the total population, while Fairfax County, Virginia, almost approached this figure, with 24 percent foreign-born. Prince George's County, although equally proximate to the District of Columbia, had a foreign-born population that is only slightly higher (13.8 percent) than the proportion of the district (U.S. Bureau of the Census 2000).

African and Asian immigrants, and in particular Ethiopians and Koreans, the two nationalities under consideration in this chapter, exhibit somewhat different settlement patterns, even though fitting in with the dominant configuration of heterolocal suburban settlement. In the District of Columbia, Africans are found in the Adams Morgan, Kalorama Heights, and Lanier Heights neighborhoods, where they account for 25.2 percent of the foreign-born. Ethiopians in the district favor the neighborhoods of Adams Morgan, Columbia Heights, and Brightwood. In the state of Virginia, the city of Alexandria has a strong African population. Proportionally, Ethiopians (7.5 percent) and Ghanaians (4.4 percent) account for the largest African subgroups in Alexandria. In the Silver Spring area of Maryland, 35.2 percent of all foreign-born are from African countries, with Ethiopians leading, with 5.6 percent of this population.

Unlike Ethiopians, who have a strong presence in the city of Washington, Koreans, like most Asian immigrants, tend to be scattered in the outer suburbs, primarily in Fairfax and Montgomery counties. However, in Annandale, Virginia, an immigrant Mecca with foreign-born accounting for approximately 33 percent of the total population, Koreans tie with Vietnamese as the largest nationality group. It is only in Annandale that a single census tract has a reported Korean population of more than 1,000 people.

ETHNIC ENCLAVES AND SOCIOCOMMERSCAPES

An increase in the strength of an ethnic community, especially in American cities in the nineteenth and early twentieth centuries, was usually accompanied by greater visibility, owing to clustering in inner-city neighborhoods. The spatial organization of growing immigrant groups in enclaves marked by the concentration of ethnic residence, economy, and services was considered part of the dynamics of neighborhood change by Robert E. Park and his associates at the University of Chicago in their urban ecological model. Premised on the biological processes of "invasion and succession" in changing ecosystems, this model deemed immigrant settlement to be transitional in nature. The Chicago model presupposed that the populations of urban ethnic enclaves were replenished by new immigrant groups, even as assimilation and upward socioeconomic mobility drew former enclave dwellers into mainstream residential areas and occupations as they became more established and Americanized (Park, Burgess, and Mackenzie 1925). Spaces that assisted new immigrants in adjusting to the new setting by providing the necessary sociocultural and economic resources, ethnic enclaves continue to facilitate acculturation and integration (Marcuse 1997; Portes and Rumbaut 1990). The Chicago model was widely applied to explain immigrant settlement patterns in other early-twentieth-century gateway cities such as New York, Boston, and Philadelphia.

Although still applied to contemporary gateway cities, the model does not neatly fit the experience of newer destinations such as Washington, D.C., or even Los Angeles. For example, scholars have noted the tendency of new immigrants to bypass the inner and central cities, traditionally domains of the newly arrived, to settle in the suburbs of major metropolitan areas. Geographer Wei Li (1998) coined the term *ethnoburb* for the concentrations of ethnic populations and businesses in suburban settings that were the result of deliberate choice rather than forced segregation. She noted that these voluntary concentrations of ethnic groups were part of a strategy to maximize ethnic personal and social networks, as well as business connections, and to create a place with a familiar culture. Immigrants of varying nationalities and ethnicities banded together in various ways for social, economic, and cultural reasons as they adjusted to life in the host country. Often they were associated with niche occupations that employed a substantial percentage of a nationality or an ethnic group. Traditionally, ethnic groups practiced their niche occupations within or close to residential ethnic enclaves. The greater residential dispersion of ethnic or nationality groups in the United States has not been accompanied by the fading away of ethnic economies. Indeed, even within a scattered immigrant group, ethnic businesses may be clustered in a commercial ethnic enclave. Locked out of well-paying professional jobs because their foreign university degrees are not always recognized in the United States or because of limited proficiency in English, many first-generation Asian and African immigrants have turned to entrepreneurship as a pathway to upward socioeconomic mobility. These immigrants have established stores, restaurants, beauty salons, clubs, and other businesses, often using capital from communal rotating savings funds or using financial support from their families.

Many of these ethnic enterprises cater to the needs of the diasporic immigrant population by offering ethnic groceries, food, household goods, music, and clothing. Small clusters of stores and restaurants become loci for commercial ethnic neighborhoods and enclaves. For example, Ethiopian restaurants and stores were thickly clustered in a commercial enclave on Eighteenth Street in the Adams Morgan neighborhood of Washington, D.C., until gentrification and a rise in property values diluted their ethnic presence there (Chacko 2003). Groups like the Vietnamese Americans have succeeded in creating more lasting ethnic spaces in suburban Washington through the establishment of a concentration of Vietnamese stores and eating places in Eden Center in the city of Falls Church, Virginia (Wood 1997).

Regardless of whether these incipient ethnic enclaves are located in urban or suburban settings, they provide spaces for expressing and negotiating meanings of identity, ethnicity, and belonging. Ethnic neighborhoods and enclaves are distinguished both by an internalized sense of place that its residents embody in the course of their daily lives (Eyles 1985) and by the perceptions of nonethnics of them as locales marked by the conspicuous presence of the ethnic "other" (Anderson 1988). Arjun Appadurai conceptualizes ethnoscapes as dynamic "landscapes for group identity" that are constantly being shaped by a globalized and deterritorialized world (1996, 48). Geographical spaces are associated with particular values, historical events, and feelings (Shields 1991), and the ethnic enclave is no exception. In neighborhoods in cities and suburbs, populations, images, and ideas collide with each other as space is transformed by immigrant groups who imbue it with ethnic flavor. Change in neighborhoods that have undergone pronounced demographic, cultural, and economic shifts may be simultaneously embraced and abhorred. City officials are likely to welcome the economic revitalization and rise in property values that sometimes accompany settlement by new immigrants. Conversely, native-born groups with more "mainstream" identities and attachment to local histories through forebears who lived in the city or neighborhood for many decades may resent cultural changes brought about by groups they consider less U.S.-centered in their identity and ethnicity. As Richard Wright and Mark Ellis assert, "Territorial politics become particularly pressing in city-regions and states" (2000, 206).

CONTESTED ETHNOSCAPES: ANNANDALE, VIRGINIA, AND U STREET, WASHINGTON, D.C.

Annandale, located in Fairfax County in Virginia, has been a distinct geographical entity since 1830. Located on the site of a former tobacco plantation, parcels of which were sold to farmers and small-scale manufacturers, it remained a small town on the periphery of Washington for much of its history. An almost exclusively white community until after 1970, by 2000, it had a total population of 55,041 persons, of which 11,087 were born in Asia, accounting for 56 percent of the area's foreign-born population.

Koreans began moving to Annandale in the 1980s. Today, a one-mile stretch of Little River Turnpike in Annandale is the locale of the Washington area's first "Koreatown," even though Koreans are not in the majority in the area. Although Koreans in Annandale (with an official count of 3,184 persons) account for 16 percent of the foreign-born population and more than a quarter of the Asian foreign-born, they make up only 6 percent of the community's total population. Korean foreign-born share the Annandale ZIP code (52353) with sizable numbers of immigrants from other countries such as Vietnam, India, and El Salvador (U.S. Bureau of the Census 2000).

Downtown Annandale had a small, aging business district when the first Korean businesses began locating in its office complexes and strip malls in the late 1980s (Pan and Pae 1999). The infusion of new capital and businesses was an economic boon for the city, which had been hemorrhaging commercial enterprises for several years, losing even its only movie theater by the end of the 1980s. Attracted by a good geographic location with excellent access to the Capital Beltway and other highways, as well as affordable commercial space, in less than a decade, Korean immigrants had turned the business district around into a viable commercial area (fig. 9.4).

The dramatic economic revitalization of the area is evident in an abundance of ethnic businesses and services that serve primarily Korean patrons. Today, Korean enterprises that have found a home in the city range from restaurants, karaoke bars, and grocery and video rental stores to specialized legal, health, and realty services and large supermarkets, catering to a large but dispersed Korean clientele throughout the metropolitan region (Cho 2005). Annandale has become a Korean sociocommerscape, an area "with concentrations of ethnic businesses that provide not only goods and services but also meeting places for the community" (Chacko 2003, 29). The draw of Annandale as a sociocommerscape is clear from the fact that in addition to patrons from the Washington metropolitan area, the locality

Fig. 9.4. Korean stores and signage in the Great World Plaza, Annandale, Virginia. Photo by the author.

attracts shoppers from as far afield as Richmond and Baltimore. Chartered buses bring Korean customers from these cities to Annandale every weekend (Nicholls 2000).

Somewhat comparable to the transformation of suburban Annandale by Korean immigrants is a growing concentration of Ethiopian businesses and restaurants in the Shaw neighborhood in the central city of Washington, D.C. Centered on U Street, which was once called the district's "black Broadway," the Shaw neighborhood rivaled Harlem in New York City as a center of black American culture. A showcase of successful black enterprises during the early twentieth century, with black-owned clubs, theaters, stores, banks, and a large hotel, the U Street corridor began its decline as middle-class white and black families began leaving the district for suburban locations in the 1950s. Rioting, looting, and arson that occurred in the aftermath of Dr. Martin Luther King Jr.'s assassination in 1968 accelerated the neighborhood's downward slide, as abandoned buildings were boarded up for decades and empty lots testified to the neighborhood's lack of appeal to potential residents and commercial enterprises alike.

In the mid- to late 1990s, the Shaw neighborhood began to exhibit signs of revitalization and gentrification. New upscale stores made an appearance on U Street, landmarks that are of significance to the native black community such as the Lincoln Theater and the True Reformer Building (which now houses the African American Civil War Memorial Museum) were restored, the number of music clubs on U Street rose, and young professionals began buying residential property in the area. Among the agents of revitalization were Ethiopians who bought old, deteriorated buildings in the U Street area and converted them into offices, restaurants, and cafes after restoring and refurbishing them. However, most of these Ethiopian entrepreneurs did not live in the area. In the neighborhood bounded by Fourteenth and Eighth streets, N.W., on the west and east, respectively, and Florida Avenue and T Street on the north and south, the population is overwhelmingly (85 percent) native-born and black. Even among the foreign-born here, Salvadorans, who constitute 6 percent of the total population, outnumber Ethiopians by a ratio of six to one (U.S. Bureau of the Census 2000).

Like their Korean counterparts in Annandale, by locating their businesses in a low-rent area with fairly good access to public transportation and a growing clientele, Ethiopians were following strategies employed by generations of immigrant entrepreneurs in other cities whose limited capital reserves prevented them from locating their establishments in higher-rent districts. Ethiopians, though not the sole or even primary driving force of revitalization, were significant contributors to the improved economic viability of the U Street area.

PLACE, NOMENCLATURE, AND IDENTITY

Geographer Carl Sauer considered the cultural landscape with its natural as well as man-made elements emblematic of the essential character of a place. Sauer's understanding of place is echoed in the writings of Henri Lefebvre who, in defining social space, referred to it as an entity that is "permeated with social relations" and "shaped and molded from historical and natural elements" (1976, 31). However, the notion of territoriality is also embedded in social and cultural space. Robert Sack defines territoriality as "the attempt of an individual or a group to affect, influence, or control people, phenomena, and relationships, by delimiting and asserting control over a geographical area" (1986, 19).

These ideas of space and place as expressions of culture, social interactions, and a desire to exert control over territory converge and overlap in both incipient and established ethnic enclaves. Both in the past, when the ethnic neighborhood or enclave was a site of sequestration of groups that were deemed unassimilable or suspect (Craddock 1999), and currently, when new immigrant groups are clamoring for the demarcation and naming of ethnic spaces (Chacko and Cheung 2006), issues of cultural representation, relations between different groups, and the relative power they wield permeate ethnic space.

Demarcating space as a bounded entity and bestowing it with the name of a nationality or ethnic group can lead to conflicts between an area's residents, owing to perceptions that one people's history and culture are being privileged over another's. The place that is most likely to be the focus of such cultural contestations is a prominent street in the changing neighborhood. Streets are often the organizing basis of aspirations, meanings, emotions, and anxieties (Crouch 1998), a space where collective memory can be expressed and celebrated (Hebbert 2005). Therefore, it is not surprising that the main street is the locus of the spatial expression of tensions between long-standing communities and newcomers in the U Street neighborhood and Annandale.

The Korean sociocommerscape in Annandale is often referred to by Korean immigrants as Hanintown or Koreatown. Although there are no markers to designate the enclave, the neighborhood abounds in Korean ethnic signatures. Signs and billboards in malls such as the Korean-owned Great World Plaza and in Korean chain supermarkets such Lotte, Super H-Mart, and Grand Mart as well as a plethora of other ethnic commercial and retail enterprises are usually in both Hangul and English, though in select cases, only the Korean script is used. The latter tend to be businesses with an exclusively Korean clientele. Signs that do not offer an English translation are a contentious issue in Koreatown. Specialty food stores and restaurants are well known among expatriates, but do not always advertise their wares or presence in English. Non-Korean locals who wish to sample ethnic cuisine or other cultural offerings complain that Korean immigrants are being exclusive. County officials routinely receive complaints about Korean signs and restaurant menus without English translations, as well as salesclerks who do not speak English.

With several hundred Annandale businesses listed in the Korean yellow pages, there is no denying that the neighborhood has become a specialty office and shopping district with a distinct Korean essence. However, the transition of Annandale's demographic makeup and changes in its cultural presentation have been noted and challenged. In particular, cultural differences between the Korean immigrant community and the local non-Hispanic white population are evident in the meanings and memories each attaches to Annandale. Although "Koreatown" is used only informally to refer to the area, city officials and many residents who are not of Korean extraction object to this ethnic characterization of the area. Eileen Garnett, a local civic leader, made a case for greater inclusivity and a community that saw itself as more than a thriving ethnic enclave. To her, *Koreatown* is a "divisive word." Non-Hispanic white natives who make up 65 percent of the population feel that their city has been taken over by the immigrants. A white resident stated that he no longer felt a part of the community; the Korean immigrants gave others the impression that they could get along quite well without them (Cho 2005).

Leaders of local civic associations and local government invited Korean entrepreneurs along with other area business owners to contribute to the planning of a new downtown, hoping to transform Annandale from a "pass-through" town to a destination with special features. Most Koreans, however, did not participate in these efforts, citing long hours at work in family-run businesses that prevented them from attending planning meetings regularly. Moreover, Korean entrepreneurs who use ethnic networks and ethnic media to advertise their services and products see no gain in participating in the local Chamber of Commerce, leading to further accusations of insularity and exclusivity. Korean business owners who work in the offices and stores of Annandale, on the other hand, feel that their success in reviving a dying business district is being overlooked or, worse, deprecated (ibid.).

Older city centers are often looked upon as focal points to draw on the resources of collective memory (Hayden 1995). Annandale's Chamber of Commerce wants to reconfigure the city's downtown and encourage greater civic involvement in city life. In an attempt to recapture Annandale's past as a traditional American town centered on a main street that acted as a locus for commercial and social activities, the Chamber of Commerce proposes to convert at least part of the business district into a walking city. City officials are promoting the concept of the "Annandale Village Center," an area in downtown Annandale at the intersection of Little River Turnpike and Annandale Road. The Village Center would hark back to a period when a slower pace of life and a greater concentration of religious, political, and commercial services attracted pedestrians to a recreated main street with brick sidewalks, specialty stores, and historic buildings. On its Web site, the Chamber of Commerce uses icons such as a Civil War–era chapel, aged barns, a large clock on a wrought-iron pedestal, and a Civil War canon—symbols of the city's nineteenth-century history and rustic origins. Clearly, the collective memory endorsed by Annandale city officials is of its distant, rather than recent, past. Conspicuous by their absence on the organization's Web site are a Korean Methodist church located just behind the white chapel dating from the Civil War and Korean-owned stores in the strip malls that dominate the streetscape of this section of Little River Turnpike. The juxtaposition of the Chamber of Commerce's vision of a new central business district that will attract people from the larger metropolitan area, and the Korean business owners' vision of a small ethnic enclave that will be a draw for not just coethnics but people from across the region, underscores the cultural differences between native and immigrant groups in Annandale.

Like the Koreans in Annandale, Ethiopian businesses have a clear visual presence in the District of Columbia (Ungar 1995). The community's initial strong cluster of stores and restaurants in Adams Morgan along Eighteenth Street has been diluted as new businesses, both "mainstream" and multiethnic restaurants and clubs, have edged out smaller Ethiopian enterprises (Chacko 2003). However, beginning in the late 1990s, a new cluster of Ethiopian businesses emerged in the U Street area of the Shaw neighborhood in Washington, D.C. Eighteen Ethiopian businesses in the neighborhood are listed in the 2005–2006 Ethiopian yellow pages. Ethiopian restaurants in particular exhibit prominent ethnic signatures through signage in Amharic and English; the prevalence of red, yellow, and green, colors of the Ethiopian flag, on awnings and signs; and the use of symbols such as the national flag itself and the Lion of Judah, emblem of Ethiopia's monarchy and the Ethiopian Orthodox Church (fig. 9.5). As the visibility of their businesses on the streetscape increased, so did the Ethiopian immigrant community's desire to establish officially recognized ethnic space in Shaw. Local Ethiopian leaders called on the diasporic community to push for a city-designated ethnic space via an online petition for naming a block of Ninth Street, a road that stems off of U Street, "Little Ethiopia." Community leaders also lobbied local politicians to support them in this endeavor.

The Ethiopians' efforts to carve official ethnic space in Shaw were vigorously resisted by the primarily African American population of the

Fig. 9.5. Salome Ethiopian restaurant on U Street, Washington, D.C. Photo by the author.

neighborhood, despite tentative support from a local city council member. The native population was concerned that the immigrant community's endeavors would detract from the recognition of U Street's role in Washington's history, particularly the contributions of its African American residents. A Shaw community activist's statement resonates with many locals: successful entrepreneurs, Ethiopians have left their mark on the commercial landscape of the neighborhood, but they have not "paid their dues" (Schwartzman 2005, B1). The schisms between native-born and immigrant blacks in the area have also been amplified by the fact that the immigrant business owners do not live in the neighborhood.

Unlike the traditional ethnic enclave where residential and occupational spaces overlapped, the new ethnic enclaves in U Street and Annandale are commercial with limited residential presence in the neighborhoods. Whereas Koreans account for 6 percent of the total population in Annandale, in the U Street area Ethiopians make up only 1 percent of the residents. Ethnic business owners who work but do not live in a neighborhood tend to be regarded by local residents as sojourners rather than settlers, individuals who are not integrated into the local community. This view does not bode well for strong support from the natives for the official endorsement of commercial ethnic enclaves and their incorporation into the official historical and cultural narratives of these neighborhoods. There have been arguments between the African American and Ethiopian communities as to why Shaw's distinctive black heritage should be preserved without distraction from competing ethnic groups, and counterarguments that the space on Ninth Street between U and T streets that the Ethiopians wish to designate as "Little Ethiopia" would add to the visibility and draw of the neighborhood without clashing with the narrative of the older historic neighborhood. However, escalating tensions between these two groups of protagonists in Shaw resulted in the Ethiopians' dropping their plans to push for the official demarcation of an Ethiopian ethnic enclave.

CONCLUSION

New immigrants of color such as Ethiopians and Koreans are changing the complexion of America's metropolitan areas in multiple and sometimes unexpected ways. In addition to racial tensions over city space that have roots in the perceived advantages of dominant (usually white) groups relative to minorities (traditionally, blacks), new configurations of privilege and power have emerged in both urban and suburban settings as new immigrant populations add to the existing racial and ethnic mix. Additionally, as immigrant groups increase in size and visibility, they are likely to wish to leave a permanent imprint on the areas where they live and work.

Experiences of urban and suburban space are products of a sequence of political, economic, racial, and class-based decisions. The varied use of space itself is an outcome of power functioning within a social system. In America's multiethnic cities, long-held binaries of black versus white and privileged natives versus disadvantaged immigrants are being disrupted and overturned. Longevity of a group in an area and a strong economic presence vie with each other as primary factors in formulating place meaning and place memories. The codification of these meanings and memories in neighborhoods and streets through the naming or renaming of streets and neighborhoods and the commemoration of landmarks and features provide physical evidence of the imprint of different racial, ethnic, and cultural entities.

In areas with multiple groups, each with its own history, culture, symbols, and memories, neighborhoods and streetscapes are likely to be palimpsests rather than montages of discrete cultural units. In immigrant gateways, waves of immigrants leave impresses on the urban landscape's built environment, history, and cultural geography. The urban landscape in a gateway city is like a palimpsest—a canvas that has been used over and over and still bears the marks of the different ethnic groups even though many of the ethnic signatures may have been all but erased or have faded over time. Moreover, ethnic spaces in immigrant gateways are likely to overlap and have blurred boundaries rather than form neat mosaics of distinct and separate spatial entities.

Cultural clashes such as the ones between Korean immigrants and native whites on Little River Turnpike in Annandale and between native-born and immigrant blacks on the U Street corridor stem from a dissonance in the meanings that disputed space holds for different groups. Transitional neighborhoods in particular resonate with contested meanings and memories.

The controlled image of the neighborhood that groups like Annandale natives and African Americans in Shaw wish to preserve and project also brings issues of nonrepresentation of other groups that share the space to the fore.

Form, function, and spatial identity jointly determine urban meaning. Identity as it plays out in metropolitan settings and the power it confers are ultimately a reflection of collective social imaginings and memories. Annandale city officials want to retain the tangibles and the intangibles of their image of an old southern settlement, steeped in history, by using symbols such as Main Street from a traditional past. They resist the obvious and robust Korean presence on the city's main arteries through their particular interpretation and memories of the city's culture, calling attention to historically significant landmarks in physical space and the electronic space of official Web sites. Lacking control over the Korean immigrants' use of buildings, signage in Hangul, and other physical expressions of Korean culture, the native population and city officials are clearly attempting to use the Annandale Village Center as a symbolic counterargument, a spatial representation of their vision of Annandale and the culture of its majority population. Although city officials accept the limited use of symbols of Korean culture in the area, they are opposed to the naming and demarcation of a street or place as "Koreatown," citing ethnic diversity among the area's residents and their desire not to privilege one immigrant group over another.

The two cases presented in the emerging immigrant gateway that is Washington, D.C., demonstrate the effects of recent immigrant populations on the use of public spaces, streets, and neighborhoods. Debates about the history and culture of neighborhoods will continue in the ever changing terrain of race and ethnicity and class in the United States. Just as individuals and communities can subscribe to several identities, played out differently in varied settings, the same physical space can hold different meanings for various groups, who formulate place identity and express it through distinctive material and abstract symbols. As sites of the expression of group identity, streets and neighborhoods should be viewed not merely as components of the built environment but as sites where community memories and community pride are articulated. Sharon Zukin (1995) notes that cultures are constantly being negotiated in the city as urban places are reshaped and revitalized. The same could also be said of central places in suburban areas. Greater awareness of the diverse heritage of a neighborhood and a willingness to acknowledge and publicly commemorate multiple remembrances appears to be the only path toward socioculturally inclusive space that truly manifests shared meanings in multiethnic cities and suburbs.

Emerging gateways are ideal settings in which to investigate the ongoing cultural, political, and historical processes of the carving of ethnic space by different immigrant groups. Although all cities retain memories in their streets and public, residential, and commercial spaces, emerging gateways with their relatively recent influxes of immigrant populations are laboratories where the unfolding meanings and memories associated with place can be observed, studied, and understood. The attempts of natives to reclaim space and the efforts of immigrants to claim territory in cities and suburbs speak to the complex relations between immigrant and nonimmigrant groups, between majority and minority populations, and the effects of these interactions on place.

As the examples of U Street and Annandale demonstrate, in emerging gateways and heterolocal metropolises such as Washington, D.C., the residential and commercial spaces occupied by an ethnic group are less likely to overlap. The separation of these two ethnic spaces makes it difficult for an ethnic group to gain local support in their efforts to mark sociocommerscapes as officially recognized ethnic places with street signs and other markers that proclaim their ethnic affiliation, whether it is a "Koreatown" or a "Little Ethiopia."

10

Dublin

An Emerging Gateway

MARY GILMARTIN

One of Dublin's most striking public sculptures is found at the edge of the city's International Financial Services Centre (IFSC). The IFSC is the iconic symbol of Ireland's Celtic Tiger economy and the sculpture—*Famine*, by Rowan Gillespie—is often photographed against its backdrop. The juxtaposition of Dublin's past and Dublin's present in these photographs is a stark representation of how gateways change—from an exit turnstile to a contemporary entrée point (fig. 10.1). The location for *Famine* was deliberately chosen because it was the site from which many famine emigrants departed for Liverpool and the "New World" (Kelleher 2002, 261). It was one of many gateways for emigration from Ireland during the nineteenth and twentieth centuries, a period when rates of emigration were so high that the country was described as an "emigrant nursery" (MacLaughlin 1994). Today, the IFSC facilitates the migration of capital to Ireland's low-tax economy, and provides employment for some of the many new migrants recently arrived in the country.

The first significant change in gateway status is Ireland's shift from being a country of net emigration to one of net immigration. For decades, Ireland had been exporting its population: to the UK, North America, Australia, and elsewhere. Emigration rates from Ireland had periodic peaks, often associated with difficult economic conditions. In 1989, for example, at the height of the last recession in Ireland, more than 70,000 people—2 percent of the population—emigrated in that year alone. The year 1995,

Fig. 10.1. *Famine* (1997), by sculptor Rowan Gillespie. Photo by the author.

however, was the last year in which Ireland experienced net emigration. Since then, individuals moving to Ireland have led to a net increase in migration rates (table 10.1).

The Irish Central Statistics Office (CSO) estimates of the nationalities of these migrants are shown in figure 10.2. There are three interesting points to note. The first is the high proportion of Irish nationals in the immigrant population. The majority are return migrants and their families, and many of the return migrants are those individuals who emigrated during the 1980s and 1990s. This number has been decreasing in the past three years. The second is the growing proportion of immigrants in the

TABLE 10.1

MIGRATION TO AND FROM IRELAND, 1995–2005

Year	Net migration	Emigration	Immigration
1995	-1.9	33.1	31.2
1996	8.0	31.2	39.2
1997	19.2	25.3	44.5
1998	17.4	28.6	46.0
1999	17.3	31.5	48.9
2000	26.0	26.6	52.6
2001	32.8	26.2	59.0
2002	41.3	25.6	66.9
2003	29.8	20.7	50.5
2004	31.6	18.5	50.1
2005	53.4	16.6	70.0

Source: Central Statistics Office 2006.
Note: Figures are in thousands.

"Rest of World" category (ROW). In 1996, for example, there were almost as many immigrants from the United States (a traditional source of immigration to Ireland) as from the ROW, but by 2004 there were ten times as many immigrants from the ROW as from the United States. The third is the new category of EU-10, immigrants from the ten new European Union accession countries. This category was first included in 2005. Prior to 2005, immigrants from these countries were included in the ROW.

The second significant change in gateway status is economic. During the last recession in the 1980s, unemployment rates were close to 20 percent, national debt per capita was for a period the highest in the world, and commentators seriously asked whether Ireland could be considered a third world country (Coulter 2004, 3). Since then, Ireland has experienced dramatic economic growth. Fueled by foreign direct investment (particularly from the United States), and enabled by social partnership, this economic transformation has been labeled the Celtic Tiger. Now, the unemployment rate is just over 4 percent, debt levels are among the lowest in Europe, and the AT Kearney/Foreign Policy Globalization Index regularly ranks Ireland as the most globalized nation in the world. The successful globalization of

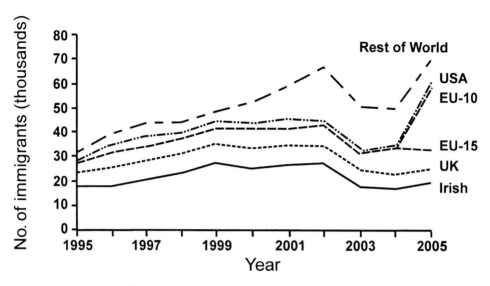

Fig. 10.2. Nationality of immigrants to Ireland, 1995–2005.

Ireland is thus proudly announced by politicians and pundits alike, proof of just how far the nation has come.

This chapter examines the changing status of Dublin as an immigrant gateway. It begins with a description of the changes that have occurred to the landscape of Dublin over the past decade. It continues with an analysis of these changes with reference to the differential status of different migrant groups, and concludes with an examination of the reactions to these changes and a speculation on how they might affect Dublin's future status as a gateway city.

BOOMTOWN: DUBLIN AS A TRANSFORMED GATEWAY

Dublin—the capital city, with more than a quarter of the population of the Irish Republic—has been at the center of Ireland's rapid economic transformation. Urban-renewal schemes, underpinned by a broad range of tax incentives, have facilitated the material transformation of certain parts of the city: inner-city gentrification, apartment building, dockland development schemes, investment in hotels, and multistory car parks, all fueled by private investment (Punch 2005). The extent of Dublin has also spread through the development of low-lying extensive suburbs to the west and south of the city. In addition, the Dublin commuting belt has extended to include not just the Greater Dublin region (Dublin and the neighboring counties of Wicklow, Kildare, Meath, and Louth) but also areas within a sixty-mile distance of Dublin, such as Westmeath, Longford, Laois, Offaly, and Kilkenny.[1] In these ways, Dublin has become an economic gateway: for inward and internal investment, for profit transfer, and for exports of goods and services.

Dublin has always been a destination for migrants from other parts of Ireland: the city provided educational, economic, and social opportunities for people, particularly women, with limited opportunities in the areas in which they grew up. However, Dublin has also become an important destination for new immigrants to Ireland: it is now an emerging immigrant gateway. Some evidence for this argument is available from the 2002 census (table 10.2). Out of a total population of around 3.8 million, in a question on nationality 93 percent self-identified as Irish, 2.7 percent as British, 0.8 percent as other EU, 0.6 percent as other European, 0.3 percent as American, 0.5 percent as African, 0.6 percent as Asian, 0.3 percent as Other, and 1.3 percent as Not Stated. Since the population of Dublin is 28.6 percent, and the population of the Greater Dublin region (including counties Meath, Louth, Kildare, and Wicklow) 41.8 percent, of the total population of Ireland, a normal spatial distribution would suggest that each of the nationality categories would be represented to this extent in Dublin and in the Greater Dublin region. However, table 10.2 clearly shows an overrepresentation in Dublin and in the Greater Dublin region of people with European (other than UK), African, and particularly Asian nationalities.

Figures for foreign-born residents of Dublin provide another insight into new migrant communities in Dublin. Excluding the UK and the United States, the highest proportion of foreign-born residents come from China,

---

1. Much of this change has been fueled by the increase in housing prices: the average cost of a house in Dublin today is €384,000 (US$491,000), compared to the average cost in the rest of Ireland of €249,000 (US$318,000) (Permanent TSB 2006).

TABLE 10.2

RESIDENT NATIONALITIES IN IRELAND AND DUBLIN, 2002

Nationality	Ireland Resident Population	Resident population (as % of total population)	Dublin Resident population (as % of total population)	Greater Dublin region Resident population (as % of total population)
Irish	3,584,975	93.0	28	39
UK	103,476	2.7	21	33
Other EU	29,960	0.8	47	56
Other European	23,105	0.6	47	59
United States	11,384	0.3	28	40
African	20,981	0.5	45	64
Asian	21,779	0.6	62	70
Other	14,423	0.4	46	59
Not stated	48,412	1.3	43	53
Total	3,858,495	100		

Source: Central Statistics Office, 2002 Census.

Nigeria, France, Romania, Germany, South Africa, Spain, Philippines, Australia, Italy, India, and Pakistan. These numbers are relatively small, but they do suggest heterogeneity in terms of place of birth for non-Irish residents of Dublin (fig. 10.3). It is expected that these numbers have significantly increased since 2002—more detailed information will be available from the 2006 census, due to be published in late 2007.

Non-Irish residents of Dublin are also spatially concentrated: in the inner city, in the west and southwest of the city (Tallaght, Lucan), and in small pockets in the north of the city (Finglas and Swords) (fig. 10.4). Non-Irish residents of Dublin are also significantly more likely to be living in private rented accommodations since the alternatives are difficult to access, either because of cost (owner occupation) or supply (limited social housing) (Humphries 2005).

It appears that a significant number of new migrants to Ireland move initially to Dublin. Some official statistics are available to support this assertion. Almost half of work permits are issued to companies in Dublin,

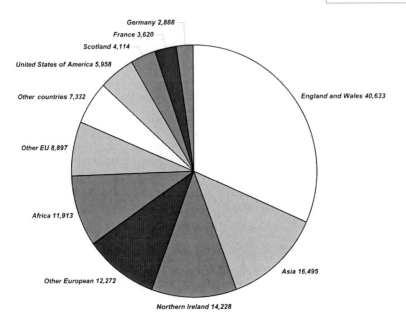

Total foreign-born:	128,350
Total population:	1,105,134
Percentage foreign-born:	11.61%

Germany 2,888
France 3,620
Scotland 4,114
United States of America 5,958
Other countries 7,332
England and Wales 40,633
Other EU 8,897
Africa 11,913
Asia 16,495
Other European 12,272
Northern Ireland 14,228

Fig. 10.3. Birthplace of foreign-born residents of Dublin, 2002. *Source:* Central Statistics Office 2002.

and many asylum seekers and residents are housed in Dublin under direct provision. Census 2002 figures suggest that Dublin and the Greater Dublin region are home to a high proportion of immigrants from the EU (excluding the UK), Europe, Asia, and Africa. However, in Dublin as in Ireland more generally, there is an information vacuum in relation to immigration. Government bodies either do not collect and compile relevant data, do not make relevant data publicly available, or make data available at very general levels, such as province and county. As interest in migration grows, these bodies are increasingly reluctant to provide information, even on an informal basis. From recent conversations with statisticians in the Irish Central Statistics Office, it appears that even they are facing considerable difficulties in accessing information about migration.

Apart from official statistics, however, other evidence is available through observation. In this regard, the everyday landscapes of Dublin have

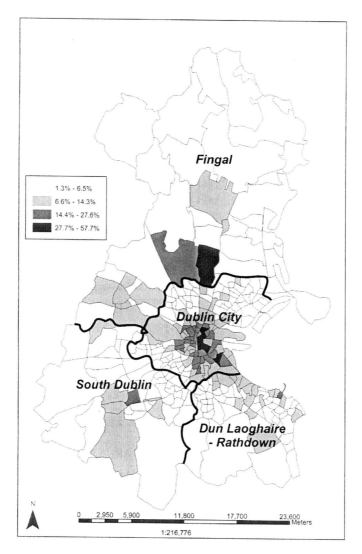

Fig. 10.4. Percentage of non-Irish households in Dublin, 2002.
Source: Adapted from Humphries 2005.

certainly changed over the past ten years. Many observers use Moore Street in Dublin's north inner city as evidence of this change (see White 2002). The site of Dublin's longest-lasting outdoor market, the shops surrounding the market are increasingly immigrant-run, offering services such as food, beauty, communications, and money transfer (figs. 10.5 and 10.6).

Fig. 10.5. Moore Street, Dublin, July 2006. Photo courtesy of Shane Willoughby, Karen O'Connell, and Eoin Hughes.

This immigrant entrepreneurial presence is visible in more low-rent areas of Dublin: rent for Moore Street and other sites in the north inner city is cheap, and leases are short-term because of uncertainty over the area's future, whereas other cluster locations for immigrant entrepreneurs include Inchicore, Phibsborough, and the South Circular Road area, also lower-rent areas. In addition, a range of other services has developed to meet the needs of immigrant communities; one example is the proliferation of Western Union money-transfer facilities. Spaces of leisure are also developing and adapting. Specific spaces for immigrant communities include restaurants and bars: the Forum on Parnell Street was Dublin's first Nigerian bar, whereas Kanal in Capel Street was Dublin's first Polish bar and restaurant (Buttimer 2005). A range of Dublin pubs and nightclubs regularly host themed nights, such as Polish and Lithuanian nights in city-center music venues and pubs.

The religious landscape of Dublin is also changing. Religious services for Polish, Lithuanian, and Filipino communities are regularly held

Fig. 10.6. Abbey Street, Dublin, July 2006. Photo by author.

in Dublin city-center churches, and unused Protestant churches are being taken over by immigrant religious groups, such as the Russian Orthodox in Harold's Cross. There is a purpose-built mosque in Clonskeagh, in the southern suburbs, and plans for another new mosque in Fingal. In addition, some Protestant congregations are reporting significant increases in service attendance because of the influence of new immigrants.

Media responses to immigration and immigrant communities have been rapid and include magazines, newspaper supplements, and television and radio programs. Immigrant-led initiatives include Metro Éireann, a monthly newspaper established in 2000 by two Nigerian immigrants; *StrefaEire,* a Polish-language newspaper; and *Saloje,* a Lithuanian-language newspaper. Mainstream initiatives include Mono, an RTE television program that has been running for five years, and Spectrum, an RTE radio program recently established. Others include a weekly supplement in the *Evening Herald*—a national daily newspaper—in Polish.

Less obviously visible, however, are two sets of difficulties associated with immigration to Dublin. The first is the increased pressure on public services, particularly education, health care, and the judicial system. Studies of recent teaching graduates suggest that their biggest challenge on graduation is dealing with new immigrant communities: these difficulties arise because of lack of experience and lack of resources, particularly in relation to language (Clarke, Lodge, and Shevlin 2004). Hospitals and the health care sector are also experiencing difficulties in the provision of services to an extremely broad range of migrants: translation services are overburdened, and there is limited capacity for dealing with newly emerging cultural issues such as male circumcision. The legal system also reports difficulties in access to translation services. Housing is also an issue, and migrants are experiencing both obvious and hidden homelessness (O'Brien 2006c; Humphries 2005).

The second is the increasing number of racist incidents and attacks. The Central Statistics Office (2004) reports that nonnationals are more likely to experience crime and victimization than their Irish counterparts, while the twice-yearly report from the National Consultative Committee on Racism and Interculturalism (NCCRI) (2005) suggests an increase in reported racist abuse and attacks. Meanwhile, reports of exploitation of migrant workers periodically surface in the print media. Underpinning all of these issues is the broader silence on the question of integration: there is, as yet, no government policy on integration or multiculturalism, which helps perpetuate the myth that immigration to Dublin and to Ireland will be temporary.

Dublin—particularly its city center—now feels more like a multicultural city than at any time since Irish independence. Walking around its streets, in shops or restaurants or pubs, on signs and in newspapers, or on public transportation, the impact of new immigrants is always visible. However, the benign face of immigration in the form of new and accessible landscapes of consumption mask other, less desirable, landscapes. These hidden or obscured landscapes of immigration to Dublin—of intimidation, exploitation, and obstacles to integration—are crucial to understand in the context of Dublin's changing status as a gateway city. State categorization of immigration is central to this process.

WHO COMES IN? CATEGORIZING MIGRANTS

The material presence of new immigrants means that immigration is now one of the key subjects of public debate in contemporary Ireland. Despite immigration's constant presence in media and other discourses, our knowledge of immigration to Dublin and Ireland, and of the experiences of migrants, is patchy and ad hoc. In particular, discussions of migration often focus on a few of the categories of migrants, thus creating the impression that the migrant experience is relatively homogenous. As a consequence, relatively little is known about most migrants, and limited attention is paid to the differential treatment immigrants experience in Dublin. The categorization of migrants is important, because their status in Ireland has an impact on their ability to establish networks and connections, thus influencing the form and extent of future immigration. In addition, the categorization of immigrants is important because it happens centrally but has significant localized effects. For this reason, it is impossible to understand Dublin as an emerging immigrant gateway without first understanding the Irish state's selection and categorization of immigrants.

Encouraged Immigration

Two particular groups of immigrants are seen as desirable and worthy of encouragement. The first is returning Irish; the second is immigrants with working visas or work authorizations. For these immigrants, the possibility of belonging in Dublin is high: they may have already existing links to place, to family, or to friends; they may be highly skilled and thus able to command substantial salaries; or they may have high levels of cultural capital—in particular, good proficiency in English.

   Returning Irish. As can be seen from figure 10.2, almost 50 percent of immigrants to Ireland in the period since 1995 have been of Irish nationality. These are mostly returning emigrants and their families, though some of these immigrants—from countries such as the United States, Australia, New Zealand, and South Africa—have qualified for Irish citizenship on the basis of the foreign-births register. Many of these new immigrants were recruited by Irish state agencies in the 1990s, particularly the Industrial Development

Authority, as part of their campaign to attract foreign direct investment
to Ireland. According to Denis O'Hearn, labor flexibility in Ireland was
traditionally and is currently based on Irish emigrants and return migrants
(1998, 167). In other words, periodic improvements in the Irish economy
have, in the past, provided sufficient encouragement for recent emigrants to
return to the country, and the current economic boom offers no exception
to this pattern. However, analysis by Caitriona Ní Laoire (2004) has highlighted the higher than expected proportion of female return migrants, suggesting that not all decisions about return are fundamentally economic. In
addition, research by Ní Laoire (2004) and Mary Corcoran (2002) suggests
that although returning Irish are "an invisible layer of society" (Ní Laoire
2004, n.p.), they have specific issues, problems, and concerns relating to the
process and experience of migration, return migration, and integration.

   Working Visas and Work Authorization. For a number of years, the Irish
government's economic migration policy had two strands. One scheme targeted lower-skilled workers, and is addressed in the next section. The second, the Working Visa/Work Authorization (WV/WA) program, targeted
highly skilled, well-educated workers required for the information technology, medical, and construction sectors (Department of Enterprise, Trade,
and Employment 2005b). The WV/WA was a fast-track program where
the migrant worker applies for a visa or authorization through the Irish
Embassy in their country. WV/WA workers could change their employers
within the same skills category as long as they continued to have permission
to work and reside in the country (Department of Enterprise, Trade, and
Employment 2005c). They were in a more privileged position than many
other immigrants in relation to family-reunification procedures and spou-
sal work authorization. The average number of people admitted to Ireland
under the WV/WA program was relatively low, averaging around 2,000
per annum between 2000 and 2005 (ibid.). Because of their skills, WV/WA
workers in Ireland were welcomed and their presence encouraged.

   Since February 2007, the WV/WA scheme has been replaced by the
Green Card Permit Scheme. Under this scheme, anyone earning between
€30,000 (US$37,000) and €60,000 (US$75,000) per annum, working in
an area of skills shortage (information technology, health care, finance,
research, engineering, or construction), will qualify for a Green Card Permit,

as will anyone earning over €60,000 per annum regardless of occupation (Department of Enterprise, Trade, and Employment 2007a).

Tolerated Immigration

As the nature and extent of migration to Ireland change, certain migrant groups are increasingly tolerated. Their extent is not publicly quantified, and this relative (official) invisibility means that concerns about their presence are rarely used to mobilize public outrage against immigration levels.

EU Citizens. Prior to the EU enlargement on May 1, 2004, this category was dominated by immigrants from the UK, traditionally the largest immigrant grouping in Ireland. With enlargement, Ireland granted immediate access to its labor markets for all EU citizens (along with the UK and Sweden; however, access to social welfare is restricted) (Ruhs 2005). From this period, it appears that there has been a dramatic increase in the numbers of accession-country citizens migrating to Ireland. A rough measure of this change is provided by PPS (Personal Public Service) application figures. Since accession, more than 230,000 PPS numbers have been issued to people from the new member states. Of these PPS numbers, around 130,000 were issued to Polish, 38,000 to Lithuanian, and 19,000 each to Latvian and Slovakian citizens (O'Brien 2006a, 2006b). Although PPS numbers provide only a rough measure of immigration—they record only those individuals who apply for numbers, and give no indication of the length of their stay in Ireland—they certainly suggest new and significant migration streams from Poland, Latvia, and Lithuania in particular. And each of these new migrant groups has been active in creating a sense of community and in advocating for that community's rights. Polish immigrants have been in the forefront of this activity, setting up advice centers, newspapers, bars, and shops and becoming actively involved in campaigns against exploitation of workers and in the mobilization of employees to join trade unions.

Working Holiday Visas. Young people from Australia, Canada, and New Zealand, and since 2005 Hong Kong, may travel to Ireland under a Working Holiday Authorisation Scheme, which allows them to work in Ireland for one year. Reciprocal schemes exist for Irish citizens in each of these countries. It is difficult to quantify the numbers availing of this scheme, but the Consular Office in Auckland has an annual allocation of 2,000 visas, while 100 visas are currently allocated annually to Hong Kong. Anecdotal evidence suggests that many overstay the terms of their visa, but there is no conclusive evidence. Working Holiday visa holders often work in service-sector jobs, and they provide a temporary workforce with limited concern for working conditions and work practices beyond timely and appropriate payment. As a consequence, they receive little attention in public discourses about immigration, and may also be tolerated because of the reciprocal nature of this visa—the Australian working holiday, in particular, has become a rite of passage for many young Irish.

Tourist Visas. There are more than eighty countries whose passport holders do not require visas to enter Ireland, predominantly European and Commonwealth countries but also the United States. All other passport holders require visas, including tourist visas. These visas are now issued by the Department of Justice, Equality, and Law Reform (DJELR). The DJELR has started to publish a list of visa applications and decisions, but this information is not classified by visa type. As a consequence, there are— as yet—no publicly available figures on the numbers of tourist visas issued (and refused) annually. It is believed that many undocumented migrants enter Ireland on tourist visas, but again there is no evidence. Because tourism is crucial to the Irish economy, it is unlikely that there will be public or political pressure for a clampdown on the issuing of tourist visas.

Expedient Immigration

Work Permits. In an earlier section, I discussed the WV/WA scheme, which targeted highly skilled workers and offered them significant benefits. The second component of the Irish government's economic migration policy was, until February 2007, its Work Permits scheme, administered by the Department of Enterprise, Trade, and Employment (DETE). This scheme targeted lower-skilled workers, from outside the European Economic Area,[2] needed in the service sectors, catering, agriculture, industry,

2. This area includes the EU, plus Norway, Iceland, Liechtenstein, and, under a separate agreement, Switzerland.

nursing, and domestic home help. Prior to EU enlargement, citizens of
Poland, Lithuania, and Latvia were the main recipients of Work Permits.
Since enlargement, the Philippines, Romania, Ukraine, and South Africa
have been in the top ranking, but India, Brazil, and China also figure
highly (see tables 10.3 and 10.4).

The Work Permits scheme was significantly different from the WV/WA
scheme. It could not be applied for by a potential migrant. Instead, the prospective employer applied, with the permit held by the employer, not the
worker (Department of Enterprise, Trade, and Employment 2005d). This situation meant that the worker was tied to that site of work and could not seek

TABLE 10.3

WORK PERMITS ISSUED IN IRELAND, 1999–2005

Year	New permits	Renewals	Renewals (as % of total)	Group permits	Total	Dublin	Dublin (as % of total)
1999	4,328	1,653	26.4	269	6,250		
2000	15,434	2,271	12.6	301	18,006		
2001	29,594	6,485	17.8	357	36,436		
2002	23,326	16,562	41.1	433	40,321	16,367	41
2003	21,965	25,039	52.3	547	47,551	18,971	40
2004	10,020	23,246	68.2	801	34,067	15,531	46
2005	7,354	18,970	69.9	812	27,136	13,023	48

Source: Department of Enterprise, Trade, and Employment 2007c.

TABLE 10.4

TOP-FIVE COUNTRIES RECEIVING WORK PERMITS IN IRELAND,
2002–2005

Year	Top countries
2002	Latvia, Lithuania, Philippines, Poland, Romania
2003	Poland, Lithuania, Latvia, Philippines, Ukraine
2004	Philippines, Ukraine, Romania, South Africa, Poland
2005	Philippines, Ukraine, Romania, South Africa, India

Source: Department of Enterprise, Trade, and Employment 2007c.

work elsewhere, creating a large power differential that was clearly exploited by some employers. Holders of Work Permits had significantly fewer rights, particularly in relation to family reunification, than WV/WA workers.

New legislation provides more rights for Work Permit holders, but also makes Work Permits more difficult to achieve. From February 2007, only a limited number of Work Permits will be issued to occupations with salaries of less than €30,000 (Department of Enterprise, Trade, and Employment 2007b). No Work Permits will be issued to a range of occupations, including retail, tourism, and child care—low-wage occupations where many Work Permit holders are currently employed. This new legislation continues the treatment of Work Permit holders as economically expedient, admitted to Ireland to provide labor, at low cost, in areas of shortage, for temporary periods only.

Student Visas. Student Visas for Ireland are issued on the basis of enrollment in a recognized course of study. Holders of Student Visas can work for up to twenty hours a week. One of the largest groups of student visa holders in Ireland is the Chinese. It is estimated that between 25,000 and 30,000 Chinese in Ireland hold student visas. Of these, around 3,000 are enrolled in third-level institutions, while the remainder are enrolled in language schools. However, Irish third-level institutions are stepping up active recruitment in a range of non-EU countries—such as China and Malaysia—as a means of increasing their fee income. There is no publicly available record of Student Visas issued annually (personal communication, CSO, January 2006).

Student Visa holders are expedient because, in the main, they provide cheap labor in a range of services, such as retail and cleaning. They have limited rights to state services other than education, for which they pay significantly more than Irish students. For example, Student Visa holders are now required to have private health insurance. Their time in Ireland is not counted as residency if they later wish to apply for Irish citizenship.

Discouraged Immigration

Refugees and asylum seekers receive a disproportionate amount of attention in public debates about migration, and they take the brunt of anti-immigration sentiment. Claims for asylum have certainly increased since the early

1990s, with 39 applications in 1992 rising to a peak of 11,634 in 2002. Since that year, applications for asylum have dropped considerably (table 10.5). It appears that roughly 7 percent of applications for asylum are successful in the first instance, with another 13 percent successful on appeal.

Since early 2000, asylum seekers have been accommodated under a direct-provision and dispersal program, designed to cope with accommodation shortages in Dublin. The Reception and Integration Agency (RIA) operates three reception centers (all in Dublin, one state-owned), sixty-four direct-provision accommodation centers (in twenty-four counties, eight state-owned), and eight self-catering accommodation centers (six in Dublin, one in Cork, and one in Roscommon, none state-owned). Asylum seekers are provided with bed and board, and with a weekly cash allowance of €19.10 per adult and €9.50 per child.

Both the increase and the decrease in asylum applications mirror trends in other European countries. Despite this trend, public discourses in Ireland often focus on what is deemed to be the country's exceptional

TABLE 10.5

ASYLUM APPLICATIONS IN IRELAND, JANUARY 1992–NOVEMBER 2005

Year	Number of applications	Top five countries of origin
1992	39	Not available
1993	91	Not available
1994	362	Not available
1995	424	Not available
1996	1,179	Not available
1997	3,883	Not available
1998	4,626	Not available
1999	7,724	Not available
2000	10,938	Nigeria, Romania, Czech Republic, Moldova, DR Congo
2001	10,325	Nigeria, Romania, Moldova, Ukraine, Russia
2002	11,634	Nigeria, Romania, Moldova, Zimbabwe, Ukraine
2003	7,900	Nigeria, Romania, DR Congo, Moldova, Czech Republic
2004	4,766	Nigeria, Romania, Somalia, China, Sudan
2005	4,323	Nigeria, Romania, Somalia, Sudan, Iran

Source: ORAC 2007.

244 | *Mary Gilmartin*

experience and, as a consequence, its attraction to "bogus asylum seekers." The former minister for justice, equality, and law reform, Michael McDowell, articulated this point in a 2005 meeting with a parliamentary committee. Responding to questions from other politicians, McDowell outlined the "cock and bull stories" told by asylum applicants. "If the Irish people had even the remotest idea of the nonsense that lies behind a huge amount of these bogus claims," he claimed, "it would try their patience to the limit." He continued to say that he "would much prefer to have a system whereby we could interview people at the airport, find out their cock and bull story and say 'You're going home on the next flight.' Unfortunately, however the UN convention requires me to go through due process in respect of all these claims" (Select Committee on Justice, Equality, Defence, and Women's Rights 2005). In part as a response to fears about "bogus asylum seekers," the basis for claiming Irish citizenship was recently changed. The drop in asylum applications, rather than being understood as part of a wider pattern, is thus described as a favorable consequence of the government's hard line on dealing with asylum applicants.

The state, enabled by the media and other discourses, has thus facilitated the categorization and differential treatment of immigrants to Ireland. Desirable immigrants—returning Irish, or highly skilled—are encouraged, whereas asylum seekers are discouraged through the proliferation of discourses of fraud and through deliberate acts of legislation or enforcement. Other immigrants, such as Work Permit or Student Visa holders, are accepted only for as long as they are of economic use. This point has relevance for Dublin, because the city is home to significant numbers of asylum seekers, Work Permit holders, and Student Visa holders. If many immigrants to Dublin are constructed—through political and public discourses—as undesirable, or are understood as filling a temporary need, it has implications for Dublin's future status as an immigrant gateway city.

RESPONDING TO MIGRATION

Dublin is one of a number of European cities experiencing a growth in immigration and a redesignation as an emerging gateway. What distinguishes

Dublin from many of these cities is the rapidity of change: preliminary population estimates from the 2006 census suggest net migration to Dublin of more than 20,000 in the period from 2002 to 2006. For the Greater Dublin region, net migration in the same period is estimated at more than 65,000. The CSO estimates that the number of non-Irish nationals in the country will have increased from around 220,000 in 2002 to 400,000 in 2006 (Central Statistics Office 2006). Dublin and Dubliners have struggled to cope with this significant change. Many of the political, social, and cultural responses to immigration have been ad hoc and reactionary, and have drawn on the more restrictive European and worldwide responses to migration rather than develop a distinctive Dublin or Irish approach. Examples include the direct-provision program mentioned earlier, which mirrors a similar initiative in the UK, and the development of dedicated "reception centers" in Dublin that are not unlike detention centers in the UK or Australia. These responses are often national in scale and often focused on asylum seekers: an example is the dispersal of many asylum seekers out of Dublin, which was a state-led, not a city-led, initiative. The dearth of strategic planning in Dublin in relation to migration is sadly evident in the development plans for each of Dublin's four local government regions.[3] Despite being drafted and adopted when it was clear that immigration to Dublin was likely to be a lasting phenomenon, the plans make scant reference to the issue. One plan makes no reference to migration, but instead uses the phrase "ethnic minority," and its only substantial policy in relation to ethnic minorities comments that in light of the growing ethnic minority population in the area, it is important to "recognise the need to acknowledge and embrace cultural diversity in planning for the needs of Fingal's community" (Fingal County Council 2005). This aspirational statement provides little in the way of guidance for how cultural diversity might be acknowledged, embraced, or put into practice. It also illustrates the limits to debates about integration and multiculturalism in Dublin (see Lentin 2002).

3. Each of the regions—Dublin City, Fingal, South Dublin, and Dun Laoghaire–Rathdown—was required to produce a development plan for the period from 2005 to 2011.

There is thus little formal evidence at the local government level that Dublin is learning much from the experiences of other cities.[4] It is at other scales where this point is more apparent. In particular, state responses to immigration—both in terms of the categorization of immigration and in terms of regulation and control—draw heavily on European experience. At the same time, civil society responses draw on broader national and international networks and experiences, but they are often locally based and locally grounded. In the following section, I highlight the state and civil society responses to migration. By focusing on these responses, I want to highlight the discrepancies between national policies and local action, suggesting that these discrepancies allow for the continued intensification of the regulation of migration.

State Controls

Irish politicians, across the political spectrum, publicly recognize that immigration is necessary for the purposes of economic growth. In this way, immigration is seen as economically expedient, and support for immigration is couched in terms of the broader desire to ensure a profitable and growing economy. However, at the same time as accepting the need for immigration, politicians—particularly in the ruling coalition of Fianna Fáil and the Progressive Democrats—have been in the forefront in imposing restrictions on immigration and (certain) immigrants, and in changing or refusing to change the legislative framework within which migration occurs. I want to highlight three such areas that point to political reluctance to engage with immigrants and immigrant rights, and political involvement in the construction of (certain) immigrants as problematic.

  Citizenship Referendum. The 2004 Citizenship Referendum fundamentally altered the basis for Irish citizenship. Prior to the referendum, any child born on the island of Ireland was entitled to Irish citizenship. After the referendum, citizenship was on the basis of blood ties. The Citizenship

---

4. This statement is not to deny the excellent efforts being made by some local government officials in relation to immigration and integration, but their work is often hampered by the fragmented nature of local government in Ireland.

Referendum was approved by the electorate by a margin of four to one. It was justified by the government for two reasons. The first was the need to bring Irish legislation into line with other EU countries (Brennock 2004). The second was the need to close a legislative "loophole" that had led to "citizenship tourism": heavily pregnant women traveling to Ireland to give birth so their child could be granted Irish citizenship. It emerged after the referendum that the figures used by the minister for justice to justify the need for the constitutional change were flawed. Rather than the thousands of citizenship tourists suggested by early press releases, it became clear that maternity-hospital statistics identified only the nationality, not the residency status, of mothers (Coulter 2004). Thus, a fundamental change to Irish citizenship was made on the basis of misinformation and scare-mongering, involving the introduction of the issue of "citizenship tourism" for a number of months prior to the referendum, the deliberate misuse or obfuscation of statistics in relation to "citizenship tourism," and the mobilization of fear of asylum seekers and refugees, and of racial prejudice (for further discussion, see Garner 2005; Lentin 2005).

Labor Migration. The older system of labor migration to Ireland, with different rights for different categories of workers, was patently unfair. In particular, workers traveling to Ireland under Work Permits were subject to exploitation. Work Permits were granted for less skilled work, and they were granted to employers rather than to employees. In many instances, employees ended up as indentured labor, repaying recruitment agencies and their employers and facing substantial deductions from often below-minimum-wage rates for accommodations, training, and so on. If the employee left the position, she could stay in Ireland only if another employer applied for and received a Work Permit on his behalf. Work Permit holders had limited family-reunification rights and limited access to Irish social welfare services, though they were entitled to the same workplace protection as other workers.

The new Employment Permits Act, which came into force in February 2007, makes few changes to the existing system (Department of Enterprise, Trade, and Employment 2005a). It introduces the concept of a Green Card Permit to replace the WV/WA, but retains the Work Permit, albeit with improved rights for Work Permit holders. Distinctions between the two categories of permit are based on salary levels and skills. A significant difference relates to residency rights. Green Card Permit holders can apply for permanent residency after two years, whereas Work Permit holders can apply for an unlimited permit after five years of employment, but their access to permanent residency is unclear. What this differentiated status suggests is a two-tier system of labor migration, clearly highlighting a distinction between desirable (skilled) and less desirable (unskilled) immigrants. Although it is clear from the experiences of many cities and countries that so-called temporary migration is rarely temporary, this possibility is not addressed in the proposed legislation. In this way, Ireland's approach to labor migration is not unlike Germany's Gastarbeiter program, and is similar to contemporary programs in other "Tiger" economies such as Singapore and South Korea (see Chapters 8 and 14).

Enforcement. A particular feature of the Irish political scene in relation to migration is the enhanced involvement of the state in the enforcement of migration legislation. Key to this feature was the former minister for justice, equality, and law reform, Michael McDowell. McDowell was a central figure in the Citizenship Referendum, and continued to be a central figure in the regulation and enforcement of what he described as "the State's restrictive immigration policy" ("Racism Fight Stepped Up" 2005). The need for rigorous enforcement of this policy was defended by McDowell in the following terms: "Holland, Austria and Denmark, all countries which Ireland would consider reasonably enlightened, learned the lesson of what happens when the laws are not strictly enforced" (Corcoran and Sheehan 2005).

Enforcement has been, in recent years, through deportation. Two groups of people are generally deported: the largest group is those immigrants whose asylum applications have been refused. A significantly smaller group (perhaps fewer than 10 cases) are those individuals whose parents' applications were refused though the deportees were, themselves, Irish citizens by birth. Deportation of people who have entered Ireland on tourist visas, Working Holiday Visas, or Work Permits/Visas and overstayed or violated the conditions of the visa is extremely rare, and the DETE, with the responsibility for issuing Work Permits/Visas, has no information on enforcement of immigration legislation in these instances. Between 2000 and 2004, 2,262 deportations were carried out (from more than 10,700 deportation orders signed by the minister for justice)—mainly to Romania, Nigeria, China, Moldova, and Poland. Another 2,483 people left the state voluntarily (Irish Refugee Council 2004). The cost of deportation is high: Department of Justice figures show that between the beginning of 1999 and the end of August 2004, almost €6.5 million—excluding Garda (police force) payments—has been spent deporting 2,059 individuals (Lally 2004). And the cost of enforcement is further increased when detention is taken into account: official figures for 2003 show that almost 20 percent of committals to prison (1,852 in total) were under immigration laws (O'Brien 2005).

However, just as the state is increasingly involved in the (selective) enforcement of migration legislation, it has also been putting in place a range of legislation that serves to protect a range of general human rights. This legislation includes the Incitement to Hatred Act in 1989, outlawing the incitement of hatred against people on the basis of race, color, nationality, religion, ethnic or national origins, or membership in the traveling community; the Employment Equality Act of 1998, which prohibits some types of discrimination in some public- and private-sector employment (Tannam 2002, 197); and the Equal Status Act of 2000, which extends the prohibition on discrimination to the purchase of goods, the use of services, access to accommodation, and participation in education. Together, the acts prohibit discrimination on nine grounds: race, gender, marital status, family status, sexual orientation, religious belief, age, disability, and membership in the traveling community. The government also established two bodies with responsibility for monitoring these acts and for providing guidance on issues of equality, race, and interculturalism: the National Consultative Committee on Racism and Interculturalism, established in 1997, a policy advisory body charged with developing antiracist programs; and the Equality Authority, established in 1999, charged with promoting and defending equality rights. At the same time, however, a range of legislation was introduced to tackle the perceived problem with asylum: the Immigration Act of 1999 and the amendment of the Refugee Act in 2000 together served to make it more difficult to claim asylum successfully in Ireland and to increase deportation rates. Bryan Fanning argued in relation to asylum seekers that "policies aimed at promoting inclusiveness and at contesting racism . . . co-existed with policies aimed at promoting the exclusion of asylum seekers from Irish society" (2002, 108). His argument is now applicable to a range of other migrants.

Civil Society Responses

There are three significant sets of civil-society responses to migration: immigrant-led and mainstream organizations (Feldman et al. 2005), trade unions, and the emerging trend of local place-based mobilization. Many civil society activists are themselves migrants, and they draw on the experiences of other countries and cities in their advocacy efforts, but these efforts are often curtailed or hampered by insecure funding. As a consequence, civil society responses are also often ad hoc and localized, and civil society activists often end up providing services and assistance during localized crises, rather than devoting more energy and attention to interventions in state policy.

Immigrant-Led and Mainstream Organizations. A recent survey by the Immigrant Council of Ireland suggests that there are more than one hundred immigrant-led organizations (ILOs) in Ireland. ILOs range from region- or country-specific (for example, the Nigerian Support Group, Congolese Irish Partnership, and Polish Information and Cultural Center) to issue-based (for instance, organizations concerned with asylum seekers and refugees) and umbrella organizations (such as Integrating Ireland). As Alice Feldman (2007) points out, most ILOs, though small organizations, are involved in a wide range of activities, including service provision, campaigning, education, and community development. Umbrella organizations that are not necessarily ILOs also exist to deal specifically with issues of migration and discrimination. These organizations include the Immigrant Council of Ireland, Residents Against Racism, and the Migrant Rights Center.

In addition to ILOs, a broad range of mainstream groups and organizations, both nongovernmental organizations and semistate organizations, are involved in lobbying, campaigning, and serving a range of immigrants. These efforts are both local and national, and include support groups for refugees, asylum seekers, and immigrants across Irish towns and cities, as well as becoming involved in lobbying for migrant rights, for changes in migration policy, and around the broader issues of human rights. Examples include church groups (for example, the Catholic Church's Conference of Religious in Ireland), St. Vincent De Paul, homeless agencies (such as Focus), Amnesty, Comhlamh, as well as statutory bodies such as the Equality Authority and NCCRI as well as FÁS and Comhairle.

Trade Unions. Recently, trade unions have become actively involved in campaigning for migrant employment rights. One of the most high-profile cases was that of Irish Ferries, a passenger and freight shipping company that offered redundancy deals to its Irish workers. In their place, the company proposed hiring workers from eastern Europe for significantly lower wages and with more restrictive conditions. Workers protested and the Irish Congress of Trade Unions (ICTU) and SIPTU, Ireland's largest trade union, organized a protest march in Dublin attended by up to 100,000 people. The message of the march was described by David Begg, general secretary of the ICTU, as follows: "We have a message which is fundamental for every employer in the country, that there is a threshold of decency below which the Irish people will not accept anybody being dragged, no matter where they come from" (Dooley 2005). The agreement reached by Irish Ferries and SIPTU currently guarantees Irish minimum wage for workers on Irish Ferries. Trade unions also became involved in the Gama dispute: Gama, a Turkish construction company, was accused of underpaying its workers, and forcing them to work excessive hours. Trade unions are now actively involved in recruiting migrant workers, particularly through the provision of information on workers' rights in a range of languages and through on-site recruitment. The rights of migrant workers are to the forefront in the current round of partnership negotiations.

Local Mobilization. One of the interesting developments in terms of civil society is the advent of place-based support groups for asylum seekers, refugees, and other migrants. These localized responses to immigration are often associated with direct provision: as local communities begin to receive migrants, local activists—sometimes, though not inevitably, church related—become involved in attempting to actively welcome these migrants. These groups initially tend to provide information and services (often language and cultural), but often are forced into advocacy through the attempted deportation of failed asylum seekers. Often, mobilization occurs spontaneously, as in the recent protests over the deportation of Olu-kunle Elukanlo: Michael McDowell, following protests by school students, overturned the deportation of Elukanlo, a failed asylum seeker who had lived in Dublin and gone to school there for a few years.

Local responses, mobilization, and protests may often result in improved conditions for individual migrants. They provide little in the way of sustained national engagement with broader issues around migra-tion, migrant rights, or integration. This tactic, however, is not unusual in the Irish political landscape, where traditional "parish pump politics" results in people elected to the national parliament on the basis of intensely local issues (such as potholes in roads). There is, however, some evidence of increased immigrant political mobilization, particularly in the numbers of immigrant candidates for local elections.[5] No immigrant candidate was elected in Dublin.

Local and national responses to political initiatives that impose restric-tions on immigration have had some successes. These successes are often small-scale: the overturning of a deportation order, the sheltering of people under threat of deportation, or support for migrant workers who are being exploited by their employers. Other examples exist in small communities of their concern for immigrants, such as the provision of financial support for families of immigrants killed in Ireland. The safeguarding of employment rights for immigrant workers has also been highlighted in recent partner-ship negotiations. These successes are minimal, however, in light of new and proposed immigration legislation, and in light of dominant discourses about particular kinds of immigrants that are widely uttered and widely believed. In this way, the possibility for local pressure groups to achieve some form of localized response to a system or an outcome they perceive as unfair or unjust abrogates the need for national-level action on the issue.

---

5. Elections in Ireland operate under the Anti-Racism Protocol, signed by all political parties. The protocol commits signatories to ensuring that election campaigns do not incite hatred or prejudice (Hughes and Quinn 2004, 31). In the most recent elections, held in June 2004, six independent Nigerians were candidates (a total of nineteen immigrant candidates stood, eleven of whom were Green Party candidates). Of them, two were elected, both in smaller urban areas (Ennis and Portlaoise) (Quinn and Hughes 2005a, 2005b).

CONCLUSION

Given the rapidity of change, it is difficult to predict the extent to which migration to Ireland and Dublin in particular will increase, and the extent to which current migrant groups will consolidate or new migrant groups will emerge. In 2002, the proportion of non-Irish residents of Dublin was around 9 percent, and it is expected that this proportion will be significantly higher in the 2006 census, reflecting the recent in-migration of EU citizens in particular. It appears that this growth in immigration will continue in the short to medium term: labor-market predictions suggest that the need for migrant labor will continue to be strong, with the suggestion that Ireland will need 420,000 additional workers between 2001 and 2010 (Feldman 2006).

Continued economic growth will certainly create conditions for continued immigration to Ireland. Whether immigrants are temporary or permanent is still unclear. It appears that many of the postaccession EU migrants are temporary—for instance, university students from Poland looking for summer work in Ireland (FÁS 2005). Work Permit statistics suggest that significant numbers of recent immigrants remain in Ireland to work after their initial permit expires, but it is still too early to speculate on the extent to which they may remain in Ireland on a more permanent basis. Similarly, initial holders of Work Visas/Authorizations are only now in a position to apply for Irish citizenship, and anecdotal evidence suggests that many are intending to leave Ireland for the UK and elsewhere on receipt of citizenship. Changes to labor-migration legislation will also affect the nature of migration to Ireland, particularly in the distinction between "green card" and permit holders. Whether Ireland and Dublin continue to be important destinations for migrants will depend on political, economic, and social factors. Political factors include migration and citizenship legislation and enforcement. Economic factors relate to the availability of work and other opportunities in Ireland, often in relation to the home country. Social factors are broader: they include the extent to which migrants feel at home or a sense of belonging, the extent to which Ireland and Dublin are represented and experienced as a welcoming place, and the extent to which networks and linkages develop with the migrants' countries of origin.

The intersections of capital and labor migration have redefined the gateway status of Dublin. The two are interdependent, yet public debates on the topic of migration often praise the effects of capital migration while expressing concern or hostility about the impacts of labor migration. While Ireland's economic growth continues, labor migration may well be tolerated, but labor migrants—and their families—may well be considered surplus if economic growth slows or reverses. The current categorization of immigrants, and the immigration hierarchies that are being constructed through political and public discourse, will facilitate this process. A recent controversy in Dublin poignantly illustrated this speculation. When a group of Afghan asylum seekers recently went on a hunger strike in a city-center church to draw attention to their plight, some local residents protested outside, carrying posters that read, "Get them out. Let them die" (Bracken 2006). Dublin is certainly an emerging immigrant gateway, probably the most recent one discussed in this volume. Whether it remains so will depend on an intersection of a range of factors, some of which are firmly within the control of Dublin residents.

11

Mean Streets

Johannesburg as an Emergent Gateway

JONATHAN CRUSH

The emergence of new immigrant gateway cities is integrally related to the accelerating pace of globalization and the new global mobility of people (Benton-Short, Price, and Friedman 2005). Immigrant gateway cities typically have large numbers and proportions of foreign-born residents from a diverse range of countries. They are also hyperdiverse, globally linked through transnational networks, and a stage on which ideas about identity, nationalism, and citizenship are actively negotiated. Further, immigrant gateway cities are "critical nodes" of cultural and economic globalization. Before the 1990s, few of these defining characteristics of global gateways could be found in the insular and isolated city of Johannesburg, with its strong siege mentality and hostility to globalization and mobility (Beavon 1997, 1998; Parnell and Pirie 1991; Parnell and Crankshaw 2004). Racist policies restricted immigration to whites from Europe (Peberdy 1999), and African migrants could only enter the country to work for short periods

I would like to thank Sally Peberdy and Ntombi Msibi for their assistance in the drafting of a report for the City of Johannesburg on which this chapter draws. My thanks too to the Canadian International Development Agency and the UK Department for International Development for its support of the Southern African Migration Project's (SAMP) Migration and Urban Governance Project. I would also like to thank the Social Science and Humanities Research Council of Canada for its support of my ongoing research on the politics of xenophobia in South Africa.

(Crush, Jeeves, and Yudelman 1991). South African cities grew but not at the rate they would have because of the regulatory discriminations. The foreign-born remained a small proportion of cities like Johannesburg.

The collapse of apartheid has fundamentally redefined Johannesburg, opening it up to the transforming power of globalization. As Graeme Gotz and Loren Landau have recently commented: "Once isolated and shunned by the world, Johannesburg has been at the forefront of South Africa's reintegration into the global community" (2004). Jennifer Robinson has referred to it as a "not quite global city" (2003). However, only a decade after the historic elections of 1994, the city may increasingly lay claim to being not only a "global city" but a true "immigrant gateway." Many of the prototypical features of gateway status are very much in their infancy. But if these features continue to intensify, Johannesburg has the potential to move very quickly from its current status as an emergent gateway to a full-fledged immigrant gateway city.

Since the collapse of apartheid, Johannesburg has become a new migrant destination for people from throughout the world, and the rest of Africa in particular. Although the numbers involved are often exaggerated, new African immigrants and their transnational linkages are extremely visible (Morris and Bouillon 2001; Crush and McDonald 2002). The distinguishing feature of Johannesburg's emergence as an immigrant gateway city is the impermanence of many of its new foreign residents. Diversity, global connectivity, and intense negotiation about the meanings of nationalism and citizenship are very much present (Peberdy 2001). The economic and cultural signatures of globalization are everywhere inscribed on the landscape. But these defining features are played out against a backdrop of immigrant transience.

Johannesburg's older and more established white immigrant population has gone into decline since 1990 (McDonald and Crush 2001). Immigration from Europe all but ceased in the 1990s, and the stock of white immigrants and their descendants has been depleted by a large outflow to the United Kingdom, North America, and Australia—these immigrants are the so-called refugees from democracy. Johannesburg's new foreign-born residents are, in behavior and intention, sojourners, not settlers. Permanence is neither desired nor encouraged by the postapartheid state. And most migrants see the city as a temporary residence or a transit point to somewhere else. The city is therefore best viewed as a sojourner, rather than settler, gateway, with considerable implications for how it engages with globalization, how it is governed, and how inclusive it is of newcomers. Indeed, most foreign-born migrants cling together for protection in a city characterized by extremely high levels of intolerance and xenophobia (Crush 2000).

EMERGENT JOHANNESBURG

Of the 3,225,816 people recorded as living in the city of Johannesburg at the time of the 2001 census, only 216,715 (6.7 percent) were born outside South Africa (table 11.1). This figure is certainly a far cry from a typical gateway city, where the foreign-born population often exceeds 25 percent (Benton-Short, Price, and Friedman 2005, 953). Nearly 60 percent of Johannesburg's foreign-born migrants were from neighboring Southern African Development Community (SADC) countries. Around a quarter of Johannesburg's foreign-born residents were pre-1994 white immigrants from Europe, primarily the United Kingdom, Germany, and Portugal (table 11.2). Those

TABLE 11.1

REGION OF BIRTH OF JOHANNESBURG MIGRANTS, 2001

Region of birth	Born outside South Africa	Proportion of total city population
South Africa	—	93.3
SADC countries	58.7	4.0
Rest of Africa	6.8	0.5
Europe	26.0	1.7
Asia	5.7	0.4
North America	1.2	<0.1
Central and South America	1.2	<0.1
Australia and New Zealand	0.5	<0.1
Total born outside South Africa	100.0	6.7

Source: 2001 Census, Statistics South Africa, 2004.
Note: Figures are percentages.

TABLE 11.2

COUNTRY OF BIRTH OF JOHANNESBURG MIGRANTS, 2001

	Male	*Female*	*Total*
SADC			
Angola	1,050	732	1,782
Botswana	516	421	937
DRC	799	479	1,278
Lesotho	2,013	3,869	5,882
Malawi	3937	874	4811
Mozambique	15,182	4,802	19,984
Namibia	106	93	199
Swaziland	615	554	1,169
Tanzania	540	91	631
Zambia	849	828	1677
Zimbabwe	10,975	6,420	17,395
REST OF AFRICA			
Congo	1,371	954	2,325
Ethiopia	333	155	488
Kenya	419	338	757
Nigeria	2,297	281	2,578
Rwanda	123	99	222
Somalia	130	77	207
EUROPE			
Germany	1,316	1,103	2,419
Portugal	1,015	751	1,766
United Kingdom	6,079	5,707	11,786
ASIA			
China	299	231	530
India	936	508	1,444
Pakistan	549	105	654
Taiwan	134	108	242

Source: Census 2001, Statistics South Africa, 2004.

immigrants from the rest of Africa and from Asia officially made up only 7 percent and 6 percent of the foreign-born population, respectively.

The primary reason for the disproportionate representation of the European-born in Johannesburg's immigrant ranks is the legacy of racial selectivity in apartheid immigration policy. Many immigrants held on to their

European citizenship, and they and their children quickly joined the ranks of a sizable postapartheid out-migration back to Europe, North America, and Australasia after 1990 (McDonald and Crush 2001). At the same time, white immigration virtually halted in the 1990s (table 11.3). Between 1996 and 2001, the foreign-born white population of South Africa increased by only 11,000.

In other words, the opening up of postapartheid South Africa virtually closed the city down to traditional forms of white immigration. In part, it was a result of declining interest in South Africa as an immigrant destination from Europe. But it was also because the first postapartheid government deliberately sought to undo decades of racist immigration policy by making it more difficult for Europeans to enter as easily and freely as before (Mattes, Crush, and Richmond 2001). The white immigrant population of Johannesburg is therefore a community in decline, a creation not so much of globalization as of racism. If anything, globalization has provided them

TABLE 11.3

LEGAL IMMIGRATION TO SOUTH AFRICA, 1990–2004

Year	Immigrants	African immigrants	Percentage African
1990	14,499	1,628	11.2
1991	12,379	2,065	16.7
1992	8,686	1,266	14.8
1993	9,824	1,701	17.3
1994	6,220	1,656	26.6
1995	5,221	1,388	26.6
1996	5,608	1,667	29.7
1997	4,271	1,413	33.1
1998	4,711	1,234	26.2
1999	3,367	1,486	44.1
2000	2,456	855	34.8
2001	5,030	1,648	32.8
2002	7,176	3,164	44.1
2003	10,578	5,019	47.4
2004	10,159	4,569	45.0
Total	110,185	30,759	27.9

Source: Census 2001, Statistics South Africa, 2004.

with a route out of Johannesburg and South Africa, since their skills are in high demand in the global labor market (Crush 2002).

Since the collapse of apartheid, migration to South Africa from the southern African region, the African continent, and the rest of the world has diversified and dramatically increased. The movements are complex and multidimensional, as recent research has begun to show.[1] Some forms represent the continuation and intensification of long-standing intraregional circular migration; others are associated with the collapse of apartheid, globalization, and the opening up of the country to Africa and the world.

Johannesburg's foreign-born, non-European migrant population is growing in numbers and diversity. The city itself was built on the backs of migrant mine workers from neighboring countries (Crush, Jeeves, and Yudelman 1991). However, there are no longer any active mines within the city limits. Consequently, one of the most enduring and historically important forms of migration to South Africa no longer directly impacts the makeup of the city population.

Many predicted that the end of apartheid would bring a flood of people into the country from the rest of Africa. Certainly, there were widespread fears in the rest of Africa of an unstoppable brain drain to newly liberated South Africa. This depletion has not transpired to date, primarily because the first decade of democratic rule was characterized by a strong anti-immigration impulse at the national level. As table 11.3 shows, legal immigration from Africa to South Africa fell throughout the 1990s. However, South Africa's 2002 Immigration Act addressed a perceived national skills crisis and should make future immigration to South Africa much easier for those individuals with the required skills. The initial impact of the new legislation can be seen in increased legal immigration from Africa (see table 11.3). The number of skilled temporary migrants to South Africa also stalled after the end of apartheid. Indeed, the number of work permits issued in 2000 was only a third of the number issued in 1996 (table 11.4). In other words, official figures for temporary skilled in-migration also give very little support to

---

1. The Southern African Migration Project has conducted extensive research on the dynamics of postapartheid migration to South Africa. SAMP's Migration Policy Series is a particularly useful resource; see http://www.queensu.ca/samp.

TABLE II.4

WORK PERMITS ISSUED AND RENEWED, 1990–2001

Year	New work permits	Renewals	Total
1990	7,657	30,915	38,571
1991	4,117	32,763	36,880
1992	5,581	33,318	38,899
1993	5,741	30,810	36,551
1994	8,714	29,352	38,066
1995	11,053	32,838	43,891
1996	19,498	33,206	52,704
1997	11,361	17,129	28,490
1998	10,828	11,207	22,035
1999	13,163	10,136	23,299
2000[a]	6,643	9,191	15,834
Total	104,356	270,865	394,650

Source: DHA Annual Reports.
[a]The figure for 2000 is based on new work permits and renewals issued abroad. Figures for new permits issued and renewals obtained inside SA are not available.

the idea that South Africa (and Johannesburg as its industrial heartland) has been experiencing a major inflow of skilled migrants since 1994.

Census data show that the number of foreign-born in South Africa as a whole increased by 211,000 between 1996 and 2001 (from 814,000 to 1,025,000). The number of SADC-born immigrants increased by 161,000 (from 527,000 to 688,000). In Gauteng Province (in which Johannesburg is located), the number of foreign-born people increased by 130,000 (from 343,000 to 473,000). These numbers hardly support the popular image that millions of migrants have flooded the country since 1994 (Crush 2001). Equally, they are inconsistent with official immigration figures that show only 19,000 immigrants and 61,000 new work permits issued in the same time period. Statistics South Africa and SAMP estimated the number of irregular migrants in South Africa at around 500,000 in 2002. The number may well be closer to a million at the present time, given the Zimbabwean influx to the country.

The discrepancy between official immigration figures and the census is partly explained by the presence of at least two other types of migrants in

Johannesburg. First, there are growing numbers of international students in the country (Kirshun 2006). Since the end of apartheid, South African universities and training colleges have been favorably disposed to the presence of international students on campus. Johannesburg's numerous training institutions therefore have sizable "foreign student" populations.

Second, there are refugees from Africa's political "hot spots" of the 1990s: Angola, the Democratic Republic of the Congo (DRC), Rwanda, and Somalia. Asylum seekers have arrived from many other African and Asian countries as well (table 11.5). Until 1997, refugee claimants were dealt with under harsh immigration laws. Thereafter, with the passage of South Africa's first Refugees Act, forced migrants have been managed under separate legislation (Handmaker 2001).

Forced migrants make up a significant proportion of Johannesburg's new African migrant community. Many refugees are highly educated with significant training and skills. The 2003 National Refugee Baseline Survey found that only 2 percent of refugees had been in "unskilled" occupations in their home countries (Community Agency for Social Enquiry 2003, 49–52). As many as 37 percent were students, while the rest worked in a range of skilled jobs, including teachers (6 percent), mechanics (4 percent), health professionals (2 percent), electricians (2 percent), and so on. National employment and refugee legislation makes it difficult for them to work at jobs in South Africa appropriate to their skill sets. Nearly a quarter (24 percent) are unemployed in South Africa, and 52 percent are in unskilled occupations (including 25 percent as street traders).

A final reason for the discrepancy between official immigration data and census figures is irregular migration.[2] Indeed, the presence of irregular migrants is probably not fully reflected in the census figures either. The census involves voluntary disclosure of place of birth. In a climate of xenophobia and fear of deportation, some people are obviously reluctant to disclose where they came from. The actual numbers of irregular migrants in the city are unknown. Some enter legally as visitors and then work, others cross borders illegally and work illegally, and still others tap

---

2. The term *irregular migrant* is widely used by the United Nations to denote an immigrant whose status is either illegal or undocumented.

TABLE 11.5

REFUGEE APPLICATIONS IN SOUTH AFRICA BY COUNTRY OF ORIGIN,
1994–2004

| | Applications | |
Country	Number	Percentage
Africa		
DRC	24,808	15.7
Angola	12,192	7.7
Somalia	14,998	9.5
Nigeria	12,219	7.7
Kenya	10,553	6.7
Zimbabwe	6,857	4.3
Ethiopia	6,537	4.1
Tanzania	4,821	3.1
Senegal	4,724	3.0
Burundi	4,570	2.9
Congo-Brazzaville	3,823	2.4
Malawi	2,765	1.8
Rwanda	2,167	1.4
Ghana	2,114	1.3
Cameroon	2,011	1.3
Ivory Coast	1,006	0.6
Asia		
Pakistan	12,576	8.0
India	10,472	6.6
Bangladesh	4,173	2.6
China	2,846	1.8
Bulgaria	1,616	1.0
Others	10,098	6.4
Total	157,946	100

Source: DHA.

into a large underground trade in forged documentation or make bogus asylum claims. The national origins of undocumented migrants are also unknown and most likely unknowable, although most appear to be from the SADC region. They certainly have no interest in declaring their status to the authorities or census administrators.

Since 2000 the implosion of the Zimbabwean economy has certainly brought more irregular Zimbabweans to the city. However, it is also apparent that increasing numbers of irregular migrants have arrived in Johannesburg from other parts of Africa and the globe. Overland entry to South Africa is relatively easy, as is access to illegal identity documentation, so that the country now attracts at least some economic migrants from almost everywhere. These migrants have quite high rates of employment compared with South Africans and tend to work in construction, manufacturing industry, domestic work, and the services industry (Crush 1999). Many also work in the informal sector (Rogerson 1998).

Johannesburg is host to a large circulating population of migrants and visitors from other countries. These people include large numbers of informal traders who regularly cross South Africa's borders on a short-term basis to trade, shop, and buy and sell (Msibi and Peberdy 2005). Networks of informal cross-border trade span the entire continent but have grown particularly dense in southern Africa since 1990. Informal cross-border trade is layered and complex. Certain sectors of the trade are increasingly dominated by foreign women. The traders face numerous obstacles crossing borders and expanding their enterprises, but it is clear that Johannesburg has emerged as a major hub of informal trading for the subcontinent.

A final category of foreign-born urban residents in Johannesburg consists of those individuals who relocate to the city from elsewhere in South Africa. In the 1980s, for example, the civil war in Mozambique forced more than three hundred thousand people to flee their homes for South Africa (Azevedo 2002). The South African government allowed them to stay, provided they remained in the eastern border areas. Most did, but a considerable number migrated to cities such as Johannesburg, especially after 1994. A regularization program in 2000 through 2001 gave legal status to approximately one hundred thousand former refugees who had previously been living a precarious existence as irregular migrants (Johnston 2003).

This brief overview of postapartheid immigration to Johannesburg illustrates the varied nature and complex forms of migration to the city. There is no single form of migration and no single set of impacts. Equally, there can be no single, uniform policy response to suit all. Major tendencies in postapartheid South Africa include a failure to disaggregate migration into its various components and the assumption that one policy response will work for all. This trend is consistent with the tendency on the street to lump all "foreigners" together as uniformly undesirable and a threat to the interests of South Africans. Clearly, different groups of migrants have different reasons for being in the city, engaging in different activities, placing different demands on city services, and having variable requirements of city government.

MIGRANTS IN PROFILE

The 2001 census permits the construction of a socioeconomic, demographic profile of a significant sample of Johannesburg's new and old migrant populations. The census shows that the majority of Johannesburg's migrants are from neighboring countries in the Southern African Development Community (59 percent in 2001). European-born residents make up 26 percent, followed by those individuals from the rest of Africa (7 percent) and Asia (6 percent). The majority of migrants are from the neighboring countries of Mozambique (19,984), Zimbabwe (17,395), Lesotho (5,882), and Malawi (4,811). In terms of the rest of Africa, the most important source countries are Nigeria, the Congo, Zambia, the DRC, and Swaziland. Smaller numbers of migrants (less than 1,000) were recorded from a variety of other African countries. The main refugee-generating countries with a presence in Johannesburg included Angola (1,782), the DRC (1,278), Somalia (207), and Rwanda (222). The major shift since 2001, not yet reflected in official statistics, is a considerable growth in migration from Zimbabwe.

Intraregional migration in southern Africa was traditionally male-dominated (Dodson 1998). It remains the case, although female migration is on the increase. The European-born population of Johannesburg is gender-balanced, reflecting an older pattern of family immigration. But, as figure 11.1 shows, male migrants predominate from the SADC (62 percent of the total), the rest of Africa (70 percent), and Asia (55 percent). Other evidence shows that refugees and asylum seekers are more likely to be men (Community Agency for Social Enquiry 2003). Male refugees from Africa tend to move first to establish themselves in South Africa before being joined by their partners and children.

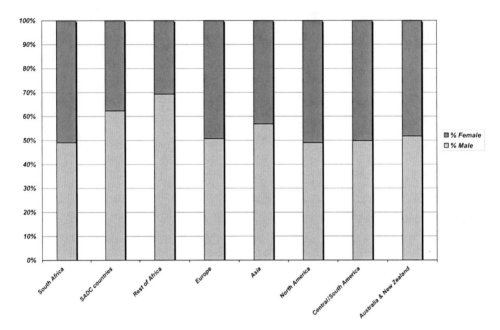

Fig. 11.1. Gender breakdown of migration. *Source:* Statistics South Africa 2004, 2001 Census.

A common perception in South Africa is that the country is a magnet for Africa's poor and uneducated (Crush 2000). However, the 2001 census shows that migrants are more likely to have tertiary education than South Africans (22 percent with postsecondary educational qualifications compared with 10 percent of the locally born) and that female migrants have higher levels of educational achievement than male migrants and female South Africans. This finding is confirmed in sample research with migrants and refugees. One study found that only 5 percent of forced migrants in Johannesburg had no education (Landau 2004). More than half (54 percent) had completed secondary education, and another 18 percent had completed tertiary education.

Migrants are more likely to be productively employed than nonmigrants. More than 60 percent of foreign-born adult migrants are formally employed (compared to 50 percent of internal migrants and only 40 percent of local residents). There are also significant gender and regional differences between the employment levels of migrants from different regions. Female migrants are more likely than their male counterparts to be unemployed. This pattern does not mean that they are not economically active, since many work in the city's informal sector. Migrants from Europe and Asia show very low levels of unemployment. Female migrants from SADC countries show the highest level of unemployment, followed by male migrants from the rest of Africa.

Refugees and asylum seekers generally find it harder to access formal employment than other cross-border migrants. Their identification documents are often not recognized by employers, and they may also find it difficult to get their qualifications verified and recognized in South Africa.

The dominant sectors of migrant employment in Johannesburg are services, domestic work, finance and business, community services, manufacturing, and construction. An important means of making a livelihood for many migrants is in the informal sector (Rogerson 1998). Street trading was banned from the streets of apartheid Johannesburg before 1990. The deregulation of the informal sector led to an explosion of street-level activity. Immigrants have inserted themselves into this sector in large numbers. They dominate certain city spaces and streets and, in many cases, are prominent in particular sectors such as import-export activity, handicrafts trading, and the secondhand clothing market (Peberdy and Rogerson 2002). Francophone migrants, in particular, are integrated into regional, continental, and even international trading networks, receiving goods and start-up capital from abroad. Other common informal-sector niches include hairdressing, taxi driving, food preparation and selling, and commercial sex work. Migrant women from neighboring countries such as Swaziland, Mozambique, and Zimbabwe sell goods made in their own countries (often clothing or handicrafts) and travel home with bought consumer goods for resale. Poorer migrants buy fruit and vegetables from wholesalers and resell them on the streets along major shopping and commuter routes.

In contrast to the informal sector in many developing country cities, Johannesburg has a disproportionate number of well-educated migrants working on the streets. As in many gateway cities, immigrants often work "below" their educational or professional qualifications. In some cases, it happens because they cannot find suitable jobs or, because of irregular status, are unemployable. Forced migrants often have few alternatives

(Landau 2005). The evidence shows, however, that the most successful traders can do extremely well on the streets.

Although the 2001 census challenges the popular idea that migrants from Africa are all living in penury and on the margins, a significant number do struggle economically. By and large these migrants are from South Africa's immediate neighbors. Migrants from elsewhere tend to be better off, although many (particularly forced migrants) are unable to secure jobs and livelihoods commensurate with their training and skills. The census does confirm that the migrant population is extremely heterogeneous both economically and socially.

MOBILE STRANGERS

During the apartheid era, Johannesburg was one of the most racially segregated and unequal cities in the world (Parnell and Pirie 1991). The city is divided into eleven administrative regions with their own management structures. The challenge of undoing the legacy of the past and uplifting the urban poor is a massive one. Economic exploitation, social exclusion, and deepening poverty are written into the highly inequitable urban landscape of Johannesburg. In the wealthiest region of Sandton and Rosebank, which is mostly white, average annual household income is over R230,000 (the equivalent of US$32,500 or €24,000), and the unemployment rate is 6 percent. By contrast, in Ennerdale and Orange Farm, annual household income is only R12,307 (US$1,700 or €1,300), and the unemployment rate is nearly 50 percent. Unemployment rates are more than 50 percent in Doornkop and Soweto and in Diepkloof and Meadowlands as well. These settlements are home to the most socially and economically marginalized, whether local-born, internal, or foreign migrants.

The collapse of apartheid has precipitated a reconfiguration of the racial geography of the city (Tomlinson et al. 2003; Murray 2004). First, the new black middle class initiated a slow process of deracialization in the wealthy northern suburbs. Second, traditional black townships such as Soweto and Alexandra continue to grow primarily through internal migration. Housing delivery failed to keep pace with demand, so a significant proportion of the population now lives in informal, backyard shacks. Third, numerous informal shack settlements have sprung up on the periphery of the city. These settlements are home to new migrants as well as people relocating from backyard shacks in the townships. Some 57,000 informal shack dwellings were erected between 1996 and 2001, raising the total number of families living in shacks to more than 212,000. Finally, there has been a rapid process of deracialization of the inner city. Suburbs formerly reserved for whites are now inhabited predominantly by black residents.

The inner-city area of Johannesburg (Hillbrow, Berea, Yeoville, Betrams) consists primarily of high-rise rental accommodations. In 2001, the area was host to just over 250,000 people, with a black population of 82 percent. In the previous five years, the "Central" region of Johannesburg had a 26 percent population increase, with the African population growing by 82 percent and the white population decreasing by 20 percent. This change simply reinforced a trend first evident in the 1980s (Morris 1999, 53–88). The rapidity of change in the demographic profile of the inner city has been accompanied by serious economic and social decline. A number of studies have painted a graphic picture of neighborhoods experiencing infrastructural deterioration, advancing dilapidation of the housing stock, and high crime rates (Morris 1999; Bremner 2000; Tomlinson et al. 2003; Oelefse 2003). The "ghettoization" of the inner city has been rapid and dramatic.

Migration to and throughout the city is also reshaping the geography of Johannesburg. Johannesburg's new postapartheid migrants confront a metropolis in a process of rapid change and are drawn to certain areas of the city. In general, skilled migrants go to the suburbs and gated communities of the northern suburbs, semiskilled and unskilled migrants from certain countries go to the townships and informal settlements, and refugees and Francophone and West African migrants go to the inner city. The process of uneven spatial insertion into the everyday life of the city presents a significant challenge to city managers seeking to develop coherent policy responses to in-migration.

Although Soweto is a major destination for internal migrants, it is not a particularly hospitable environment for foreign migrants unless they are from countries such as Botswana, Lesotho, and Swaziland, where their "invisibility" is more ensured because of cultural and language affinity (Parnell 2001a). A study of Soweto in 2000 found that backyard rental shacks made up 20 percent of all residential structures and that 37 percent of Sowetans lived in these "backyards" (Crankshaw, Gilbert, and Morris 2000). Across the city, 108,000 households live in backyards. Another study concluded that "at least 16 percent" of Soweto's backyard residents are foreign (Parnell and Wooldridge 2001, 12). The other major apartheid-era township of Alexandra is close to the northern suburbs and industrial employment opportunities. Although the reception from locals is no more hospitable than in Soweto, there are clusters of foreign migrants in Alexandra, particularly from Mozambique.

Internal and external migration to Johannesburg has fueled the growth of informal settlements on the city periphery. In 2001, more than 200,000 households lived in informal shacks, primarily in the regions of Ennerdale and Orange Farm and in Diepkloof and Meadowlands, some of the most socially and economically marginalized areas of metropolitan Johannesburg. Migrants from the SADC are more likely to live in informal settlements than migrants from the rest of Africa. A study of one informal settlement (Hospital Hill) found significant numbers of nonnationals, particularly from Lesotho, Mozambique, and Swaziland, as well as Nigeria. In this "unplanned, unregulated settlement," conditions are "abysmal," social pathologies "shocking," and the prospects for infrastructural and social betterment "bleak" (Parnell 2001b, 5). The study found that residents could afford to live nowhere else but that some found it a useful place to live, as they could avoid legal scrutiny—whether they were in the country illegally or involved in illegal activities. Foreign migrants tend to cluster in certain areas within the shack settlements. Tension between foreign and local migrants is often high, given the poverty of all and the extremely limited economic and social resources in these areas, and on occasion has exploded into violent confrontation.

The most visible change associated with new African migration to Johannesburg has been the transformation of the inner city. Just as black South Africans displaced whites in the late 1980s, so, in the ensuing decade, have foreign migrants moved into these areas en masse. A study of the inner-city residential district of Hillbrow found that foreign migrants, particularly those individuals without papers or from outside the SADC, find it easier to get accommodation in the inner city (Wooldridge 2001). Refugees and asylum seekers also find it difficult to find accommodation outside these areas. In popular consciousness, the inner-city, high-rise area of Hillbrow is now associated almost exclusively and extremely negatively with non–South African migrants (Morris 1999). Other inner-city suburbs of Berea, Yeoville, and Melville have also attracted increasing numbers of transnational migrants. The appeal of the inner city to migrants has been explained as a combination of affordable rental accommodation, proximity to economic opportunity, solidarity in the face of police harassment, and migrant networking (Sadie and Borger 2004). Although the precise national composition of the migrant population of the inner city is unknown, the majority appear to be from West and Francophone Africa and, more recently, Zimbabwe.

Most migrants in the inner city live in overcrowded conditions in deteriorating buildings owned largely by white slumlords. One study of Somalian refugees found that 70 percent lived in one room in a house and 11 percent in one room in a flat, and that 77 percent had access to only that one room (Peberdy and Majodina 2000). A study of forced migrants across four South African cities, including Johannesburg, similarly found that 75 percent rented a room in a house or flat and that more than 33 percent shared that room with at least one other person (Community Agency for Social Enquiry 2003, 135).

INTEGRATION, TRANSIENCE, AND XENOPHOBIA

The integration of migrants and immigrants is a major issue for gateway cities worldwide. Theories of integration tend to assume the existence of a stable, urbanized population with a clear identity and embedded cultural practices. The challenge is how to incorporate newcomers into neighborhoods and communities in a way that maximizes acceptance and tolerance, fosters diversity, builds social capital and promotes multiculturalism (Anisef and Lamphier 2003). Some of Johannesburg's older and more stable residential areas (whether Soweto or Sandton) might be amenable to this kind of approach. Indeed, South Africa's black townships are generally quite ethnically diverse and have achieved degrees of informal integration despite the best efforts of the apartheid state to keep people apart.

However, there is some question as to whether traditional concepts and policies of "integration" and "inclusion" have much applicability (Tomlinson 1999; Beall, Crankshaw, and Parnell 2003a). The core issue is that modern Johannesburg, like many other developing cities, is a city of migrants. As noted earlier, some 40 percent of the city's population are "migrants." Neither internal nor international migrants are entering a city with a stable, urban population of long and continuous residence. Although, as noted, parts of the city have relatively stable urban populations, these areas are not where new migrants tend to cluster. Many (if not most) are sojourners, not settlers intending to stay. They are in the city for particular reasons and see their time in Johannesburg as temporary. They are there to earn, to remit, and to accumulate resources to improve livelihoods in rural areas or the home country. They want to minimize urban outlays and expenditures.

The general evidence on migrant behavior suggests that most migrants from the southern African region are involved in a form of circular migration of varying periodicity (McDonald 2000). Refugees and migrants from the rest of Africa are less likely to be engaged in circular migration of the same regularity and frequency, but they, too, do not see South Africa as their final stopping point (Araia 2005). Most see the country, and the city, as a stopping point on the way to somewhere else (particularly the favored destinations of Europe and North America), although many feel marooned in the country (Kihato and Landau 2006). One result is that immigrants are neither disposed nor likely to want to "integrate." As Graeme Gotz notes, "Municipalities are more or less comfortable responding to the well-recognized household-focused service requirements of paying 'customers' but a little bewildered when faced with the needs of as yet unincorporated, and probably temporary, new residents" (2004).

The depiction of Johannesburg as a "city yet to come" provides a prescient perspective of transnationalism and "transience" brought about by migration (Simone 2001, 2004). AbdouMaliq Simone argues that transnational migration has substantially reshaped inner-city life and commerce in Johannesburg. At the same time, the city is "becoming an increasingly desperate place, living in the edge without a core of cohesiveness" (2001, 152). The rapidity of the transition, depreciating infrastructure, and absence of social cohesion means that "conventional mechanisms for monitoring and assessing social change have proved largely inadequate" (153). As a result:

> More than anything else, Johannesburg is being treated as a necessary elaboration of migrant circuits—a place where it is still best to remain a stranger. The primary feeling among many migrants in Johannesburg's inner city is that the social, political and economic situation in the city will grow worse with time, and that their objective is to take advantage of the short-term opportunities. While it is an African city, there is a pervasive feeling that its lack of cosmopolitaness and pervasive xenophobia makes it difficult to establish multifaceted African communities. (ibid., 164)

Johannesburg is not a permanent home but "a place to pass through—to run from—not a place to collaboratively contest or co-invest in for the longer term" (Gotz and Simone 2003, 134). At best, it is a temporary site of opportunity. Among the fluidity and transience, there is great tension and hostility between the foreigner and the local and "between some sections of the more marginalized sectors of the foreign community" (Simone 2001, 167). As such, concludes Simone, there are too many hurdles for the residents to be interested in set formulas for stabilizing the area. Transnational migrants are active agents, remaking the city, enriching its cultural life and creating new forms of associational life. Yet, as Gotz and Simone pessimistically observe, there is "precious little sense of community" in inner-city Johannesburg, "a felt deficit of belonging," and "few grounds for any established sense of social cohesiveness" (2003, 129).

The growth of antiforeign intolerance in South Africa after 1990 has been dissected in numerous quantitative surveys and qualitative studies (Crush 2000; Valji 2003; Nyamnjoh 2006). This prejudice is not simply indifference or coldness to the stranger—it is active, aggressive, and often vitriolic. In many societies, the most xenophobic citizens are the ones most threatened in material or cultural terms by the advent and proximity of unwanted immigrants. Extensive research by SAMP on this subject failed to identify a typical xenophobic profile in South Africa (Crush 2000). In other words, all South Africans, irrespective of race, gender, education, and class, hold remarkably similar antiforeign attitudes. In addition, xenophobia is directed primarily at black African migrants.

Attitudes translate easily into action. African migrants are victimized by criminals and are targets of daily verbal and physical abuse from citizens (Mang'ana 2004; Misago 2005). Unsurprisingly, xenophobic sentiments permeate the attitudes of the media and the institutions of governance (Danso and McDonald 2001; McDonald and Jacobs 2005). Recent studies of the access to health and educational facilities show that at public hospitals, clinics, and schools, migrants are sometimes denied health care and educational services guaranteed by law and the constitution (Pursell 2005; Winterstein and Stone 2004). No one has suggested that the local government of Johannesburg is any more xenophobic than other tiers of government, but there is clear evidence that within Johannesburg, migrants do have to cope with the playing out of xenophobic sentiments by officials and employees of all three levels: national, provincial, and local.

In general, the problem of xenophobia runs completely counter to the self-image of Johannesburg as a "global city" welcoming foreign investments and visitors. The press regularly carries reports of the bad experiences of visitors to the city at the hands of officials and South African citizens. Yet there has been very little recognition of the magnitude and impact of this problem, much less any strategizing about how it might be countered or eliminated. Whatever the truth of these claims, a city that wishes to project a cosmopolitan image as a global gateway would do well to look at its own backyard and develop strategies to mitigate xenophobia in the corridors of local government and on the streets.

GOVERNING THE GATEWAY

The postapartheid state—at national, provincial, and local levels—is committed to reversing decades of discrimination and economic exploitation through black empowerment, poverty alleviation, delivery of basic services, and the extension of rights enshrined in the constitution. A number of studies have evaluated the achievements of a decade of democratic local government in Johannesburg in alleviating the plight of South Africa's poor

(Beall, Crankshaw, and Parnell 2000a, 2000b, 2003b, 2003c). Whatever the successes and failures, the priority of city governments remains an enhanced quality of life for the disadvantaged *South African* urban poor. The task of improving the lives of South Africans is seen as so urgent that the "foreigner" is explicitly or implicitly precluded from plans and strategies for sustainable urban development. More often, migrants are actually seen as a threat to poor South Africans and to city plans to better the quality of life of citizens.

Graeme Gotz advances several important arguments about why migrants should be taken more seriously and effectively mainstreamed into all areas of city government. First, domestic and international migration to Johannesburg is likely to continue and even accelerate in the future. To ignore the challenges and opportunities presented by migration would be inconsistent with the responsibilities of effective, development-oriented city management. Second, Johannesburg has certain development obligations to all communities, migrants included, flowing from national and provincial policy and legislation, as well as the bill of rights in the constitution. Third, the city needs to work with communities to "facilitate the development of denser networks of social capital" (2004, 30). Fourth, the city should address the "blight" and inner-city decay that has accompanied the rapid transformation of migrant spaces. Fifth, the city has a legal and constitutional responsibility to counter the rampant xenophobia that infests its own ranks as well as a highly fractious civil society. Sixth, the city needs to recognize and develop strategies to maximize the benefits of the presence of transmigrants in terms of investment, skills deployment, entrepreneurship, and job creation. In sum, migrants need to be seen primarily as an opportunity, not an obstruction.

In 2004, the Corporate Planning Unit in the city manager's office included "migration" as a theme in a broader project aimed at supporting the development, refinement, and implementation of a new long-term Human Development Strategy for the city (Peberdy, Crush, and Msibi 2004).[3] Although the contribution highlights the importance of migration

3. See http://www.joburg.org.za/corporate_planning/corpplan_initiatives.stm. Other themes on which the Corporate Planning Unit collected information included HIV/AIDS, urban poverty, children, persons with disabilities, social services, women, and youth.

for the city, it is clear that the formulation of concrete policy recommendations has been hampered by the fact that there has been no systematic city-wide research dealing specifically with international migration. In August 2006, the mayor of Johannesburg announced that the city was formulating a new plan for immigrant integration.[4]

In an analysis of the "competencies" of city government, Gotz points out that unlike systems elsewhere in the world, "South African local government is not defined by national or provincial government" (2004, 25). The independent status of local government is constitutionally guaranteed and protected. Municipalities have legislative and executive authority over the delivery of "basic needs" services, local tourism, municipal planning, public transport, infrastructure, building regulations, and street trading. All of these areas are germane to immigrants. So, too, are a set of issues that are the domain of provincial and national government, such as access to education and health care, safety and security, and administrative justice.

Yet Johannesburg does not have control over a number of key issues relating to immigration, even though decisions made at other levels of government have profound implications for city management. For example, immigration and refugee policies (defining who is allowed into the country, for how long, and for what purposes) are national responsibilities, the key pieces of legislation being the Refugees Act of 1997 (implemented on May 1, 2000), the repealed Aliens Control Act (1991–2002), and the new Immigration Act of 2002 (as amended in 2004). Once legally admitted, migrants effectively enjoy freedom of movement (a right constitutionally guaranteed to all persons in the country). The effectiveness, or lack thereof, of central government in deterring irregular migration also impacts who arrives in the city. Local government, therefore, has no say or control over who arrives in Johannesburg (which is as it should be, given the city's sordid apartheid-era history of influx controls and forced removals) or where they will go once there. In practice, this means the city cannot project or plan for future newcomers, or predict the demand and allocation of services. This problem is not unique to Johannesburg but shared by most gateway cities.

4. See http://www.joburg.org.za/2006/aug/aug22_workshop.stm.

Similarly, the rounding up and "expulsion" of irregular migrants from the city (and the country as a whole) is in the hands of the national Department of Home Affairs and South African Police Services (SAPS). This process has been characterized by coercion, corruption, and an almost complete absence of due process (Human Rights Watch 1998; Leggett 2003; Palmary 2004; Klaaren and Algottson 2004; Madsen 2004). Some legal scholars, commenting on the scope and scale of the abuse, have even referred to them as the actions of a "criminal state" (Klaaren and Ramji 2001). South Africa deports between 150,000 and 200,000 migrants a year (the vast majority to neighboring countries). Most migrants are arrested on the streets or in their workplaces and dispatched to a privately owned holding center to the west of the city called Lindela. This center has been beset by controversy and is regularly the subject of human rights investigations over the treatment of migrants (South African Human Rights Commission 2000). At Lindela, detainees are held until their identity is established and then either released or deported. Since the police engage in unabashed "racial profiling" in identifying "foreigners," up to 20 percent of their arrests turn out to be South African citizens. Because the SAPS have free rein on the streets of Johannesburg and consider the apprehension of irregular migrants a key element in fighting crime, considerable disruption and even chaos occur in inner-city neighborhoods and workplaces.

The city does have its own police department, the Johannesburg Metropolitan Police Department (JMPD), which is responsible for bylaw enforcement and crime prevention. In practice, the JMPD often conducts joint crime-prevention operations with the SAPS. Since, in police circles, irregular migration is a crime against the state, arresting migrants is viewed as a crime-prevention activity. The JMPD, therefore, also regularly accosts and detains citizens and noncitizens suspected of being in the country illegally. A recent study of relations between the police and forced migrants in Johannesburg found that nearly 70 percent had been stopped at least once and asked for identity documents (compared to only 12 percent of South Africans) (Palmary 2004). The JMPD has been accused of being derelict in its duties to offer protection to migrants. This charge takes on extra significance, given that migrants are more likely to be the victims of violence and crime than local residents (Palmary, Rauch, and Simpson 2003). Migrants are typecast as the perpetrators of crime rather than as people requiring protection from local or foreign criminals.

Studies of the treatment of forced migrants in Johannesburg show that refugees and asylum seekers face additional problems in their interactions with the national Department of Home Affairs, national and city police, and other authorities. Abeda Bhamjee and Jonathan Klaaren (2004) provide a lengthy list of social problems faced by asylum seekers and refugees in Johannesburg, including difficulties accessing identification documentation, limited access to basic health services, exclusion of refugee children from schools, denial of foster care grants, inability to open bank accounts, and denial of employment opportunities (Jacobsen and Bailey 2004; Winterstein and Stone 2004; Pursell 2005). Unaccompanied minors face additional problems of survival and potential abuse (Eyber 2004). Nongovernmental organizations, faith-based organizations, and migrant associations all work in trying circumstances and with limited resources to provide support, shelter, and legal advice to asylum seekers and refugees (Tlou 2004; Segale 2004). The challenge confronting local government is that many of the policies and practices that impact forced migrants are nationally set and enforced. What the city needs to ensure is that its own social and economic policies vis-à-vis refugees are nondiscriminatory, constitutionally sound, and consistent with basic human rights principles.

CONCLUSION

The number of migrants in the city of Johannesburg is consistently overestimated by officials, the public, and the media. Certainly, on these grounds alone, the classification of Johannesburg as an immigrant gateway city is debatable. Yet this reservation does not mean that immigration is not of growing importance, and that Johannesburg is best seen as an emergent gateway. One could argue that the presence of immigrants in the city is entirely consistent with a country and city that aspire toward cosmopolitanism, global status, regional solidarity, and pan-Africanism. Yet there is probably not a single immigrant in Johannesburg who feels comfortable being there, does not fear the heavy hand of corrupt law enforcers, and does not worry that they will be the next victim of violent crime (Dirsuweit

2002; Madsen 2004; Winkler 2006). This perception cannot be the reputation that Johannesburg wants to project to the rest of Africa and beyond, but it is. It is a dangerous place to try to make a living. African migrants in particular feel like pariahs in the new South Africa.

The migrant population of the city is relatively small in absolute numbers, but is also extremely heterogeneous, in terms of both national origin and life skills. Consequently, migrants do not disperse evenly across the city. They are drawn by affordability, social networks, and, in many cases, absence of choice to certain city neighborhoods. They are an extremely significant force in those parts of the city in which they cluster, especially in the inner city, where the foreign presence is highly visible. In the more impoverished informal settlements and backyards of the city, immigrants cluster together for reasons of affinity and self-protection.

Johannesburg is, or aspires to be, a global city. One of the major consequences of globalization, porous borders, and a location on a fractured continent is increased human mobility. Johannesburg is not insulated from the world. Migrants are a fact of modern, global-city life. They can be wished away, but they will not disappear. Among the citizenry and within the corridors of power, there is a pervasive insularity—a failure to see the city in its global and African context. Migration certainly brings problems and challenges, but it also offers rich economic, social, and cultural opportunities. A fundamental rethinking of the potential and opportunity of the transnationally mobile sojourner has recently been promised by the mayor of Johannesburg.

Given the magnitude of the postapartheid challenges confronting local government, it is perhaps unsurprising that the issue of migration management has been relatively low on the list of priorities to date. Policies have been ad hoc and reactive rather than systematic and proactive. This chapter argues that, in common with many gateway cities in the developing world, transnational migration has largely been ignored by Johannesburg city managers and precluded from developmental efforts to formulate and implement a coordinated response to good city governance.

To the extent that xenophobia is driven by notions of nationalism, identity, and citizenship, it is also another defining feature of the urban immigrant gateway. In Johannesburg, xenophobic sentiment has reached a fever pitch in postapartheid South Africa, making it one of the least-immigrant-friendly cities in the world.

Earlier conceptualizations of gateway cities tended to assume that new urban immigrants came to stay. This kind of model may be appropriate to Toronto or Washington, D.C., but has much less purchase in developing country cities such as Accra or Johannesburg (Grant and Nijman 2002). As other case studies in this book demonstrate, immigrant gateways are not always end points, per se, but part of a transnational urban network more like a turnstile than a place of permanent settlement. In this respect, Johannesburg is more of a regional and global turnstile than a place in which new migrants intend to put down roots. Johannesburg is a quintessentially migrant city, a fact that existing strategies, plans, and visions largely ignore, whereas officials see a city largely disconnected from the countryside, the region, the continent, and the world. At the same time, impermanence does not mean that immigrants hover like ghosts through the urban landscape without leaving a trace. Johannesburg may be a turnstile, but for many it is also a marooned community. Migrants may not want to stay, but many do not know how to leave. Even those migrants who successfully pass through the city to other cities in the global network leave many transnational connections and traces. Despite all the transience and impermanence, this emergent gateway city is being profoundly reshaped by its new immigrants.

PART THREE | Exceptional Gateways

12

In the Margins of Riyadh

Indonesian Domestic Workers in Saudi Arabia

RACHEL SILVEY

The Kingdom of Saudi Arabia receives more immigrants than most countries in the world. In absolute terms, it ranks sixth in the world, with nearly 7 million international migrants resident in the kingdom in 2005, more than many widely recognized immigrant receiving countries, such as Canada and the United Kingdom. Saudi Arabia also ranks sixth in the world in its percentage of international migrants, who constitute 25 percent of its total population, making its percentage of foreign-born twice the figure for the United States (United Nations 2005). It is also the second most important source of immigrant remittances (US$15 billion in 2003) in the world, with only migrants in the United States sending a larger total sum of money home to origin countries (International Organization of Migration 2005, 65). Despite Saudi Arabia's significance as an immigrant destination, the kingdom's immigration policies and dynamics remain relatively understudied, particularly in English-language immigration literature.[1]

Immigration to Saudi Arabia is distinctive in several respects. First, immigration has grown extremely rapidly, rising from 63,389 in 1960 to 6,360,730 in 2005 (United Nations 2005). Second, this increase has

1. The main reason for the relative dearth of literature on immigration in Saudi Arabia is the Saudi government's refusal to allow foreign researchers to examine the topic. Scholars have published several important exceptions, which are discussed in the chapter.

happened quite recently relative to many other major global immigrant-receiving nations, which began receiving large numbers of immigrants in earlier historical periods. Third, the Saudi Arabian government has instituted particularly restrictive immigration policies and exclusionary practices. Saudi cities do not operate as gateways in the same manner as some cities in the United States such as Los Angeles and New York. Rather, as the rate of immigration has increased rapidly in recent years, Saudi Arabia has excluded immigrants from various paths toward social and political incorporation. As this chapter explores, Saudi Arabia stands out from other major immigrant destinations in the extent to which it has drawn on high rates of temporary guest workers while excluding immigrants from more permanent, or even partially integrated, membership into Saudi society.

Saudi Arabia's capital city, Riyadh, has the country's largest number of immigrants. Riyadh's proportion of foreign-born people is quite high, comparable to the proportion of Chicago in the United States. Approximately 31 percent of Riyadh's population, or 1.47 million of its 4.73 million inhabitants, are foreign-born (Benton-Short, Price, and Friedman 2005, 953). The city depends on this immigrant workforce to fulfill private-sector activities, including highly skilled technical work in the oil industry, as well as lower-skilled positions in construction, gardening, transportation, janitorial, and domestic service work. Low-wage jobs are filled primarily by migrants from neighboring Gulf states, as well as an increasing proportion of migrants from South and Southeast Asia since the 1970s (Shadid, Spaan, and Speckman 1990). Immigrants are employed as guest workers, and they generally serve contracts of two to three years.

More overtly than other major immigrant gateway cities, Riyadh is highly segregated along the lines of ethnicity and nationality. The segregation that characterizes Riyadh's housing and urban planning, the kingdom's exclusionary citizenship and labor policies, and the history of national labor-market segmentation serve to keep Saudi citizens largely socially and spatially distant from immigrants. The kingdom's immigration policy has encouraged immigrants to come as guest workers and simultaneously refused to allow them to apply for citizenship. Immigrant workers are kept on the margins of social and political life in the kingdom and its capital city, and they face heightened exploitation and abuse in conjunction with their lack of legal protection (Human Rights Watch 2004). Riyadh thus serves as a case study of a city that draws large numbers of immigrant workers whom it actively excludes from political and economic incorporation.

Female immigrant domestic workers face particular exclusions in Saudi Arabia. In that domestic workers are restricted to the homes of their employers and refused entry to public space, they remain politically excluded from and socially subordinated to the Saudi citizenry. The complex of sociospatial forces that serve to marginalize domestic workers is indicative of the pressures that make Riyadh a gateway for large-scale temporary employment yet persistently exclude and marginalize immigrants.

In this chapter, I examine Riyadh's operation as an immigrant gateway city by focusing on Indonesian domestic workers who have returned from overseas contracts in Saudi Arabia. I base the analysis on long-term (1995–present) field research with rural-urban and transnational migrants in West Java and South Sulawesi, as well as interviews with nongovernmental migrant-rights organizations, government officials, and migrant recruitment agents (Silvey 2004b). By examining migrants' memories of Riyadh, it is possible to explain the forces influencing gendered migration and immigrant exclusion in Saudi Arabia.

The analysis of migrants' narrated memories is a methodological approach aimed at shedding light on the subjective dimensions of migration and place meaning. Migrants' narrations contribute to our understanding of their positionality and situation, which can yield insights into broader processes of immigrant inclusion and exclusion (Silvey and Lawson 1999). As Roger Rouse has argued, critical ethnographies of migration not only provide depth and nuance to structural and quantitative accounts but can also "challenge spatial images. [Migration] highlights the social nature of space as something created and produced through collective human agency" (1991, 11). Interviewing returned migrants about their perceptions of place and their personal histories of mobility can provide ground from which theorists may rethink teleological metanarratives and spatial dualisms, such as immigrant assimilation and inclusion and exclusion (Lawson 2000). The narratives of female migrant domestic workers in Riyadh contribute to understanding how the city operates in excluding workers from participation in civil society, in part through confining migrants to the spaces of their employers' homes.

This chapter is organized into five sections. First, it provides a review of the theoretical literature on immigrant exclusion, particularly in terms of the gendered marginalization associated with immigrant domestic labor. It argues that "gateways" can serve as spaces of segregation, producing difference and inequality more than social incorporation. Second, it analyzes the immigration data, the history and policies of Saudi Arabia, and the urban development history of Riyadh, as they affect immigrant nonincorporation. Third, it provides some background on Indonesia's overseas migration program. Fourth, it examines narratives of Indonesian female migrants who have returned from contract work in Saudi Arabia and their memories of working and living in Riyadh in particular. Finally, the chapter concludes by returning to the question of how a gateway city reproduces marginality and exclusion even as its economy relies on the labor of immigrants.

THEORIZING IMMIGRANT EXCLUSION THROUGH GATEWAYS

Early theories of immigrant incorporation and analyses of gateway cities were based primarily on the history of immigration to the United States. Major U.S. port cities, such as New York, Chicago, and Boston, where the majority of immigrants settled in the early part of the twentieth century, provided the case studies on which theories of assimilation were written (Goździak 2005, 3). The basic ideas behind assimilation theory were that immigrants would eventually join the culture, society, and political system of the dominant host society. From this perspective, a gateway city should provide the space through which immigrants can assimilate into the majority population.

For many decades now, assimilation theory has been critiqued for both assuming an Anglo-American norm from which immigrants were understood to aspire as well as presupposing that flows of immigrants would produce "unilinear, nonreversible, and continuous" social change (Suàrez-Orozco 2000, p). Similar critiques apply to assimilationist conceptions of "gateway cities," which critics argue should not be presumed to be sites of straightforward incorporation. Critics argue that immigrant receiving spaces should instead be conceptualized in relation to social networks and political contestation (Yeoh, Willis, and Fakhri 2003). Geraldine Pratt and Brenda Yeoh, for example, question any blanketing assessments of the effects of transnational migration, emphasizing the need to pay closer attention to the "particular and concrete specificity of daily experience" (2003, 160).

A growing body of feminist migration research has worked to theorize the ways that bodies of both migrants and nonmigrants are produced through hierarchical social spaces (Silvey 2004a). Recent scholarship on domestic immigrants points to the ways in which crossing national borders not only changes migrants' political status but also locally defines levels of spatial constraint or opportunity. Power relations and local norms may limit immigrants' rights and even control over their own bodies. Geraldine Pratt's work on Filipina domestic workers in Vancouver illustrates this coupling of mobility-immobility through her analysis of migrants' daily lives (2004). She demonstrates the ways in which female migrants' labor is devalued through their work as live-in caregivers. Her work shows that these women's transnational border crossings lead them into spatial entrapment within their employers' homes. Similarly, Melissa Wright's work on the U.S.-Mexican border reveals the ways in which low-income female migrants' work is "erased" and devalued, and how these processes lead to women workers' heightened vulnerability to murder and rape (1999). Both authors illuminate the spatial entrapment and exploitation of specific groups of migrant women.

Recent research calls for analyses of transnationalism and mobility that specify the power relations that position migrants in particular socio-spatial situations. As Brenda Yeoh, Katie Willis, and S. M. Abdul Khader Fakhri have argued, "Transnational spaces are clearly non-isotropic, but contain 'centres' and 'margins' of different kinds" (2003, 210). Although some groups may be able to create and sustain strong social networks that link families across transnational space, there are others who cannot participate so actively in such networks. Multiple legal policies and regulatory procedures serve to differentiate between those individuals who belong and those who are excluded from the rights and privileges of citizenship. This chapter aims to disentangle some of the ways in which social and spatial inequalities shape the localized experience of transnationalism. This research is interested in the structures of inequality in gateway cities such as Riyadh that actively discourage immigrant incorporation. Migrant women's views of cities tend to be marginalized in the historical geographic literature on immigration. Thus, this work aims to add migrant women's "subaltern spatialities" to the analysis of Riyadh as an immigrant gateway city (Featherstone 2003), and then ask how this addition contributes to theorizing the roles of gendered exclusion through immigrant gateways.

IMMIGRATION TO RIYADH, SAUDI ARABIA

Riyadh has been a major center for commercial activity in the kingdom, and served as a key site of political influence since it was proclaimed the capital of the Saudi state in 1823 (Al-Hemaidi 2001, 182). In the early 1900s, Riyadh remained only a small town, with approximately 20,000 residents (Glasze and Alkhayyal 2002, 322). Indeed, prior to the 1950s, almost everyone living in Riyadh was a Saudi national, and Riyadh was composed of "clusters of courtyard houses, which jointly surrounded common urban spaces" (ibid., 323). In the spaces between the housing clusters, members of the extended families of Saudi nationals congregated and let their children play together.

Following the major oil discoveries of the 1930s, the Saudi state began to invest in the modernization and development of Riyadh. Strong linkages developed between the U.S. and Saudi governments via the Arab-American Oil Company, ARAMCO. The Saudi government invited the U.S. Army Corps of Engineers to plan and develop Riyadh's first housing project for government employees, Al Malaz, and ARAMCO began building housing compounds for its employees in the 1940s. The Saudi government required companies with more than 50 expatriate workers to provide employee housing, "in order to limit and control the cultural influences of Western foreigners on Saudi society" (ibid., 325). Riyadh's urban fabric is today punctuated by small gated communities in the center of the city and larger, more expensive gated communities located on the periphery. These gated compounds house highly skilled, high-income expatriate workers, who make up less than 1 percent of the population (ibid.).

In the 1960s Saudi Arabian oil income funded rapid national economic development. Riyadh's urban development accelerated particularly strikingly after OPEC doubled the price of oil in the 1970s and foreign workers began to migrate to the city at high rates. Many researchers have noted the difficulty of finding accurate and reliable data on labor migration to the Gulf (Gamburd 2000, 32). More conservative estimates indicate that 55.9 percent of the Saudi labor force is foreign-born (Winckler 2005, 89). Immigrant workers compose the distinct majority—between 80 and 90 percent—of Saudi Arabia's private-sector labor force, whereas public-sector jobs are filled almost entirely (97 percent) by Saudi citizens (Struyk 2005, 143). The number of foreign-born in Saudi Arabia has risen extremely rapidly from 1960, when the total was just above 60,000 (63,389), to more than 6 million (6,360,730) in 2005 (fig. 12.1).

In recent years, the government has attempted to implement a policy of "Saudization," a development strategy aimed at replacing foreign workers with Saudi nationals. The Saudization program is intended to reduce and reverse the country's heavy reliance on foreign workers, and to redirect the flow of remittance incomes back into the national economy (Looney

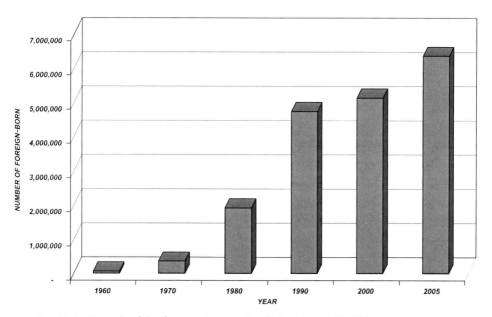

Fig. 12.1. Growth of the foreign-born in Saudi Arabia, 1960–2005.

2004, 3). The program is not expected to be particularly successful, given that despite efforts to nationalize the workforce, the numbers of expatriate workers have continued to increase in recent years. Foreign workers fill both the high-skilled positions for which Saudi nationals often lack training as well as the physically demanding and menial jobs that Saudis are not interested in taking (Atiyyah 1990).

By the late 1990s, Riyadh had attracted more than 1.4 million foreign-born people, in light of a total 4.7 million residents (http://www.gstudynet. org/gum) (fig. 12.2). Throughout the Gulf states, populations have wide-based age pyramids and are predicted to see continuing high rates of natural population increase (Winckler 2002, 617). Indeed, Saudi Arabia has a fertility rate of 6.25 children per woman, which ranks it among the highest in the world (Doumato 1999, 580). Therefore, the average family size is large, and families have heavy domestic labor loads. The nation as a whole has a high ratio of dependents per each breadwinner (Winckler 2002).

The United Nations has projected that Saudi Arabia's population, including foreigners, will rise rapidly between now and 2025. Estimated

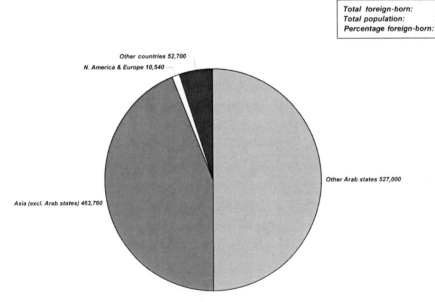

Total foreign-born: 1,054,000
Total population: 3,100,000
Percentage foreign-born: 34.0%

Other countries 52,700
N. America & Europe 10,540
Other Arab states 527,000
Asia (excl. Arab states) 463,760

Fig. 12.2. Composition of the foreign-born in Riyadh, 1997. *Source:* Ar-Riyadh Development Authority 1997.

at 3.2 million in 1950, the population rose to 20.3 million in 2000, and it is projected to increase to 31.7 million by 2015 and 40.5 million by 2025 (United Nations 2001). The Saudi labor force grew at an annual rate of 4.9 percent between 1980 and 1997. Of this growth, the native-born labor-force participation rate increased from 29.5 percent in 1980 to 32.6 percent in 1997 (Winckler 2002, 622). For 2000, the International Organization of Migration (2005) reported that the native Saudi labor force had risen to 44.2 percent, which suggests an overall trend toward Saudization of the labor force despite the persistently increasing numbers of migrant laborers. The kingdom has seen particularly rapid rates of increase in the Saudi female labor-force participation rates, which rose from 4.9 percent in 1980 to 10.4 percent in 1997 (Winckler 2002, 621).

Like other Persian Gulf countries, the Saudi monarchy limits citizenship and its benefits and privileges to Saudi nationals (Shadid, Spaan, and Speckman 1990). Saudi citizens benefit from the government's provision of substantial social services, including free public education, medical care, and public service jobs (Winckler 2005). Such state benefits are not provided to foreign workers, many of whom live in poverty. Indeed, the division between Saudi national and foreigners is the most pronounced social distinction in the kingdom.

Foreign workers are required to have contracts for their specific positions, and employers have the power to decide whether a worker can move to another job position (Struyk 2005, 144). The relationship between the employer and the employee is institutionalized via formal sponsorship, known in Arabic as the *kafala* system (Longva 1997). A person from outside of the Gulf Cooperation Council (GCC) states is legally required to have a *kafeel* (sponsor or employer) in order to gain access to employment or be permitted a residence permit *(iqama)* in any of the GCC states. The *kafeel* and the employee are required to sign a work contract that declares that the employee works for the employer and covers the terms of the work contract. The *kafeel* often retains the employees' passports, which further strengthens the power he or she wields over the workers (Shadid, Spaan, and Speckman 1990).

Many migrants are housed in worker camps or informally in shops or additional rooms within employer homes. Virtually no foreigners own their own homes in Riyadh, nor are they permitted to own property, a stipulation that effectively excludes them from the local landed class. Saudi nationals, by comparison, have high rates (56 percent) of home ownership in Riyadh (Struyk 2005).

In addition to differentiating between citizens and noncitizens, the Saudi state has supported a number of policies that segregate women from men across the kingdom. The government restricts women's independent mobility through laws that forbid women to drive or travel alone without written permission from a *muhrim* (male relative). The *mutawaa'in,* the officials representing the state's Committee for the Promotion of Virtue and the Prevention of Vice (Hai'at al-amr bi al-ma'ruf wa al-nahia 'an al-munkar), are charged with upholding the laws requiring that women wear the *hijab* and travel accompanied by a male relative (Doumato 2000). Although these laws are not equally strictly upheld on an everyday basis in all neighborhoods of Riyadh, they do intensify the isolation and immobility of women in general, and female domestic workers in particular. Among immigrant workers, migrant domestic workers are particularly vulnerable because they are not protected by any labor laws in Saudi Arabia, and are thus left particularly dependent on their employers (Atiyyah 1990). They are required to live with their employers, who then determine unilaterally the employees' living and working conditions.

INDONESIAN DOMESTIC WORKERS IN SAUDI ARABIA, 1983–2006

The Indonesian government began formally permitting recruitment agents from Middle Eastern countries to enlist Indonesian nationals for overseas work in 1983. The state's hope was that, like the model of overseas contract work promoted by the Philippines, overseas employment could alleviate unemployment and contribute to the national economy through remittances (K. Robinson 1991). In the first year of the program, Indonesia placed 47,000 migrant workers in Saudi Arabia. Potential migrants in Indonesia enthusiastically embraced the opportunity to work in Saudi Arabia both in order to escape unemployment and also because they were attracted to promises of incomes five to fifteen times higher than what they would earn in Indonesia. Between 1989 and 1994, Saudi Arabia was the single largest national recipient of Indonesian overseas workers, with 59 percent of all documented overseas Indonesian workers contracted to work there (Hugo 1995, 280). In 1983, Pakistan and Bangladesh banned the out-migration of women workers (Chin 1998, 102), thereby increasing the demand for workers from other countries. In addition, the inter-Arab tensions associated with the Gulf War underpinned a shift away from hiring domestic workers from neighboring Arab countries and toward hiring Southeast Asian laborers (Gamburd 2000, 33–34).

The number of Indonesian-Saudi female migrants grew quickly to a total of 186,052 between 1984 and 1989, and then rose again from 342,048 between 1989 and 1994 to 507,113 in the 1994–1999 period. Most recently, between 1999 and 2004, women from Indonesia working in the informal sector rose to 844,118 (Hugo 2005, 60; Depnaker 2006). No other country has received so many migrants from Indonesia. Women make up the distinct majority of Indonesian migrants to Saudi Arabia, with a sex ratio ranging from 8.5 women to 1 man between 1994 and 1999, and rising as high as 20.2 women to 1 man between 1984 to 1989 (Hugo 2005, 60). Migrant workers have also sent substantial remittances back to their countries of origin. Between 2001 and 2004, the Indonesian government reported receiving almost US$3 billion in remittances (Depnaker 2006). Because migrants commonly hide earnings from the government, actual incomes earned and contributed are certainly higher than the formal estimates. From migrants' perspectives, the incomes possible in Saudi Arabia serve as a strong pull factor. Rianto Adi found that households in West Java with overseas migrants enjoyed average household incomes that were twice as high as households without migrants (1995, 226).

Actual numbers of migrants are also higher than the formal state figures, because many migrants travel without work visas. Migrants commonly enter the country on *hajj* or *umrah* visas, intended for travelers making religious pilgrimages, and then stay beyond the allotted time and seek work. Hugo writes that "undocumented migrants certainly outnumber documented migrants" abroad (2002, 159; see also Spaan 1999; Jones 2000), though there are probably fewer undocumented migrants in Saudi Arabia than other countries where the undocumented are less penalized. Migrants without work visas are particularly vulnerable to abuse, given their illegal status in the country. Employers who know that a migrant is in the country without a work visa can threaten to report the migrant to the police for any reason, and therefore wield exceptional power over undocumented migrant employees. If arrested, undocumented workers are imprisoned and deported.

Neither the Indonesian nor the Saudi government has provided protection to domestic workers. Domestic service jobs are unregulated in Saudi Arabia, such that even those domestic workers who have work visas or contracts do not have an institutionalized right to legal employee protections (Huang and Yeoh 1996). Domestic workers are additionally vulnerable because their work takes place within the home, defined by the state as the "private" sphere. Indonesian domestic workers have faced numerous abuses in Saudi Arabia. Migrants are commonly sexually abused, overworked, underpaid, and often forbidden to leave their employers' domiciles (K. Robinson 2000, 255). There are also high suicide rates reported and deaths from unknown causes. Various public officials have called for a ban on the export of Indonesian women as low-skilled laborers (Spaan 1999), and others have made motions for more rigorous regulation and monitoring of recruitment agencies. Despite widespread popular and government pressure to stop sending women overseas, the export of female domestic laborers continues to dominate the official outflow of migrants from Indonesia (Depnaker 2006).

REMEMBERING RIYADH: MIGRANTS' NARRATIONS
OF HOME AND WORK SPACE

In order to better understand Indonesian women's migration, I have employed multiple methods over a series of return fieldwork visits over the course of the past decade. I began focused fieldwork in West Java and South Sulawesi in 1994 through 1995, during which time I lived in major female migrant-receiving destinations and interviewed migrants about gendered mobility and economic development. I returned to carry out follow-up fieldwork in 1998 to examine the "Asian economic crisis" and the gender politics of labor organizing. In 2000, I carried out a survey (total number of 185 for two villages in West Java, based on random sampling via village registers), which found growing numbers of women migrating abroad on contracts as domestic workers. I then returned to reinterview a subsample of the overseas workers in 2002, and in 2004, I spent two months, mostly in Jakarta, interviewing government officials and nongovernmental organizations working on migrant women's rights. In the paragraphs that follow, I illustrate the overall findings of this work with excerpts and observations developed over the course of this long-term project.

Most migrant households in Rancaekek are very low-income. The families of migrants subsist primarily on their farming incomes and produce, which some subsidize with factory wages or a household member's income earned in the urban informal sector. Of the 185 respondents interviewed in 2000, all viewed overseas migration as a *necessary* strategy for increasing household income rather than one among many livelihood possibilities. Each possible destination held its particular appeal, but Saudi Arabia was especially attractive to migrants because of its status as the holy land of Islam and the possibility of earning relatively large earnings (Silvey 2005).[2]

However, in contrast to their hopes, migrants recalled their time in Riyadh primarily in terms of their relationships with employers and the spaces of the homes in which they worked. Most migrant workers spent very little time outside of their employers' homes, and few had recollections of the city streets other than their initial travel from the airport. A small number of migrants had employers who accompanied them on occasional trips outside of the home, and they remembered the opulence of the shopping malls in Riyadh. Overall, migrants' impressions of the city reflected the overt spatial constraints that they faced as foreign workers and as women, as well as their internalized senses of exclusion and alienation. Unlike domestic workers in Singapore and Hong Kong who congregate in parks or city squares with their conationals on days when they are free from work, in Saudi Arabia domestic workers remain largely isolated in the homes of their employers.

Yet in some cases, migrants found ways to create spaces of belonging for themselves in relation to the larger imagined *umma,* or "community

2. For further discussion of the role of religion in marketing Saudi Arabia as a destination site, see Silvey 2005.

of all Muslims." Their capacity to imagine themselves out of the city of Riyadh, and into the geographically abstract space of the *umma,* served to both sustain them spiritually and also, ironically, to keep them subordinate to their Saudi employers in their places of employment.

When interviewed about their migration experiences in Saudi Arabia, most migrants emphasized the extreme heat and their lack of mobility in the country. Mariati, who was twenty-seven when she migrated, told a common story:

> My sponsor picked me up at the airport in Riyadh and drove me to my employer's house. It was the first time I had seen the desert. The traffic jams were not as bad as those I had seen in Jakarta, but the heat on the walk from the airport to the car was unbearable. I thanked God for the air-conditioned car, and I prayed that I'd never have to walk anywhere in the middle of the day because I didn't think I'd be able to stand it. When we arrived at my employer's home, my boss showed me the small washroom in the back of the house where I was expected to sleep. For two years I never left the house, not even to go to the grocery store. That is my memory of Riyadh: the walls of that house were my world.

Mariati's view of the city was confined to the home of her employer where she worked long hours and was forbidden to leave.

Migrants spoke of their heavy workloads as central to their memories of the city. Ita, a thirty-one-year-old migrant from West Java, put it this way: "I try not to remember my time in Saudi because I was so exhausted from working there for so long. Even though my contract stated that I would work eight hours per day, in fact I worked twelve hour days. I began preparing the morning meal and washing clothes before dawn and was still cleaning dishes after the children went to bed. I became so fatigued that it was hard for me to move my body." Such exhaustion and long work hours were not unique to migrants who had worked in Saudi Arabia, but they were characteristic of the stories people told about work abroad.

When migrants were able to imagine escaping the confinement of their employers' homes, they recalled a generalized fear of the streets of Riyadh. Their fear took several forms. Most basically, migrant domestic workers were afraid of being lost if they tried to navigate the streets on their own. As one return migrant, Siri, put it, "I only speak a few words of Arabic. So, if I'd lost my way, I couldn't have asked anyone for help. I couldn't read a map in Arabic." In addition to fear of being lost, women spoke of their gender-specific fears. As Siri said, "If a woman goes out alone in Riyadh, she will be stopped by the police. I heard terrible stories from my friends about what the police do to women in prison. People will think you are a prostitute [if you are a woman out alone], and you might be arrested." She was thus disciplined by both the formal regulations against women's independent travel as well as her fears of abuse by police and her anxiety about the social stigma that might accompany her if she were to leave the home.

Migrants also feared the vulnerability associated with poverty. Siri explained, "I didn't have any money because my employer was holding my pay until the end of my contract. So, I couldn't have even paid for transportation to the embassy or the airport. How would I have fed myself if I'd left the house? Where would I have slept?" Given her situation, she said she felt safer staying at home. Like Siri, Indonesian migrant domestic workers in Riyadh are constrained by the gendered, class-based, and racialized inequalities that affect their mobility on the streets of the city.

Migrant women's Muslim faith helped them in their efforts to cope with isolation, homesickness, workloads, and abuse. All migrants from West Java who had worked in Saudi Arabia were professed Muslims, and their selection of Saudi Arabia as a destination had been influenced, in part, by their interest in visiting the holy land of Islam (Silvey 2005). Returned migrants claimed to have prayed five times a day and to have felt supported by their employers in this practice. As one returnee, Riyani, who was thirty-five years old put it, "I could not have survived without prayer. It gave me strength to continue to work. It helped me accept my fate. I prayed every time the family prayed, and I was grateful to them for allowing me to do it." Another returnee, Tati, twenty-four years old, said that the regular calls to prayer that echoed from loudspeakers from all over the city helped her to feel at home: "When the mosques would echo the call to prayer, starting early in the day, they reminded me that Allah is with me everywhere." Such faith in Allah's universal presence helped migrants manage their sense of dislocation.

Migrants also invoked the *umma,* the "imagined community of Muslims at large," "'the nation of Islam,' 'the totality of all Muslims,' 'irrespective of place or origin,'" in their efforts to make Riyadh feel more like home
(Grillo 2004, 866, 867). Tati said, "I've come to work here with people of
the same religion, because we share faith. All overseas workers long for
their homes, but here we are part of the *umma.*" For some migrants, the
abstract vision of a transnational "community" of Muslims was solidified
through the holy *hajj* pilgrimage to Mecca. Eight percent of migrants flew
into Riyadh on *hajj* visas rather than work visas and overstayed their visas
in order to work, though two who entered on regular contracts were able
to convince their employers to permit them to make the pilgrimage after the
conclusion of their contracts (see also Diedrich 2005).[3]

Migrants reported that their religious observances were respected
because they were shared by their employers, though they also perceived
Indonesian Islam as religiously subordinate to Saudi Islam. Ita, who was
thirty-eight years old, said: "In Riyadh, my boss was Muslim, and so the
household did not have dogs and I did not have to prepare pork for the family to eat. I was able to remain true to my religion there. My religious training was strengthened there, as I learned the correct way to read the Koran,
and as I learned that my religious training in Indonesia had been poor."
Migrants were attracted to Saudi Arabia because of its status as the home
and center of Islam. Yet Indonesian workers' social subordination was
perpetuated through the international religious hierarchy that positioned
Saudi Islam as superior to, and more authentic than, Indonesian Islam.
"We belonged to the same religion," said Ita in reference to her employers,
"but they did not see us as equals even in our religious training."

Overall, domestic workers in Saudi Arabia are extremely socially and
spatially segregated. Most respondents said little to nothing about the city,
because most had experienced only the homes of their employers during
their sojourns abroad. Their coping strategies were based on faith and collective imaginings of a shared *umma* rather than any shared experienced
with coethnic workers in Riyadh. Immigrant women's spatial mobility and
social interaction were extremely limited as a result of strict immigration

3. These data are based on the author's survey of 185 migrants.

controls, norms of female sequestration, and the enforced immobility placed on them as domestic workers.

CONCLUSION

Women are located in gender-specific social spaces within cities, and immigrants face multiple exclusions from Riyadh's urban social fabric. Indonesian female domestic workers are incorporated into Riyadh's temporary labor force as contract workers, yet they, like other migrants to Saudi Arabia, remain excluded from the privileges of citizenship and from the kingdom's public, social, and political life. The state-supported regulations on women's independent mobility, the lack of labor regulations for the domestic sphere, and the policies that keep migrants dependent on the goodwill of their employers combine to marginalize foreign domestic workers in Riyadh and elsewhere in the kingdom. Riyadh as a gateway city permits labor in the domestic spaces and labor pools of the city, but controls against immigrant workers' further social integration.

Indonesian migrant-rights nongovernmental organizations are working to improve the treatment of overseas migrant workers. They are "demanding moral guarantees of biological welfare, not rights of citizenship for migrant workers as members of a global humanity" (Ong 2006, 215). Activists frame their arguments in terms of individual migrants' rights to physical protection and freedom from abuse and overwork, but they do not pressure receiving states to grant migrants the rights of citizenship. In limiting the substance of their claims, nongovernmental organizations challenge neither the interests of the Indonesian state in profiting from overseas workers' remittances nor the Saudi state in its exploitation of the foreign guest-worker labor force.

The exclusionary character of Riyadh's urban fabric for Indonesian women reveals the limits to transnational labor migration. Though migrants travel transnationally, they are disallowed from creating and maintaining the multistranded social ties across national boundaries that have come to define transnationality. Moreover, within Saudi Arabia, they are restricted from access to the social and public life that characterizes overseas communities in other major destinations of transnational migrants. Their labor is crucial for the social reproduction of the Saudi economy, yet they have no hope of citizenship rights or occupational mobility. They reside in the intimate domestic spaces of their employers, yet they remain excluded from the family's activities and forms of exchange. As women, they are excluded from the streets of the city, and as Indonesians abroad they are stigmatized and denied membership in the social and political life of the nation. As an immigrant gateway city, Riyadh works to both funnel migrants into the country as domestic laborers and simultaneously restrict their mobility almost entirely to domestic spaces. Examining such tensions inherent in the production of the immigrant gateway from the perspectives of foreign female domestic workers provides insight into the interdependencies tying together global accelerations of transnational labor migration and local intensifications of limitations on mobility.

13

Immigrants and Natives in Tel Aviv

What's the Difference?

DAVID BARTRAM

The United States is often described as the quintessential "land of immigration." But if we look at the proportion of immigrants in the total population,
then Israel is more deserving of such a title. At present, the vast majority
of Americans are native-born (88 percent); this point is true even of a significant proportion of American ethnic minorities (and not just blacks). In
Israel, by contrast, the foreign-born constitute more than half of the population, and many of those immigrants are recent arrivals: immigrants who
have arrived since 1989 constitute 20 percent of the population. Immigration rates have decreased in recent years, and it seems unlikely that there
will ever again be inflows on the scale of the 1990s. But the impact of those
inflows will be felt for decades to come, especially because of how their
composition differs from the makeup of previous immigration waves.

   A substantial proportion of immigrants settle in Tel Aviv (especially
the recently arrived noncitizen foreign workers).[1] Tel Aviv is also Israel's
major metropolis, home to almost one-third of the country's population
(depending on how one draws the boundaries) and to its primary institutions (even some major government ministries). It is a global city, not on the
scale of New York or London, but it is a key player in some of the activities that constitute the global economy, such as technological innovation

---

1. As discussed below, noncitizen foreign workers are non-Jews imported on temporary
work visas, from countries such as Thailand, Romania, and the Philippines.

and financial and producer services. It also contains an impressive range of ethnic diversity, with immigrants from many sending countries. Some of these immigrants—the noncitizen foreign workers, in particular—are heavily concentrated in certain neighborhoods.

Is Tel Aviv, therefore, an immigrant gateway in the way that term is applied to cities like London and New York? On the surface, the answer is indisputably yes. But to describe Tel Aviv as an immigrant gateway (or Israel as an immigration country) constitutes a "chutzpah." In a mainstream (Zionist) Israeli perspective, there are no immigrants in the normal sense of the term, only Jews returning to their homeland. To be an immigrant, one must first be a foreigner—but if Israel is the Jewish homeland, Jews there cannot really be foreign. Indeed, in the dominant version of Israeli history, the problem that Israel was created to solve was the fact that Jews were foreigners everywhere else. And although Israel has non-citizen (non-Jewish) foreign workers, they are hardly immigrants either: rather, they are temporary residents, an aberration that will be resolved when (not if) they return home. Not to coin a phrase, but Israel is not an immigration country.

There are indeed peculiarities here that might complicate efforts to apply migration scholars' vocabulary to the Israeli case, and they are the focus of the first part of this chapter, which challenges often unexamined assumptions about key terms and definitions used by migration scholars. If Tel Aviv is an immigrant gateway, it has in some respects been an ambiguous one, particularly because of the reception afforded to Jewish immigrants.

But there have been significant changes in the nature of immigration to Israel in recent years, and the result is that those peculiarities no longer amount to a significant difference between Israel and other countries, and therefore between Tel Aviv and, say, Los Angeles or Toronto. If anything, a perspective denying the existence of immigration exacerbates certain features of what we might call the immigration problem in Israel, insofar as it highlights and reinforces the foreignness of immigrants.

In other words, Israel has in certain key respects become a normal immigration country, with Tel Aviv functioning as a typical immigrant gateway. In some ways, it is a strange shift in direction for the world's only "Jewish state," a description that one might assume necessarily depends on the maintenance of a high degree of ethnic closure. On the other hand, with hindsight it becomes clear that Israel was always going to have difficulty resisting the forces of globalization (Shalev 1999), which have helped produce new migration flows to previously unaffected regions.[2] With immigration comes a familiar set of challenges, particularly for Tel Aviv, and the purpose of this chapter is to describe how those challenges are being addressed in a context that might seem to embody some significant unfavorable conditions—unfavorable precisely because hegemonic notions of what Israel is make it difficult to think about immigrants in ways that incorporate certain key lessons that have emerged from the experience of other immigration countries. The two groups to be discussed here are the non-Jewish component of the Russian immigrants who began entering in large numbers in 1989 and the foreign workers who have arrived from all over the world beginning in 1993.[3]

IMMIGRATION TO ISRAEL: HISTORY AND CONCEPTS

There is a dimension of Israel's official ideology that will strike many readers as familiar yet perhaps ironic and puzzling: Israel is "not an immigration country" (Rosenhek 1999). Most Israelis—with the significant exception of the country's Palestinian citizens—are either immigrants or the descendants of quite recent immigrants. Instead of dismissing this contention out of hand, however, I propose to consider it on its own terms, at least for the purpose of trying to learn something about the more recent immigration history of Israel.

If Israel is officially not an immigration country, then what is it? Officially, of course, it is the Jewish state, the Jewish homeland. Jews from abroad who move to Israel, then, do not immigrate—instead, they "return"

---

2. In contrast to some scholars, I do not take the view that globalization makes immigration inevitable or ubiquitous. Several countries, including Japan and Finland, remain relatively untouched by immigration. See Bartram 2000, 2005b.

3. Another group that could be discussed are the Ethiopians, whose Jewishness is considered doubtful by some. I do not treat them here because their numbers are much smaller, and because of lack of space and expertise.

(see Joppke 2005 for an incisive analysis of this point and ethnic migration more generally). The institutional foundation of this idea is the Law of Return, according to which any Jew has the right to enter Israel without restriction and acquire immediate citizenship (and some substantial resources designed to facilitate settlement and integration).[4] Other commonly used terms embody this perspective: in particular, in place of immigration *(hagirah)*, Israelis speak of *aliyah,* meaning ascent (see Shuval 1998). The word has distinct religious connotations: in a synagogue service that includes a reading from the Torah, members of the congregation are invited for "an *aliyah,*" wherein one ascends to a raised platform (the *bimah*) and recites a blessing before and after the reading. Likewise with *olim* (the word applied to new immigrants, derived from the same "roots" as *aliyah*): they are ascending to a holy place (the "Holy Land," after all). Emigration *(yeridah,* literally, descent), unsurprisingly, carries strongly negative connotations, though the stigma attached to emigrants has declined in recent years (Gold 2002). The late Prime Minister Yitzhak Rabin once referred to emigrants in terms variously translated as "the lowliest of parasites" and "gutless scum."

As this use of language implies, Jewish immigrants in Israel are perceived and treated differently from immigrants in many other contexts. Although many countries welcome and encourage immigration, most immigrants are nonetheless definitively *foreign,* at least upon arrival. In Israel, Jewish immigrants are, to a significant extent, viewed as *compatriots* from the moment they arrive and declare their intention to settle—or even before, as residents of the diaspora. This perspective is embodied in the granting of instant citizenship; it is also apparent in the attitudes of veteran (Jewish) Israelis, most of whom do not question the notion that new Jewish immigrants genuinely *belong* in Israel. Though newcomers are understood to be different in some respects (culture, language, and so on) as a result of having lived in other places, new Jewish immigrants typically begin life in Israel with the sense that they share a great deal with the

---

4. As frequently noted, the Law of Return is therefore intimately connected with the thorny question of "Who is a Jew?" Whereas we will discuss the genealogical aspects of this question, it also relates to conversion, an issue well beyond the scope of this paper.

existing population—something that immigrants in other settings generally must *achieve*. To this extent, new Jewish immigrants in Israel are less foreign than immigrants in other contexts.

Foreignness is an essential component of any discussion of international migration. This point is sometimes overlooked, even in scholarly discussions. It is sometimes assumed that "immigrants" are equivalent to "foreign-born" individuals. This equation makes for simpler measurement and data collection, but it might fail to capture what is truly interesting and important about international migration. The term refers to more than simple geographic relocation: inter*national* migration is inescapably bound up with questions of belonging, of membership in a nation (see, for example, Castles and Miller 1998). This point is an empirical one, not a normative one. It is reinforced by the reasonable claim that if the membership of new immigrants were not a significant and sometimes even contentious issue, then the entire question would have much less political salience (and probably attract less scholarly interest as well).

It is also worth repeating that most Jews in Israel are either themselves immigrants or descendants of recent immigrants: being an immigrant does not by itself make one terribly different from other Jewish Israelis. The onset of Zionist immigration to Palestine is generally dated to the 1880s. Prior to that decade, Palestine was home to a small number of Jews—fewer than 30,000 (approximately 6 percent of the total population; see Schölch 1985). When Israel became an independent country in 1948, the Jewish population was approximately 700,000—most of whom were immigrants. This figure was doubled by 1951, mainly via the immigration of Sephardic Jews who left (and in some cases were expelled from) Arab countries. In other words, very few Israeli Jews can trace their family's history in Israel-Palestine back more than just a couple of generations: immigration is a part of most family histories.

As such, this history is constitutive of Israeli identity. Modern Israel is seen as the product of Jews' return to their ancient homeland. This language is important: it bears emphasizing that Israel is "home" for many Jews, even for some Jews who do not live there. When Jews move to Israel, then, their social position as "immigrants" is different in certain respects from the social position of immigrants in most other contexts. Specifically,

Jewish immigrants can make a claim of "belonging" in Israel to a degree that probably exceeds the weight of that sort of claim by immigrants in other countries. This is not to say that integration of Jewish immigrants is unproblematic or even that their presence is accepted without resentment by more veteran Israelis. Moreover, some immigrants, from North America in particular, decide rather quickly that they don't feel they belong there and so return to their countries of origin. But this sense of belonging, embodied as it is in the substantial rights and benefits accorded to new immigrants, means that immigration has posed less of a challenge to identity in Israel than it does in many other contexts. Sephardic Jews (from North Africa, in particular) might feel they were treated poorly by the Ashkenazi elite in the 1950s and that they still suffer the consequences of chauvinism and economic marginalization—but no one disputes that Sephardic Jews are as Israeli as the Ashkenazis. Being immigrants of more recent entry simply doesn't matter in this regard.

These points indicate that there is some merit in the Israeli view by which Jewish immigrants are not really immigrants in the normal sense. This perspective contains ideological components that migration scholars (among others) might well find unhelpful. Nonetheless, the perspective cannot be dismissed simply because it can be identified as ideological. On the contrary: the ideology has significant concrete impacts, as described above. The point should not be overstated: *olim* are immigrants to some degree and do resemble immigrants elsewhere to some degree. But there are some important differences.

The key fact for this chapter, however, is that things have changed significantly in recent years. The discussion to this point implies that, to some degree, describing Israel as an immigration country (particularly in the emphatic language I used at the beginning of this paper) is not quite right.[5] But recently Israel's experience with immigration has taken a dra-

---

5. There is another reason for this position, which will be only mentioned here (rather than explored in depth) because of space limitations. Newcomers who can definitively be described as foreign are immigrants—but for how long? When (if ever) does one stop being an immigrant? It violates common sense to describe as an immigrant someone who moved to Israel in the 1950s. Such persons are universally described in Israel as "veterans"—the

matic turn—by virtue of the fact that, for the first time, a significant number of people entering and settling in the country are not Jewish. It is in this context that it begins to make undisputed sense to think of Tel Aviv as an immigrant gateway, as many non-Jewish immigrants make up the resident population of Tel Aviv.

RUSSIAN IMMIGRANTS, JEWISH AND NON-JEWISH

The largest group of immigrants in Israel today is from the former Soviet Union (commonly referred to as Russians, even if many are from other countries such as Ukraine, in which case one of their primary languages is indeed Russian). Most people who have immigrated from these countries entered and gained citizenship under the Law of Return.[6] As such, they are ostensibly not different from the vast majority of the rest of Israeli Jews.[7] In principle, the more recent arrival of Russians is merely a continuation of earlier trends. If Israeli society—the dominant Jewish population component, in particular—is the product of continual immigration, then the immigration of another group poses no more of a challenge to the existing society than did the immigration of previous groups.

In practice, however, things are not so straightforward: the immigration of Russians in the 1990s constitutes a decisive break with the previous immigration history of Israel. Israeli history prior to 1989 might be different from the history of most other receiving countries,[8] but in the 1990s

---

opposite of a new immigrant *(vatik* vs. *oleh)*. The foreign-born proportion of the Israeli population is quite high, but the proportion who are immigrants is reasonably asserted to be lower.

6. There are others who could not establish Jewish links and belong instead to the foreign-worker category, as discussed below.

7. They are, of course, different from another important group of Israelis: the Arab-Palestinian citizens of Israel, most of whom have no recent history of immigration (whatever Alan Dershowitz might say).

8. Christian Joppke (2005) compares Israel to Germany's experience with the *Aussiedler* (returnees) but properly notes the difference in the scale of the phenomenon. One might also discuss Australian migration to Britain and the more recent return of Irish and Finnish emigrants.

Israel began to be marked by strong similarities to other immigration countries. The immigration of Russians poses a challenge to Israeli identity to a much greater degree than did previous immigration waves.

This challenge emerges from the fact that a substantial portion—approximately 30 percent—of Russian immigrants are not Jewish. Non-Jewish Russians have entered Israel under the Law of Return by virtue of having a close Jewish relative; the Law of Return, as amended in 1970, grants this right to anyone with a Jewish spouse, parent, or grandparent. Of course, if the maternal grandmother is Jewish, then the grandchild is Jewish, according to religious law—but the Law of Return does not distinguish between matrilineal and patrilineal descent.[9] The result is that there are approximately 300,000 Russian immigrants in Israel who are not recognized as Jewish by the religious authorities (out of the almost 1 million Russians who arrived in the 1990s); some of them consider themselves Jewish (and were treated as such in the USSR and Russia), whereas others are active Christians. This group alone amounts to more than 4 percent of the Israeli population, and there are widespread predictions that it will continue to grow, perhaps to 400,000 by 2020 (*HaAretz*, December 1, 2005). Figure 13.1 depicts the immigrant population of Tel Aviv; most of those individuals in the category "from Europe or America" are "Russian" immigrants, particularly the non-Jews.

In certain respects, this population has been welcomed as a way of coping with what is often referred to as the "demographic problem"—the fact that the birthrate of Arab and Palestinian citizens is higher than the birthrate of the Jews and therefore portends a diminished Jewish majority, with attendant political consequences in a democratic context.[10] Russian immigrants, whether religiously Jewish or not, are counted as part of the Jewish population group: the Statistical Abstract of Israel makes a major distinction between "Jews and others" and "Arabs." This point might be surprising: in the Israeli context, one might expect population figures to

9. In the United States, patrilineal descent is recognized by Reform Jews—but in Israel the only religious authorities that matter recognize matrilineal descent only.

10. See Ghanem, Rouhana, and Yiftachel 1998 for a critique of claims about Israel's democratic nature, and Gavison 1999 for a response.

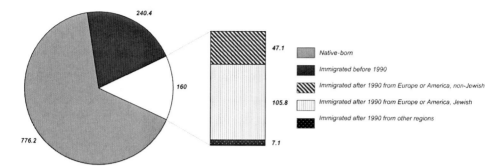

Fig. 13.1. Composition of Tel Aviv district population (in thousands). *Source:* Israel Central Bureau of Statistics.

refer to Jews and non-Jews. In some ways, however, it makes sense: many non-Jews are family members of Jews and certainly identify more closely with Jews than with Arabs. On a political level, the logic is clear: the government prefers to maximize the "Jewish" component of the population and to minimize the Arab component (on these grounds, Ian Lustick [1999] cleverly refers to "Israel as a non-Arab state"). Israeli Jewish political leaders are keen to integrate the Russians at least for this purpose.

But in other respects, the presence of non-Jewish immigrants is experienced as unnerving or even provocative by some veteran Israelis. Churches have proliferated in recent years. There have always been churches, as part of the Arab population is Christian, but churches now appear in wholly "Jewish" (that is, non-Arab) areas. Moreover, the ambiguous personal status of non-Jewish Russians means that they cannot legally get married in Israel. The problem is self-perpetuating, as there are many long-term relationships, leading to family formation, between non-Jewish Russians and Jews (mainly of Russian background themselves), so that, if the woman is not Jewish, the children will carry ambiguous status as well. From the point of view of firmly religious Jews, the entire Russian population is considered suspect—for instance, definitively unsuitable as prospective marriage partners.

Indeed, it is common in Israel to think of the Russians as a separate group, without distinguishing between Jews and non-Jews (as against the alternative of considering Jewish Russians as akin to other Jewish Israelis).

Russians are a large, distinct ethnic group in Israel (Al-Haj 2004): they have their own cultural institutions and media, they consider it important to transmit their distinct culture (including language) to their children, and they live in patterns of high residential segregation. In this regard they are quite different from the Russians who immigrated to Israel from the Soviet Union in the 1970s. These factors lead to the conclusion that the impact of the non-Jewish Russians is greater than their numbers alone would suggest: they constitute just over 4 percent of the population, but the Russians as a whole are more than 12 percent, and in some respects being Russian matters more than being Jewish.

Prior to the 1990s, it would have been possible to describe Israel as an immigration country—but doing so would have been more than a bit simplistic, insofar as it implies that Israel was similar to other immigration countries. Only in the 1990s did Israel become a destination for immigration in the more generic sense of the term. Some implications of that fact are discussed below.

FOREIGN WORKERS AND THE NEW UNDERCLASS

In the past decade, Israel has become even more "normal" as an immigration country, with the entry of hundreds of thousands of foreign workers of a very traditional type (Bartram 1998, 2005a). Workers were recruited at first to replace Palestinians from the Occupied Territories, who were prevented from entering Israel by border closures intended to stop the suicide bombings of the mid-1990s. The phenomenon then transcended a mere replacement function, as the numbers went well beyond the previous employment of Palestinians and began to touch sectors in which Palestinians had never been employed (such as caring for elderly relatives). In addition, the border closures affecting Palestinians were eventually relaxed, so that foreign workers should be considered a substantial net addition to the labor force and not simply replacements. According to official estimates, in 2002 there were more than 225,000 foreign workers in Israel, and more than half did not have legal status (Bar-Tsuri 2003). Primary sectors of employment (in addition to care work) are construction and agriculture, though not manufacturing (see table 13.1). Originally, workers came primarily from three

TABLE 13.1

FOREIGN WORKERS IN ISRAEL

	Total	Agriculture	Construction	Hotels and restaurants	Health services[a]	Other[b]
1994	30.5	6.5	5.6	2.9	1.5	14.0
1995	59.9	13.1	15.5	3.8	2.1	25.4
1996	79.8	17.0	29.3	4.4	2.8	26.2
1997	83.0	18.5	30.7	4.6	3.8	25.4
1998	79.3	20.1	29.4	4.4	5.2	20.2
1999	76.5	20.4	25.0	4.5	5.8	20.8
2000	78.0	20.6	23.4	4.9	7.3	21.8
2001	88.8	21.9	29.7	4.4	9.3	23.5
2002	93.0	22.8	29.8	3.8	10.6	26.1
2003	72.3	23.7	16.7	2.4	11.1	18.5
2004	64.0	24.5	11.2	2.4	13.0	12.9

Source: Israel Central Bureau of Statistics 1994-2004.
Note: Figures are in thousands. These official data do not capture the large number of undocumented workers.
[a] Includes home-care services (for example, for the elderly). However, such workers are not included in these figures if they are insured by the employer.
[b] Most in this category are assumed to be working in construction, via employment agency intermediaries.

countries (Romania, Thailand, and the Philippines), but more recently the origins have become much more diverse, with workers coming from Colombia, Nigeria, and China, among many others.

As noted above, foreign workers are generally not described as immigrants in Israel. Most Israelis would find it difficult to imagine that noncitizen foreign workers will ever be granted an official status that allows them to remain in Israel in the long term. This prospect would seem to violate deeply the understanding most Jewish Israelis have concerning Israel as a Jewish state. Even without this population, many Israelis fear the "demographic problem." Though only roughly 3 percent of the population, foreign workers would appear to exacerbate that concern. Beyond the numbers, however, non-Jewish foreigners simply do not "belong": from a traditional Zionist perspective, the presence of Arabs in Israel is unfortunate but unavoidable, given that their presence mostly predated the presence of most Jews—but the notion that other non-Jews (particularly individuals who have no Jewish family connections, unlike the Russians) would come to form a significant part of the population is quite disturbing for many Jewish Israelis.

This point is reinforced by a government decision in June 2005 that grants Israeli citizenship to the children of foreign workers, but only under very restrictive conditions. Citizenship is now available to children ages ten and above who were born in Israel and whose parents entered the country legally (*HaAretz,* November 1, 2005). The number of children eligible under these provisions is very small, probably well below 1,000 and thus small as a proportion of the total as well. In other words, the government recognizes that it is impossible not to address the question, but it is addressing it in a way that mostly confirms existing (highly restrictionist) principles. Here, the exception truly proves the rule—and confirms the exclusion of the workers themselves as well.

But the failure to see possibilities for settlement and integration is perhaps simply an indication that Israel is at an earlier point on the learning curve in relation to this issue. In a comparative perspective, there is no reason to think that Israel's version of this problem is unique. It seems likely that the implausibility of integrating foreign workers was just as pronounced in West Germany in the 1970s, though of course this sort of thing would be difficult to measure.

Many foreign workers in Israel want to remain (others are focused on achieving an income or savings target and do return home voluntarily, though the supply is generally replenished by new entrants). Some believe they can achieve a secure permanent status; they certainly believe they deserve such a status, despite not being Jewish. This belief is particularly true of some strongly religious Christians: members of evangelical churches in Tel Aviv have developed a version of Christian Zionism that combines right-wing political beliefs with the use of Jewish ritual elements in religious services, even to the point of wearing *kippot* (skullcaps) and *tallitot* (prayer shawls) (Raijman and Kemp 2004). In their eyes, these beliefs and practices make them Israeli; some of South American origin go so far as to identify themselves as descendants of Marranos (Jews who were forced to convert to Christianity during the Spanish Inquisition but who continued to practice Judaism in private). As such, they believe they are entitled to stay in Israel under the Law of Return.

The factual and legal validity of these claims is, of course, doubtful, and there are no signs that they carry any weight whatsoever with Israeli authorities such as the Interior Ministry. But there are features of Israeli politics that might work in their favor. As described above, because so many of the Russian immigrants who entered under the Law of Return in the 1990s were non-Jewish, official Israeli population statistics refer to two main categories: "Jews and others" and "Arabs." If one counts Russian Christians (that is, those immigrants with Jewish family members) as part of the "Jewish" group, it is perhaps only a small step to counting strongly Zionist South American Christians as part of the "Jewish" group as well—especially when we keep in mind that they are "non-Arabs." In other words, they and perhaps other foreign workers as well might come to be viewed as useful recruits in the demographic war.

Moreover, it is difficult to imagine that the constellation of political interests that brought foreign workers to Israel in the first place will change sufficiently to alter government policy. Successive governments have made very public pronouncements to the effect that permit quotas for employing foreigners will be minimized and workers will be deported. Deportations have indeed taken place—and senior government figures have gleefully claimed that, as an important side effect, the resulting climate of fear has led many others to leave "voluntarily." But it would be difficult to argue that stocks have been reduced at a rate exceeding what would have occurred simply as a result of economic recession (a decline in construction activity, in particular). Moreover, although the government declared a moratorium on allocating new permits to construction employers in 2002, it then resumed allowing new workers to be imported (*HaAretz*, October 26, 2005). (In practice, employers found ways to circumvent the ostensible ban all along.) The interests of the employers have not changed—nor has the institutional context that enables them to transform their interests into policy. There is no reason to think that Israel will succeed (where so many others have failed) in ridding itself of this type of immigrant.

In short, it seems highly likely that foreign workers will be a significant presence in Israel for many years to come. Foreign workers in Israel are not a temporary aberration; rather, they are immigrants. The word carries a sense of permanence appropriate to the case: we might recall Philip Martin's "iron law of labor immigration: there is nothing more permanent than temporary workers" (1994, 221). They are having a profound transformative impact on Tel Aviv, in particular. The Israeli government's insistence on treating them as foreigners who do not belong simply intensifies that impact: if they continue to be foreigners, then it is as foreigners that they make their presence felt.

TEL AVIV: FROM "FIRST HEBREW CITY" TO GLOBAL CITY

These two groups—Russian immigrants and foreign workers—are challenging the nature of Israeli identity and citizenship. These concepts are best treated as continua rather than dichotomies. As in other countries, in Israel there are varying degrees of citizenship, for citizens and noncitizens alike (Shachar 1999). As formal citizens, non-Jewish Russians enjoy a relatively high level of membership in Israeli society, though being non-Jewish their membership is significantly compromised. Because the Russians in general are viewed as a distinct group, this taint then applies to Jewish Russians as well.[11] The foreign workers are noncitizens, but despite that formal status they possess some attributes of membership, as "denizens" or "margizens" (Jacobson 1996). But the truly interesting question is not simply the addition of populations with varying degrees of membership, but how their presence is affecting the definition of "Israeliness" more generally for the entire population.

These changes are apparent most of all in Tel Aviv, which is commonly described as an emerging world city (for example, Kipnis 2005; Menachem 2000). Nurit Alfasi and Tovi Fenster (2005) draw a contrast between Tel Aviv as a global city and Jerusalem as a national city: the former has a strong outward orientation, whereas the latter is the primary symbol of national

11. After all, one does not normally inquire into the formal religious status of an acquaintance, and a Russian name or accent is often sufficient to lodge a question in the mind of a veteran Israeli (particularly if the latter is religiously observant).

identity and sovereignty.[12] The distinction is much more than symbolic: it rests on Tel Aviv's development into a center for technology, finance, and producer services (Shachar and Felsenstein 2002).

It is unsurprising that a large proportion of foreign workers in Israel are found in Tel Aviv. If one defines the city narrowly, referring only to the municipality of Tel Aviv–Jaffa, foreign workers amount to approximately 20 percent of the population (roughly 70,000 out of 370,000).[13] Of course, the metropolitan area is much larger, with a population of more than 2 million, in which case the percentage of foreign workers is much lower, between 3 and 4 percent. They are highly concentrated in an area around the Old Central Bus Station: this area has been utterly transformed in the past ten years (figs. 13.2 and 13.3).

As the site of internationally oriented economic activity, Tel Aviv generates significant revenue in terms of both volume and type (for instance, hard currency, as sales revenue, and foreign investment). With this economic base, the city has achieved a significant degree of financial independence from the national government, which gives it a substantial degree of autonomy on policy as well (Ben Elia 1993). The city has used this autonomy in its handling of matters relating to foreign workers. As noted earlier, national policy is to reduce the number of foreign workers (and to deport illegal ones, in particular) and to exclude them from the benefits of citizenship (both formal and substantive). The Tel Aviv municipality, in contrast, has made considerable efforts to extend some rights and benefits to foreign workers, in some cases without reference to their legal status (Willen 2006). Most significant in this context is the city's establishment of the Forum for Foreign Workers, which was later superseded by the Aid

12. On the other hand, Jerusalem's international status as a major religious site for Muslims, Jews, and Christians, combined with its disputed political status following the annexation of East Jerusalem after 1967, lends some ambiguity to the notion that it is a "national" city.

13. Adriana Kemp and Natan Marom (2006) report that, in addition to the resident population, a large number of foreign workers travel to Tel Aviv on weekends for social activities.

Fig. 13.2. Foreign workers in a Tel Aviv market. Photo by Karyn Aviani.

and Information Center for the Foreign Community in Tel Aviv–Jaffa, known by the Hebrew acronym MESILA (Kemp and Raijman 2004). These organizations act as a channel for foreign workers to express their views on matters of city policy; they have also accelerated the organization and mobilization of the foreign-worker community and thus help to entrench the city's need to listen to this community (Kemp et al. 2000). As the name indicates, MESILA also acts as an information center, enabling foreign workers to learn about opportunities and benefits available to them, including enrollment of children in city schools and assistance with health care issues. In addition, the city decided, without being prodded by the workers themselves, to include foreign workers in the planning consultation process for formulation of proposals to redevelop the area around the Old Central Bus Station (Fenster and Yacobi 2005). The existence of these policies leads to the conclusion that foreign workers enjoy a certain degree of citizenship in the city (Kemp and Raijman 2004).[14]

14. It is common in this type of juncture to note that the word *citizenship* itself is closely connected to the word *city* (see Holston 1999).

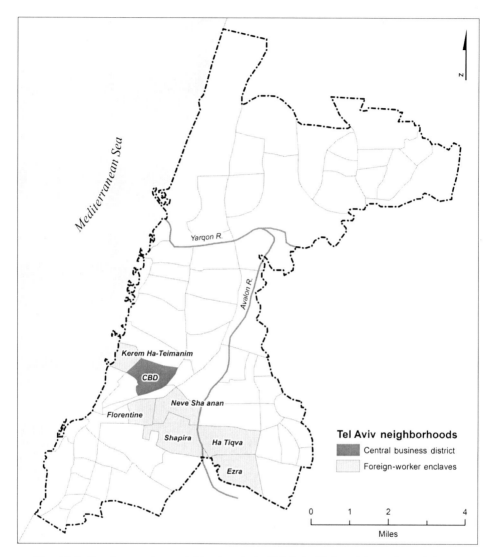

Fig. 13.3. Foreign-worker neighborhoods in Tel Aviv–Yafo, 1998. Adapted from several sources.

The inclusion of children in schools is especially significant in the long run, as the foreign-worker population inevitably includes couples who have brought or produced children. As noted above, national policy is, with few exceptions, to deny citizenship to children of foreign workers. Already this approach is being challenged and reconsidered, both in the parliament and in the supreme court; the latter was the site of a demonstration by children, who predictably made the point that they cannot be sent "home" because they have never had any home but Israel (*HaAretz,* November 28, 2005). That point shows that any formal decision to withhold national citizenship is bound to have only partial success, especially when institutions at other levels—cities, in particular—adopt a contrary approach.

But the changes wrought by immigration of non-Jewish foreign workers go well beyond policy—and indeed demonstrate the growing weakness of government policy, in the face of a type of immigration that is difficult for governments everywhere to control. Although many Israelis adhere to a traditional ethnonationalist view of the country and believe that foreign workers (and non-Jews generally) do not belong there, this view is not universally shared even among Jews. Some have adopted a multiculturalist attitude commonly found in places like New York and Toronto and see no problem in the presence of non-Jews. Tovi Fenster and Haim Yacobi quote a resident of the Old Central Bus Station area as follows: "I do not have any problem with the foreign workers. . . . On Saturday you see colours, it's fun to see. I feel as if I live in a city like New York" (2005, 206). (One sometimes hears Israelis refer to Tel Aviv as the "Big Orange.") The idea that Tel Aviv is like New York did not arise because of foreign workers, but their presence is reinforcing that notion. Tel Aviv now has a much more cosmopolitan feel, owing in part to secular Israelis' own increasing appetite for foreign travel and culture, but in more recent years it is also the product of immigration, particularly of non-Jews (Berthomière 2003).

Of course, a contrary perspective contains more weight: foreign workers in Israel are a marginalized minority, often persecuted and mistreated, possessing few rights and opportunities. Most citizens do not consider them as members of Israeli society, and most of the workers do not see themselves as Israeli. What is worth noting in this context, however, is the fact that a significant part of the population recognizes that there is a problem the society will have to deal with, that is, that it is unacceptable for Israel to contain a substantial number of people with few rights and no sense of belonging. Although many think it means the foreign workers should simply be deported, others recognize this option is impossible or believe it would be wrong, and therefore believe an inclusive approach will be necessary. This recognition extends in some cases to an understanding that accepting their presence means the society itself will have to adapt. So, although it is important not to overstate the extent of change, there is no question that the presence of foreign workers has already produced significant changes in Israeli society.

The challenge posed by the non-Jewish Russians is no less significant. This part of the population is unquestionably Israeli. Moreover, as "non-Arabs," they are more of an "us" than a "them"; the Arabs may be citizens, but one seldom describes them simply as Israelis—rather as "Israeli Arabs," the term typically used by Israeli Jews, though often rejected by the Arabs themselves. The Russians as a whole constitute a new ethnic group: the term *Israeli* no longer comprises only Ashkenazis and Sephardim, as there is a new group that does not fit easily into either category. Though the implications of this fact are not yet entirely clear, it is inevitable that this new addition will alter the content of the other two identities and the more general notion of "Israeliness" as well.

One issue that holds special urgency is the inability of some Russians to marry legally in Israel, as noted above. Marriage is controlled by the various religious authorities; there is no provision for civil marriage, and no possibility for intermarriage. The Jewish religious authorities are very strict in determining who is allowed to marry under their auspices: they will not conduct a wedding for anyone who is not Jewish according to the Orthodox standard (having a Jewish mother, or Orthodox conversion). For the large number of Russians who do not meet that criterion but nonetheless consider themselves Jewish (and therefore would be unwilling to try to marry in a Christian context), it is impossible to get married in the country.

Two responses to the difficulty have emerged. For many years, a small number of secular Israelis have traveled abroad to get married (often to Cyprus), simply to avoid what is often described as the "religious coercion" of the authorities; a civil marriage conducted abroad is then recognized by the Israeli state (though not by the religious authorities). That trend has increased markedly since the arrival of the Russian immigrants. The second response has been a significant rise in the rate of cohabitation without marriage. In practice, the result in both cases is an increase in de facto civil marriages among the "Jews and others" population (though with substantially impaired legal rights for those individuals who cohabitate) and a corresponding decline in religious marriage. Many who are compelled to use these routes are deeply unhappy about it; moreover, some predict that the distress will be even more acute for the non-Jewish children of such couples, who will be raised as Israelis but will be unable to enjoy the right to marry like others in their communities.

The movement for institution of proper civil marriage is therefore gaining steam. If it succeeds, one may confidently predict that it will be used by a vastly increased number of secular Israeli Jews, which would significantly undermine the power of the religious authorities in this and other spheres (and of course it is being resisted precisely for that reason). Even if this outcome were the only consequence of the immigration of non-Jewish Russians, it would amount to a very significant transformation of Israeli society. This issue was particularly salient in the campaigns for the elections in March 2006, with several political parties raising it as a central concern.

CONCLUSION

In the eyes of many, being Jewish is a fundamental component of Israeli identity. Some observers even forget that a significant proportion of the country's citizens are not Jewish,[15] and the membership of Arabs in Israeli society is best considered as a question fraught with difficulty (not least by many Arabs themselves). Many Israeli Jews adhere to the notion that Israel is "Jewish and democratic," but as Christian Joppke notes (2005), the phrase bespeaks a difficulty, a problem to resolve rather than the resolution itself: the very need to conjoin the words indicates there is a problem in doing so. This problem emerges most of all in the perspective of Arab citizens, many of whom would prefer to redefine Israel as "the state of all its citizens." Israeli society, even the Jewish portion, is hardly homogenous, and Baruch Kimmerling has recently argued (2001) that there is no longer

15. I have reviewed several manuscripts by scholars who use the term *Israeli* in a way that makes it clear they mean Jewish Israelis only. The distinction has more than political implications: if one speaks of "Israeli public opinion," one's findings will likely be very different depending on whether the population being surveyed is all Israelis or only Jewish Israelis.

any unified notion of "Israeliness" even among the country's Jewish citizens. All the same, it has long seemed safe to regard the Jewish element as fundamental and lending at least some degree of coherence.

The recent immigration of large numbers of non-Jews complicates these matters significantly. The non-Jewish immigrants do not fit into key Israeli institutions that take for granted the Jewish identity of the citizens they address. As in other countries, those institutions are therefore changing, in ways that affect the population more generally. Tel Aviv is at the forefront of the trends identified in this paper: as a global city, it has been the site of most of the economic changes that have led to the importation of foreign workers, and it also contains the kind of native population that is most open to the sociocultural changes that immigration typically produces. As in other contexts, immigration is leading many Israelis to rethink key components of their identity. Jewishness will likely remain a central component of that identity for many, but it is becoming more difficult to take it for granted.

14

Keeping the Gateway Shut

Regulating Global City-ness in Seoul

YEONG-HYUN KIM

At the heart of the global-cities literature lies a rather simple acknowledgment that many large cities around the world, with their distinctive histories and sociopolitical systems, are undergoing similar economic, cultural, and spatial changes as a result of globalization. Despite its immense contribution to a better understanding of globalization as well as contemporary urbanization, the global-cities literature has received mixed reviews so far. Serious concerns have been raised about the dominance of cities such as London and New York in this literature that may overwhelm or distort an understanding of globalization's impact on other cities, including those cities in the developing world, particularly smaller ones (Gugler 2004; McCann 2004; J. Robinson 2002a). Another criticism of the global-cities literature is that it emphasizes the economic aspects of urban life while neglecting various cultural, social, and material expressions of urban change (Keith 2005; Krause and Petro 2003; Smith 2001).

Although global cities have always been associated with the existence of immigrant workers, transnational communities, and cosmopolitan cultures (Hannerz 1996; King 1996; Sassen 1991; Vertovec and Cohen 2002), few studies have attempted to examine how different global cities rate in their reliance on immigrant labor (Benton-Short, Price, and Friedman 2005). Even fewer studies have examined the interface of immigration and urban changes in so-called nonglobal cities or globalizing cities beyond the West.

This chapter examines the *absence* of labor migration and immigration in the global city of Seoul, the capital city of South Korea (hereafter Korea). Seoul has been considered an emerging economic powerhouse in the Asian Pacific (Lo and Yeung 1996), yet, in terms of ethnic diversity, it is still a strongly Korean city rather than a cosmopolitan one. Almost all residents of Seoul are native-born Koreans, whereas foreigners make up a mere 1 percent of the population. Viewed from the perspective of economic globalization, Seoul, home to many large multinational firms, banks, and related business services, is clearly a global city. In addition, the city's consumer and youth culture has become remarkably Westernized, if not globalized, in recent years. The images of Seoul featuring office buildings, high-end stores, and night-life scenes have much in common with other culturally globalized places. However, it has not fostered a cosmopolitan demographic that would welcome a diverse immigrant population. This research looks into the Korean government's policies on labor migration and immigration in the context of Seoul's global aspirations but its desire for cultural homogeneity.

In pursuit of boosting Seoul's international status, the Korean government, a prototype of the strong state in the newly industrializing economies in East Asia, has undertaken numerous megaurban projects, such as the upgrade of mass-transit systems and the hosting of high-profile sports competitions (Kim 2004). However, the notions of multicultural and immigrant communities, which are often seen as essential elements in global city-ness, have received little attention in Seoul's global-city endeavor. Instead, the Korean government has effectively closed its borders against migrant workers and immigrants alike. Without any significant history of immigration or the government's intention to change its 99 percent ethnic homogeneity, Seoul remains rather exceptional to the ethnic diversity often associated with global cities.

Since the early 1990s, however, Seoul has been receiving a small but growing number of migrant workers from the developing areas of Asia, including China and Southeast Asian countries. Most of the migrant workers have been recruited by small- and medium-size manufacturing firms located in industrial cities outside Seoul, collectively called Outer Seoul. Despite the Korean government's restrictive policies on labor migration and immigration, the number of migrant workers, especially illegal ones, has grown rapidly in recent years. Given the acute labor shortage in low-skilled jobs in Korea, labor migration from developing Asian countries is likely to grow even faster in the next decade, as demonstrated by established immigrant flows to Singapore, Hong Kong, and cities in Japan (Castles and Miller 1998). The growing number of migrant workers has, in a few settings, added greater ethnic diversity to Seoul. However, a multicultural, multiethnic society has yet to be recognized as a desirable project by the Korean government as Seoul aspires to global-city status. Seoul is not so much a bypassed immigrant gateway as a closed one, where government officials maintain strict control of foreign workers in the metropolitan area.

This chapter is organized into five sections. The first section provides an overview of recent urban changes in Seoul, which has experienced a mix of decentralization, deindustrialization, and globalization in the past two decades. Particular attention is paid to the city's quest for global-city status and the politics behind it. The second section explores the issue of immigration in Korean society where various sociopolitical conditions have contributed to making Seoul a "closed immigrant gateway" where few foreign workers settle. In the next section, the recent increase in migrants from developing Asian countries is examined in the context of the Korean government's efforts to regulate it. The fourth section examines the settlement of migrant workers in industrial cities in Outer Seoul. The fifth and final section concludes with a discussion of ongoing public debates in Seoul over the relationship between global city-ness and immigration.

SEOUL AND GLOBAL-CITY STATUS

Greater Seoul, commonly called the "Capital Region," consists of Seoul and Outer Seoul (fig. 14.1). The city of Seoul once dominated the extended metropolitan area in all aspects of urban growth and development. Yet, as decentralization and deindustrialization began to take place, the balance between Seoul and Outer Seoul changed considerably in a relatively short period. In 2005, Greater Seoul housed 22.6 million people and accounted for 48.1 percent of the national population, making it one of the largest metropolitan areas in the world (table 14.1). As large and fast growing as

Greater Seoul's population is, it is owing to internal migration and natural growth, not to immigration. Key to Korea's economic success was the explosive growth of export-oriented manufacturing, much of which was established around Seoul. The capital city naturally became a primary magnet for migrants from rural areas in the 1960s and 1970s. Despite

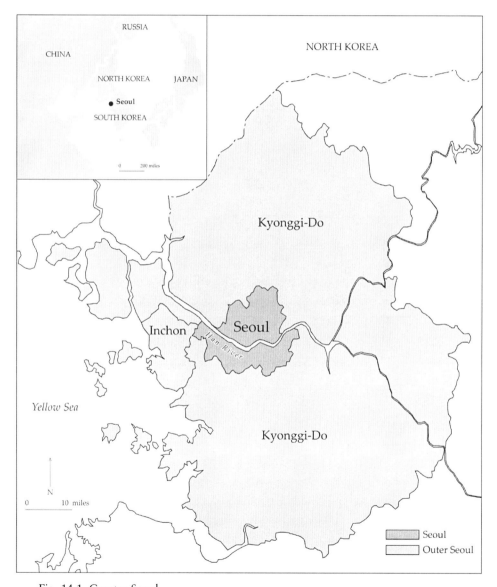

Fig. 14.1. Greater Seoul.

TABLE 14.1

POPULATION IN SEOUL AND OUTER SEOUL, 1949–2005

	Seoul	Outer Seoul	Greater Seoul	Share of national population (%)
1949	1,446,019	2,740,594	4,186,613	20.8
1955	1,574,868	2,363,660	3,938,528	18.3
1960	2,445,402	2,748,765	5,194,167	20.8
1965	3,793,280	3,102,325	6,895,605	23.6
1970	5,535,725	3,358,022	8,893,747	28.3
1975	6,889,502	4,039,132	10,928,634	31.5
1980	8,364,379	4,933,862	13,298,241	35.5
1985	9,639,110	6,181,046	15,820,156	39.1
1990	10,612,577	7,973,551	18,586,128	42.8
1995	10,231,217	9,957,929	20,189,146	45.3
2000	9,895,217	11,459,273	21,354,490	46.3
2005	9,762,546	12,858,686	22,621,232	48.1

Source: National Statistical Office, Census of Population and Housing, Republic of Korea, 2006.

various government policies designed to curtail the flow of rural migrants, Seoul's population grew rapidly through the 1980s and reached the 10 million mark in 1988.

Although Seoul's once seemingly uncontrollable population growth has shown signs of slowing and, indeed, decline in the past couple of decades, Outer Seoul has experienced large population gains in the corresponding years. Outer Seoul is a combined area of Inchon and Kyonggi-Do. Home to Korea's largest airport and seaport, the city of Inchon has long served as the gateway for Seoul's international trade. Seoul is literally surrounded by Kyonggi-Do, a province in which twenty-five cities contain more than 100,000 residents. The recent growth of Outer Seoul has been attributed to mounting megacity problems in Seoul and the resulting relocation of residents and businesses, government restrictions on the (re)location of manufacturing industries inside Seoul, and new construction of large-scale apartment buildings throughout cities in Kyonggi-Do (Kwon 1995). Outer Seoul has received a large number of manufacturing firms relocating from traditional industrial districts in Seoul, most of which shut down in the wave of deindustrialization in the late 1980s. Thanks to its geographical proximity to the east coast of China, where a large proportion of Chinese manufacturing production takes place, the southwestern part of Outer Seoul has emerged as a primary site for small- and medium-size manufacturing firms in Korea.

Alongside decentralization and deindustrialization, globalization has played a key role in transforming the landscape of Seoul. The 1988 Summer Olympics was a truly landmark event in Seoul's international visibility, as the city used the global spectacle to showcase the phenomenal economic success that Koreans have achieved since the Korean War (Kim 1997). Capitalizing on Seoul's enhanced international profile following the Olympics, local and national politicians of all political affiliations made the most of the phrase "Seoul as a world-class city" and demonstrated support for Seoul's drive to global-city status. Indeed, the phrase was well received and widely quoted in the local media and among residents in the early 1990s. Seoul was often benchmarked against well-known world cities, such as New York and Tokyo, for various indicators ranging from mass transit systems to financial districts and sports stadiums. The projected image of Seoul as a world-class city was highlighted whenever city planners bid to host international events, including the 2002 World Cup Finals (Kim 2004).

More recently, cashing in on the rhetoric of global city-ness, the city government embarked on a highly controversial waterfront revitalization project in the city's center (Seoul Metropolitan Government 2006). The project, named Cheonggyecheon Restoration, planned to open more public spaces and historic sites and replace a century-old wholesale market of apparel and watches with a state-of-the-art business district in which high-rise office buildings would stand next to upscale shopping areas. Facing mounting protests from the existing residents and businesses in the area, the mayor, who later ran for, and won, the 2007 presidential election, skillfully linked the redevelopment project to Seoul's global-city status, and eventually won both public and media support.

It is not uncommon for local and national politicians to make somewhat arbitrary claims about their particular city's importance in the global economic system (Paul 2004). The designation of global-city status is often aggressively sought, especially by political leaders aspiring for such recognition (Short 2004; Yeoh 2004). In the case of Seoul, however, the projects that have been identified and subsequently promoted have stressed the physical and economic aspects of urban development. High-profile, international events and local businesses' global competitiveness have received strong political support, whereas ethnic diversity and multiculturalism are not addressed.

That cosmopolitanism is missing from Seoul's global-city project is evident by how the Korean government is dealing with the recent rise of labor migration. Seoul, particularly Outer Seoul, has been receiving a steady stream of low-skilled migrant workers from various Asian countries. Their arrival marks the first large addition of non-Korean people to the metropolitan area. Migrant workers are contributing to the diversification of Seoul's homogenous culture. However, there is no connection made between the government's efforts to enhance globalness and the newly forming communities of migrant workers that are culturally changing the city. Few steps have been taken to incorporate labor migration and immigration into Seoul's global city endeavor, although vibrant immigrant communities are key features of global city-ness. Instead, the Korean government has undertaken enormous efforts to impede the transition of the migrant workers into permanent settlers in Greater Seoul.

IMMIGRATION TO KOREA

Korea has long been a major source of international migration flows. The number of ethnic Koreans residing overseas is estimated at 6.6 million, including 1.2 million residents of other countries who have maintained their Korean citizenship (Overseas Korean Foundation 2006). Approximately 2 million ethnic Koreans reside in China, another 2 million in the United States, 1 million in Japan, and 500,000 in Russia. The existence of such a large Korean diaspora is a product of the economic and political difficulties that Koreans endured during the twentieth century, including Japanese colonialism and the 1950–1953 Korean War, followed by dire poverty (Bergsten and Choi 2003). During the 1970s and early 1980s, nearly 2 million Koreans migrated to the Middle East for construction work, but almost all of them returned home upon the completion of their contracts (Park 1998).

Contrary to the sheer presence of ethnic Koreans overseas, the population of foreign nationals residing in Korea is estimated at a mere half million, including some 200,000 illegal migrant workers. Foreigners make up about 1 percent of the country's total population, which is now 47 million. Although the number of foreigners is fairly small by international standards, it has increased almost ten times in the past decade, as the 1995 census reported 55,016 foreigners living in Korea (National Statistical Office 2006).[1] As of the 2005 census, the number of naturalized citizens has been considered too minimal to be counted separately, although the Korean government plans to include that statistic in the next census, scheduled for 2010. In the meantime, there are about 160,000 North Korean–born Koreans currently living in Korea, most of whom migrated south before or during the Korean War. Unlike other immigrants, they have been accepted legally, socially, and politically into Korean society, and, more important, they have never been considered foreign-born.

In the case of Seoul, foreign nationals made up less than 0.2 percent of its population in 1970 when they were counted for the first time. The presence of foreigners remained statistically insignificant through the next three decades until the late 1990s. When Seoul started globalizing its economic and political relations immediately following the 1988 Summer Olympics, the city's ethnic composition remained solidly Korean. According to the latest official data available, foreign nationals make up 1.1 percent of Seoul's population and 1.5 percent of Outer Seoul's. These figures are much lower than the world average of 2.9 percent, although the past few years have witnessed a surge in the arrival of international migrant workers from many developing Asian countries (fig. 14.2).

In order to better understand the recent rise of labor migration to Seoul, it is necessary to examine the lack of it in previous decades. Indeed, Seoul was one of the very few large cities in Asia that did not develop an

---

1. The census count of foreign nationals tends to be much smaller than the number of migrant workers, both legal and illegal, reported by the Immigration Bureau that collects migrant data from the arrival and departure records of work-visa holders.

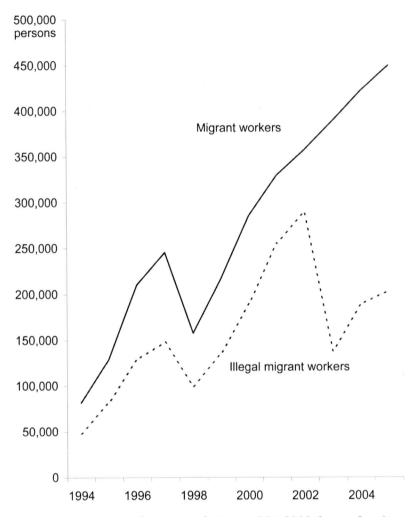

Fig. 14.2. Foreign labor force in South Korea, 1994–2005. *Source:* Immigration Bureau, Ministry of Justice, Republic of Korea, 2006.

economically vibrant Chinese community in the 1950s and 1960s. The city was virtually bypassed by Vietnamese refugees in the 1970s, as the Korean government staunchly refused to offer them assistance for permanent settlement. Until recently, Seoul was not a major destination of Filipino workers whose presence in large Asian cities, such as Hong Kong, Singapore, and Tokyo, grew dramatically in the 1990s. In sum, Seoul remained for a long period of time a Korean-only city, with the exception of a small number of foreigners whose occupations were limited mostly to diplomats, corporate expatriates, and language instructors.

The weak presence of the foreign-born in Seoul has been attributed mainly to the Korean government's restrictive immigration policies aimed at preserving ethnic homogeneity within the nation. Much like Japan, Korea has developed its national culture and identity based primarily on the notion of "one language, one ethnicity" (Brody 2002; Choi et al. 2004; Douglass and Roberts 2000). Korean society, typical of a nation-state in a traditional sense, is tightly knit among insiders while fairly exclusive to outsiders. The fact that Korea has been a divided nation for almost six decades has been used to justify the tight state control over its borders and immigration. Along with these unique cultural and political conditions, economic difficulties following the Korean War, coupled with high population density, helped shape Korea as a country of emigration rather than a destination country for international labor migration.

The Korean government has maintained the strict rule of ethnic citizenship, under which citizenship is granted only to children of Korean parents, or least a Korean father. Consequently, the country's formal citizenship process excludes the immigration or naturalization of non-Korean people, regardless their birthplace. Indeed, the Korean-born overseas Chinese, estimated at a little more than 20,000, had not been granted either citizenship or permanent residency until 2002, when a reform of immigration laws allowed their pursuit of naturalization upon further review.[2] Given that third- and fourth-generation overseas Chinese in Korea have had such difficulty obtaining Korean citizenship, it is difficult to imagine that recently arrived migrant workers could be integrated into Korean society.

Korea has a long history of producing emigrants who have settled in many parts of the world, however controversial their settlement in the host

2. Almost all overseas Chinese residing in Korea are officially Taiwanese citizens, because the Korean government that was at odds with People's Republic of China during the cold war period forced them to take passports issued by the Taiwanese government. Until recently, they were requested to renew their residency permit in Korea every three to five years (Chinese Residents' Association in Seoul 2005).

society might have been. Rapid economic growth has now resulted in both the decline of Korean emigration flows and the rise of immigrant arrivals in Korea. The country's past experience with emigration seems to have little bearing on the Korean government's policies toward labor migration and immigration, as it is still very reluctant to accept migrant workers.

Efforts to improve the legal status of foreign residents have been led by various nongovernmental, human rights, and religious organizations since the mid-1990s. Lawmakers and policy makers have recently responded to requests to ease the immigration procedures for both those individuals who have been residing in Korea for an extended period of time and those who are married to a Korean. There are signs of changes in policies and attitudes towards nonnatives, but the traditional nation-state strategies to control ethnic, racial, and cultural difference within the country are still very much at work in Korean society. The controllability of difference has been challenged in many developed countries (Castles 2004), yet the Korean government believes that such control is possible.

LABOR MIGRATION FROM DEVELOPING ASIAN COUNTRIES

Despite the reluctance to admit foreign labor, particularly low-skilled labor, a small but growing number of migrant workers have entered Korea from the early 1990s onward. Korea's economic success became common knowledge throughout Asia in the late 1980s, which made the country, and particularly Seoul, a new destination for international labor migrants (Hugo 2004). Recognizing the growing demand for cheap labor, the Korean government has taken a course of measured actions to bring in guest workers who could help relieve labor-shortage problems but would return home upon the completion of their contracts. However, the conventional wisdom that strict (im)migration regulations, accompanied with substantial labor shortages in low-skilled jobs, could actually encourage illegal movement from labor-surplus countries has proved true in Korea during the past decade. The number of illegal migrants who entered Korea legally but have overstayed their temporary work or tourist visas has grown rapidly in recent years, accounting for more than two-thirds of the foreign labor force.

In 1991, the Korean government decided to allow migrant workers to fill low-skill, entry-level jobs, departing from its traditional employment policy that limited foreign workers to jobs that required special skills, such as native fluency in a foreign language. This new policy stemmed from a serious labor shortage facing traditional manufacturing industries and the resulting capital outflows to low-wage countries.[3] The Korean manufacturing industry underwent an extensive restructuring in the late 1980s and early 1990s, as its labor-intensive sectors were giving way to high-tech, capital-intensive sectors, such as the semiconductor industry and the automobile industry. In addition, thanks to the decadelong economic boom in the 1980s, the country's average wage levels increased during that period. Consequently, more and more local manufacturing firms started exploring investment opportunities in China and Southeast Asian countries. Fearing the exodus of labor-intensive industries to neighboring countries, the government allowed small- and medium-size manufacturing firms to hire a limited number of foreign workers on condition that the firms would not reduce or shut down their domestic production lines.

The Industrial Training System was introduced to authorize local companies to recruit low-wage foreign workers through their overseas operations, under the name of "employee training." The program was amended a few times in the mid 1990s-so that any manufacturing firms, regardless their status of overseas operation, could hire foreign workers for the purpose of training. But, in reality, these trainees were carrying out low-wage, undesirable jobs that were shunned by domestic workers (Suk et al. 2003). The trainees were not permitted to settle or to bring their families. The annual number of trainees brought in through this program ranged from 1,700 to 30,000, amounting to a total of 145,500

---

3. A rapidly aging population has been another factor in Korea's labor-shortage problems. The country's total dependency ratio (the ratio of the number of individuals aged below fifteen or above sixty-four divided by the number of individuals ages fifteen to sixty-four) has been recorded around 40 percent in the past decade, and is predicted to remain at this level for the next decade or so. However, its elderly dependency ratio has increased from 7.4 percent in 1990 to 12.6 percent in 2005, and is predicted to reach 21.8 percent by 2020, causing serious concerns about a labor shortage in the future.

by the end of 2002, when it was phased out for a series of new migrant-labor programs.

The Industrial Training System tried to control foreign labor, but in the end it was the many loopholes the participating companies and the trainees took advantage of that forced its demise. In addition, the trainees were exposed to the dangers of exploitation at all stages of recruitment and training, since their "trainee" status made them ineligible for most of the legal protections that domestic workers received (Korea Labor Institute 2004). Meanwhile, a large number of trainees disappeared from their designated workplaces in Korea, turning into illegal migrants by overstaying their trainee visas. Indeed, the Industrial Training System was blamed for having played an instrumental role in the rapid growth of illegal migrant workers in the past six years, as more than half of the trainees did not leave the country after their training visa expired, thus becoming illegal in the eyes of the state (Ministry of Justice, Republic of Korea, 2006).

Tables 14.2 and 14.3 show the rapid growth of foreign labor in Korea in the past decade, in which the share of illegal migrant workers has been alarmingly high. Official estimates in 2002 put the number of illegal migrant workers at 289,239, which made up almost 80 percent of the foreign workforce in Korea.[4] Anxious to bring order to this chaotic situation, the Korean government took a drastic measure to grant all illegal migrant workers legal status, on the condition that they report to designated government offices within a specified grace period. A total of 256,107 people, more than 90 percent of the estimated number of illegal migrant workers, took action on this legal arrangement and received temporary work visas. This one-time amnesty measure, which was a desperate attempt by the government to regain control over migrant labor, reduced the portion of illegal migrant workers in the total foreign labor force from a record high of 79.8 percent in 2002 to 35.5 percent in 2003. The dramatic drop in the number of illegal

---

4. The estimate was based on the arrival and departure records of foreigners. Those immigrants who were overstaying their trainee or work visas were automatically considered illegal migrant workers. Although there seemed to be an exaggeration in labeling all foreigners with expired work visa as illegal migrant workers, this estimate might have undercounted those individuals who worked illegally on other types of visas, such as tourist visas.

TABLE 14.2

FOREIGN LABOR FORCE IN KOREA

	Foreign labor	Illegal migrant workers[a]	Share of total foreign labor (%)
1994	81,824	48,231	58.9
1995	128,906	81,866	63.5
1996	210,494	129,054	61.3
1997	245,399	148,048	60.3
1998	157,689	99,537	63.1
1999	217,384	135,338	62.3
2000	285,506	188,995	66.2
2001	329,555	255,206	77.4
2002	357,460	289,239	79.8
2003	388,816	138,056	35.5
2004	421,641	188,483	44.7
2005	337,325	187,908	55.7

Source: Ministry of Justice, Republic of Korea, 2006.
[a]Workers who are overstaying their specified contract term.

migrant workers afforded the Korean government a belief, however misguided, in the controllability of labor migration, though the numbers of illegal migrants began to rise again the very next year.

Table 14.3 lists major source countries of those illegal-turned-legal migrant workers, based on the information that they provided while applying for legal status. The vast majority of them are from developing countries in Asia, including China, Bangladesh, the Philippines, Mongolia, Vietnam, and Thailand. China is by far the top sending country of migrant workers, both legal and illegal. More than half of the Chinese workers coming to Korea are indeed ethnic Koreans (Korean Chinese), most of whom are children or grandchildren of Korean peasants who migrated to northeastern China during the Japanese colonial period (1910–1945). Their return migration began in the late 1980s when the Korean government allowed visitors from then socialist countries, including China, for the first time in decades. Soon after, many ethnic Koreans visited Korea looking for their immediate relatives, and some started working while still on visitor or tourist visas. Compared to other migrant workers, they have certainly benefited from

TABLE 14.3

COUNTRIES OF ORIGIN OF ILLEGAL MIGRANT WORKERS
IN KOREA, 2002

	Workers	*Percentage of total*
China	151,361	59.1
(Korean Chinese)	(91,770)	(35.8)
Bangladesh	17,092	6.7
Philippines	16,094	6.3
Mongolia	13,967	5.5
Vietnam	10,618	4.1
Thailand	9,666	3.8
Pakistan	6,974	2.7
Indonesia	6,806	2.7
Uzbekistan	6,209	2.4
India	2,781	1.1
Sri Lanka	2,290	0.9
Others	12,249	4.8
Total	257,107	100.0

Source: Ministry of Justice, Republic of Korea, 2006.
Note: Information based on the data of the illegal workers who applied for legal status during the grace period, March 25–May 29, 2002.

government policies favoring migrants of Korean decent. They have, since 2002, been allowed to work in the service sector and construction industry as well as in the manufacturing sector, whereas other migrant groups have been limited to the latter.[5] Hoping for the Korean government's decision to grant ethnic Koreans citizenship, many Korean Chinese workers have overstayed their visas, becoming the single largest group among illegal migrant workers. Whereas Bangladesh and the Philippines have a long-established history of labor migration to developed Western economies and oil-producing countries in the Middle East (Hugo 2004), Korea has emerged in the past decade as another destination for these migration flows.

Despite the government's desperate efforts to keep low-skilled migrant labor under control, the number of overstaying illegal migrant workers is

5. Whereas foreign workers need to obtain E-9 visas to work in Korea, ethnic Koreans need F-1-4 visas (Ministry of Labor, Republic of Korea, 2006).

TABLE 14.4

DOCUMENTED FOREIGN NATIONALS IN SEOUL AND OUTER SEOUL, 1970–2004

	Seoul		Outer Seoul	
	Foreigners	Share of foreigners in total population (%)	Foreigners	Share of foreigners in total population (%)
1970	10,463	0.19	4,750	0.14
1975	10,038	0.15	4,425	0.11
1980	13,763	0.16	3,527	0.07
1985	13,355	0.14	3,513	0.06
1990	9,327	0.09	2,864	0.04
1995	14,040	0.14	15,811	0.16
2000	41,245	0.42	55,183	0.48
2004[a]	114,685	1.11	197,820	1.49

Source: National Statistical Office, Census of Population and Housing, Republic of Korea, 2006.

[a]Data compiled from government Web sites of Seoul, Inchon, and Kyonggi Province.

rising after a brief decline in 2003. The Korean government embarked in the summer of 2004 on a new program named the Employment Permit System in an effort to expand legal avenues for migrant workers while toughening law enforcement against illegal migrants. Replicating the guest worker policies of western Europe, the Korean government currently permits the recruitment of needed manual workers, not trainees, from labor-surplus countries, who can be hired by small- and medium-size manufacturing firms on a temporary contract basis. It now mandates that employers of contract workers meet the minimum-wage requirement and pay health and social security benefits. In a continuing effort to reduce illegal migration, policy reforms include hefty penalties for the employment of undocumented migrant workers. Although the new program has clearly responded to business interests by loosening restrictions on the employment of low-skilled foreign labor, it has also addressed some social concerns, such as incentives for foreign labor, ending the exploitative industrial trainee system and reducing the flow of illegal migrants.

While the latest employment act is more realistic than the infamous Industrial Training System, it demonstrates the Korean government's firm belief in the controllability of labor migration and immigration. Fearful of the possibility of domestic workers being crowded out, the government set a cap of two percent of the total workforce on the number of recruited migrant workers. In addition, the provisions contain no legal consideration for migrant workers who might pursue permanent resident status, and subsequently naturalized citizenship, in Korea. Indeed, it effectively prevents any employment permit holders from taking a path to permanency or citizenship. Foreign labor is contracted to work in Korea for a maximum of three years. Workers may renew their contract one more time after that initial period, but only after leaving the country to do so. This particular requirement is a critical measure to prevent migrant workers from obtaining permanent residence in Korea; the law requires legal residence in the country for five consecutive years before permanent residency can be considered. As the demand for migrant labor in low-skilled jobs is quickly growing, however, it remains to be seen whether the Korean government can be as effective as it has been in the past in regulating labor migration and immigration.

MIGRANT WORKERS IN OUTER SEOUL

For nearly twenty years, both Seoul and Outer Seoul have received labor migrants from developing Asian countries, as well as some migrants from Russia and Africa. Most foreign laborers came to Korea as temporary contract workers, including industrial trainees and low-skilled labor. After having barred labor migration for decades, the Korean government finally agreed, partly owing to concern with domestic business interests, to accept migrant workers within strict functional and temporal limits. Put simply, they have been accepted to help relieve a severe labor shortage in the manufacturing sector but not to settle permanently.[6] This policy has impacted

6. In 2005, the first full year of implementation, the Employment Permit System brought in 116,000 workers from eight countries: Cambodia, China, Indonesia, Mongolia, Philippines, Sri Lanka, Thailand, and Vietnam. Of those recruited workers, 38,000 were ethnic Koreans who could choose a wider range of jobs, while the remaining 78,000 workers were hired by manufacturing firms (Ministry of Labor, Republic of Korea, 2006).

the ethnic and gender makeup of migrant workers and their geographical distribution in Korea. This section examines the concentration of low-skilled migrant labor in Outer Seoul, which has recently emerged as the most ethnically diverse place in the entire country.

As shown in table 14.4, the number of documented foreign nationals residing in Greater Seoul has increased more than ten times in the past decade, jumping from a mere 29,850 in 1995 to 312,505 in 2004. Until recently, more than two-thirds of all foreigners entering Korea settled in Seoul, although their proportional numbers remained minimal because of the city's enormous population. With growing arrivals of migrant workers from developing Asian countries, however, Outer Seoul has emerged as a major destination of the newly arrived. According to the latest official figures provided by local governments, about 200,000 foreigners reside in Outer Seoul, accounting for 1.49 percent of the total population. Considering that illegal migrant workers have outnumbered legal ones for the majority of the past decade, the foreign population in Outer Seoul, documented and undocumented combined, could be as large as 400,000.

Since the bulk of migrant workers are housed in dormlike accommodations near their place of employment, distinctive ethnic enclaves have not yet formed for any particular origin group. However, some ethnic business districts have taken shape near subway stations in many industrial cities in Outer Seoul. The city of Ansan, for example, home to around 5,000 manufacturing firms, has developed the country's largest Southeast Asian shopping street in Wonkok Dong, where a number of ethnic grocery stores and restaurants, bars, Internet cafés, and game clubs are clustered together (fig. 14.3).

With growing numbers of foreign-born industrial workers, Outer Seoul houses a very different migrant population than central Seoul. Figure 14.4 demonstrates a stark difference between Seoul and Outer Seoul in the national origin of their foreign-born residents. The main sources of migrants to Seoul include China, the United States, Taiwan, and Japan, which together account for about 80 percent of the city's foreign-born population. In contrast, sources of migrants to Outer Seoul include China, the Philippines, Thailand, Indonesia, and Vietnam. Outer Seoul has a more diverse stock of foreign migrants than Seoul, although neither area attracts

Fig. 14.3. Ethnic business center in Ansan, Outer Seoul. Photo by the author.

a significant number of migrants outside Asia, with the exception of a few U.S. migrants.

Different country groups show a preference for either Seoul or Outer Seoul (table 14.5). For example, American, Taiwanese, Japanese, British, and French nationals are more likely to live in Seoul, whereas the vast majority of the Thai, Vietnamese, Indonesian, Bangladeshi, Uzbeki, Sri Lankan, and Kazakh live in Outer Seoul. The Chinese are the only exception to this distribution pattern, as they are distributed evenly between Seoul and Outer Seoul. Chinese nationals make up almost half of the documented foreigners residing in Greater Seoul, reflecting a number of factors that have fostered Chinese migration to the metropolitan area. A sharp increase in economic transactions between the two countries has obviously factored into the growing arrival of Chinese migrant workers to Korea, as has the ever growing return migration of ethnic Koreans. Since the government allows ethnic Koreans, if they wish, to work in service industries, including restaurants, hotels and retail stores, their employment and settlement are

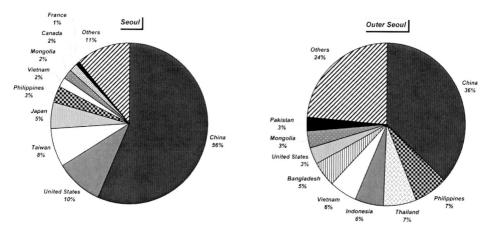

Fig. 14.4. Immigrant populations in Seoul and Outer Seoul. *Source:* Compiled from government Web sites of Seoul, Inchon, and Kyonggi-Do.

not limited to the location of factories. Indeed, most Korean Chinese are working in Seoul where more service job opportunities exist, which factors into the distribution of Chinese workers as a whole.

The Korean government's hands-on approach to labor migration has also had some effect on the gender distribution of migrant workers entering the country and particularly those settling in Outer Seoul. As shown in table 14.6, two-thirds of documented foreigners in Outer Seoul are male, yet the gender ratio of foreign labor in Seoul is fairly even. More than 70 percent of employment permits are granted to manufacturing firms, including auto component and machinery manufacturers, which tend to seek young male workers in the recruitment process. The growth of female domestic workers from the Philippines and Indonesia has been identified as one of the most significant developments in labor migration in Asia (Hugo 2004; Organization for Economic Co-operation and Development 1998). Korea, however, does not issue employment permits for domestic laborers yet, so there are relatively few female migrant laborers in Seoul. Because of the government's tight control over labor migration, Outer Seoul receives highly male-dominated migration flows, which is somewhat exceptional to the widespread feminization trend of migrant workers in large Asian cities.

TABLE 14.5

COUNTRIES OF ORIGIN OF DOCUMENTED FOREIGN NATIONALS
IN GREATER SEOUL, 2004

	Seoul	*Outer Seoul*	*Greater Seoul*
China	64,762	73,132	137,894
United States	10,959	6,785	17,744
Philippines	3,740	13,705	17,445
Taiwan[a]	8,899	5,254	14,153
Thailand	977	13,062	14,039
Vietnam	2,216	10,980	13,196
Indonesia	770	11,503	12,273
Bangladesh	634	9,991	10,625
Japan	6,271	3,555	9,826
Mongolia	2,128	6,344	8,472
Pakistan	887	5,603	6,490
Uzbekistan	539	5,499	6,038
Nepal	380	3,167	3,547
Canada	1,893	1,552	3,445
India	828	2,551	3,379
Sri Lanka	230	2,799	3,029
Russia	927	1,899	2,826
Kazakhstan	108	1,494	1,602
Myanmar	143	1,279	1,422
Iran	367	956	1,323
UK	848	255	1,103
France	1,015	60	1,075
Total foreign population	114,685	197,820	312,505

Sources: Compiled from government Web sites of Seoul, Inchon, and Kyonggi-Do.
[a] Taiwanese nationals include overseas Chinese who have lived in Seoul over generations.

TABLE 14.6

GENDER IN DOCUMENTED FOREIGN NATIONALS
IN GREATER SEOUL, 2004

	Seoul	*Outer Seoul*	*Greater Seoul*
Female	60,619	69,856	130,475
Male	54,066	127,964	182,030
Total	114,685	197,820	312,505

Source: Data compiled from government Web sites of Seoul, Inchon, and Kyonggi Province.

Korean government officials and politicians across the political spectrum take pleasure in comparing Seoul to other large cities, and particularly Asian regional rivals, in terms of global city-ness. Much attention is paid to how they have hosted international sports competitions, upgraded infrastructure, and increased foreign investment. Little is said about the number of migrant workers they have received, how migrant workers have contributed to a cosmopolitan culture, or what policy provisions have been drafted to protect migrant workers from potentially exploitative situations. Instead, the frequent sights of migrant workers in Outer Seoul have been associated with crime and prostitution in local media accounts. For example, the ethnic shopping district in Ansan is repeatedly portrayed as an exotic but high-crime area in the national media, which prompted local politicians to vow for better policing of alien residents.

CONCLUSION

For a booming economy in the age of global migration, Korea has maintained an exceptionally low level of immigration. Its capital city, Seoul, has been recognized for successfully bidding and hosting major sports events, which, along with the success of homegrown multinational firms, has placed the city on the map of global cities. Whereas the economic globalization of Seoul has escalated dramatically in the past two decades, its cosmopolitanism, in part measured by ethnic diversity, remains very limited. The absence of immigrant communities in Seoul has often been attributed to the political and economic situation that Koreans endured during the cold war period, which was indeed very unusual. However, this research argues that the Korean government has played a key role in keeping the gateway shut to immigration.

The Korean government has maintained highly restrictive policies on labor migration and immigration. Since the mid-1990s, however, Seoul and Outer Seoul have received a growing number of low-skilled migrant workers from labor-surplus countries in Asia. The Korean government, wanting to meet the business world's demand for a stable supply of cheap labor while, at the same time, not wanting to change its ethnic-national identity, has decided to accept a limited number of migrant workers for low-wage jobs in the manufacturing sector on a temporary basis. The political reluctance to allow migrant workers to settle has been unmistakably evident in government policies on labor migration. Although the newly forming migrant communities in Outer Seoul could make significant contributions to Seoul's global city-ness in terms of multiculturalism, the Korean government stresses other aspects of global city-ness than cultural diversity.

Public discourse over the permanent settlement of migrant workers has ranged widely from an antiglobalization, nationalistic rhetoric to a proglobalization one. Many have focused on whether the economic benefits of migrant labor would be neutralized by the perceived, and often imagined, social costs, yet little thought is given to the sociocultural benefits that migrant workers could bring to Seoul.

Seoul has been fairly well connected to the global networks of corporations, financial services, and consumer goods, but closed to the latest waves of migrant workers and immigrants. This situation might be exactly what the Korean government has intended for its capital city. It is very doubtful, however, that Seoul can remain closed in the future. Recent trends in labor migration indicate that major changes are under way, which may eventually have significant impacts on the city's ethnic diversity and immigrant stock. The Korean government may insist on its traditional immigration policies for a short period of time, but their effectiveness in keeping migrant workers from settling in Seoul in the long run will be undercut by both the demand and supply sides of migrant workers. Viewed from the demand side, the Korean economy, with its aging population and labor shortages, will grow increasingly dependent on migrant labor for low-skilled, low-wage jobs. Pressure will placed on the Korean government to loosen up control over labor migration in order to fill the gaps in the labor market. Developing countries in Asia, including China and Vietnam, continue to provide immigrants to Korea. Migrant communities have already emerged in industrial cities in Outer Seoul, which indicates that the settlement process of temporary migrant workers, both legal and illegal, has already taken shape. Once those communities expand and become permanent, Seoul will no longer be able to keep the gateway shut.

15

São Paulo

Historic Immigrant Gateway
to Contemporary Emigrant Outpost

EMILY SKOP and SARAH ZELL

Today's immigrant gateways are shaped through various globalizing processes and transnational connections. But urban theorists sometimes neglect the powerful role of global economic cycles and immigrant social networks in prompting the growth of urban immigrant gateways, both now and in the past. In the last great "Age of Migration" (whose zenith persisted from the late 1880s to the early 1920s), various cities around the world attracted millions of immigrants seeking reprieve from poverty and hardship. That migration was part of a common economic system and global demographic transformation that prompted individuals and families to cross oceans in search of better living and working conditions. The sudden surge in immigrant flows to cities resulted in large numbers of foreign-born settling in places that often had little previous history with immigration.

Despite changing world events and new immigrant cohorts, many of these cities, such as New York City, Toronto, and Sydney, have continued to act as immigrant gateways and have become well-known, established destinations. At the same time, some of these former gateways have lost their magnetism. These cities may still be considered global cities, in the sense that they are major sites for the accumulation of capital and command points in the world economy, but they no longer attract many international migrants (Singer 2004). In fact, ironically enough, in many of these cities, out-migration now predominates. Native-born residents (who are often the second-, third-, and fourth-generational offspring of previous international migrants) are creating new waves of emigration, whether to various metropolises within the country or to other destinations overseas.

Since the 1960s, São Paulo has changed from a net importer to a net exporter of international migrants. Thus, it is an excellent exemplar of a former immigrant gateway that has become a contemporary emigrant outpost. This chapter provides evidence of the key role of former gateways in (re)creating both old and new transnational links. On the one hand, connections from the past have prompted new emigration flows generations later. On the other, contemporary global economic linkages provide a context that promotes the creation of alternative transnational linkages and additional flows of emigration. The chapter begins with an exploration of the historical role of immigration *to* São Paulo in the late nineteenth and early twentieth centuries. Then, we jump ahead nearly one hundred years and describe the ways in which those small numbers of foreign-born that do live in São Paulo today make their mark on the cultural landscape. Subsequently, we contend that despite the nearly 200,000 immigrants living in São Paulo, mostly from Europe, Asia, and South America, the metropolis should be considered a former immigrant gateway, since it continues to lose migrants (both foreign- and native-born) every year. We examine the contemporary role of emigration *from* São Paulo in the late twentieth and early twenty-first centuries to suggest that this former immigrant gateway is now an emigrant outpost. Guiding the paper is the theoretical principle of social networks and transnational theory, which helps to make clear how this process happens.

Social network theory is predicated on the idea that migrant connections allow for the substitution of social capital for human capital over time. Migrant networks are sets of interpersonal ties that connect migrants, former migrants, and non-migrants in origin and destination areas through ties of kinship, friendship, and shared community origin (Massey et al. 1998). These networks increase the likelihood of international migration because they lower the costs and risks of movement across borders. Drawing on the social ties of relatives and friends who have migrated before, nonmigrants can gain access to knowledge, assistance, and other resources that ease the process of migration. Douglas Massey (1987) was the first to identify these networks as a form of social capital. To people seeking to migrate abroad, everyday networks of friendship or kinship provide few advantages. However, once someone makes the decision to migrate, these social ties can be transformed, or converted, into a resource that can be used to gain access to opportunities abroad. Each act of migration creates social capital among people to whom the new migrant is related, thereby raising the odds of their migration (Massey et al. 1994).

In transnational migration theory there exists a pattern whereby people, although they move across international borders and settle in a new state, maintain social connections with their country of origin. People literally live their lives across international borders, straddling two worlds. This process by which "immigrants forge and sustain multi-stranded social relations that link together their societies of origin and settlement" (Waters 2002) challenges the classic definition of migration as a single and permanent change of residence, occurring only once. These transmigrants maintain and (re)create familial, economic, religious, political, or social relations, or a combination thereof, in the state from which they moved even as they form similar relationships in the destination (Glick-Schiller, Basch, and Blanc-Szanton 1992b). Interestingly, early studies of transnationalism were begun by scholars working in immigrant communities in New York City, a classic immigrant gateway, and later were tested in other settings. To understand the different types of connections that transmigrants maintain in the places that they left behind, many scholars of transnational migration began to use the concept of "transnational community" (Nagengast and Kearney 1990). The concept of a transnational community directs attention to transmigrant connections to two or more states at the same time and the political and social implication of such connections.

Social network theory and transnationalism both help bridge our understanding of how people operate on both micro and macro levels to organize migration, as Weber Soares (2003) suggests. He asserts that the study of social networks in international migration can yield information regarding the causes and nature of migration, as well as the perpetuation and stabilization of flows. Still, what is missing from these theories is an understanding of how historical networks can lead to contemporary patterns. In other words, how do connections from the past operate in the present as migrants decide where to move?[1] At the same time, how do contemporary linkages forge new connections and migration flows to alternative destinations? To answer these questions, we outline how the migration process works in São Paulo, looking specifically at ethnic "return" flows to Japan and largely illegal "new" flows to the United States.

SÃO PAULO: ESTABLISHED IMMIGRANT GATEWAY

Historically, São Paulo has been considered a city of net immigration. In the past, the city's population was comprised of a diverse mixture of labor migrants mostly from Portugal, Germany, Italy, Spain, Japan, Syria, and Lebanon. Indeed, in the half century before the Great Depression, Brazil received the third-largest number of immigrants in the Western hemisphere (after the United States and Argentina), and a large number of these migrants settled in São Paulo (Holloway 1978). Between 1890 and 1923, nearly 4 million immigrants arrived in São Paulo, from a multitude of sending communities, as table 15.1 illustrates.

The decision to take on immigrant laborers en masse directly stemmed from the urgent need to replace slaves following the demise of the slave trade and the abolition of slavery in 1889 (Holloway 1980; Andrews 1988). At the same time, the Brazilian state hoped to populate the south of the country and ensure possession of its territory. The desire by the state to "whiten" Brazilian society and develop a homogeneous national culture also may have served to motivate national immigration policy at the time (Safa 2005).

The first mass immigration movement came with the prohibition of slave trafficking in 1850. Sensing a move toward abolition (which would come in 1889), plantation owners in São Paulo began to look for alternative sources of labor. They solved the problem by pushing the government

1. World-systems theory does address how decolonization, national consolidation, military interventions, and capital penetration forge connections *through time* at the scale of the state (Massey 1999; Castles and Miller 2003). Yet we are particularly interested in how the migration process works in more intimate ways, through social networks, especially at the household level.

TABLE 15.1

IMMIGRATION TO SÃO PAULO, BY NATIONALITY, 1884–1923

Nationality	Decade			
	1884–1893	*1894–1903*	*1904–1913*	*1914–1923*
Germans	22,778	6,698	33,859	29,339
Spaniards	113,116	102,142	224,672	94,779
Italians	510,533	537,784	196,521	86,320
Japanese	—	—	11,868	20,398
Portuguese	170,621	155,542	384,672	201,252
Middle Easterners	96	7,124	45,803	20,400
Other	66,524	42,820	109,222	51,493
Total	883,668	852,110	1,006,617	503,981

Source: Brazilian Institute for Geography and Statistics, various years.

to recruit foreign labor, primarily from Europe and, later, Japan (Conrad 1975; Holloway 1978; Bassanezi 2001). In 1840 the first immigration recruitment company was established by planters in São Paulo; these companies played an increasingly important role in stimulating and shaping Brazilian migration patterns through the end of the nineteenth century.

At the same time, to attract European immigrants to the country, the Brazilian government offered small plots of land. In the 1870s, German immigrants were the first to come, followed by the Spaniards and Italians. But after the abolition of slavery in 1889, planters urged the government to address the labor scarcity, and in the early 1890s the state began to take over and expand the functions of the planters' recruitment companies, sending representatives to Europe to promote emigration to Brazil (Holloway 1978; Lesser 1999). The aim was no longer to attract families to set up small holdings but instead to hire hands to tend the coffee plantations, which were in their heyday.

The government not only staged a major advertising campaign throughout Europe but also offered travel subsidies for emigrant families, especially for those who engaged in labor contracts with plantation owners (Conrad 1975). The subsidy consisted of a free sea passage for a family group and free transportation to the plantations (Andrews 1988). This subsidization lasted until 1927, perhaps because it was a sure way of attracting poor immigrants to a country whose climate and sanitary conditions were hardly alluring (Fausto 1991; Holloway 1978). Widespread immigration was encouraged and the promotion and transportation costs of recruitment were fully subsidized with government revenues; state support was seen as necessary to overcome the reluctance of Europeans to migrate to Brazil.

A massive wave of overseas emigration swept across Europe during this period. This wave of emigration was set in motion by socioeconomic and demographic transformations under way in several European countries (Ostergren 1988). It was further facilitated by the spread of steamships and the consequent drop in the cost of sea passages. The arrival of the first large groups of immigrants to São Paulo triggered a chain reaction, as settlers in the new land persuaded relatives and friends to follow suit, significantly increasing the number of immigrants arriving in São Paulo. Indeed, nearly 2.3 million disembarked as third-class passengers at the port of Santos in São Paulo state in the late nineteenth century alone (Fausto 1991).

Planter interests remained important in São Paulo's immigration policy through the early twentieth century, and when complaints arose that European immigrants (especially Italians) proved to be too demanding and rebellious (protesting low wages and poor working conditions), planters began to look elsewhere. The Chinese option was discussed, but international pressures against "coolie" contract labor pushed Brazil in the direction of Japan. Japan, like China, had a large and restless rural population, and when the United States banned Japanese entry in 1907, the directors of Brazilian immigration recruitment companies convinced the Japanese to divert their migration to Brazil (Lesser 1999). Also, at the same time that Brazilian planters complained about the instability of European (especially Italian) workers, the Italian government had prohibited their citizens from working in Brazil (because of the working conditions), so Brazil was even more in need of Japanese labor. Japanese first arrived in São Paulo as contract labor in 1908, and their numbers increased through the 1930s, though World War II and the end of official relations between the countries ended the migration flow by the 1940s (Santos 1997; Lone 2001).

From the 1930s onward, the number of immigrants began to subside, as figure 15.1 demonstrates. Nationalist policies, massive worldwide depression, and political instability in several European countries hampered emigration to Latin America (and elsewhere). In São Paulo specifically, the burgeoning demand for labor to boost industrial development was increasingly satisfied by means of internal migration (Graham 1970). Indeed, from the 1930s to the 1970s, the process of urbanization in São Paulo was remarkable. Postwar government policies that stimulated economic growth, along with private industrial and commercial expansion, prompted dramatic flows of migration from the countryside to Brazil's large and intermediate-sized cities, especially to the rapidly growing city of São Paulo. From the early 1950s onward, deteriorating economic, social, and environmental conditions in many parts of rural Brazil triggered even more growth in São Paulo. Large numbers of rural migrants from all parts of the country (but particularly from the most poverty stricken states in the Northeast) used improved roads and expanding transportation networks to enter São Paulo. As Alan Marcus (2004) explains, among other reasons, harsh droughts, desertification, and hunger pushed the *nordestinos* (Northeasterners) from the *sertão* (that is, the interior or backlands) to search for employment opportunities in São Paulo's industrial hub. A fully integrated sociospatial system ensured the process

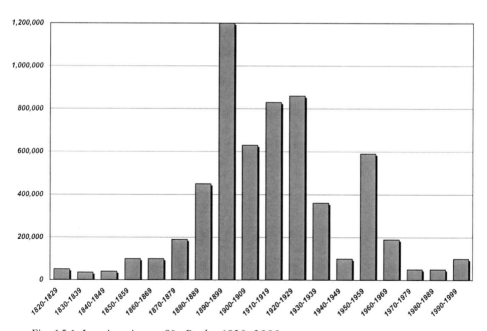

Fig. 15.1. Immigration to São Paulo, 1820–2000.

of internal migration to São Paulo. During the 1950s, a small spike in new immigrant arrivals occurred as well, largely a response to the Brazilian economic miracle. But this flow rapidly waned after 1959, when the country started to experience serious economic and political difficulties. Eventually, the pace of internal migration also declined, though the movement of Brazilians to São Paulo has had, and continues to have, a tremendous impact on the composition of the resident population (Skop et al. 2006a). Yet natural increase, especially in the urban core, is currently the most important factor in fueling the growth in the metropolis. Today, more than 81 percent of Brazilians reside in a metropolitan area, 20 million of whom (or 11 percent of the total population) live in the São Paulo metropolitan area alone.

SÃO PAULO: FORMER IMMIGRANT GATEWAY

By the second half of the twentieth century, immigration to Brazil was greatly reduced, in part because economic opportunities decreased and checks on entrance of foreigners became more rigid, but also because immigration pressures decreased as wealth and political and economical stability increased in those sending countries which had contributed the most immigrants. The only immigrants that continued to arrive in significant numbers were the Japanese, who came to till small farms in the states of São Paulo and Paraná to the south (Sakurai 1998).

Following the hardships of the early years—no different from those adversities facing most newcomers in other countries—most immigrants gradually integrated into Brazil's multiethnic society (Fausto 1991). In reality, various nationalistic governments strongly encouraged Europeans to assimilate into Brazilian culture. The goal was to replace the immigrants' home cultures by forcing them to learn Portuguese, prohibiting them to organize their own political groups, and forbidding them to publish foreign-language magazines and newspapers, or to instruct classes in languages other than Portuguese (Amaral and Fusco 2005). Massive campaigns have created national propaganda that on the one hand, celebrate the ethnic and racial diversity so prevalent in Brazilian society, but on the other, force large communities of immigrants to give up their cultural identities (at least publicly) in order to succeed.

Over time, this policy worked, and the majority of immigrants (and their descendants) integrated into Brazilian society. The majority also managed to move up the social ladder. In fact, immigrants were responsible for galvanizing much of the development of trade and industry in São Paulo. Most European groups concentrated in commerce activities and started both small businesses and larger enterprises (Truzzi 1991; Vilela 2002). Many Japanese immigrants, too, eventually left coffee plantations and either moved from the countryside to the city of São Paulo or became tenant farmers. In the 1930s Japanese farmers were responsible for 35 percent of vegetable and fruit production in the greater São Paulo area; currently, that number has grown to nearly 70 percent (Page 1995).

Today, immigration to São Paulo has all but stopped. In fact, according to the most recent UN Population Division data on net migration (2000–2005), Brazil loses more migrants than it gains every year. The dearth of immigrants in the metropolis is reflected in the Brazilian census displayed in table 15.2, which indicates that only 195,643 foreign-born individuals were residing in the city of São Paulo in 2000, constituting less than 2 percent of the city's total population. The vast majority of these immigrants come from Europe (59.9 percent), and it is likely that some of these individuals are not recent arrivals, but rather aging immigrants who came to the city many years ago. Other immigrants hail from several other regions, including Asia and Oceania (18.4 percent), South and Central America (12.9 percent), Africa and the Middle East (5.2 percent), and North America (1.6 percent). These newcomers most likely arrived more recently, especially since the 1990s, when Brazil began to receive both legal and illegal migration flows from all of these regions (Amaral and Fusco 2005).

Those immigrants living in São Paulo come from more than seventy different countries, the most significant of which are shown in figure 15.2. The largest proportions originate from Portugal (32.3 percent), Japan (11.2 percent), Italy (10 percent), and Spain (7 percent), with smaller numbers arriving from Bolivia, Korea, Chile, Argentina, China, Libya, and Germany. Most of these immigrants have crossed the border for economic reasons. For instance, a small number of highly skilled migrants from Europe and North America have found their way to São Paulo recently,

TABLE 15.2

NUMBER OF FOREIGN-BORN RESIDENTS BY COUNTRY OF BIRTH
IN SÃO PAULO, 2000

Country of birth	Population in 2000	Percentage of total foreign-born
Europe	117,279	59.9
Portugal	63,274	31.4
Italy	19,786	10.1
Spain	13,782	7.0
Germany	4,527	2.3
France	2,595	1.3
Russia	2,364	1.2
Poland	2,159	1.1
Romania	1,729	0.9
Hungary	1,375	0.7
Greece	1,235	0.6
Rest of Europe	4,453	2.3
Asia/Oceania	35,991	18.4
Japan	22,005	11.2
Korea	7,029	3.6
China	4,799	2.5
Taiwan	1,820	0.9
Rest of Asia/Oceania	258	0.1
South/Central America	25,203	12.9
Bolivia	7,722	3.9
Chile	5,189	2.7
Argentina	5,183	2.6
Uruguay	2,277	1.2
Peru	1,834	0.9
Paraguay	1,420	0.7
Rest of South/Central America	1,578	0.7
Africa/Middle East	10,153	5.2
Libya	4,615	2.4
Egypt	2,126	1.1
Angola	1,191	0.6
Syria	1,070	0.5
Rest of Africa/Middle East	1,144	0.6

(Continued)

TABLE 15.2 *(continued)*

North America	3,113	1.6
United States	2,551	1.3
Canada	282	0.1
Mexico	280	0.1
Other countries	3,893	2.0
Total foreign-born	195,643	100.00
Total city population	10,435,546	1.9

Source: Brazilian Institute for Geography and Statistics 2000.

primarily as members of an international class of highly skilled laborers. These immigrants, as a part of the "information elite," build professional and social networks that span national boundaries (Castells 1996). As major multinational corporations seek to gain market share and expand internationally, they recruit the most highly skilled workers to facilitate flows of capital, skill, and technology (Sassen 2004). Though not a huge community, the impact of this small group of immigrants is significant enough that the Brazilian Government has created a special department within the Labor Ministry to help the highly skilled newcomers (Amaral and Fusco 2005).

At the same time, immigrants arrive (oftentimes illegally) from neighboring countries such as Argentina, Uruguay, Chile, and Bolivia (Vilela 2002). The development of a common economic market beginning in the early 1990s with the "Asunción Agreement" in southern cone countries like Uruguay, Brazil, Argentina, and Paraguay (collectively known as the Mercosur) appears to drive these recent migration flows (Amaral and Fusco 2005). Yet because the Brazilian government has no policies either encouraging or discouraging regional migration, illegal immigrants from neighboring countries account for the majority of new arrivals. This increasing trend (the extent of which may be masked since government census data fails to include most undocumented migrants) suggests the possibility that São Paulo is becoming a regional immigrant gateway, but because the city continues to experience more emigration than immigration (including a significant flow of migration to Paraguay that began in the 1960s),

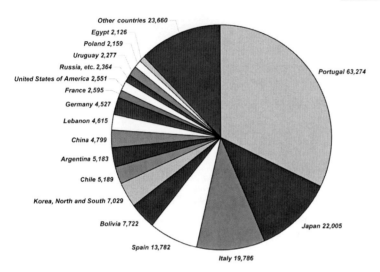

Total foreign-born:	195,643
Total population:	10,435,546
Percentage foreign-born:	1.87%

Other countries 23,660
Egypt 2,126
Poland 2,159
Uruguay 2,277
Russia, etc. 2,364
United States of America 2,551
France 2,595
Germany 4,527
Lebanon 4,615
China 4,799
Argentina 5,183
Chile 5,189
Korea, North and South 7,029
Bolivia 7,722
Spain 13,782
Italy 19,786
Japan 22,005
Portugal 63,274

Fig. 15.2. Foreign-born residents in São Paulo by country of birth, 2000. *Source:*
Instituto Brasile de Geografia e estatistica, 2000 Census.

only time will tell if the metropolis will retain more regional migrants
than it loses.

Foreign-born migrants constitute such a small minority of São Paulo
today that there are very few studies about them (for exceptions see Decol
1999; Figoli and Vilela 2003; Patarra 2004). Even so, new immigrants
continue to transform the economic and cultural landscapes of São Paulo,
though their "imprint" is slight, if not invisible. For instance, Koreans have
made their mark in the city as they engage in textiles and the restaurant
business (Patarra and Baeninger 1995). And as Sakurai (1998) discovered,
although Japanese immigrants in São Paulo may have started as very low-
skilled workers, at the bottom of the economic scale, they quickly achieved
a high socioeconomic status because they lacked notable competition or
conflict with other members of the larger society. Individuals within the
group were also highly successful in creating an ethnic economy, the primary function of which is to serve the immediate, specialized consumption

Fig. 15.3. A Japanese store specializing in imported goods. Photo by Sarah Zell.

needs of the Japanese population living in São Paulo, like the Japanese specialty goods store illustrated in figure 15.3. There is even one neighborhood in São Paulo, Liberdade (also a stop on the metro), that has been known as "the" Japanese neighborhood ever since the first migrants began to arrive.

In terms of foreign-born migrants' geographic distributions within the metropolis, Emily Skop and colleagues (2006b) discovered that they are highly concentrated in particular areas of São Paulo, especially in the central city, as figure 15.4 demonstrates. Indeed, amongst all migrants living in the city, the foreign-born are the most highly segregated group, according to both traditional and newer indices of dissimilarity. This point is significant, and suggests a couple of possibilities: São Paulo is not as welcoming to immigrants as it may have once been, so immigrants are forced to concentrate in particular neighborhoods where the foreign-born make up a significant proportion of the population, or immigrants self-segregate because they would rather interact with their own group than seek out others in the metropolis.

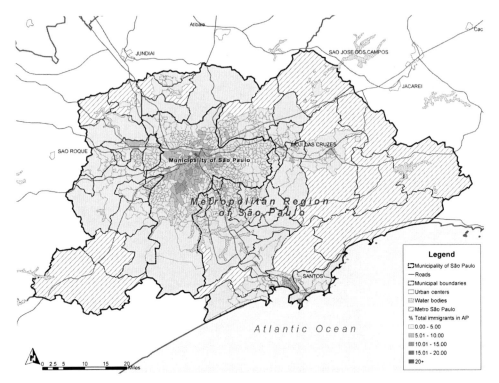

Fig. 15.4. Immigrants in São Paulo as a percentage of each *Area de Ponderaçao*, 2000.

SÃO PAULO: EMIGRANT OUTPOST

During the 1980s, Brazil entered a severe economic recession, which left thousands jobless. The economic crisis worsened the position of Brazil's middle class, and in the mid-1980s many primarily middle-class Brazilians began to seek opportunities in other global cities. As a result, for the first time in its history, São Paulo has gone from being a city of net immigration to one of net emigration. Currently, according to the latest Brazilian Consulate Report and data from the UN Population Division, more than 1.8 million Brazilians are living outside the country (Levitt and de la Dehesa 2003). Many of these emigrants take advantage of historical connections and ongoing social ties to migrate back to the countries of their ancestors, including Japan. They also forge new ties as they begin to migrate to the United States. Interestingly enough, however, while many of the forces prompting migrants to move to these countries are similar, the nature of migration is starkly different, as Japan-bound Brazilians are formally recruited by the Japanese government, whereas U.S.-bound Brazilians must negotiate their own way into the United States, often illegally. The two groups of emigrants rely on vastly different social networks and thus are different types of movers.

The Japan Case: Ethnic "Return" Migration

Though they share weak contemporary economic or political ties, Brazil and Japan are connected through a historical legacy of migration. Many Brazilians, especially in the state of São Paulo, are descendants of Japanese who migrated to Brazil in the early 1900s to work in mining and on agricultural plantations, and many of these past migrants have maintained contact with family and social connections in Japan. The first organized group sailed from Japan in 1908 (the same year that Japanese migration to the United States was banned), arriving as contract labor for coffee plantations in the state of São Paulo. According to Stewart Lone (2001), from 1908 to 1940, 190,000 men, women, and children migrated from Japan to Brazil, creating the largest expatriate Japanese community outside East Asia. The migration flow halted after 1941, however, with war in the Pacific. The two countries reached a peace treaty in 1952, and the migrant flow actually reversed in the 1980s as more and more individuals moved from Brazil to Japan.

For a long time, Japan was unique in the world in that it was a developed country whose industrialized economy did not rely on foreign labor. With economic growth in the 1980s, however, complaints of labor shortages in manufacturing escalated. A declining fertility rate, increasing life expectancy, and depletion of rural labor sources, combined with increased female labor participation, created a labor shortage so acute that many small- and medium-sized businesses would soon have to close their doors (Tsuda 1999a). Many large companies were able to automate or to transfer production abroad, but for those not able to do so, foreign workers became the only realistic and cost-effective source of labor.

In response, the Japanese government amended the Immigration Control and Refugee Recognition Act in 1990. In an effort to maintain Japan's ethnic homogeneity, the act created a new visa category, which in effect instituted a labor recruitment plan whereby descendants of Japanese born abroad *(Nikkeijin)*, up to the third generation, as well as their spouses may enter Japan legally to work for up to three years (Yamanaka 2002; Tsuda 1999a, 1999b; Spencer 1992). Because the visa is renewable, it in effect grants *Nikkeijin* quasi-permanent resident status, with no restrictions on employment, and the opportunity to apply for citizenship over time. Spouses or children of Japanese residents may also achieve alien resident status, and after three years of residency may apply for permanent resident status.

With the reformed immigration policy allowing for ethnic "return" migration, the population of foreign-born Brazilian residents in Japan greatly increased. According to the 2000 Japanese Census, from 1995 to 2000 the increase of foreign-born residents who were Brazilian nationals was 55,000, second only to that of the Chinese. Today, Brazilians constitute more than 14.4 percent of the total foreign-born population in Japan, making them the third-largest foreign-born group in the country after Chinese and Koreans (Japanese Census 2000). Naoto Higuchi and Kiyoto Tanno (2003) estimate that approximately one-fifth of Japanese descendants in Brazil are now living in Japan. Because labor recruitment in "return" migration to Japan operates along explicitly ethnic lines, those migrants who have maintained social networks through generations are also likely to be those most readily able to emigrate.

In designing immigration policy, the Japanese government appears to be negotiating between labor needs and ethnic xenophobia. The official explanation for granting residence-work permits to *Nikkeijin* is to provide opportunities to visit relatives in Japan, though the Japanese government may have the hidden motive of stopping the entry of additional illegal workers and solving the labor shortage problem (Kondo 2002). Officially referred to as "visitors," many *Nikkeijin* immigrants are in fact sources of flexible and cost-effective foreign labor for Japanese businesses (Tsuda and Cornelius 2004). As a result, these migrants have become structurally embedded in the Japanese labor market, since the introduction of cost-effective foreign labor has created a reliance on Brazilian labor in Japan, generating a self-perpetuating demand for immigration (Tsuda 1999b; Martin 1991; Higuchi and Tanno 2003). Mizuho Matsuda (2003) notes that 73.1 percent of the 40,033 immigrants that arrived in Japan as "long-term residents" were Brazilian (followed by Chinese, Filipinos, and Peruvians). Likewise, the largest percentage (43.9 percent) of the newcomers who were granted visas as spouses of Japanese residents was Brazilian.

In the original formulation of the new immigration policy, the Japanese government believed that Brazilians were likely to be "temporary" migrants, as most Brazilians who initially migrated to Japan were members of the middle class temporarily escaping the economic recession in Brazil in the 1980s (Morita 1992; Spencer 1992; Tsuda 1999a). Indeed, the original intention of a large majority of Brazilian migrants was to stay for short periods of time, saving up money for their return to Brazil (Higuchi and Tanno 2003; Morita 1993; Morita and Sassen 1994; Yamanaka 2002). However, Takeyuki Tsuda (1999a, 1999b) has shown that this intention has changed over time, and many more migrants are moving to Japan with longer-term intentions. Because work visas to Japan are renewable, Brazilian immigrants may in fact become de facto long-term Japanese residents, and as the duration of the average Brazilian migrant's stay has increased, many migrants have brought their family members to Japan. Indeed, Brazilian census estimates reveal that fewer than 20 percent of those who reported residing in another country less than 10 years before the 2000 census came from Japan, suggesting the fact that many are deciding to stay in Japan rather than return to Brazil.

Tsuda (1999b) argues that a "culture of migration" has developed in many sending communities in Brazil, though this migration flow is still limited to a certain extent by the ethnic restrictions placed on the migration flow (one must prove Japanese ancestry, to the third generation, or be a spouse or child of an ethnic descendent). Significantly, Japan also holds the power to increase or decrease the numbers of migrants to be admitted at any time, and labor recruiters who process visa applications act as a sort of additional filter that governs who will go abroad to Japan, oftentimes allowing individuals to go simply if they have a Japanese-sounding last name or "look" Japanese (Roth 2002).

Even as the Japanese economy has worsened and the Brazilian economic situation has improved, Brazilians continued to migrate to Japan. Migrant social networks linking the two countries are now so well established that a self-perpetuating process has begun. In fact, Higuchi and Tanno (2003) show that a "Brazilian niche" has developed in certain industries in Japan, socially labeling particular jobs (especially in the automobile and electronics manufacturing sectors) as "immigrant jobs" and concentrating foreign labor in those occupational areas.

To a certain extent, as family connections have been maintained through the years, Brazilian migration of *Nikkeijin* to Japan may be seen as family reunification. However, because the emigration to Brazil took place many generations before and emigrants lost their Japanese citizenship, it is unlikely that family reunification rather than economic rationale

Fig. 15.5. Numerous labor-broker offices recruit *Nikkeijin* through advertisements in Brazil's major newspapers.

is the primary motive for Brazilian migration (though "family reunification" or "visits" are the official reasons given by the Japanese government
for the granting of resident status to *Nikkeijin*). So, although some potential emigrants take advantage of their ties as second- and third-generation
descendants of those original São Paulo–bound immigrants to "return" to
Japan, they have also begun to utilize extensive migrant social networks
and transnational labor brokerage firms, like the ones featured in figure
15.5, to move to Japan.

The United States: New Transnational Linkages

Contemporary transnational linkages between the United States and Brazil have begun to fuel an alternative setting whereby the back-and-forth
exchanges of money, capital, and technologies have also created and now
perpetuate the flows of people between the two countries. Especially in
the past two decades, the push toward neoliberal reform and structural
adjustment programs has increased the connections between Brazil and
the United States, which in turn has prompted large numbers of people in
Brazil to become displaced from more secure livelihoods as peasant farmers, family artisans, and employees of state-owned industries (Castells
and Laserna 1989; Massey et al. 1998). As a result, a mobilized population prone to migrate both internally and internationally has emerged in
Brazil, especially in the recent era. Many of these migrants move to the
United States.

It is apparent that migration from São Paulo and other parts of Brazil
to the United States constitutes a complicated system that involves many
different players and diverse types of movement. The original migrants to
the United States arrived mostly in the late 1960s and 1970s, after the
1965 Immigration and Naturalization Act opened the doors to migrants
from South America. These "pioneer" migrants created new transnational
connections with their friends and family in Brazil, who later transformed
these linkages into channels by which new migrants could find their way
to the United States.

With the onset of the Brazilian economic crisis of the 1980s, the number of Brazilian-born immigrants in the United States increased rapidly, as

newcomers took advantage of newly crafted connections to move abroad (Goza 1994; Margolis 1994, 1998). Because of the combining function of decreasing opportunities in Brazil, increasing opportunities in the United States, as well as the emergence of a well-defined web of social networks, the volume of Brazilian migration to the United States has grown and expanded, and a "culture of migration" exists in many sending communities, including São Paulo. More and more often, migration has become a more integral part of the life cycle for *Paulista* (that is, São Paulo) residents, and migrants rely extensively on social networks to help them in the migration process, which is oftentimes illegal. In São Paulo, and in other Brazilian cities like Governador Valadares, illegal immigration to the United States has become so common that it has become next to impossible to obtain a non-immigrant visa to the United States (Beserra 2003). Consequently, Brazilian migration to the United States, which has not been preceded by the kinds of historical transnational linkages present in the Japanese case, is, in contrast to the Japanese case, generally characterized by illegality. Estimates of the proportion of Brazilian immigrants who are residing in the United States illegally range from 30 to 70 percent of the total Brazilian-born population (Margolis 1998). Most migrants arrive with either a tourist or a student visa and simply remain in the country after the visa expires, though some arrive undocumented or clandestinely cross the Mexican border (Amaral and Fusco 2005). Other migrants, descendants of Italian immigrants in Brazil, use their Italian passports to enter the United States illegally (Assis 2003).

No matter how they arrive, the financial cost of unauthorized migration to the United States is high; estimates given by Maxine Margolis (1998) range from $1,000 to $2,000 for a round-trip flight to as high as $10,000 for transportation across the Mexican border (Zell 2006). But the economic benefit can be great, as migrants are able to save money, much of which they remit home (recent estimates by the Inter-American Development Bank suggest that remittances by Brazilian emigrants topped $7.4 billion in 2006). They can also enjoy middle-class luxuries not available to them in Brazil (Margolis 1994, 1998). A popular Brazilian soap opera, *America,* has even dealt with the perils and romance of the northward passage in recent episodes. The soap opera chronicles illegal immigrants risking their lives to enter the United States to find jobs and romance, even as they experience hardship.

Franklin Goza (1994) demonstrates that Brazilian immigration to the United States was relatively small prior to the 1980s (only slightly more than 50,000 Brazilian-born individuals lived in the United States at the time of the 1980 U.S. Census). But today, significant migration flows between Brazil and the United States exist. Margolis (1998) estimates that there were around 350,000 to 400,000 Brazilians in the United States in the late 1990s, many of whom had arrived in the mid- to late 1980s. The most current estimates of the Brazilian-born population in the United States range from 328,510 (U.S. Census 2005) to 799,000 (Brazilian Ministry of Foreign Affairs, cited in Beserra 2003), and the true number probably lies somewhere in between. But the majority arrived in the past twenty years, as Teresa Sales (1999) found in her study of a Brazilian migrant community in a Massachusetts community, where the bulk of her sample arrived in the United States between 1985 and 1989. Similarly, Bernadete Beserra (2003) found that 76 percent of her sample of Brazilian migrants in Los Angeles arrived in the country between 1981 and 1999.

The migration flow to the United States appears to be influenced primarily by economic conditions in Brazil and immigration policy and legal conditions operating in the United States. In her case study of Brazilian migrants in New York, Margolis (1994) illustrates that, similar to the Japanese case, migrants during this period were generally well educated and middle-class Brazilians who had been squeezed out of the country by economic depression, and migration to the United States became a "safety valve" for many of them, most of whom arrived on nonimmigrant visas and stayed in the country. As migrant social networks expanded through time, however, the diversity in migrant selectivity also grew, especially as Brazilian migrants sought out family, friends, and even distant acquaintances already living in the United States (Zell 2006). In fact, social capital has begun to act as a substitute for human capital as social networks strengthen, and the process becomes self-perpetuating.

New transnational linkages between these two countries, forged over time through migrant social networks, have resulted in a particular geography of Brazilian communities in the United States. Historically, Brazilian immigration has been concentrated in major metropolitan areas in New England, New York, California, and Florida. In fact, Brazilians are very much clustered in three U.S. "immigrant gateways"—New York, Boston, and Miami. Margolis (1998) estimates that five states—New York, New Jersey, California, Florida, and Massachusetts—are home to approximately two-thirds of all Brazilians living in the United States, though smaller and more recently developed enclaves can also be found in Chicago; Philadelphia; Washington, D.C.; Roanoke, Virginia; and Houston and Austin, Texas. The residential concentration of Brazilian migrants in specific geographic areas suggests the existence and expansion of migrant social networks through time, all the while accompanied by a marked increase in the volume (and illegality) of Brazilian migration to the United States in recent years.

CONCLUSION

Although the connection between Brazil and Japan has a longer history than that with the United States, significant contemporary Brazilian migration flows to both countries appear to have risen around the same point in time, coinciding with the economic crisis of Brazil in the mid-1980s. A cursory glance might suggest that traditional neoclassical economics are at work here, as individuals balance the costs and benefits of moving to maximize expected incomes. Thus, Brazilians go to Japan and the United States because they expect to see the highest gains by choosing these two destination countries and perhaps because they think it is easier to go to these two countries than to most others, though flows to Paraguay and Europe are on the rise, and likely to increase, as new social networks and transnational linkages emerge.

However, the two migration flows discussed in this book chapter are characterized by different kinds of transnational connections, one historical and one recently established. The migration flow to Japan was formally state-induced, and resulting emigrant flows from São Paulo are shaped by both historical linkages between the two countries as well as antecedent social connections that span generations, linking origins and destinations. In the case of emigration to the United States, social networks are still at play, channeling migrants to concentrated communities of Brazilians in the country. However, these social networks formed more recently, out of transnational social connections forged by pioneer migrants who made their way to U.S. immigrant gateways in recent times.

Japanese immigration policy, because of its state-initiated nature, is more overtly selective than that of the United States (Zell 2006). Japan permits legal access to labor recruitment networks only if the migrant is ethnically Japanese (defined as a person of Japanese descendent up to three generations) or a spouse or child of such a descendent. Though it has maintained relatively restrictive immigration policies, the Japanese government has legally allowed for Brazilian immigration, with ethnicity as the primary determinant of access. But Brazilian migration to the United States (where historical and ethnic ties are weaker) is characterized by illegality, primarily because immigrants are relying on more informal social networks to facilitate movement.

Thus, the legal frameworks operating to shape or "manage" each migration flow shed light on the significant role of both previous and current political and cultural connections in understanding contemporary migration patterns. São Paulo, as a former immigrant gateway, saw the arrival of several hundred thousand Japanese in the late nineteenth and early twentieth centuries. These immigrants created large ethnic communities while also maintaining home ties and social networks that extended across international borders. While their transnational activities and political projects may have gone largely unnoticed by political leaders, scholars, and even some of the immigrants themselves, many Japanese Brazilians maintained connections that transcended both space and time. Today, their descendants, many of whom remain in the São Paulo metropolitan area, are testament to this continuous back-and-forth participation across borders, and to the ways in which transnational linkages can carry through (and even be reinvented) from one generation to the next. At the same time, the recent movement of Brazilians to the United States is a testament to the ways in which new transnational linkages can emerge and create alternative migration flows in a very short period of time.

Today, São Paulo clearly operates as an emigrant outpost that is not attracting large numbers of globally diverse migrants like other global cities.

The metropolis is instead feeding the global migration system with emigrants and pushing them towards other global cities. The foreign-born (and their descendants) are (re)creating old ties and fashioning new transnational networks that in turn create alternative migration flows. Thus, the metropolis still performs an important function in the global circulation of labor, and remains an essential part of that system. Simultaneously, it appears as though São Paulo could be at the threshold of remaking itself as a regional immigrant gateway, especially for immigrants coming from South America, though it is too early to tell how this trend will play out in the coming years. Nonetheless, this new trend could mean the creation of even more migrant linkages across space and through time, adding to the complexity of an already complicated global migration system.

Former immigrant gateways should not be written off as "has-beens." True, they no longer hold the power and attraction that they once did for potential immigrants, but these cities remain a part of the migrant circuit and their influence is likely to persist into the future. Although these cities have seen their foreign-born populations decline for more than a half century, the descendants of immigrants have come to constitute a significant proportion of the population through time. When given the opportunity or pushed by necessity to emigrate, some of these individuals seek out new destinations, as in the case of the Brazilian-U.S. migration flow. But others rely on the social networks that have persisted through time, and return to their original homelands, even if generations removed, as in the Brazilian-Japanese case. This fluid constellation of movement between various sending and receiving communities perpetuates migration and represents just how bounded to each other global cities have become in this era of economic globalization.

APPENDIX

REFERENCES

INDEX

Appendix

CITIES WITH MORE THAN 100,000 FOREIGN-BORN

City	Country	Census year	Metropolitan population[a]	Foreign-born	Percentage foreign-born
New York	United States	2005	18,351,099	5,117,290	27.9
Los Angeles	United States	2005	12,703,423	4,407,353	34.7
Hong Kong	China	2005	7,039,169	2,998,686	42.6
Toronto	Canada	2001	4,647,960	2,091,100	45.0
Miami	United States	2005	5,334,685	1,949,629	36.5
London	United Kingdom	2001	7,172,091	1,940,390	27.0
Chicago	United States	2005	9,272,117	1,625,649	17.5
Moscow	Russia	2002	10,382,754	1,586,068	15.3
Riyadh	Saudi Arabia	2000	4,730,330	1,477,601	31.2
Singapore	Singapore	2000	4,017,733	1,350,632	33.6
Sydney	Australia	2001	3,961,451	1,235,908	31.2
San Francisco	United States	2005	4,071,751	1,201,209	29.5
Jiddah	Saudi Arabia	1998	3,171,000	1,186,600	37.4
Houston	United States	2005	5,193,448	1,113,875	21.4
Paris	France	1999	6,161,887	1,081,611	17.5
Dubai	United Arab Emirates	2005	1,272,000	1,056,000	83.0

(Continued)

City	Country	Census year	Metropolitan population[a]	Foreign-born	Percentage foreign-born
Washington, D.C.	United States	2005	5,119,490	1,017,432	19.9
Dallas	United States	2005	5,727,391	1,016,221	17.7
Melbourne	Australia	2001	3,367,169	960,145	28.5
Buenos Aries	Argentina	2001	11,460,625	917,491	8.0
Riverside	United States	2005	3,827,946	827,584	21.6
Vancouver	Canada	2001	1,967,475	767,715	39.0
Tel Aviv–Yafo	Israel	2002	2,075,500	747,400	36.0
St. Petersburg	Russia	2000	4,661,219	711,596	15.3
Boston	United States	2005	4,270,631	684,165	16.0
Montreal	Canada	2001	3,388,640	664,435	19.6
San Diego	United States	2005	2,824,259	659,731	23.4
San Jose	United States	2005	1,726,057	614,304	35.6
Phoenix	United States	2005	3,805,123	612,850	16.1
Atlanta	United States	2005	4,828,838	612,759	12.7
Philadelphia	United States	2005	5,644,383	485,800	8.6
Seattle	United States	2005	3,133,715	479,913	15.3
Kiev	Ukraine	2001	2,566,953	456,186	17.8
Berlin	Germany	2001	3,337,000	435,117	13.0
Perth	Australia	2001	1,336,239	422,547	31.6
Mecca	Saudi Arabia	1998	1,326,000	397,800	30.0
Detroit	United States	2005	4,428,941	387,027	8.7
Johannesburg	South Africa	2001	6,664,427	375,169	5.6
Karachi	Pakistan	1998	9,339,023	371,611	4.0
Tbilisi	Georgia	1999	1,339,105	370,932	27.7
Auckland	New Zealand	2001	1,103,466	354,126	32.1

(Continued)

City	Country	Census year	Metropolitan population[a]	Foreign-born	Percentage foreign-born
Sacramento	United States	2005	2,004,476	353,592	17.6
Stockholm	Sweden	2003	1,693,946	340,852	20.1
Brisbane	Australia	2001	1,609,116	338,150	21.0
Las Vegas	United States	2005	1,691,213	334,087	19.8
Istanbul	Turkey	1990	7,309,190	327,647	4.5
Orlando	United States	2005	1,903,273	302,323	15.9
Muscat	Oman	2000	661,000	294,881	44.6
Tampa	United States	2005	2,596,556	294,848	11.4
Denver	United States	2005	2,327,901	290,765	12.5
Munich	Germany	2001	1,247,934	282,148	22.6
Zurich	Switzerland	2003	1,249,893	279,633	22.4
Athens	Greece	2001	2,805,262	275,080	9.8
Madrid	Spain	2002	5,423,384	272,692	5.0
Hamburg	Germany	2000	1,707,901	272,604	16.0
São Paulo	Brazil	2000	19,198,273	271,506	1.4
Minneapolis	United States	2005	3,076,239	267,368	8.7
Brussels	Belgium	2005	1,006,749	265,211	26.3
Portland	United States	2005	2,063,277	250,955	12.2
Vienna	Austria	2001	1,550,123	248,264	16.0
Medina	Saudi Arabia	1998	885,000	247,252	27.9
Barcelona	Spain	2002	4,805,927	237,513	4.9
Accra	Ghana	2000	2,905,726	225,735	7.8
Copenhagen	Denmark	2006	1,633,565	222,248	13.6
Tokyo	Japan	2000	12,064,101	212,975	1.8
San Antonio	United States	2005	1,844,018	211,579	11.5
Amsterdam	Netherlands	2005	742,951	211,260	28.4
Jerusalem	Israel	2002	678,300	208,700	30.8
Calgary	Canada	2001	943,310	205,000	21.7
Providence	United States	2005	1,565,972	198,286	12.7

(Continued)

City	Country	Census year	Metropolitan population[a]	Foreign-born	Percentage foreign-born
Ottawa	Canada	2001	1,050,755	193,665	18.4
Austin	United States	2005	1,406,364	192,738	13.7
Baltimore	United States	2005	2,583,923	184,439	7.1
Cologne	Germany	2001	1,019,049	182,456	17.9
Seoul	South Korea	2000	9,853,972	181,391	1.8
Frankfurt	Germany	2000	650,705	181,184	27.8
Manchester	United Kingdom	2001	2,482,328	179,927	7.2
Marseille	France	1999	1,834,026	175,779	9.6
Edmonton	Canada	2001	927,020	171,055	18.4
Osaka	Japan	2000	8,805,081	170,877	1.9
Rome	Italy	2000	2,655,970	169,064	6.4
Caracas	Venezuela	2001	1,836,286	166,669	9.1
Birmingham	United Kingdom	2001	977,087	161,250	16.5
Rotterdam	Netherlands	2005	596,597	157,395	26.4
Lyon	France	1999	1,579,237	156,518	9.9
Charlotte	United States	2005	1,491,330	134,749	9.0
Lisbon	Portugal	2000	3,926,000	134,485	3.4
Taipei	Taiwan	2000	6,646,503	129,152	1.9
Dublin	Ireland	2002	1,105,134	128,350	11.6
Hartford	United States	2005	1,140,319	127,212	11.2
Rio de Janeiro	Brazil	2000	11,546,023	125,887	1.1
Amman	Jordan	1994	1,387,440	124,360	9.0
Milan	Italy	2000	1,301,551	117,691	9.0
Bern	Switzerland	2003	951,957	117,094	12.3
Cleveland	United States	2005	2,082,379	115,897	5.6
Salt Lake City	United States	2005	1,017,572	112,628	11.1
Nagoya (Aichi Ken)	Japan	2000	7,043,300	110,298	1.6
Saint Louis	United States	2005	2,725,336	108,621	4.0

(Continued)

City	Country	Census year	Metropolitan population[a]	Foreign-born	Percentage foreign-born
Kansas City	United States	2005	1,909,666	103,618	5.4
San Juan	United States	2005	2,546,200	103,105	4.0
Columbus	United States	2005	1,665,428	101,891	6.1

Source: Editors, using various national census data. For more information, go to the editors' Web site, http://www.gstudynet.org/gum.

[a] Some cities on this list are less than 1 million people. They are included because they represent metropolitan areas of more than 1 million people, but we were unable to get metropolitan-level data.

References

Aalbers, Manuel, Ellen van Beckhoven, Ronald van Kempen, Sako Musterd, and Wim Ostendorf. 2003. "Large Housing Estates in the Netherlands: Overview of Developments and Problems in Amsterdam and Utrecht." RESTATE 2d report. Utrecht: Faculty of Geosciences.

Adi, Rianto. 1995. *Migrasi internasional tenaga kerja Indonesia: Harapan dan kenyataan* [International Migration of Indonesian Migrant Workers: Expectation and Reality]. Jakarta: Pusat Penelitian Unika Atma Jaya.

Afroza, Akhter, Rajgopal Chakrawarti, and Nikhat Rasheed. 2006. *A Review of Bridge Training Programs for Immigrants with Professional Backgrounds in Ontario: Exploratory Findings.* Toronto: Policy Roundtable Mobilizing Professions and Trades (PROMPT).

Agnew, John A. 1987. *Place and Politics: The Geographical Mediation of State and Society.* Boston and London: Allen and Unwin.

Aguilar, Filomeno V., Jr. 1999. "The Triumph of Instrumental Citizenship? Migrations, Identities, and the Nation-State in Southeast Asia." *Asian Studies Review* 23, no. 3: 307–36.

Alba, Richard, Nancy Denton, Shu-yin Leung, and John R. Logan. 1995. "Neighborhood Change under Conditions of Mass Immigration: The New York City Region, 1970–1990." *International Migration Review* 29, no. 3: 625–56.

Alba, Richard, John Logan, Wenquan Zhang, and Brian J. Stults. 1999. "Strangers Next Door: Immigrant Groups and Suburbs in Los Angeles and New York." In *A Nation Divided: Diversity, Inequality, and Community in American Society,* edited by Phyllis Moen, Donna Dempster-McClain, and Henry A. Walker, 108–32. Ithaca: Cornell Univ. Press.

Alfasi, Nurit. and Tovi Fenster. 2005. "A Tale of Two Cities: Jerusalem and Tel Aviv in an Age of Globalization." *Cities* 22, no. 5: 351–63.

Amaral, Ernesto Friedrich, and Wilson Fusco. 2005. "Shaping Brazil: The Role of International Migration." http://www.migrationinformation.org/feature/dis play.cfm?ID=311.

Amin, Ash. 1997. "Placing Globalization." *Theory, Culture, and Society* 14: 123–37.

———. 2002. "Ethnicity and the Multicultural City: Living with Diversity." *Environment and Planning A* 34: 959–80.

———. 2003. "Unruly Strangers? The 2001 Urban Riots in Britain." *International Journal of Urban and Regional Research* 27, no. 2: 460–63.

———. 2004. "Regions Unbound: Towards a New Politics of Place." *Geografiska Annaler* 86B: 33–44.

Amin, Ash, and Nigel Thrift. 2002. "Guest Editorial: Cities and Ethnicities." *Ethnicities* 2, no. 3: 291–300.

Anderson, Benedict. 1983. *Imagined Communities: Reflections on the Origins and Spread of Nationalism*. London: Verso.

Anderson, Kay. 1988. "Cultural Hegemony and the Race Definition Process in Chinatown, Vancouver, 1880–1980." *Environment and Planning D: Society and Space* 6: 127–49.

Andrews, George Reid. 1988. "Black and White Workers: São Paulo, Brazil, 1888–1928." *Hispanic American Historical Review* 68, no. 3: 491–524.

Ang, Ien. 1998. "Can One Say No to Chineseness? Pushing the Limits of the Diasporic Paradigm." *Boundary* 25, no. 3: 213–27.

Anisef, Paul, and Michael Lanphier, eds. 2003. *The World in a City*. Toronto: Univ. of Toronto Press.

Appadurai, Arjun. 1990. "Disjuncture and Difference in the Global Cultural Economy." *Public Culture* 2, no. 2: 1–21.

———. 1996. *Modernity at Large: Cultural Dimensions of Globalization*. Minneapolis: Univ. of Minnesota Press.

Araia, Testalem Tekleab. 2005. "Routes, Motivations, and Duration: Explaining Eritrean Forced Migrants' Journeys to Johannesburg." Master's thesis, Wits Univ., Johannesburg.

Arumainathan, P. 1970. *Census of Population, 1970: Singapore*. Singapore: Singapore Department of Statistics.

Atiyyah, Hamid S. 1990. "The Sponsorship System and Infringements of the Rights of Foreign Workers in the Gulf Countries." *Employee Responsibilities and Rights Journal* 3, no. 4: 267–76.

Azevedo, Mario. 2002. *Tragedy and Triumph: Mozambique Refugees in Southern Africa, 1977–2001*. Portsmouth, N.H.: Heinemann.

Badets, Janes, and Linda Howaston-Leo. 1999. "Recent Immigrants in the Work Force." *Canadian Social Trends* 52: 16–22.

Balz, Dan, and Darryl Fears. 2006. "We Decided Not to Be Invisible Anymore." *Washington Post*, Apr. 11, A1.

Barclay, Ryan, and Peter West. 2006. "Racism or Patriotism? An Eyewitness Account of the Cronulla Demonstration of 11th December, 2005." *People and Place* 14, no. 1: 75–85.

Bardsley, Martin, and Marian Storkey. 2000. "Estimating the Numbers of Refugees in London." *Journal of Public Health Medicine* 22, no. 3: 406.

Bartram, David. 1998. "Foreign Workers in Israel: History and Theory." *International Migration Review* 32, no. 2: 303–25.

———. 2000. "Japan and Labor Migration: Theoretical and Methodological Implications of Negative Cases." *International Migration Review* 34, no. 1: 5–32.

———. 2005a. *International Labor Migration: Foreign Workers and Public Policy*. New York: Palgrave Macmillan.

———. 2005b. "Une absence remarquée: Pourquoi si peu de travailleurs étrangers en Finlande?" *Migrations Société* 17, no. 102: 125–45.

Bar-Tsuri, Roni. 2003. *Foreign Workers Deported from Israel in 2002* [in Hebrew]. Jerusalem: Manpower Planning Authority, Ministry of Labour and Social Affairs.

Bassanezi, Maria Silvia C. Beozzo. 2001. "Family and Immigration in the Brazilian Past." In *Population Change in Brazil: Contemporary Perspectives*, edited by Daniel J. Hogan, 61–80. Campinas, Brazil: Population Studies Center (Nepo/Unicamp).

Beall, Jo, Owen Crankshaw, and Susan Parnell. 2000a. "The Causes of Unemployment in Post-apartheid Johannesburg and the Livelihood Strategies of the Poor." *Journal of Economic and Social Geography* 91, no. 4: 379–96.

———. 2000b. "Local Government, Poverty Reduction, and Inequality in Johannesburg." *Environment and Urbanisation* 12: 107–22.

———. 2003a. *Uniting a Divided City: Governance and Social Exclusion in Johannesburg*. London: Earthscan.

———. 2003b. "Urban Water Supply, Sanitation, and Social Policy: Lessons from Johannesburg, South Africa." In *World Poverty: New Policies to Defeat an*

Old Enemy, edited by Peter Townsend and Dave Gordon, 251–70. London: Polity Press.

———. 2003c. "Victims, Villians, and Fixers: The Urban Environment and Johannesburg's Poor." In *Human Settlements and Sustainability,* edited by Saskia Sassen and P. Marcotullio, 833–55. New York: UNESCO.

Beaverstock, Jonathan, and Joanne Smith. 1996. "Lending Jobs to Global Cities: Skilled International Labour Migration, Investment Banking, and the City of London." *Urban Studies* 33, no. 8: 1377–1400.

Beaverstock, Jonathon, Richard Smith, and Peter Taylor. 1999. "A Roster of World Cities." *Cities* 16, no. 6: 445–58.

———. 2000. "World City Network: A New Metageography." *Annals of the Association of American Geographers* 90, no. 1: 123–34.

Beaverstock, Jonathan, Richard Smith, Peter J. Taylor, David Walker, and Hayden Lorimer. 2000. "Globalization and World Cities: Some Measures and Methodologies." *Applied Geography* 20, no. 1: 43–63.

Beavon, Keith. 1997. "Johannesburg: A City and Metropolitan Area in Transformation." In *The Urban Challenge in Africa,* edited by Carole Rakodi, 150–91. Tokyo: UN Univ. Press.

———. 1998. "Johannesburg: Coming to Grips with Globalization from an Abnormal Base." In *Globalization and the World of Large Cities,* edited by Fu-chen Lo and Yue-man Yeung, 352–88. Tokyo: UN Univ. Press.

Bell, Martin. 1995. *Internal Migration in Australia, 1986–1991: Overview Report.* Canberra: Australian Government Publishing Service.

Bell, Martin, and Jim Cooper. 1995. *Internal Migration in Australia, 1986–1991: The Overseas-Born.* Canberra: Australian Government Publishing Service.

Bell, Martin, and Graeme Hugo. 2000. *Internal Migration in Australia, 1991–1996.* Canberra: Australian Government Publishing Service.

Ben Elia, Nahum. 1993. "Policy Making and Management in Israeli Local Government: Evolving Trends and Strategies." *Policy Studies Journal* 21: 115–25.

Benton-Short, Lisa, Marie D. Price, and Samantha Friedman. 2005. "Globalization from Below: The Ranking of Global Immigrant Cities." *International Journal of Urban and Regional Research* 29, no. 4: 945–59.

Bergsten, C. Fred, and Inbom Choi, eds. 2003. *The Korean Diaspora in the World Economy.* Special Report 15. Washington, D.C.: Institute for International Economies.

Berthomière, William. 2003. "L'emergence d'une Tel Aviv cosmopolite ou les effets d'un fin melange entre reconfigurations sociopolitiques internes et externes."

Cahiers de la Méditerranée 67. http://revel.unice.fr/cmedi/sommaire.html?id =169.

Beserra, Bernadete. 2003. *Brazilian Immigrants in the United States: Cultural Imperialism and Social Class.* New York: LFB Scholarly Publishing.

Betts, Katherine. 2005. "Cosmopolitan and Patriots: Australia's Cultural Divide and Attitudes to Immigration." *People and Place* 13, no. 2: 29–40.

Bhamjee, Abeda, and Jonathan Klaaren. 2004. "Legal Problems Facing Refugees in Johannesburg." In *Forced Migrants in the New Johannesburg,* edited by Loren Landau, 54–60. Johannesburg: Forced Migration Programme, Wits Univ.

Binnie, Jon, Julian Holloway, Steve Millington, and Craig Young, eds. 2006. *Cosmopolitan Urbanism.* London: Routledge.

"Birmingham: From Workshop to Melting Pot." 1998. *Economist,* Aug. 8, 22–23.

Birmingham City Council. 2001a. *Population Census in Birmingham: Asian Groups.* Birmingham: Birmingham City Council.

———. 2001b. *Population Census in Birmingham: Black Groups.* Birmingham: Birmingham City Council.

———. 2001c. *Population Census in Birmingham: Chinese Groups.* Birmingham: Birmingham City Council.

———. 2001d. *Population Census in Birmingham: Other Ethnic Groups.* Birmingham: Birmingham City Council.

———. 2001e. *Population Census in Birmingham: White Groups.* Birmingham: Birmingham City Council.

Birmingham Government Web Site. N.d. http://www.birmingham.gov.uk/.

Birrell, Bob. 1990. "Population Growth and Urban Problems." In *Regional Policies: Future Directions,* 62–75. Papers presented at the Office of EPAC Seminar. Canberra, Australia: Australian Government Publishing Service.

———. 1991. "Infrastructure Costs on the Urban Fringe: Sydney and Melbourne Compared." In *Background Papers on Urban and Regional Issues: Studies Prepared for the Office of EPAC,* 203–34. Background Paper no. 10. Canberra: Australian Government Publishing Service.

Blainey, Geoffrey. 1993. "A Critique of Indo-Chinese in Australia: The Issues of Unemployment and Residential Concentration." *BIPR Bulletin* (Bureau of Immigration and Population Research) 9 (July): 42–45.

———. 1994. "Melting Pot on the Boil." *Bulletin,* Aug. 30, 22–27.

Blair, T. L., and Edward D. Hulsbergen. 1993. "Designing Renewal on Europe's Multi-ethnic Urban Edge: The Case of Bijlmermeer, Amsterdam." *Cities* 6: 283–98.

Board of Education of the City of New York. 1999. *Facts and Figures: Answers to Frequently Asked Questions about Limited English Proficient Students and Bilingual/ESL Programs, 1997–1998.* New York: Office of Bilingual Education.

Bodaar, Annemarie. 2006. "Multicultural Urban Space and the Cosmopolitan 'Other': The Contested Revitalization of Amsterdam's Bijlmermeer." In *Cosmopolitan Urbanism,* edited by Jon Binnie, Julian Holloway, Steve Millington, and Craig Young, 171–86. London: Routledge.

Body-Gendrot, Sophie. 2002. "Living Apart or Together with Our Differences? French Cities at a Crossroads." *Ethnicities* 2, no. 3: 367–85.

Bracken, Ali. 2006. "Angry Exchanges as Afghans Are Removed." *Irish Times,* May 22.

Brah, Avtar. 1996. *Cartographies of Diaspora: Contesting Identities.* London: Routledge.

Braichevska, Olena, Halyna Volosiuk, Olena Malynovska, Yaroslav Pylynskyi, Nancy Popson, and Blair Ruble. 2004. *Nontraditional Immigrants in Kiev.* Washington, D.C.: Woodrow Wilson International Center for Scholars.

Bremner, L. 2000. "Reinventing the Johannesburg Inner City." *Cities* 17, no. 3: 185–93.

Brennock, Mark. 2004. "Ahern Welcomes Referendum Poll Support." *Irish Times,* June 8.

Breton, Raymond. 1992. *Report of the Academic Advisory Panel on the Social and Cultural Impacts of Immigration: Meeting on Indicators of Integration.* Ottawa: Research Division, Strategic Planning and Research.

Breton, Raymond, Wsevolod Isajiw, Warren Kalbach, and Jeffrey Reitz. 1990. *Ethnic Identity and Equality: Varieties of Experiences in a Canadian City.* Toronto: Univ. of Toronto Press.

Brettell, Caroline. 2003. "Bringing the City Back In: Cities as Context for Immigrant Incorporation." In *American Arrivals: Anthropology Engages the New Immigration,* edited by Nancy Foner, 163–95. Santa Fe: School of American Research.

———. 2005. "The Spatial, Social, and Political Incorporation of Asian Indian Immigrants in Dallas, Texas." *Urban Anthropology* 34, nos. 2–3: 247–80.

Brody, Betsy. 2002. *Opening the Door: Immigration, Ethnicity, and Globalization in Japan.* New York: Routledge.

Brubaker, Rogers. 2003. "The Return of Assimilation? Changing Perspectives on Immigration and Its Sequels in France, Germany, and the United States." In *Toward Assimilation and Citizenship: Immigrants in Liberal Nation-States,* edited by Christian Joppke and Ewa Morawska, 39–58. Basingstoke: Palgrave Macmillan.

Bryson, John, Peter Daniels, and Nick Henry. 1996. "From Widgets to Where? The Birmingham Economy in the 1990s." In *Managing a Conurbation: Birmingham and Its Region,* edited by A. John Gerrard and Terry Slater, 156–68. Studley, England: Brewin Books.

Burghardt, Andrew F. 1971. "A Hypothesis about Gateway Cities." *Annals of the Association of American Geographers* 61, no. 2: 269–85.

Burnley, Ian. 1989. "Settlement Dimensions of the Vietnam-Born Population in Sydney." *Australian Geographical Studies* 27, no. 2: 129–54.

———. 1996. *Atlas of Australian People, 1991 Census: New South Wales.* Canberra: Australian Government Publishing Service.

———. 1998. "Immigrant City, Global City? Advantage and Disadvantage among Communities from Asia in Sydney." *Australian Geographer* 29, no. 1: 49–70.

———. 1999. "Levels of Immigrant Residential Concentration in Sydney and Their Relationship with Disadvantage." *Urban Studies* 36, no. 8: 1295–1315.

———. 2004. "Migration Processes and Geographies of Population Diversity in Sydney, Australia: A 2001 Census Evaluation." Presentation to conference of New Zealand Geographical Society, Auckland.

Burnley, Ian, and Peter Murphy. 1994. *Immigration, Housing Costs, and Population Dynamics in Sydney.* Canberra: Australian Government Publishing Service.

———. 2004. *Sea Change: Movement from Metropolitan to Arcadian Australia.* Sydney: Univ. of New South Wales Press.

Business Times, various issues.

Buttimer, Avril. 2005. "The Hidden Community: Polish Migrants in Ireland." Master's thesis, Univ. College, Dublin.

Carney, Judith, and Robert Voeks. 2003. "Landscape Legacies of the African Diaspora in Brazil." *Progress in Human Geography* 27, no. 2: 139–52.

Castells, Manuel. 1975. "Immigrant Workers and Class Struggles in Advanced Capitalism: The Western European Experience." *Politics and Society* 5, no. 1: 32–66.

———. 1996a. "The Net and the Self: Working Notes for a Critical Theory of the Informational Society." *Critique of Anthropology* 16, no. 1: 9–38.

———. 1996b. *The Rise of the Network Society.* Blackwell: Oxford.

Castells, Manuel, and Roberto Laserna. 1989. "The New Dependency: Technological Change and Socioeconomic Restructuring in Latin America." *Sociological Forum* 4, no. 4: 535–60.

Castles, Stephen. 2004. The "Myth of the Controllability of Difference: Labour Migration, Transnational Communities, and State Strategies in the Asia-Pacific Region." In *State/Nation/Transnation: Perspectives on Transnationalism in the Asia-Pacific*, edited by Brenda S. A. Yeoh and Katie Willis, 16–36. London: Routledge.

Castles, Stephen, and Alastair Davidson. 2000. *Citizenship and Migration: Globalization and the Politics of Belonging*. New York: Routledge.

Castles, Stephen, and Mark J. Miller. 1993. *The Age of Migration: International Population Movements in the Modern World*. Basingstoke: MacMillan.

———. 1998. *The Age of Migration: International Population Movements in the Modern World*. London: MacMillan.

———. 2003. *The Age of Migration*. 3d ed. New York: Guildford Press.

Central Bureau of Statistics. 2005. "Several Data Sheets StatLine." http://www.cbs.nl.

Central Statistics Office. 2004. *Quarterly National Household Survey: Crime and Victimisation*. Cork and Dublin: Central Statistics Office, Ireland. http://www.cso.ie/qnhs/documents/qnhscrimeandvictimisation.pdf.

———. 2006. *Census 2006 Preliminary Report*. Cork and Dublin: Central Statistics Office Ireland. http://www.cso.ie/census/documents/2006PreliminaryReport.pdf.

Chacko, Elizabeth. 2003. "Ethiopian Ethos and the Creation of Ethnic Places in the Washington Metropolitan Area." *Journal of Cultural Geography* 20, no. 2: 21–42.

Chacko, Elizabeth, and Ivan Cheung. 2006. "The Formation of a Contemporary Ethnic Enclave: The Case of 'Little Ethiopia' in Los Angeles." In *Race, Ethnicity, and Place in a Changing America*, edited by John S. Frazier and Eugene Tettey-Fio, 131–39. Binghamton, N.Y.: Global Academic Publishing.

Champion, Anthony. 2004. "Testing the Return Migration Element of the 'Escalator Region' Model: An Analysis of Migration into and Out of South East England, 1996–2001." Paper presented at the L5 2001 Census Launch Conference, London School of Hygiene and Tropical Medicine, Sept. 21.

Chan, Raymond K. H., and Moha Asri Abdullah. 1999. *Foreign Labour in Asia: Issues and Challenges*. Commack, N.Y.: Nova Science.

Chan, Sewell, and Fernanda Santos. 2005. "Transit Union and M.T.A. Are Drawing Closer to a Contract Deal." *New York Times,* Dec. 24.

Chew, Soon-Beng, and Rosalind Chew. 1995. "Immigration and Foreign Labour in Singapore." *Asean Economic Bulletin* 12, no. 2: 191–200.

Chin, Christine 1998. *In Service and Servitude: Foreign Female Domestic Workers and the Malaysian "Modernity" Project.* New York: Columbia Univ. Press.

Chinese Residents' Association in Seoul. 2005. "Chinese in Korea." http://www .crask.or.kr/.

Chinn, Carl. 1994. *Birmingham: The Great Working City.* Birmingham: Birmingham City Council.

Cho, David. 2005. "'Koreantown' Image Splits Annandale: Immigrant Retailers, Civic Groups at Odds." *Washington Post,* Mar. 14, Metro section, B1.

Choi, Hyup, Sung-Kook Kim, Keun-Sik Jung, and Myung-Ki Yu, eds. 2004. *Minority in Korea, Past and Future* [in Korean]. Seoul: Hanul.

Chow, Esther Ngan-ling. 1996. "From Pennsylvania Avenue to H Street, NW: The Transformation of Washington's Chinatown." In *Urban Odyssey: Migration to Washington, D.C.,* edited by Frances Carey, 190–207. Washington, D.C.: Smithsonian Institution Press.

Chua, Beng Huat. 1998. "World Cities, Globalisation, and the Spread of Consumerism: A View from Singapore." *Urban Studies* 35, nos. 5–6: 981–1000.

Citizenship and Immigration Canada. 2005. *Recent Immigrants in Metropolitan Areas: Toronto, a Comparative Profile Based on the 2001 Census.* Ottawa: Minister of Public Works and Government Services Canada.

Clark, William, and Sarah A. Blue. 2004. "Race, Class, and Segregation Patterns in U.S. Immigrant Gateway Cities." *Urban Affairs Review* 39, no. 6: 667–88.

Clarke, Marie, Anne Lodge, and Michael Shevlin. 2004. "The Profiles, Motivations, and Experiences of Higher Diploma in Education Participants in Three Universities, 2002–2003." Paper presented to the Annual Conference of the Educational Studies Association of Ireland, NUI Maynooth, Apr. 1–3.

Coe, Neil M., and Philip F. Kelly. 2002. "Languages of Labour: Representational Strategies in Singapore's Labour Control Regime." *Political Geography* 21: 341–71.

Community Agency for Social Enquiry. 2003. *National Refugee Baseline Survey: Final Report.* Braamfontein: Community Agency for Social Enquiry.

Conrad, Robert. 1975. "The Planter Class and the Debate over Chinese Immigration to Brazil, 1850–1893." *International Migration Review* 9, no. 1: 41–55.

Corcoran, Jody, and Maeve Sheehan. 2005. "McDowell's Warning on Abuse of Race." *Sunday Independent,* Mar. 27.

Corcoran, Mary. 2002. The Process of Migration and the Reinvention of Self: The Experiences of Returning Irish Emigrants. *Éire-Ireland* 37: 175–91.

Coulter, Carol. 2004. "Figures Do Not Identify Status of Non-national Mothers." *Irish Times,* June 17.

Craddock, Susan. 1999. "Embodying Place: Pathologizing Chinese and Chinatown in Nineteenth-Century San Francisco." *Antipode* 31, no. 4: 351–71.

Crankshaw, Owen, Alan Gilbert, and Alan Morris. 2000. "Backyard Soweto." *International Journal of Urban and Regional Research* 24: 841–57.

Crouch, David. 1998. "The Street in the Making of Popular Geographical Knowledge." In *Images of the Street,* edited by Nicholas Fyfe, 160–75. London: Routledge Press.

Crowder, Kyle, and Lucky Tedrow. 2001. "West Indians and the Residential Landscape of New York." In *Islands in the City: West Indian Migration to New York,* edited by Nancy Foner, 81–114. Berkeley and Los Angeles: Univ. of California Press.

Crush, Jonathan. 1999. "The Discourse and Dimensions of Irregularity in Post-apartheid South Africa." *International Migration* 37: 125–51.

———. 2000. "The Dark Side of Democracy: Migration, Xenophobia, and Human Rights in South Africa." *International Migration* 38: 196–218.

———. 2001. *Making Up the Numbers: Measuring Illegal Immigration to South Africa.* Migration Policy Brief no. 3. Cape Town: Southern African Migration Project.

———. 2002. "The Global Raiders: Nationalism, Globalization, and the South African Brain Drain." *Journal of International Affairs* 56, no. 1: 147–72.

Crush, Jonathan, Alan Jeeves, and David Yudelman. 1991. *South Africa's Labor Empire: A History of Black Migrancy to the Gold Mines.* Boulder: Westview Press.

Crush, Jonathan, and David McDonald, eds. 2002. *Transnationalism and New African Immigration to South Africa.* Toronto: Canadian Association of African Studies.

Danso, Ransford, and David McDonald. 2001. "Writing Xenophobia: Immigrants and the Print Media in Post-apartheid South Africa." *Africa Today* 48: 115–38.

Darden, Joe T. 2004. *The Significance of White Supremacy in the Canadian Metropolis of Toronto.* Lewiston, N.Y.: E. Mellen Press.

Dean, Simon. 1997. "Constructing Chinatown: Capital and Culture in Birmingham's Chinese Quarter." Master's thesis, Univ. of Birmingham.

Dear, Michael, ed. 2002. *From Chicago to L.A.: Making Sense of Urban Theory.* Thousand Oaks, Calif.: Sage Publications.

Decol, René D. 1999. *Imigraçõtes Urbanas para o Brasil: O caso dos judeus*. Campinas, Brazil: Departamento de Sociologia, Instituto de Filosofia e Ciências Humanas da UNICAMP (Tese de Doutorado em Sociologia).

del Tufo, M. V. 1949. *Malaya, Comprising the Federation of Malaya and the Colony of Singapore: A Report on the 1947 Census of Population*. London: Crown Agents for the Colonies.

Department of Enterprise, Trade, and Employment. 2005a. *Employment Permits Bill, 2005*. Dublin: Department of Enterprise, Trade, and Employment. http://www.entemp.ie/publications/employment/2005/employmentpermitsvill.pdf.

———. 2005b. *Labour Migration and Employment Permits in Ireland*. Dublin: Department of Enterprise, Trade, and Employment. http://www.entemp.ie/labour/workpermits/elements/employmentpermit.htm.

———. 2005c. *Working Visas/Work Authorisations for Employment in Ireland*. Dublin: Department of Enterprise, Trade, and Employment.http://www.entemp.ie/labour/workpermits/authorisation.htm.

———. 2005d. *Work Permits Section*. Dublin: Department of Enterprise, Trade, and Employment. http://www.entemp.ie/labour/workpermits/index.htm.

———. 2007a. *Employment Permits Arrangements: Guide to Green Card Permits*. Dublin: Department of Enterprise, Trade, and Employment. http://www.entemp.ie/publications/labour/2007/guidegreencards.pdf.

———. 2007b. *Employment Permits Arrangements: Guide to Work Permits*. Dublin: Department of Enterprise, Trade, and Employment. http://www.entemp.ie/publications/labour/2007/guideworkpermits.pdf.

———. 2007c. *Statistical Tables and Company Listings for the Employment Permits Section*. Dublin: Department of Enterprise, Trade, and Employment. http://www.entemp.ie/labour/workpermits/statistics.htm.

Department of Immigration and Multicultural and Indigenous Affairs. 2005. *Population Flows Immigration Aspects, 2003–04 Edition*. Canberra, Australia: Department of Immigration and Multicultural and Indigenous Affairs.

Depnaker. 2006. *Department of Labor and Transmigration (Departemen Tenaga Kerja dan Transmigrasi, DEPNAKERTRANS)*. http://www.nakertrans.go.id/pusdatinnaker/tki/index_tki.php.

Deurloo, Rinus, and Sako Musterd. 2001. "Residential Profiles of Surinamese and Moroccans in Amsterdam." *Urban Studies* 38, no. 3: 467–85.

DeVoretz, Don J. 1995. *Diminishing Returns: The Economics of Canada's Recent Immigration Policy*. Toronto: C. D. Howe Institute.

Diedrich, Mathias. 2005. "Indonesians in Saudi Arabia: Religious and Economic Connections." In *Transnational Connections and the Arab Gulf*, edited by Madawi Al-Rasheed, 128–46. London: Routledge.

Dienst Onderzoek en Statistiek. 2004. "Kerncijfers Amsterdam 24."

Dikotter, Frank. 1996. "Culture, 'Race,' and Nation: The Formation of National Identity in Twentieth Century China." *Journal of International Affairs Online* 49, no. 2: 590–601.

Dion, Kenneth. 2001. "Immigrants' Perception of Housing Discrimination in Toronto: The Housing New Canadians Project." *Journal of Social Issues* 57: 523–39.

Dirsuweit, Teresa. 2002. "Johannesburg: Fearful City?" *Urban Forum* 13, no. 2: 3–19.

Dodson, Belinda. 1998. *Women on the Move: Gender and Cross-Border Migration to South Africa*. Migration Policy Series no. 9. Cape Town: Southern African Migration Project.

Dooley, Chris. 2005. "Further Effort to End Ferry Row as Thousands March in Protest." *Irish Times*, Dec. 10.

Douglass, Mike, and Glenda S. Roberts, eds. 2000. *Japan and Global Migration: Foreign Workers and the Advent of a Multicultural Society*. London: Routledge.

Doumato, Eleanor Abdella. 1999. "Women and Work in Saudi Arabia: How Flexible Are Islamic Margins?" *Middle East Journal* 53, no. 4: 568–83.

———. 2000. *Getting God's Ear: Women, Islam, and Healing in Saudi Arabia and the Gulf*. New York: Columbia Univ. Press.

Drummond, Don, Derek Burleton, Gillian Manning, and Karen Richardson. 2002. "The Greater Toronto Area (GTA): Canada's Primary Economic Locomotive in Need of Repairs." *TD Economics Special Report*.

Dudrah, Rajinder K. 2000. *Birmingham (UK): Constructing and Contesting City Spaces*. Birmingham: Birmingham City Council. http://www.birmingham .gov.uk/GenerateContent?CONTENT_ITEM_ID-2339&CO&CONTENT _ITEM_TYPE=0&MENU_ID=10114.

Ellis, Mark. 2006. "Unsettling Immigrant Geographies: US Immigration and the Politics of Scale." *Tijdschrift voor Economische en Sociale Geografie* 97, no. 1: 49–58.

Entzinger, Han. 2003. "The Rise and Fall of Multiculturalism: The Case of the Netherlands." In *Toward Assimilation and Citizenship: Immigrants in Liberal Nation-States*, edited by Christian Joppke and Ewa Morawska, 59–86. New York: Palgrave Macmillan.

Eyber, Carola. 2004. "Forced Migrant Children and Youth in Urban Johannes-burg." In *Forced Migrants in the New Johannesburg*, edited by Loren Landau, 70–76. Johannesburg: Forced Migration Studies Programme, Wits Univ.

Eyles, John. 1985. *Sense of Place*. Warrington, England: Silverbrook.

Fan, Cindy. 2002. "The Elite, the Natives, and the Outsiders: Migration and Labor Market Segmentation in Urban China." *Annals of the Association of American Geographers* 92, no. 1: 103–24.

Fanning, Bryan. 2002. *Racism and Social Change in the Republic of Ireland*. Manchester: Manchester Univ. Press.

FÁS [Ireland's National Training and Employment Authority]. 2005. *Irish Labour Market Review, 2005*. Dublin: FÁS.

Fausto, Boris. 1991. *Historiografia da Imigração para São Paulo*. São Paulo: Sumaré/Idesp.

Featherstone, David. 2003. "Spatialities of Transnational Resistance to Globaliza-tion: The Maps of Grievance of the Inter-continental Caravan." *Transactions of the Institute of British Geographers* 28: 404–21.

Feldman, Alice. 2006. "Social Research and Immigration." In *Care and Social Change in the Irish Welfare Economy*, edited by Bryan Fanning and Michael Rush. Dublin: Univ. College Press.

———. 2007. "Immigrant Civic Mobilisation." In *Immigration and Social Change in the Republic of Ireland*, edited by Bryan Fanning. Manchester: Manchester Univ. Press.

Feldman, Alice, Deo Ladislas Ndakengerwa, Ann Nolan, and Carmen Frese. 2005. *Diversity, Civil Society, and Social Change in Ireland: A North-South Com-parison of the Role of Immigrant/"New" Minority Ethnic-Led Organisa-tions*. Dublin: Migration and Citizenship Research Initiative, Geary Institute, Univ. College.

Fenster, Tovi, and Haim Yacobi. 2005. "Whose City Is It? On Urban Planning and Local Knowledge in Globalizing Tel Aviv–Jaffa." *Planning Theory and Practice* 6, no. 2: 191–211.

Fielding, Anthony. 1992. "Migration and Social Mobility: Southeast England as an Escalator Region." *Regional Studies* 26, no. 1: 1–15.

Figoli, Leonardo H., and Elaine Meire Vilela. 2003. "Migration, identidad y multi-culturalismo: Sirios y libaneses en Brasil." *Papeles de Trabajo* 11: 27–43.

Fincher, Ruth, and Jane Jacobs, eds. 1998. *Cities of Difference*. New York: Guil-ford Press.

Fingal County Council. 2005. *Development Plan, 2005–2011*. Dublin: Fingal Country Council. http://www.fingalcoco.ie/yourlocalcouncil/services/plan ning/developmentplan2005-2011/developmentplan2005-2011content/index .aspx.

Flood, J., Chris Maher, Peter Newton, and J. Roy. 1991. *The Determinants of Internal Migration in Australia*. Melbourne: Commonwealth Scientific and Industrial Research Organisation (CSIRO), Division of Building, Construction, and Engineering.

Florida, Richard L. 2002. *The Rise of the Creative Class: And How It's Transforming Work, Leisure, Community, and Everyday Life*. New York: Basic Books.

Foley, Michael, and Dean Hoge. 2007. *Religion and the New Immigrants: How Faith Communities Form Our Newest Citizens*. Oxford: Oxford Univ. Press.

Foner, Nancy. 2000. *From Ellis Island to JFK: New York's Two Great Waves of Immigration*. New Haven: Yale Univ. Press.

———, ed. 2001. *New Immigrants in New York*. Rev. ed. New York: Columbia Univ. Press.

———. 2005. *In a New Land: A Comparative View of Immigration*. New York: New York Univ. Press.

———. 2006. "Then *and* Now or Then *to* Now: Immigration to New York in Contemporary and Historical Perspective." *Journal of American Ethnic History* 25, nos. 2–3: 33–47.

Foucault, Michel. 1995. *Discipline and Punish: The Birth of the Prison*. New York: Vintage Books.

Frey, William. 1993. The New Urban Revival in the United States. *Urban Studies* 30, nos. 4–5: 741–74.

———. 1996. *Immigration, Internal Out-Movement, and Demographic Balkanization in America: New Evidence for the 1990s*. Population Studies Center Research Report no. 96-364. Ann Arbor: Univ. of Michigan.

Frey, William, Jill H. Wilson, Alan Berube, and Audrey Singer. 2004. "Tracking Metropolitan America in the 21st Century: A Field Guide to the New Metropolitan and Micropolitan Definitions." In *The Living Cities Census Series*. Washington, D.C.: Brookings Institution.

Friedman, Thomas. 2005. *The World Is Flat: A Brief History of the Twenty-first Century*. New York: Farrar, Straus, and Giroux.

Friedmann, John. 1986. "The World City Hypothesis." *Development and Change* 17: 69–83.

Friedmann, John, and Ute Angelika Lehrer. 1997. "Urban Policy Responses to Foreign In-migration." *Journal of the American Planning Association* 63, no. 1: 61–79.

Gamburd, Michelle Ruth. 2000. *The Kitchen Spoon's Handle: Transnationalism and Sri Lanka's Migrant Housemaids.* Ithaca: Cornell Univ. Press.

Garner, Steve. 2005. "Guests of the Nation." *Irish Review* 33: 78–84.

Gask, Karen. 2006. "Population Review of 2004 and 2005: England and Wales." *Population Trends* (Office of National Statistics) 126: 8–15.

Gavison, Ruth. 1999. "A Rejoinder to the 'Ethnic Democracy' Debate." *Israel Studies* 4, no. 1: 44–72.

Gemeente Amsterdam. 2003. "Erbij horen en meedoen: Uitgangspunten voor Integratie in de Gemeente Amsterdam." *Gemeenteblad* 1, no. 214.

Ghanem, Asad, Nadim Rouhana, and Oren Yiftachel. 1998. "Questioning 'Ethnic Democracy': A Response to Sammy Smooha." *Israel Studies* 3, no. 2: 253–67.

Glancey, John. 1999. "Where Would You Rather Live?" *The Guardian,* Mar. 1.

Glasze, Georg, and Abdallah Alkhayyal. 2002. "Gated Housing Estates in the Arab World: Case Studies in Lebanon and Riyadh, Saudi Arabia." *Environment and Planning B: Planning and Design* 29: 321–36.

Glazer, Nathan, and Daniel Moynihan. 1970. *Beyond the Melting Pot.* 2d ed. Cambridge: MIT Press.

Glick-Schiller, Nina, Linda Basch, and Cristina Blanc-Szanton. 1992a. "Transnationalism: A New Analytical Framework for Understanding Migration." *Annals of the New York Academy of Sciences* 645: 1–24.

Glick-Schiller, Nina, Linda Basch, and Cristina Blanc-Szanton. 1992b. "Transnational: A New Analytic Framework for Understanding Migration." In *Towards a Transnational Perspective on Migration: Race, Class, Ethnicity, and Nationalism Reconsidered,* edited by Nina Glick-Schiller, Linda Basch, and Cristina Blanc-Szanton, 1–24. New York: New York Academy of Sciences.

Goh, Chok Tong. 1997. *Prime Minister's National Day Rally Speech 1997.* Singapore: Ministry of Information, Communication, and the Arts. http://stars .nhb.gov.sg/stars/public/.

Goździak, Elżbieta M. 2005. "New Immigrant Communities and Integration." In *Beyond the Gateway: Immigrants in a Changing America,* edited by Elżbieta Goździak and Susan Martin, 3–18. Lanham, Md.: Lexington Books.

Gold, Steven J. 2002. *The Israeli Diaspora.* London: Routledge.

Gotz, Graeme. 2004. "The Role of Local Government Towards Forced Migrants." In *Forced Migrants in the New Johannesburg,* edited by Loren Landau, 24–36. Johannesburg: Forced Migration Studies Programme, Wits Univ.

Gotz, Graeme, and Loren Landau. 2004. Introduction to *Forced Migrants in the New Johannesburg,* edited by Loren Landau, 13–23. Johannesburg: Forced Migration Studies Programme, Wits Univ.

Gotz, Graeme, and AbdouMaliq Simone. 2003. "On Belonging and Becoming in African Cities." In *Emerging Johannesburg: Perspectives on the Postapartheid City,* edited by Richard Tomlinson, Robert Beauregard, Lindsay Bremner, and Xolela Mangcu. New York: Routledge.

Government of Ontario. 2002. *The Facts Are In: A Study of the Characteristics and Experiences of Immigrants Seeking Employment in Regulated Professions in Ontario.* Toronto: Ministry of Training, Colleges, and Universities.

Goza, Franklin. 1994. "Brazilian Migration to North America." *International Migration Review* 28, no. 1: 136–52.

Goździak, Elżbieta M., and Susan F. Martin, eds. 2005. *Beyond the Gateway: Immigrants in a Changing America.* Lanham, Md.: Lexington Books.

Graham, D. H. 1970. "Divergent and Convergent Regional Economic Growth and Internal Migration in Brazil, 1940–1960." *Economic Development and Cultural Change* 18: 362–82.

Grant, Richard, and Jan Nijman. 2002. "Globalization and the Corporate Geography of Cities in the Less-Developed World." *Annals of the Association of American Geographers* 92, no. 2: 320–40.

Griffin, J. 1998. "Brum Group to Support Irish." *Birmingham Evening Mail,* Dec. 10, 43.

Grillo, Ralph. 2004. "Islam and Transnationalism." *Journal of Ethnic and Migration Studies* 30, no. 5: 861–78.

Gugler, Josef, ed. 2004. *World Cities Beyond the West: Globalization, Development, and Inequality.* Cambridge: Cambridge Univ. Press.

HaAretz, various issues.

Hagendoorn, Louk, Justus Veenman, and Wilma Vollebergh, eds. 2003. *Integrating Immigrants in the Netherlands.* Aldershot: Ashgate.

Al-Haj, Majid. 2004. *Immigration and Ethnic Formation in a Deeply Divided Society: The Case of the 1990s Immigrants from the Former Soviet Union in Israel.* Boston: Brill.

Hall, Peter. 1995. "Towards a General Urban Theory." In *Cities in Competition: Productive and Sustainable Cities for the 21st Century,* edited by John

Brotchie, Mike Batty, Ed Blakely, Peter Hall, and Peter Newton, 3–31. Melbourne: Longman.

Hall, Stuart. 1990. "Cultural Identity and Diaspora." In *Identity: Community, Culture, Difference,* edited by Jonathan. Rutherford, 222–37. London: Lawrence and Wishart.

Handmaker, Jeff. 2001. "No Easy Walk: Advancing Refugee Protection in South Africa." *Africa Today* 48: 91–114.

Hannerz, Ulf. 1996. *Transnational Connections: Culture, People, Places.* London: Routledge.

———. 2000. "Cities as Windows on the World." In *Understanding Amsterdam: Essays on Economic Vitality, City Life, and Urban Form,* edited by Leon Deben, Willem Heijnemeijer, and Dick van der Vaart, 179–96. Amsterdam: Het Spinhuis.

Harding, Glenys, and Elizabeth Webster. 2002. *The Working Holiday Maker Scheme and the Australian Labour Market.* Melbourne: Melbourne Institute of Applied Economics and Social Research, Univ. of Melbourne.

Hawthorne, Lesleyanne. 2005. "'Picking Winners': The Recent Transformation of Australia's Skilled Migration Policy," *International Migration Review* 39, no. 2: 663–96.

Hayden, Dolores. 1995. *The Power of Place: Urban Landscapes as Public History.* Cambridge: MIT Press.

Head, Wilson 1975. *The Black Presence in the Canadian Mosaic: A Study of Perception and the Practice of Discrimination Against Blacks in Metropolitan Toronto.* Toronto: Ontario Human Rights Commission.

Healy, Ernest, and Bob Birrell. 2003. "Metropolis Divided: The Political Dynamic of Spatial Inequality and Migrant Settlement in Sydney." *People and Place* 11, no. 2: 65–87.

Hebbert, Michael. 2005. "The Street as Locus of Collective Memory." *Environment and Planning D: Society and Space* 23, no. 4: 581–96.

Hedges, Chris. 2000. "Translating America for Parents and Family." *New York Times,* June 19.

Heisz,, Andrew and Logan McLeod. 2004. *Low Income in Census Metropolitan Areas, 1980–2000.* Ottawa: Statistics Canada, Analytical Studies Branch.

Held, David, Anthony McGrew, David Goldblatt, and J. Perraton. 1999. *Global Transformations: Politics, Economics, and Culture.* Cambridge: Polity Press.

Helleman, Gerben, and Frank Wassenberg. 2004. "The Renewal of What Was Tomorrow's Idealistic City: Amsterdam Bijlmermeer's High-rise." *Cities* 21: 3–17.

Al-Hemaidi, Waleed Kassab. 2001. "The Metamorphosis of the Urban Fabric in an Arab-Mulsim City: Riyadh, Saudi Arabia." *Journal of Housing and the Built Environment* 16: 179–201.

Henry, Frances. 1989. *Housing and Racial Discrimination in Canada: A Preliminary Assessment of Current Initiatives and Information*. Ottawa: Policy and Research, Multiculturalism and Citizenship.

———. 1994. *The Caribbean Diaspora in Toronto: Learning to Live with Racism*. Toronto: Univ. of Toronto Press.

Henry, Nick. 1998. "Multicultural City, Multicultural City Centre? Some Thoughts on the Future of the City Centre and Birmingham 'Going International.'" *Service Sector Commentary* (SSRU, Univ. of Birmingham) 4, no. 1.

Henry, Nick, Cheryl McEwan, and Jane Pollard. 2002. "Globalization from Below: Birmingham—Postcolonial Workshop of the World." *Area* 34, no. 2: 117–27.

Henry, Nick, and Adrian Passmore. 1999. "Rethinking 'Global' City Centres: The Example of Birmingham." *Soundings: A Journal of Politics and Culture* 13 (Autumn): 60–66.

Hesse, Barne. 1993. "Black to Front and Black Again: Racialization Through Contested Times and Spaces." In *Place and the Politics of Identity*, edited by M. Keith and S. Pile, 162–82. London: Routledge.

———. 1999. "It's Your World: Discrepant Multiculturalisms." In *New Ethnicities, Old Racisms?* edited by P. Cohen, 205–25. London: Zed Books.

Hiebert, Daniel. 1999. "Local Geographies of Labour Market Segmentation: Montreal, Toronto, and Vancouver, 1991." *Economic Geography* 75: 339–69.

Higuchi, Naoto, and Kiyoto Tanno. 2003. "What's Driving Brazil-Japan Migration? The Making and Remaking of the Brazilian Niche in Japan." *International Journal of Japanese Sociology* 12: 33–47.

Holloway, Thomas H. 1978. "Creating the Reserve Army? The Immigration Program of São Paulo, 1886–1930." *International Migration Review* 12, no. 2: 187–209.

———. 1980. *Immigrants on the Land: Coffee and Society in São Paulo, 1886–1934*. Chapel Hill: Univ. of North Carolina Press.

Holston, James. 1999. *Cities and Citizenship*. Durham: Duke Univ. Press.

Hou, Feng, and Garnett Picot. 2003. *Visible Minority Enclave Neighbourhoods and Labour Market Outcomes of Immigrants*. Ottawa: Statistics Canada, Analytical Studies Branch.

Huang, Shirlena, and Brenda S. A. Yeoh. 1996. "Ties That Bind: State Policy and Migrant Female Domestic Helpers in Singapore." *Geoforum* 27: 479–93.

———. 2005. "Transnational Families and Their Children's Education: China's Study Mothers in Singapore." *Global Networks* 5, no. 4: 379–400.

Hughes, Gerard, and Emma Quinn. 2004. *The Impact of Immigration on Europe's Societies: Ireland*. Dublin: Economic and Social Research Institute (ESRI).

Hugo, Graeme. 1992. *Atlas of the Australian People: New South Wales*. Canberra: Australian Government Publishing Service.

———. 1995. "Labour Export from Indonesia." *ASEAN Economic Bulletin* 12: 275–98.

———. 1996. "The Relationship Between Immigration and Internal Migration in Sydney, Australia." Paper presented at twenty-eighth International Geographical Congress, The Hague, Netherlands, Aug.

———. 1999. "A New Paradigm of International Migration in Australia." *New Zealand Population Review* 25, nos. 1–2: 1–39.

———. 2002. "Effects of International Migration on the Family in Indonesia." *Asian and Pacific Migration Journal* 11: 13–46.

———. 2004a. *Australia's Most Recent Immigrants, 2001*. Australian Census Analytic Program. Catalogue no. 2053.0. Canberra: Australian Bureau of Statistics.

———. 2004b. "International Migration in the Asia-Pacific Region: Emerging Trends and Issues." In *International Migration: Prospects and Policies in a Global Market*, edited by Douglas S. Massey and J. Edward Taylor, 77–103. Oxford: Oxford Univ. Press.

———. 2005a. "Indonesian International Domestic Workers: Contemporary Developments and Issues." In *Asian Women as Transnational Domestic Workers*, edited by Shirlena Huang, Brenda S. A. Yeoh, and Noor Abdul Rahman, 54–91. Singapore: Marshall Cavendish Academic.

———. 2005b. "Regionalisation of Immigration to Australia." Paper prepared for workshop on regionalization of immigration in federations and quasi federations, International Metropolis Conference, Toronto, Oct. 17–21.

———. 2006a. "Australian Demographic Change and Its Implications for Sydney." In *Talking about Sydney: Population, Community, and Culture in Contemporary Sydney*, edited by Robert Freestone, Bill Randolph, and Caroline Butler-Bowdon, 3–23. Sydney: Univ. of New South Wales Press in association with the Historic Houses Trust and the Faculty of the Built Environment, Univ. of New South Wales.

————. 2006b. "Immigration Responses to Global Change in Asia: A Review." *Geographical Research* 44, no. 2: 155–72.

————. 2006c. "Temporary Migration and the Labour Market in Australia." *Australian Geographer* 37, no. 2: 211–31.

Hugo, Graeme, Kevin Harris, Errol Bamford, and Justin Nottage. 2005. "Internal Migration in Australia: Analysis of Australia Post Mail Redirection Database, Mar.–May 2005, and Survey of Moving Households in Australia, Apr. 2004–June 2005." Report prepared for Victorian Department of Sustainability and Environment and Commonwealth Department of Transport and Regional Services.

Hugo, Graeme, Dianne Rudd, and Kevin Harris. 2003. *Australia's Diaspora: Its Size, Nature, and Policy Implications.* Information Paper no. 80. Melbourne: Committee for Economic Development of Australia.

Hui, Weng-Tat. 1997. "Regionalisation, Economic Restructuring, and Labour Migration in Singapore." *International Migration* 35, no. 1: 109–28.

————. 1998. "The Regional Economic Crisis and Singapore: Implications for Labor Migration." *Asian and Pacific Migration Journal* 7, nos. 2–3: 187–218.

————. 2000. "Foreign Manpower and Development Strategy in Singapore." Paper presented at a conference on APEC-HRD-LSP, Ninth International Workshop on International Migration and Structural Change in APEC Member Economies, the Institute of Economics, Academia Sinica, Taipei, Oct. 19–20.

Human Rights Watch. 1998. *Prohibited Persons: Abuse of Undocumented Migrants, Asylum-Seekers, and Refugees in South Africa.* New York: Human Rights Watch.

————. 2004. "Bad Dreams: Exploitation and Abuse of Migrant Workers in Saudi Arabia." Report 16(5)(E). http://hrw.org/mideast/saudi/labor/.

Humphries, Niamh. 2005. "The Importance of Housing in the Integration of Asylum Seekers and Refugees in Dublin." Ph.D. diss., Univ. College, Dublin.

Immigrant Council of Ireland. 2003. *Labour Migration into Ireland.* Dublin: Immigrant Council of Ireland.

————. 2004. *Voices of Immigrants: The Challenges of Inclusion.* Dublin: Immigrant Council of Ireland.

Immigration Bureau, Ministry of Justice, Republic of Korea. 2006. *Major Policy Guide.* http://www.immigration.go.kr/.

International Organization of Migration. 2005. *World Migration Report.* http://www.iom.int/jahia/Jahia/cache/bypass/pid/8?entryId=932.

Ireland, Patrick R. 2004. *Becoming Europe: Immigration, Integration, and the Welfare State.* Pittsburgh: Univ. of Pittsburgh Press.

Irish Refugee Council. 2004. *Asylum Statistics.* http://www.irishrefugeecouncil .ie/stats.html.

Isin, Engin F. 2002. *Being Political: Genealogies of Citizenship.* Minnesota: Univ. of Minnesota Press.

Isin, Engin F., and Myer Siemiatycki. 2002. "Making Space for Mosques: Struggles for Urban Citizenship in Diasporic Toronto." In *Race, Space, and the Law: Unmapping a White Settler Society,* edited by Sherene H. Razack, 185–209. Toronto: Between the Lines.

Itzigsohn, Jose, and Carlos Dore-Cabral. 2000. "Competing Identities? Race, Ethnicity, and Panethnicity among Dominicans in the United States." *Sociological Forum* 15, no. 2: 225–47.

Jacobs, Jane. 1996. *Edge of Empire: Postcolonialism and the City.* London: Routledge.

Jacobsen, Karen, and Sarah Bailey. 2004. "Micro-credit and Banking for Refugees in Johannesburg." In *Forced Migrants in the New Johannesburg,* edited by Loren Landau, 99–102. Johannesburg: Forced Migration Studies Programme, Wits Univ.

Jacobson, David. 1996. *Rights Across Borders: Immigration and the Decline of Citizenship.* Baltimore: Johns Hopkins Univ. Press.

Japanese Census. 2000. "Results of Special Tabulation on Foreign Residents from the 2000 Population Census." *News Bulletin* (Statistics Bureau, Ministry of Internal Affairs and Communications), no. 3 (July). 2004? http://www.stat .go/jp/english/info/news/1851.htm.

Jarvie, Wendy. 1989. "Migration and Regional Development." In *Australian Regional Development: Readings in Regional Experiences, Policies, and Prospects,* edited by Benjamin Higgins and Krzysztof Zagorski, 218–33. Canberra: Australian Government Publishing Service.

Johnston, Nicola. 2003. *The Point of No Return: Evaluating the Amnesty for Mozambican Refugees in South Africa.* Migration Policy Brief no. 6. Cape Town: Southern African Migration Project.

Jones, Sidney. 2000. *Making Money Off Migrants: The Indonesian Exodus to Malaysia.* Hong Kong and Wollongon: Asia 2000 Ltd., Hong Kong Centre for Asia Pacific Transformation, and Univ. of Wollongon.

Jones-Correa, Michael. 1998. *Between Two Nations: The Political Predicament of Latinos in New York.* Ithaca: Cornell Univ. Press.

Joppke, Christian. 2005. *Selecting by Origin: Ethnic Migration in the Liberal State*. Cambridge: Harvard Univ. Press.

Joppke, Christian, and Ewa Morawska, eds. 2003. *Toward Assimilation and Citizenship: Immigrants in Liberal Nation-States*. Basingstoke: Palgrave Macmillan.

Jupp, James. 1993. "Ethnic Concentrations: A Reply to Bob Birrell." *People and Place* 4, no. 4: 51–52.

———. 2002. *From White Australia to Woomera: The Story of Australian Immigration*. Cambridge: Cambridge Univ. Press.

Kadima, Denis. 2001. "Motivations for Emigration and Character of the Economic Contribution of Congolese Emigrants in South Africa." In *African Immigration to South Africa: Francophone Migration of the 1990s*, edited by Alan Morris and Antoine Bouillon, 90–110. Pretoria: Protea.

Kasinitz, Philip. 2000. "Children of America: The Second Generation Comes of Age." *Common Quest* 4: 32–41.

Kasinitz, Philip, John Mollenkopf, and Mary Waters. 2002. "Becoming American/Becoming New Yorkers: Immigrant Incorporation in a Majority Minority City." *International Migration Review* 36, no. 4: 1020–36.

———. 2004a. "Children of Immigrants, Children of America." In *Becoming New Yorkers: Ethnographies of the New Second Generation*, edited by Philip Kasinitz, John H. Mollenkopf, and Mary C. Waters, 393–403. New York: Russell Sage Foundation.

———. 2004b. "Worlds of the Second Generation." In *Becoming New Yorkers: Ethnographies of the New Second Generation*, edited by Philip Kasinitz, John H. Mollenkopf, and Mary C. Waters, 1–19. New York: Russell Sage Foundation.

Kee, Pookong. 1995. "The New Nanyang: Contemporary Chinese Populations in Australia." In *The Geography of Contemporary China: The Impact of Deng Xiaoping's Decade*, edited by Terry Cannon and Alan Jenkins, 266–90. London: Routledge.

Keith, Michael. 2005. *After the Cosmopolitan? Multicultural Cities and the Future of Racism*. London: Routledge.

Kelleher, Margaret. 2002. "Hunger and History: Monuments to the Great Irish Famine." *Textual Practice* 16, no. 2: 249–76.

Kemp, Adriana, and Natan Marom. 2006. "The Deportation of Labour Migrants from Israel: A 'Successful Policy'?" Paper presented at the "Conference on International Labour Migration: In Whose Interests?" Oxford: Centre for Migration, Policy, and Society.

Kemp, Adriana, and Rebeca Raijman. 2004. "'Tel Aviv Is Not Foreign to You': Urban Incorporation Policy on Labor Migrants in Israel." *International Migration Review* 38, no. 1: 26–51.

Kemp, Adriana, Rebeca Raijman, Julia Resnik, and Silvina Schammah Gesser. 2000. "Contesting the Limits of Political Participation: Latinos and Black African Migrant Workers in Israel." *Ethnic and Racial Studies* 23, no. 1: 94–119.

Kennett, Patricia, and Ray Forrest. 2006. "The neighborhood in a European Context." *Urban Studies* 43, no. 4: 713–18.

Keogan, Kevin. 2002. "A Sense of Place: The Politics of Immigration and the Symbolic Construction of Identity in Southern California and the New York Metropolitan Area." *Sociological Forum* 17, no. 2: 223–54.

Khandelwal, Madhulika. 2002. *Becoming American, Becoming Indian: An Immigrant Community in New York*. Ithaca: Cornell Univ. Press.

Khoo, Siew-Ean, Carmen Voight-Graf, Graeme Hugo, and Peter McDonald. 2003. "Temporary Skilled Migration to Australia: The 457 Visa Sub-class." *People and Place* 11, no. 4: 27–40.

Kihato, Caroline, and Loren Landau. 2006. *The Uncaptured Urbanite: Migration and State Power in Johannesburg*. Forced Migration Working Paper Series no. 25. Johannesburg: Wits Univ. Press.

Kim, Yeong-Hyun. 1997. "Interpreting the Olympic Landscape in Seoul: The Politics of Sports, Spectacle, and Landscape." *Journal of the Korean Geographical Society* 32, no. 3: 387–402.

———. 2004. "Seoul: Complementing Economic Success with Games." In *World Cities Beyond the West: Globalization, Development, and Inequality,* edited by Josef Gugler, 59–81. Cambridge: Cambridge Univ. Press.

Kimmerling, Baruch. 2001. *The Invention and Decline of Israeliness: State, Society, and the Military*. Berkeley and Los Angeles: Univ. of California Press.

King, Anthony D., ed. 1996. *Re-presenting the City: Ethnicity, Capital, and Culture in the 21st Century Metropolis*. New York: New York Univ. Press.

Kipnis, Baruch A. 2005. "The Geography of Israel's Wealthy, Influential, and Professionals: Its Impact on Tel Aviv's World City Status and on the Dwindling National Space." *GaWC Research Bulletin* 168. http://www.lboro.ac.uk/gawc/rb/rb168.html.

Kirshun, R., ed. 2006. *The Internationalization of Higher Education in South Africa*. Durban: International Education Association of South Africa.

Klaaren, Jonathan, and Emma Algottson. 2004. *Policing Migration: Immigration Enforcement and Human Rights in South Africa.* Migration Policy Brief no. 14. Cape Town: Southern African Migration Project.

Klaaren, Jonathan, and Jaya Ramji. 2001. "Inside Illegality: Migration Policing in South Africa after Apartheid." *Africa Today* 48: 35–48.

Kondo, Atsushi. 2002. "Development of Immigration Policy in Japan." *Asia and Pacific Migration Journal* 11, no. 4: 415–36.

Korea Labor Institute. 2004. *Analysis of the Unskilled Foreign Workforce and Labor Market* [in Korean]. Seoul: Korea Labor Institute.

Kraly, Ellen, and Ines Miyares. 2001. "Immigration to New York: Policy, Population, and Patterns." In *New Immigrants in New York,* edited by Nancy Foner, 33–80. Rev. ed. New York: Columbia Univ. Press.

Krause, Londa, and Patrice Petro, eds. 2003. *Global Cities: Cinema, Architecture, and Urbanism in a Digital Age.* New Brunswick: Rutgers Univ. Press.

Kwekkeboom, Willem. 2002. "Rebuilding the Bijlmermeer, 1992–2002: Spatial and Social." In *Amsterdam Southeast: Centre Area Southeast and Urban Renewal in the Bijlmermeer, 1992–2010,* edited by Dick Bruijne, Dorine van Hoogstraten, Willem Kwekkeboom, and Anne Luijten, 73–113. Bussum: TOTH Publishers.

Kwok, Kian Woon. 1998. "Being Chinese in the Modern World." In *The Encyclopedia of the Chinese Overseas,* edited by Lynn Pan, 121–26. Singapore: Archipelago Press and Landmark Books.

Kwon, Won-Yong. 1995. "Seoul: Mega-city Problems in Korea." In *Cities and Nation: Planning Issues and Policies of Korea,* edited by Gun Young Lee and Hyun Sik Kim, 177–204. Seoul: Korea Research Institute for Human Settlements.

Kymlicka, Will. 1995. *Multicultural Citizenship: A Liberal Theory of Minority Rights.* Oxford: Oxford Univ. Press.

———. 2003. "Immigration, Citizenship, Multiculturalism: Exploring the Links." *Political Quarterly* 73: 195–208.

Lally, Conor. 2004. "Asylum Process Cost State EUR 353m in 2003." *Irish Times,* Oct. 11.

Landau, Loren, ed. 2004. *Forced Migrants in the New Johannesburg.* Johannesburg: Forced Migration Studies Programme, Wits Univ.

———. 2005. "Urbanization, Nativism, and the Rule of Law in South Africa's 'Forbidden' Cities." *Third World Quarterly* 26: 1115–34.

Lawson, Victoria. 2000. "Arguments Within Geographies of Movement: The Theoretical Potential of Migrants' Stories." *Progress in Human Geography* 24, no. 2: 173–89.

Lee, Boon Yang. 2000. "Talent Capital Singapore" [speech at the AISEC Singapore 30th Anniversary Dinner, May 27, 2000]. In *Speeches: A Bimonthly Selection of Ministerial Speeches [May–June],* edited by Ministry of Information and the Arts, 65–76. Singapore: Ministry of Information and the Arts.

Lee, Kuan Yew. 2000. "Be International in Outlook" [speech to NTU/NUS students, Feb. 15, 2000]. In *Speeches: A Bimonthly Selection of Ministerial Speeches [Jan.–Feb.],* edited by Ministry of Information and the Arts, 10–15. Singapore: Ministry of Information and the Arts.

Lee, Namhee. 2002. "Anticommunism, North Korea, and Human Rights in South Korea: 'Orientalist' Discourse and Construction of South Korean Identity." In *Truth Claims: Representation and Human Rights,* edited by Mark Philip Bradley and Patrice Petro, 43–71. New Brunswick: Rutgers Univ. Press.

Lefebvre, Henri. 1976. "Reflections on the Politics of Space." Translated by M. J. Enders from the French journal *Espaces et Sociétés. Antipode* 8, no. 2: 30–37.

Leggett, Ted. 2003. *Rainbow Tenement: Crime and Policing in Inner Johannesburg.* Pretoria: Institute for Security Studies.

Lemon, James T. 1985. *Toronto since 1918: An Illustrated History.* Toronto: Lorimer.

Lentin, Ronit. 2002. "At the Heart of the Hibernian Post-metropolis: Spatial Narratives of Ethnic Minorities and Diasporic Communities in a Changing City." *City* 6, no. 2: 229–49.

———. 2005. "Black Bodies and 'Headless Hookers': Alternative Global Narratives for 21st Century Ireland." *Irish Review* 33: 1–12.

Lesser, Jeffrey. 1999. *Negotiating National Identity: Immigrants, Minorities, and the Struggle for Ethnicity in Brazil.* Durham: Duke Univ. Press.

Levitt, Peggy, and Rafael de la Dehesa. 2003. "Transnational Migration and the Redefinition of the State: Variations and Explanations." *Ethnic and Racial Studies* 26, no. 4: 587–611.

Ley, David. 1999. "Myths and Meanings of Immigration and the Metropolis." *Canadian Geographer* 43, no. 1: 2–20.

———. 2004. "Transnational Spaces and Everyday Lives." *Transactions of the Institute of British Geographers* 29, no. 2: 151–64.

Ley, David, and Peter Murphy. 2001. "Immigration in Gateway Cities: Sydney and Vancouver in Comparative Perspective." *Progress in Planning 55*, no. 3: 119–94.

Ley, David, and Heather Smith. 1997. "Immigration and Poverty in Canadian Cities, 1971–1991." *Canadian Journal of Regional Science* 20: 29–48.

Ley, David, and Judith Tutchener. 2001. "Immigration, Globalization, and House Prices in Canada's Gateway Cities." *Housing Studies* 16, no. 2: 199–223.

Li, Wei. 1998. "Anatomy of a New Ethnic Settlement: The Chinese Ethnoburb in Los Angeles." *Urban Studies* 35, no. 3: 479–501.

Li, W., G. Dymski, Y. Zhou, M. Chee, and C. Aldana. 2002. "Chinese-American Banking and Community Development in Los Angeles County." *Annals of the Association of American Geographers* 92, no. 4: 777–96.

Liang, Zai, and Naomi Ito. 1999. "Intermarriage of Asian Americans in the New York City Region: Contemporary Patterns and Future Prospects." *International Migration Review* 33, no. 4: 876–900.

Light, Ivan. 2006. *Deflecting Immigration: Networks, Markets, and Regulation in Los Angeles.* New York: Russell Sage Foundation.

Lin, Jan. 1998. "Globalization and the Revalorizing of Ethnic Places in Immigration Gateway Cities." *Urban Affairs Review* 34, no. 2: 313–39.

Liu, Xiaofeng. 1997. "Space, Mobility, and Flexibility: Chinese Villages and Scholars Negotiate Power at Home and Abroad." In *Underground Empires,* edited by A. Ong and D. Nonini, 91–114. New York: Routledge.

Lo, Fu-chen, and Yue-man Yeung, eds. 1996. *Emerging World Cities in Pacific Asia.* Tokyo: United Nations Univ. Press.

Lo, Lucia, and Lu Wang. 2004. "A Political Economy Approach to Understanding the Economic Incorporation of Chinese Sub-ethnic Groups." *Journal of International Migration and Integration* 5: 107–40.

Lo, Lucia, and Shuguang Wang. 1997. "Settlement Patterns of Toronto's Chinese Immigrants: Convergence or Divergence?" *Canadian Journal of Regional Science* 20: 49–72.

Lobo, Arun Peter, and Joseph Salvo. 2004. *The Newest New Yorkers, 2000.* New York: New York City Department of City Planning.

Logan, John, and John Mollenkopf. 2003. "People and Politics in America's Big Cities: The Challenges to Urban Democracy." Paper presented to the Russell Sage Foundation conference "The Immigrant Metropolis: The Dynamics of Intergenerational Mobility in Los Angeles and New York."

Lone, Stewart. 2001. *The Japanese Community in Brazil, 1908–1940: Between Samurai and Carnival*. Hampshire, UK: Palgrave.

"The Longest Journey: A Survey of Migration." 2002. *Economist*, Nov. 2.

Longva, Anh Nga 1997. *Walls Built on Sand: Migration, Exclusion, and Society in Kuwait*. Boulder: Westview Press.

Looney, Robert. 2004. "Saudization and Sound Economic Reforms: Are the Two Compatible?" *Strategic Insights* 3, no. 2. http://www.ccc.nps.navy.mil/si/2004/feb/looneyFeb04.pdf.

Low, Linda. 1995. "Population Movement in the Asia Pacific Region: Singapore Perspective." *International Migration Review* 29, no. 3: 745–64.

Lustick, Ian. 1999. "Israel as a Non-Arab State: The Political Implications of Mass Immigration of Non-Jews." *Middle East Journal* 53, no. 3: 101–17.

MacLaughlin, Jim. 1994. *Ireland: The Emigrant Nursery and the World Economy*. Cork: Cork Univ. Press.

Madsen, Morten Lynge, 2004. "Living for Home: Policing Immorality among Undocumented Migrants in Johannesburg." *African Studies* 63, no. 2: 173–92.

Maher, Chris, and John McKay. 1986. *1981 Internal Migration Study Final Report: Internal Migration in Australia*. Canberra, Australia: Department of Immigration and Ethnic Affairs.

Malheiros, Jorge Macaista, and Francisco Vala. 2004. "Immigration and City Change: The Lisbon Metropolis at the Turn of the Twentieth Century." *Journal of Ethnic and Migration Studies* 30, no. 6: 1065–86.

Mang'ana, John Mark. 2004. "The Effects of Migration on Human Rights Consciousness among Congolese Refugees in Johannesburg." Master's thesis, Wits Univ., Johannesburg.

Manning, Robert. 1998. "Multicultural Washington, D.C.: The Changing Social and Economic Landscape of a Post-industrial Metropolis." *Ethnic and Racial Studies* 21, no. 2: 328–55.

Marcus, Alan. 2004. "Brazil's Northeast: A Violated Land." http://www.brazzil.com/2004/html/articles/feb04/p112feb04.htm.

Marcuse, Peter. 1997. "The Enclave, the Citadel, and the Ghetto: What Has Changed in the Post-Fordist City." *Urban Affairs Review* 33, no. 2: 228–64.

Margolis, Maxine L. 1994. *Little Brazil: An Ethnography of Brazilian Immigrants in New York City*. Princeton: Princeton Univ. Press.

———. 1998. *An Invisible Minority: Brazilians in New York City*. Boston: Allyn and Bacon.

Marshall, Paule. 1987. "Black Immigrant Women in *Brown Girl, Brownstones.*" In *Caribbean Life in New York City,* edited by Constance Sutton and Elsa Chaney, 87–91. New York: Center for Migration Studies.

Martin, Philip L. 1991. Labor Migration in Asia. *International Migration Review* 25, no. 1: 176–93.

———. 1994. "Germany: Reluctant Land of Immigration." In *Controlling Immigration: A Global Perspective,* edited by Wayne A. Cornelius, Philip L. Martin, and James F. Hollifield, 189–225. Cambridge: Cambridge Univ. Press.

Marwell, Nicole. 2004. "Ethnic and Postethnic Politics in New York City: The Dominican Second Generation." In *Becoming New Yorkers: Ethnographies of the New Second Generation,* edited by Philip Kasinitz, John H. Mollenkopf, and Mary C. Waters, 227–56. New York: Russell Sage Foundation.

Marx, Anthony. 2002. "The Nation-State and Its Exclusions." *Political Science Quarterly* 117, no. 1: 103–26.

Mason, Susan. 1998. *Jewellery Making in Birmingham, 1750–1995.* Chichester, England: Phillimore.

Massey, Doreen. 1994. *Space, Place, and Gender.* Cambridge: Polity.

Massey, Douglas S. 1987. "Understanding Mexican Migration to the United States." *American Journal of Sociology* 92: 1372–1403.

Massey, Douglas S., Joaquin Arango, Graeme Hugo, Ali Kouaouci, Adela Pellegrino, and J. Edward Taylor. 1998. *Worlds in Motion: Understanding International Migration at the End of the Millennium.* Oxford: Clarendon Press.

Massey, Douglas S., and Nancy A. Denton. 1993. *American Apartheid.* Cambridge: Harvard Univ. Press.

Massey, Douglas S., Luin P. Goldring, and Jorge Durand. 1994. "Continuities in Transnational Migration: An Analysis of Nineteen Mexican Communities." *American Journal of Sociology* 99: 1492–1533.

Mata, Fernando. 1996. "Birthplace and Economic Similarities in the Labour Force." In *Immigration and Ethnicity in Canada,* edited by Anne Laperriere, Varpu Lindstrom, and Tamara Palmer Seiler. Montreal: Association for Canadian Studies.

Matsuda, Mizuho. 2003. *Japan: An Assessment of the International Labour Migration Situation: The Case of Female Labour Migrants.* Gender Promotion Programme, Series on Women and Migration. GENPROM Working Paper no. 5. Geneva: International Labour Office. http://www.ilo.org/public/english/ employment/gems/download/swmjap.pdf.

Mattes, Tobert, Jonathan Crush, and Wayne Richmond. 2001. "The Brain Gain and Legal Immigration to Post-apartheid South Africa." In *Destinations Unknown: Perspectives on the Brain Drain in Southern Africa,* edited by David A. McDonald and Jonathan Crush, 139–56. Pretoria: Africa Institute.

McAlister, Elizabeth. 1998. "The Madonna of 115th Street Revisited: Vodou and Haitian Catholicism in the Age of Transnationalism." In *Gatherings in Diaspora: Religious Communities and the New Immigration,* edited by Stephen Warner and Judith G. Witner, 123–62. Philadelphia: Temple Univ. Press.

McCann, Eugene J. 2004. "Urban Political Economy Beyond the 'Global City.'" *Urban Studies* 41, no. 12: 2315–33.

McDonald, David A. 2000. *On Borders: Perspectives on Cross Border Migration in Southern Africa.* Cape Town: Southern African Migration Project; New York: St. Martin's Press.

———. 2002. "No Money, No Service: South Africa's Poorest Citizens Lose Out under Attempts to Recover Service Costs for Water and Power." *Alternatives* 28, no. 2: 15–20.

McDonald, David A., and Jonathan Crush, eds. 2001. *Destinations Unknown: Perspectives on the Brain Drain in Southern Africa.* Pretoria: Africa Institute.

McDonald, David A., and Sean Jacobs, 2005. *Understanding Press Coverage of Cross-border Migration in Southern Africa since 2000.* Migration Policy Series no. 37. Cape Town: South African Migration Project.

McEwan, Cheryl, Jane Pollard, and Nick Henry. 2005. "Re-visioning a 'Global City': Multicultural Economic Development in Birmingham." *International Journal of Urban and Regional Research* 29, no. 4: 916–33.

McGinty, Jo Craven. 2005. "Breaking Down Hate Crime." *New York Times,* July 24.

McKay, J., and Jim Whitelaw. 1978. "Internal Migration and the Australian Urban System." *Progress in Planning* 10, no. 1: 1–83.

Melder, Keith. 1997. "The Postwar Boom and Transformation." In *City of Magnificent Intentions: A History of Washington, District of Columbia,* Unit V–World Capital, 23:499–514. Washington, D.C., and Silver Spring, Md.: Intac.

Menahem, Gila. 2000. "Jews, Arabs, Russians, and Foreigners in an Israeli City: Ethnic Divisions and the Restructuring Economy of Tel-Aviv, 1983–1996." *International Journal of Urban and Regional Research* 24, no. 3: 634–52.

"Menu Master." 2000. *Birmingham Voice,* June 7, 3.

Metropolis. 2006. "Mission Statement." http://www.metropolis.org.

Min, Pyong Gap. 2001. "Koreans: An 'Institutionally Complete Community' in New York." In *New Immigrants in New York,* edited by Nancy Foner, 173–200. Rev. ed. New York: Columbia Univ. Press.

Ministry of Big Cities and Integration Policy. 2002. *Nota integratie in het perspectief van immigratie.* Den Haag: Sdu. http://www.minbzk.nl.

Ministry of Justice, Republic of Korea. 2006. http://www.moj.go.kr/.

Ministry of Labor, Republic of Korea. 2006. "The Employment Permit System." http://www.eps.go.kr/main.html.

Misago, Pierre. 2005. "The Impact of Refugee–Host Community Interactions on Human Rights Consciousness among Congolese Refugees in Johannesburg." Master's thesis, Wits Univ., Johannesburg.

Mitchell, Katharyne. 2004. "Geographies of Identity: Multiculturalism Unplugged." *Progress in Human Geography* 28, no. 5: 641–51.

Modood, Tariq, and Pnina Werbner, eds. 1997. *The Politics of Multiculturalism in the New Europe: Racism, Identity, and Community.* London: Zed Books.

Mollenkopf, John. 1999. "Urban Political Conflicts and Alliances." In *The Handbook of International Migration,* edited by Charles Hirschman, Philip Kasinitz, and Josh DeWind, 412–22. New York: Russell Sage Foundation.

Mollenkopf, John, David Olson, and Timothy Ross. 2001. "Immigrant Political Participation in New York and Los Angeles." In *Governing American Cities: Interethnic Coalitions, Competition, and Conflict,* edited by Michael Jones-Correa, 17–70. New York: Russell Sage Foundation.

Morita, Kiriro. 1992. *Japan and the Problem of Foreign Workers.* Tokyo: Research Institute for the Japanese Economy, Faculty of Economics, Univ. of Tokyo-Hongo.

———. 1993. "Foreign Workers in Japan." In "Labor Migration and Capital Mobility, Comparing the U.S. and Japan," edited by Saskia Sassen. Special issue, *International Journal of Political Economy.*

Morita, Kiriro, and Saskia Sassen. 1994. "The New Illegal Immigration to Japan, 1980–1992." *International Migration Review* 28, no. 1: 153–63.

Morris, Alan. 1999. *Bleakness and Light: Inner-city Transition in Hillbrow, Johannesburg.* Johannesburg: Wits Univ. Press.

Morris, Alan, and Antoine Bouillon, eds. 2001. *African Immigration to South Africa: Francophone Migration of the 1990s.* Pretoria: Protea.

Msibi, Ntombikayise, and Sally Peberdy. 2005. "Female Informal Sector Cross Border Traders in Johannesburg." Unpublished paper, Southern African Migration Project, Johannesburg.

Murdie, Robert. 1996. "Economic Restructuring and Social Polarization in Toronto." In *Social Polarization in Post-industrial Metropolises,* edited by John O'Loughlin and Jurgen Friedrich. New York: Walter de Gruyter.

Murdie, Robert, and Carlos Teixeira. 2003. "Towards a Comfortable Neighbourhood and Appropriate Housing: Immigrant Experiences in Toronto." In *World in a City,* edited by Michael Lanphier and Paul Anisef, 132–91. Toronto: Univ. of Toronto Press.

Murray, Martin, 2004. *The Evolving Spatial Form of Cities in a Globalising World Economy: Johannesburg and Sao Paulo.* Pretoria: Human Sciences Research Council.

Nagengast, Carole, and Michael Kearney. 1990. "Mixtec Ethnicity: Social Identity, Political Consciousness, and Political Activism." *Latin American Research Review* 23: 61–91.

National Consultative Committee on Racism and Interculturalism. 2005. *Report on Incidents Relating to Racism in Ireland.* Dublin: National Consultative Committee on Racism and Interculturalism. http://www.nccri.ie/.

National Population Council. 1991. *Population Issues and Australia's Future: Environment, Economy, and Society, Final Report of the Population Issues Committee.* Canberra: Australian Government Publishing Service.

National Statistical Office. 2006. *2005 Census.* http://kosis.nso.go.kr.

New South Wales Department of Urban Affairs and Planning. 1995. *Demographic Change in New South Wales and Its Implications.* Sydney: Department of Urban Affairs and Planning.

New York City Housing Authority. 2006. *Fact Sheet.* New York: New York City Housing Authority. http://www.nyc.gov/html/nycha/html/about/factsheet.shtml.

Nicholls, Walter. 2000. "Opening the Door to Koreatown: From Kimchi to Karaoke, 28 Great Reasons to Head to Annandale." *Washington Post,* Sept. 20, Guidepost, F1.

Nieuwenhuysen, John. 1995. "Sydney Population Myths." *BIMPR Bulletin* (Bureau of Immigration, Multiculturalism, and Population Research) 15: 10–11.

Ní Laoire, Caitriona. 2004. "Coming 'Home': A Geography of Recent Return Migration to the Republic of Ireland." Narratives of Migration and Return Working Paper. http://migration.ucc.ie/nmr/publications1.html.

Nyamnjoh, Francis. 2006. *Insiders and Outsiders: Citizenship and Xenophobia in Contemporary Southern Africa.* London: Zed Press.

Nyiri, Pal, and Igor Saveliev, eds. 2003. *Globalizing Chinese Migration.* Aldershot: Ashgate.

O'Brien, Carl. 2005. "Need for Rescue from Unscrupulous Bosses." *Irish Times,* Nov. 12.

———. 2006a. "Former EU Accession State Workers Exceed 200,000." *Irish Times,* May 11.

———. 2006b. "Migrant Worker Numbers Continue to Surge." *Irish Times,* July 10.

———. 2006c. "600 Poles May Be Homeless in Ireland, Embassy Finds." *Irish Times,* July 29.

O'Connor, Kevin. 1991. "Economic Activity in Australian Cities: National and Local Trends in Policy." Paper presented to the joint CSIRO Department of Health, Housing, and Community Services seminar "Productive Cities of the Twenty-first Century," Sydney, Sept. 3.

O'Connor, Kevin, Robert Stimson, and Maurice Daly. 2001. *Australia's Changing Economic Geography: A Society Dividing.* Melbourne: Oxford Univ. Press.

Oelefse, Mike. 2003. "Social Justice, Social Integration, and the Compact City: Lessons from the Inner City, Johannesburg." In *Confronting Fragmentation: Housing and Urban Development in a Democratizing Society,* edited by P. Harrison, M. Huchzermeyer, and M. Mayekiso, 88–104. Cape Town: Univ. of Cape Town Press.

O'Hearn, Denis. 1998. *Inside the Celtic Tiger: The Irish Economy and the Asian Model.* London: Pluto.

O'Loughlin, John, and Jurgen Friedrich. 1996. *Social Polarization in Post-industrial Metropolises.* New York: Walter de Gruyter.

Onderzoek en Statistiek [Department of Research and Statistics, City of Amsterdam]. http://www.os.amsterdam.n1.

Ong, Aihwa 2006. *Neoliberalism as Exception: Mutations in Citizenship and Sovereignty.* Durham: Duke Univ. Press.

Ontario Minister of Citizenship and Immigration. 2006. "McGuinty Government Introduces Legislation to Break Down Barriers for Newcomers." News release. June 8.

Opoku-Dapaah, Edward. 1995. *Somali Refugees in Toronto: A Profile.* Toronto: York Lane Press.

ORAC. 2007. *Statistics.* http://www.orac.ie/pages/Stats/statistics.htm.

Organization for Economic Co-operation and Development. 1998. *Migration and Regional Economic Integration in Asia.* Paris: Organization for Economic Co-operation and Development.

Orleck, Annelise. 1987. "The Soviet Jews: Life in Brighton Beach, Brooklyn." In *New Immigrants in New York,* edited by Nancy Foner, 273–304. New York: Columbia Univ. Press.

———. 2001. "Soviet Jews: The City's Newest Immigrants Transform New York Jewish Life." In *New Immigrants in New York,* edited by Nancy Foner, 111–40. Rev. ed. New York: Columbia Univ. Press.

Ornstein, Michael. 2006. *Ethno-racial Groups in Toronto, 1971–2001: A Demographic and Socio-economic Profile.* Toronto: Institute for Social Research, York Univ.

Ostergren, Robert C. 1988. *A Community Transplanted: The Trans-Atlantic Experience of a Swedish Immigrant Settlement in the Upper Middle West, 1835–1915.* Madison: Univ. of Wisconsin Press.

Overseas Korean Foundation. 2006. *Statistics of Overseas Koreans.* http://www.okf.or.kr/data/abodeStatus.jsp.

Owusu, Thomas. 1999. "Residential Patterns and Housing Choices of Ghanian Immigrants in Toronto, Canada." *Housing Studies* 14, no. 1: 77–97.

Palmary, Ingrid. 2004. "City Policing and Forced Migrants in Johannesburg." In *Forced Migrants in the New Johannesburg,* edited by Loren Landau, 61–69. Johannesburg: Forced Migration Studies Programme, Wits Univ.

Palmary, Ingrid, Janine Rauch, and Graeme Simpson. 2003. "Violent Crime in Johannesburg." In *Emerging Johannesburg: Perspectives on the Postapartheid City,* edited by Richard Tomlinson, Robert Beauregard, Lindsay Bremner, and Xolela Mangcu, 101–22. New York: Routledge.

Pan, Philip, and Peter Pae. 1999. "Now Entering Koreatown: Immigrant Community Flourishes in Annandale." *Washington Post,* May 16, A1.

Papademetriou, Demetrios, ed. 2006. *Europe and Its Immigrants in the 21st Century: A New Deal of a Continuing Dialogue of the Deaf?* Washington, D.C.: Migration Policy Institute.

Papastergiadis, Nikos. 2000. *The Turbulence of Migration: Globalization, Deterritorialization, and Hybridity.* Cambridge: Polity Press.

Parekh, Bikhu. 2000. *Rethinking Multiculturalism: Cultural Diversity and Political Theory.* Basingstoke: Palgrave.

Park, Robert E., Eugene W. Burgess, and Robert D. Mackenzie. 1925. *The City.* Chicago: Univ. of Chicago Press.

Park, Young-bum. 1998. "The Republic of Korea: Trends and Recent Developments in International Migration." *Migration and Regional Economic Integration in Asia: OECD Proceedings*, 121–32. Washington, D.C.: Organization for Economic Co-operation and Development.

Parker, David. 1998. "Emerging British Chinese Identities: Issues and Problems." In *The Last Half Century of Chinese Overseas*, edited by Elizabeth Sinn, 91–114. Hong Kong: Hong Kong Univ. Press.

Parnell, Susan. 2001a. "The Melting Pot of Soweto: Orlando East Backyard Tenancy." Report for the City of Johannesburg.

———. 2001b. "'On the Critical List': Social Exclusion in the Informal Settlement of Hospital Hill." Report for the City of Johannesburg.

Parnell, Susan, and Owen Crankshaw. 2004. "Race, Inequality, and Urbanisation in the Johannesburg Region, 1946–1996." In *World Cities Beyond the West: Globalisation, Development, and Inequality*, edited by Josef Gugler, 348–70. Cambridge: Cambridge Univ. Press.

Parnell, Susan, and Gordon Pirie. 1991. "Johannesburg." In *Homes Apart: South Africa's Segregated Cities*, edited by Anthony Lemon, 129–45. Cape Town: David Philip.

Parnell, Susan, and Jennifer Robinson. 2006. "Development and Urban Policy: Johannesburg's City Development Strategy." *Urban Studies* 43, no. 2, 337–55.

Parnell, Susan, and Dominique Wooldridge. 2001. "Social Capital and Social Exclusion in the City of Johannesburg: The Implications for Urban Governance." Report for the City of Johannesburg.

Patarra, Neide, 2004. *Migração internacional: Questão relevante para a região centro-oeste?* http://www.codeplan.df.gov.br/pesquisas/nep/publicacoes/cad erno_04.

Patarra, Neide L., and Rosana Baeninger. 1995. "Migrações internacionais recentes: O caso do Brasil." *Programa interistitucional de avaliação e acompanhamento das migrações internacionais no Brasil* (Campinas) 1 (Sept.).

Paul, Darel E. 2004. "World Cities as Hegemonic Projects: The Politics of Global Imagineering in Montreal." *Political Geography* 23, no. 5: 571–96.

Peberdy, Sally. 1999. "Selecting Immigrants: Nationalism and National Identity in South Africa's Immigration Policies, 1910–1998." Ph.D. diss., Queen's Univ.

———. 2001. "Imagining Immigration: Inclusive Identities and Exclusive Policies in Post-1994 South Africa." *Africa Today* 48: 15–34.

Peberdy, Sally, Jonathan Crush, and Mtombikayise Msibi. 2004. "Migrants in the City of Johannesburg." Report for the City of Johannesburg.

Peberdy, Sally, and Zonke Majodina. 2000. "Just a Roof Over My Head? Housing and the Somali Refugee Community in Johannesburg. *Urban Forum* 11: 73–88.

Peberdy, Sally, and Christian Rogerson. 2002. "Transnationalism and Non–South African Entrepreneurs in South Africa's Small, Medium, and Micro-enterprise (SMME) Economy." In *Transnationalism and New African Immigration to South Africa,* edited by Jonathan Crush and David A. McDonald, 20–40. Toronto: Canadian Association of African Studies.

Pellegrino, Adela. 2004. "Migration from Latin America to Europe: Trends and Policy Challenge." Paper prepared to the International Organization of Migration, Geneva.

Pennix, Rinus, Karen Kraal, Marco Martiniello, and Steven Vertetoc, eds. 2004. *Citizenship in European Cities: Immigrants, Local Politics, and Integration Policies.* Hampshire: Ashgate.

Permanent TSB. 2006. *House Price Index, Quarter 1, 2006.* http://www.permanenttsb.ie/dynamic/pdf/Quarter1-2006.pdf.

Picot, Garnett, and Feng Hou. 2003. *The Rise in Low-Income Rates among Immigrants in Canada.* Ottawa: Statistics Canada, Analytical Studies Branch.

Porter, Catherine. 2005. "9 Communities Picked for Aid." *Toronto Star,* July 1, A4.

Portes, Alejandro, and Ruben Rumbaut. 1990. *Immigrant America: A Portrait.* Berkeley and Los Angeles: Univ. of California Press.

Poulsen, Michael, Ron Johnston, and James Forrest. 2002. "Is Sydney a Divided City Ethnically?" *Australian Geographical Review* 42, no. 3: 356–77.

———. 2004. "Plural Cities and Ethnic Enclaves: Introducing a Measurement Procedure for Comparative Study." *International Journal of Urban and Regional Research* 26, no. 2: 229–43.

Pratt, Geraldine. 2004. *Working Feminism.* Philadelphia: Temple Univ. Press.

Pratt, Geraldine, and Brenda S. A. Yeoh. 2003. "Transnational (Counter) Topographies." *Gender, Place, and Culture* 10, no. 2: 159–66.

Preston, Valerie, and Joseph C. Cox. 1999. "Immigrants and Employment: A Comparison of Montreal and Toronto Between 1981 and 1996." *Canadian Journal of Regional Science* 22: 87–112.

Preston, Valerie, and Wenona Giles. 1997. "Ethnicity, Gender, and Labour Markets in Canada: A Case Study of Immigrant Women in Toronto." *Canadian Journal of Urban Research* 6: 135–59.

Preston, Valerie, Lucia Lo, and Shuguang Wang. 2003. "Immigrants' Economic Status in Toronto: Stories of Triumph and Disappointment." In *World in a City,* edited by Michael Lanphier and Paul Anisef, 192–262. Toronto: Univ. of Toronto Press.

Price, Marie, and Lisa Benton-Short. 2007. "Immigrants and World Cities: From the Hyper-diverse to the Bypassed." *GeoJournal* 68, nos. 2–3: 103–17.

Price, Marie, Ivan Cheung, Samantha Friedman, and Audrey Singer. 2005. "The World Settles In: Washington, D.C., as an Immigrant Gateway." *Urban Geography* 26, no. 1: 61–83.

Prins, Baukje, and Boris Slijper, eds. 2002. "Inleiding." *Migrantenstudies* 18, no. 4: 194–210.

Punch, Michael. 2005. "Problem Drug Use and the Political Economy of Urban Restructuring: Heroin, Class, and Governance in Dublin." *Antipode* 37, no. 4: 754–74.

Purcell, Mark. 2003. "Citizenship and the Right to the Global City: Reimagining the Capitalist World Order." *International Journal of Urban and Regional Research* 27, no. 3: 564–90.

Pursell, Rebecca. 2005. "Access to Health Care among Somali Forced Migrants in Johannesburg." Master's thesis, Wits Univ., Johannesburg.

Qadeer, Mohammed. 2003. *Ethnic Segregation in a Multicultural City: The Case of Toronto, Canada*. Working Paper no. 28. Toronto: Centre of Excellence for Research on Immigration and Settlement.

Quinn, Emma, and Gerard Hughes. 2005a. *Policy Analysis Report on Asylum and Migration: Ireland 2003 to Mid-2004*. Dublin: ESRI.

———. 2005b. *Reception Systems, Their Capacities, and the Social Situation of Asylum Applicants Within the Reception System in Ireland*. Dublin: ESRI.

"Racism Fight Stepped Up as McDowell Unveils New Action Plan." 2005. *Irish Independent*, Jan. 28.

Rahman, Mizanur. 1999. *The Asian Economic Crisis and Bangladeshi Workers in Singapore*. Working Paper no. 147. Singapore: Department of Sociology, National Univ. of Singapore.

Raijman, Rebeca, and Adriana Kemp. 2004. "Consuming the Holy Spirit in the Holy Land: Evangelical Churches, Labor Migrants, and the Jewish State." In *Consumption and Market Society in Israel*, edited by Yoram S. Carmeli and Kalman Applbaum, 163–84. Oxford: Berg.

Ram, Monder, David Smallbone, and D. Deakins. 2002. "Access to Finance and Business Support by Ethnic Minority Firms in the UK." Report presented to the Bank of England, British Bankers Association, London.

Rath, Jan. 1991. *Minorisering: De sociale constructie van "etnische minderheden"* [Minorization: The Social Construction of "Ethnic Minorities"]. Amsterdam: SUA.

Ray, Brian. 1998. *A Comparative Study of Immigrant Housing, Neighborhoods and Social Networks in Toronto and Montreal.* Ottawa: Canada Mortgage and Housing Corporation.

Reitz, Jeffrey. 1998. *Warmth of the Welcome: The Social Causes of Economic Success for Immigrants in Different Nations and Cities.* Boulder: Westview Press.

Rex, J., and R. Moore. 1967. *Race, Community, and Conflict: A Study of Sparkbrook.* London: Oxford Univ. Press.

Rex, J., and S. Tomlinson. 1979. *Colonial Immigrants in a British City.* London: Routledge.

Richmond, Anthony. 1992. "Immigration and Structural Change: The Canadian Experience, 1971–1986." *International Migration Review* 26, no. 4: 1200–1221.

Robinson, Jennifer. 2002a. "Global and World Cities: A View from Off the Map." *International Journal of Urban and Regional Research* 26, no. 3: 531–54.

———. 2002b. "A World of Cities." *British Journal of Sociology* 55, no. 4: 569–78.

———. 2003. "Johannesburg's Futures: Beyond Developmentalism and Global Success." In *Emerging Johannesburg: Perspectives on the Postapartheid City,* edited by Richard Tomlinson, Robert Beauregard, Lindsay Bremmer, and Xolela Mangcu, 259–80. New York: Routledge.

———. 2005. *Ordinary Cities: Between Modernity and Development.* London: Routledge.

Robinson, Kathryn. 1991. "Housemaids: The Effects of Gender and Culture in the Internal and International Migration of Indonesian Women. In *Intersexions: Gender/Class/Culture/Ethnicity,* edited by G. Bottomley, M. de Lepervanche, and J. Martin, 33–51. Sydney: Allen and Unwin.

———. 2000. "Gender, Islam, and Nationality: Indonesian Domestic Servants in the Middle East." In *Home and Hegemony: Domestic Service and Identity Politics in South and Southeast Asia,* edited by K. M. Adams and S. Dickey, 249–82. Ann Arbor: Univ. of Michigan Press.

Rogerson, Christian. 1998. "Formidable Entrepreneurs: The Role of Foreigners in the Gauteng SMME Economy." *Urban Forum* 9: 143–53.

Rosenhek, Zeev. 1999. "The Politics of Claims-Making by Labour Migrants in Israel." *Journal of Ethnic and Migration Studies* 25, no. 4: 575–95.

Rosenwaike, Ira. 1972. *Population History of New York City.* Syracuse: Syracuse Univ. Press.

Roth, Joshua. 2002. *Brokered Homeland: Japanese Brazilian Migrants in Japan.* Ithaca: Cornell Univ. Press.

Rouse, Roger 1991. "Mexican Migration and the Social Space of Postmodernism." *Diaspora* (Spring): 8–23.

———. 1995. "Questions of Identity: Personhood and Collectivity in Transnational Migration to the United States." *Critique of Anthropology* 15, no. 4: 351–80.

Ruddick, Susan. 1996. "Constructing Difference in Public Spaces: Race, Class, and Gender as Interlocking Systems." *Urban Geography* 17, no. 2: 132–51.

Ruhs, Martin. 2005. *Managing the Immigration and Employment of Non-EU Nationals in Ireland.* Dublin: TCD Policy Institute.

Sack, Robert. 1986. *Human Territoriality: Its Theory and History.* Cambridge: Cambridge Univ. Press.

Sadie, Wendy, and Scott Borger. 2004. "Accessing Accommodation in Inner-City Johannesburg." In *Forced Migrants in the New Johannesburg,* edited by Loren Landau, 84–89. Johannesburg: Forced Migration Studies Programme, Wits Univ.

Safa, Helen I. 2005. "Challenging Mestizaje: A Gender Perspective on Indigenous and Afrodescendant Movements in Latin America." *Critique of Anthropology* 25, no. 3: 307–30.

Sakurai, Célia. 1998. "Imigração japonesa para o Brasil: Um exemplo de imigração tutelada, 1908–1941." In *CD. XXII Encontro Nacional da ANPOCS.* Caxambu, Minas Gerais.

Sales, Teresa. 1999. *Brasileiros longe de casa.* São Paulo: Cortez Editora.

Samers, Michael. 1999. "'Globalization,' the Geo-political Economy of Migration, and the 'Spatial Vent.'" *Review of International Political Economy* 6, no. 2: 166–99.

———. 2002. "Immigration and the Global City Hypothesis: Towards an Alternative Research Agenda." *International Journal of Urban and Regional Research* 26, no. 2: 389–402.

Sandercock, Leonie. 1998. *Towards Cosmopolis: Planning for Multicultural Cities.* Chichester: John Wiley and Sons.

———. 2003. *Cosmopolis II: Mongrel Cities of the 21st Century.* London: Continuum.

Sanjek, Roger. 1998. *The Future of Us All: Race and Neighborhood Politics in New York City.* Ithaca: Cornell Univ. Press.

Santos, Regina Bega. 1997. *Migração no Brasil.* 3d ed. São Paulo: Editora Scipione.

Sassen, Saskia. 1988. *The Mobility of Labor and Capital: A Study of International Investment and Labor Flow.* New York: Cambridge Univ. Press.

———. 1991. *The Global City: New York, London, Tokyo.* Princeton: Princeton Univ. Press.

———. 1994. *Cities in a World Economy.* London: Pine Forge Press.

———. 1998. *Globalization and Its Discontents: Essays on the New Mobility of People and Money.* New York: New Press.

———. 1999. *Guests and Aliens.* New York: New Press.

———, ed. 2002. *Global Networks, Linked Cities.* New York: Routledge.

———. 2004. "Global Cities and Survival Circuits." In *Global Woman: Nannies, Maids, and Sex Workers in the New Economy,* edited by Barbara Ehrenreich and Arlie Russell Hochschild, 254–74. New York: Metropolitan Books.

———. 2006. *Territory, Authority, Rights: From Medieval to Global Assemblages.* Princeton: Princeton Univ. Press.

Schölch, Alexander. 1985. "The Demographic Development of Palestine, 1850–1882." *International Journal of Middle East Studies* 17, no. 4: 485–505.

Schuerman, Matthew, and Ben Smith. 2005. "Sic Transit Duo: Two Guys Caught on a Third Rail." *New York Observer,* Dec. 26.

Schwartzman, Paul. 2005. "Shaw Shuns 'Little Ethiopia': Black Leaders Note Immigrants' Pride but Resist Designation." *Washington Post,* July 25, B1.

Scientific Council for Government Policy. 2001. *Nederland als immigratiesamenleving.* The Hague: WRR.

Scott, Allen, ed. 2001. *Global City-Regions: Trends, Theory, Policy.* Oxford: Oxford Univ. Press.

Searle, Glen. 1996. *Sydney as a Global City.* Sydney: New South Wales Department of Urban and Planning.

Segale, Tebogo. 2004. "Forced Migrants and Social Exclusion in Johannesburg." In *Forced Migrants in the New Johannesburg,* edited by Loren Landau, 43–45. Johannesburg: Forced Migration Studies Programme, Wits Univ.

Select Committee on Justice, Equality, Defence, and Women's Rights. 2005. *Justice, Equality, and Law Reform.* Rev. ed. May 18. http://debates.oireachtas.ie/DDebate.aspx?F=JUS20050518.xml&Node=H3#H3.

Seoul Metropolitan Government. 2006. *International Cooperation: Policy Directions and Goals.* http://english.seoul.go.kr/gover/cooper/coo_01pol.html.

Shachar, Arie, and Daniel Felsenstein. 2002. "Globalization Processes and Their Impact on the Structure of the Tel Aviv Metropolitan Area." In *Emerging Nodes in the Global Economy: Frankfurt and Tel Aviv Compared*, edited by Daniel Felsenstein, Eike W. Schamp, and Yaron Ergas, 36–56. Berlin: Springer.

Shachar, Ayelet. 1999. "Whose Republic? Citizenship and Membership in the Israeli Polity." *Georgetown Immigration Law Journal* 13, no. 2: 233–72.

Shadid, W. A., Ernst Spaan, and Johann D. Speckman 1992. "Labour Migration and the Policy of the Gulf States." In *Labour Migration to the Middle East: From Sri Lanka to the Gulf,* edited by Frank Eelens, Toon Schampers, and Johann D. Speckman, 63–86. London and New York: Kegan Paul International.

Shalev, Michael. 1999. "Have Globalization and Liberalization 'Normalized' Israel's Political Economy?" In *Israel: The Dynamics of Continuity and Change,* edited by David Levi-Faur, Gabriel Sheffer, and David Vogel. London: Frank Cass.

Shen, L. 1996. "Emigration in a Transitional Time: Hong Kong Business Migrants in Sydney, Australia." Ph.D. diss., Department of Geographical Sciences, Australian National Univ.

Shields, Rob. 1991. *Places on the Margins: Alternative Geographies of Modernity.* London: Routledge.

Short, John Rennie. 2004a. "Black Holes and Loose Connections in a Global Urban Network." *Professional Geographer* 56, no. 2: 295–302.

———. 2004b. *Global Metropolian: Globalizing Cities in a Capitalist World.* London: Routledge.

Short, John Rennie, Carrie Breitbach, Steven Buckman, and Jamey Essex. 2000. "From World Cities to Gateway Cities: Extending the Boundaries of Globalization Theory." *City* 4, no. 3: 317–40.

Short, John Rennie, and Yeong-Hyun Kim. 1999. *Globalization and the City.* Addison Wesley Longman.

Short, John Rennie, Yeong-Hyun Kim, Maria Kuus, and Heather Wells. 1996. "The Dirty Little Secret of World Cities Research: Data Problems in Comparative Analysis." *International Journal of Urban and Regional Research* 20, no. 4: 697–717.

Shoval, Noam. 2002. "A New Phase in the Competition for the Olympic Gold: The London and New York Bids for the 2012 Games." *Journal of Urban Affairs* 24, no. 5: 583–99.

Shuval, Judith. 1998. "Migration to Israel: The Mythology of 'Uniqueness.'" *International Migration* 36, no. 1: 3–24.

Silvey, Rachel 2004a. "Power, Difference, and Mobility: Feminist Advances in Migration Studies." *Progress in Human Geography* 28, no. 4: 490–506.

———. 2004b. "Transnational Domestication: Indonesian Domestic Workers in Saudi Arabia." *Political Geography* 23, no. 3: 245–64.

———. 2005. "Transnational Islam: Indonesian Migrant Domestic Workers in Saudi Arabia." In *Geographies of Muslim Women: Gender, Religion, and Space,* edited by Ghazi-Walid Falah and Caroline Nagel, 127–46. New York: Guilford.

Silvey, Rachel, and Lawson, Victoria. 1999. "Placing the Migrant." *Annals of the Association of American Geographers* 89: 121–32.

Simone, AbdouMaliq. 2001. "African Migration and the Remaking of Inner-City Johannesburg." In *African Immigration to South Africa: Francophone Migration of the 1990s,* edited by Alan Morris and Antoine Bouillon, 150–71. Pretoria: Protea.

———. 2004. *For the City Yet to Come: Changing African Life in Four Cities.* Durham: Duke Univ. Press.

Singapore Department of Statistics. 2001. *Singapore Population: Census 2000.* Singapore: Singapore Department of Statistics.

Singer, Audrey. 2003. *At Home in the Nation's Capital: Immigrant Trends in Metropolitan Washington.* Washington, D.C.: Brookings Institution Center on Urban and Metropolitan Policy.

———. 2004. "The Rise of Immigrant Gateways." *The Living Cities Census Series.* Washington, D.C.: Brookings Institution.

Singer, Audrey, and Amelia Brown. 2001. "Washington, D.C." In *Encyclopedia of American Immigration,* edited by James Ciment, 974–82. Armonk, N.Y.: Sharpe Reference.

Skop, Emily, Ernesto Amaral, Paul Peters, and Joseph Potter. 2006a. "Chain Migration and Residential Segregation of Internal Migrants in the Metropolitan Area of São Paulo, Brazil." *Urban Geography* 27, no. 5: 397–421.

Skop, Emily, and Cecilia Menjívar. 2001. "Phoenix: The Newest Latino Immigrant Gateway?" *Association of Pacific Coast Geographers Yearbook* 63: 63–76.

Skop, Emily, and Sarah Zell. 2006b. "The Migration Industry." Unpublished manuscript held at the Univ. of Texas at Austin.

Slater, Terry. 1996. "Birmingham's Black and South Asian Population." In *Managing a Conurbation: Birmingham and its Region,* edited by A. John Gerrard and Terry Slater, 140–55. Studley, England: Brewin Books.

Smith, Michael P. 2001. *Transnational Urbanism: Locating Globalization.* Oxford: Blackwell.

Smith, Robert C. 2006. *Mexican New York: Transnational Lives of New Immigrants.* Berkeley and Los Angeles: Univ. of California Press.

Soares, Weber. 2003. "A emigração valadarense à luz dos fundamentos teóricos da análise de redes sociais." In *Fronteiras cruzadas: Etnicidade, gênero e redes sociais,* edited by Ana Cristina Braga Martes and Soraya Fleischer, 231–62. São Paulo: Editora Paz e Terra.

Social and Cultural Planning Office of the Netherlands. 1995. *Rapportage Minderheden 1995.* The Hague: VUGA.

South African Human Rights Commission. 2000. *Lindela at the Crossroads for Detention and Deportation: An Assessment of the Conditions of Detention.* Johannesburg: South African Human Rights Commission.

South China Morning Post. 2003. Sept. 16.

Southern African Migration Project. 2003. *Read as Migration News.* http://www.queensu.ca/samp/.

Sowell, Thomas. 1996. *Migrations and Cultures: A World View.* New York: Basic Books.

Spaan, Ernst. 1994. "Taikongs and Calos: The Role of Middlemen and Brokers in Javanese International Migration." *International Migration Review* 28, no. 1: 93–114.

———. 1999. *Labour Circulation and Socioeconomic Transformation: The Case of East Java, Indonesia.* Groningen: Rijksuniversiteit Groningen.

Spencer, Steven A. 1992. "Illegal Migrant Laborers in Japan." *International Migration Review* 26, no. 3: 754–86.

Statistics Canada. 1971. Census.

———. 1981. Census.

———. 1991. Census.

———. 2001. Census.

———. 2003. *Canada's Ethnocultural Portrait: The Changing Mosaic.* 2001 Census Analysis Series. Ottawa: Statistics Canada, Census Operation Division.

Stewart, C. 1989. *Health Education for Owners of Greek-Cypriot Fish and Chip Shops.* Birmingham: Environmental Health Department, Birmingham City Council.

The Straits Times, various issues.

Strong Neighborhood Task Force. 2005. *Strong Neighborhood: A Call to Action.* Toronto: Strong Neighborhood Task Force.

Struyk, Raymond J. 2005. "Housing Policy Issues in a Rich Country with High Population Growth: The Case of Riyadh, Saudi Arabia." *Review of Urban and Regional Development Studies* 17, no. 2: 140–61.

Suàrez-Orozco, Marcelo M. 2000. "Everything You Ever Wanted to Know about Assimilation but Were Afraid to Ask." *Daedalus* 129, no. 4: 1–30.

Suk, Hyun-Ho, Ki-Sun Jung, Jung-Hwan Lee, Hye-Kyung Lee, and Soo-Dol Kang. 2003. *Foreign Workers' Workplace and Life* [in Korean]. Seoul: Ji Sik Ma Dang.

Tam, Suk Tak. 1998. "Representations of the 'Chinese' and 'Ethnicity' in British Racial Discourse." In *The Last Half Century of Chinese Overseas,* edited by Elizabeth Sinn, 81–90. Hong Kong: Hong Kong Univ. Press.

Tannam, Marian. 2002. "Questioning Irish Anti-racism." In *Racism and Anti-racism in Ireland,* edited by Ronit Lentin and Robbie McVeigh, 193–210. Belfast: Beyond the Pale Publications.

Taylor, Charles. 1992. "The Politics of Recognition." In *Multiculturalism and the "Politics of Recognition": An Essay,* edited by A. Gutmann. Princeton: Princeton Univ. Press.

Taylor, Peter J. 2004. *World City Network: A Global Urban Analysis.* New York: Routledge.

Teixeira, Carlos, Lucia Lo, and Marie Truelove. 2007. "Ethnic Entrepreneurship, Institutional Discrimination, and Related Policy Issues: A Case Study in Toronto." *Environment and Planning C,* 25: 176–93.

Tlou, Joyce. 2004. "Challenges Facing Forced Migrants in Johannesburg and the Non-governmental Response." In *Forced Migrants in the New Johannesburg,* edited by Loren Landau, 43–45. Johannesburg: Forced Migration Studies Programme, Wits Univ.

Tomlinson, Richard. 1999. "From Exclusion to Inclusion: Rethinking Johannesburg's Central City." *Environment and Planning A* 31: 1655–78.

Tomlinson, Richard, Robert Beauregard, Lindsay Bremner, and Xolela Mangcu, eds. 2003. *Emerging Johannesburg: Perspectives on the Postapartheid City.* New York: Routledge.

Toronto City Summit Alliance. 2003. *Enough Talk: An Action Plan for the Toronto Region.* Toronto: Toronto City Summit Alliance.

Truzzi, Oswaldo. 1991. "De mascates a doutores: Sírios e libaneses em São Paulo." In *Série Imigração,* IDESP. São Paulo: Sumaré.

Tsuda, Takeyuki. 1999a. "The Motivation to Migrate: The Ethnic and Sociocultural Constitution of the Japanese-Brazilian Return-Migration System." *Economic Development and Social Change* 48, no. 1: 1–31.

————. 1999b. "The Permanence of 'Temporary' Migration: The 'Structural Embeddedness' of Japanese-Brazilian Immigrant Workers in Japan." *Journal of Asian Studies* 58, no. 3: 687–722.

Tsuda, Takeyuki, and Wayne A. Cornelius. 2004. "Japan: Government Policy, Immigrant Reality." In *Controlling Immigration: A Global Perspective*, edited by Wayne A. Cornelius, Takeyuki Tsuda, Philip L. Martin, and James F. Hollifield, 439–76. Stanford: Stanford Univ. Press.

Tuan, Yi-Fu. 1977. *Space and Place: The Perspective of Experience.* Minneapolis: Univ. of Minnesota Press.

Tweede Kamer der Staten-Generaal. 2005 (2005: 30-304). Jaarnota Integratiebeleid 2005, vergaderjaar 2005–2006. Den Haag.

Uitermark, Justus. 2003. "'Social Mixing' and the Management of Disadvantaged Neighborhoods: The Dutch Policy of Urban Restructuring Revisited." *Urban Studies* 40, no. 3: 531–49.

Uitermark, Justus, Ugo Rossi, and Henk van Houtem. 2005. "Reinventing Multiculturalism: Urban Citizenship and the Negotiation of Ethnic Diversity in Amsterdam." *International Journal of Urban and Regional Research* 29, no. 3: 622–40.

Ungar, Sanford. 1995. "Getting Down to Business: The Ethiopians and Eritreans." In *Fresh Blood: The New American Immigrants*, edited by Sanford Ungar, 247–72. New York: Simon and Schuster.

United Nations 2001. Table 2 in *World Population Prospects: The 2000 Revision*, 27–30. New York: United Nations Department of Economic and Social Affairs.

————. 2005. *Population Division of the Department of Economic and Social Affairs of the United Nations Secretariat, Trends in Total Migrant Stock: The 2005 Revision.* http://esa.un.org/migration.

United Nations, Department of Economic and Social Affairs, Population Division. 2002. *International Migration Report, 2002.* New York: United Nations.

————. 2006a. *Migrant Stock Data, 2006.* New York: United Nations.

————. 2006b. *World Migration Data Sheet, 2006.* New York: United Nations.

United Way of Greater Toronto and the Canadian Council on Social Development. 2004. *Poverty by Postal Code: The Geography of Neighbourhood Poverty, City of Toronto, 1981–2001.* Toronto: United Way of Greater Toronto.

U.S. Bureau of the Census. 1999. *Nativity of the Population for Regions, Divisions, and States, 1850–1990.* Technical Paper 29, Table 13. http://www.census.gov/population/www/documentation/twps0029/tab13.html.

———. 2000. *U.S. Census, 2000.* http://www.census.gov/main/www/cen2000.html.

———. 2004. "Census Bureau Projects Tripling of Hispanic and Asian Populations in 50 Years: Non-Hispanic Whites May Drop to Half of Total Population." Press release, Mar. 18.

———. 2005. *American Community Survey.* http://www.census.gov/acs/www/.

Valji, Nahla. 2003. "Creating the Nation: The Rise of Violent Xenophobia in the New South Africa." M.A. thesis, York Univ.–Toronto.

Van Hook, Jennifer, Weiwei Zhang, Frank Bean, and Jeffrey Passel. 2006. "Foreign-Born Emigration: A New Approach and Estimates Based on Matched CPS Files." *Demography* 43, no. 2: 361–82.

Vertovec, Steven. 1999. "Conceiving and Researching Transnationalism." *Ethnic and Racial Studies* 22, no. 2: 447–62.

———. 2001. "Transnationalism and Identity." *Journal of Ethnic and Migration Studies* 27, no. 4: 573–82.

Vertovec, Steven, and Robin Cohen, eds. 2002. *Conceiving Cosmopolitanism: Theory, Context, and Practice.* Oxford: Oxford Univ. Press.

Vickerman, Milton. 1999. *Crosscurrents: West Indian Immigrants and Race in America.* New York: Oxford Univ. Press.

———. 2001. "Tweaking a Monolith: The West Indian Immigrant Encounter with Blackness." In *Islands in the City: West Indian Migration to New York,* edited by Nancy Foner, 237–56. Berkeley and Los Angeles: Univ. of California Press.

Vilela, Elaine. 2002. "Sirios e libaneses e o fenomeno étnico: manipulações de identidades." Ph.D. diss., Departamento de Sociologia e Antropologia—UFMG, Belo Horizonte.

Viviani, Nancy, James Coughlan, and Trevor Rowland. 1993. *Indo-Chinese in Australia: The Issues of Unemployment and Residential Concentration.* Canberra: Australian Government Publishing Service.

Vulliami, E. 2005. "Rumours of a Riot." *Guardian,* Nov. 29. http://www.guardian.co.uk/g2/story/0,1652950,00.html.

Wacquant, Loãc J. D. 1993. "Urban Outcasts: Stigma and Division in the Black American Ghetto and the French Urban Periphery." In *International Journal of Urban and Regional Research* 17, no. 3: 366–83.

Waldinger, Roger. 1996. "From Ellis Island to LAX: Immigrant Prospects in the American City." *International Migration Review* 30, no. 4: 1078–86.

———. 1997. "Immigrant Integration in the Postindustrial Metropolis: A View from the United States." Proceedings, First International Metropolis Conference, Iniziative e lo Studio sulla Multietnicita, Milan, 34–47.

Waldinger, Roger, and Jennifer Lee. 2001. "New Immigrants in Urban America." In *Strangers at the Gates: New Immigrants in Urban America,* edited by Roger Waldinger, 30–79. Berkeley and Los Angeles: Univ. of California Press.

Wang, Gungwu. 2003. *Don't Leave Home: Migration and the Chinese.* Singapore: Eastern Universities Press.

Wang, Ling-chi. 1991. "Roots and Changing Identity of the Chinese in the United States." *Daedalus* 120, no. 2: 181–206.

Ware, Helen. 1975. "Immigrant Fertility: Behaviour and Attitudes." *International Migration Review* 9, no. 3: 361–78.

Waters, Joanna L. 2002. "Flexible Families? 'Astronaut' Households and the Experiences of Lone Mothers in Vancouver, British Columbia." *Social and Cultural Geography* 3, no. 2: 117–34.

Waters, Mary, and Tomás Jimenez. 2005. "Assessing Immigrant Assimilation: New Empirical and Theoretical Challenges." *Annual Review of Sociology* 31: 105–25.

White, Elisa Joy. 2002. "Forging African Diaspora Places in Dublin's Retro-global Spaces: Minority Making in a New Global City." *City* 6, no. 2: 251–70.

Willen, Sarah S. 2006. "Perspectives on Labour Migration in Israel." *Revue Européenne des Migrations Internationales* 19, no. 3: 243–62.

Wilson, W. 1989. "Vietnamese Settlement in Sydney." *Australian Geographical Studies* 31: 94–110.

Winckler, Onn. 2002. "The Demographic Dilemma of the Arab World: The Employment Aspect." *Journal of Contemporary History* 37, no. 4: 617–36.

———. 2005. *Arab Political Demography.* Vol. 1, *Population Growth and Natalist Policies.* Brighton and Portland: Sussex Academic Press.

Winkler, T. 2006. "Kwere Kwere Journeys into Strangeness: Re-imaging Inner City Regeneration in Hillbrow, Johannesburg." Ph.D. diss., Univ. of British Columbia–Vancouver.

Winnick, Louis, 1990. *New People in Old Neighborhoods.* New York: Russell Sage Foundation.

Winterstein, Shani, and Lee Stone. 2004. "Forced Migration and Education in Johannesburg." In *Forced Migrants in the New Johannesburg,* edited by Loren Landau, 77–83. Johannesburg: Forced Migration Studies Programme, Wits Univ.

Withers, Glenn. 2004. "Migration to the Regions." Presentation to the Vital Issues Seminar, Parliament House, Mar. 10.

Withers, Glenn, and Marion Powell. 2003. *Immigration and the Regions: Taking Regional Australia Seriously.* A report prepared for the Chifley Research Centre by Applied Economics P/L. Barton, Australia: Chifley Research Centre.

Wong, Diana. 1997. "Transience and Settlement: Singapore's Foreign Labor Policy." *Asian and Pacific Migration Journal* 6, no. 2: 135–67.

———. 2000. "Men Who Built Singapore: Thai Workers in the Construction Industry." In *Thai Migrant Workers in East and Southeast Asia, 1996–97,* edited by Supang Chantavanich, A. Germershausen, and Allan Beesey, 58–105. Chulalongkorn: Asian Research Center for Migration.

Wood, Joseph. 1997. "Vietnamese American Place-Making in Northern Virginia." *Geographical Review* 87, no. 1: 58–72.

Wooden, Mark, Robert Holton, Graeme Hugo, and Judith Sloan. 1994. *Australian Immigration: A Survey of the Issues.* Canberra: Australian Government Publishing Service.

Wooldridge, Dominique. 2001. "Hillbrow: The Bleeding Edge of South African Urbanism?" Report for the City of Johannesburg, Johannesburg.

Wright, Melissa. 1999. "The Dialectics of Still Life: Murder, Women, and Maquiladoras." *Public Culture* 11: 453–74.

Wright, Richard, and Mark Ellis. 2000. "Race, Region, and the Territorial Politics of Immigration in the US." *International Journal of Population Geography* 6: 197–211.

Yamanaka, Keiko. 2002. *Ana Bortz's Law Suit and Minority Rights in Japan.* Japan Policy Research Institute. JPRI Working Paper no. 88. http://www.jpri .org/publications/workingpapers/wp88.html.

Yeoh, Brenda S. A. 2004. "Cosmopolitanism and Its Exclusion in Singapore." *Urban Studies* 41, no. 12: 2431–45.

———. 2006. "Bifurcated Labour: The Unequal Incorporation of Transmigrants in Singapore." *Tijdschrift Voor Economische en Sociale Geografie* 97, no. 1: 26–37.

Yeoh, Brenda, and Tou Chuang Chang. 2001. "Globalizing Singapore: Debating Transnational Flows in the City." *Urban Studies* 38, no. 7: 1025–44.

Yeoh, Brenda S. A., and Shirlena Huang. 2000. "'Home' and 'Away': Foreign Domestic Workers and Negotiation of Diasporic Identity in Singapore." *Women's Studies International Forum* 23, no. 4: 413–29.

Yeoh, Brenda S. A., Shirlena Huang, and Joaquin Gonzalez III. 1999. "Migrant Female Domestic Workers: Debating the Economic, Social, and Political impacts in Singapore." *International Migration Review* 33, no. 1: 114–36.

Yeoh, Brenda S. A., Katie D. Willis, and S. M. Abdul Khader Fakhri. 2003. "Intro-duction: Transnationalism and Its Edges." *Ethnic and Racial Studies* 26, no. 2: 207–17.

Young, Christabel. 1991. "Changes in the Demographic Behaviour of Migrants in Australia and the Transition Between Generations." *Population Studies* 45, no. 1: 67–90.

Zelinsky, Wilbur, and Barrett Lee. 1998. "'Heterolocalism': An Alternative Model of the Sociospatial Behaviour of Immigrant Ethnic Communities." *International Journal of Population Geography* 4, no. 4: 281–98.

Zell, Sarah. 2006. "Intersections of Social Networks and State Policy: A Compara-tive Analysis of Brazilian Migration to the United States and Japan." Master's thesis, Univ. of Texas at Austin.

Zhou, Min. 2001. "Chinese: Divergent Destinies in Immigrant New York." In *New Immigrants in New York*, edited by Nancy Foner, 141–72. Rev. ed. New York: Columbia Univ. Press.

Zolberg, Aristide. 2006. *A Nation by Design: Immigration Policy in the Fashion-ing of America*. New York: Russell Sage Foundation.

Zukin, Sharon. 1995. *The Cultures of Cities*. Oxford: Blackwell Publishers.

Index

Amsterdam: *allochtonen* (foreigner), 158–60; *autochtonen* (native), 158–60; Bijlmermeer, 166–72; death of Theo van Gogh, 150–52; foreign-born statistics, 155–57, 160; Ghanaian immigrants, 166, 169–72; immigrant settlement patterns, 156–58; immigration trends (1960s–2006), 153–56, 160; location of foreign-born, 158; multiculturalism backlash, 151–53, 161–65; Surinamese immigrants, 166; urban multiculturalism policy, 161, 165–66; urban renewal policy, 166

Australia: immigration policy, 17, 71, 75–76, 93–94; state and regional migration schemes, 94

Birmingham: *balti,* 142; banking industry, 141; Joseph Chamberlain, 134, 134n. 2; Chinese immigrants, 136; Chinese Quarter, 143–44; ethnic commodities: 10, 142–43; foreign-born statistics, 132–33, 138–39, 140n. 3; gateway status, 146–47; global city definitions, 130, 132, 146–48; historical immigration trends, 134–37; riots, 146, 146n. 4; settlement patterns, 140; South Asian immigrants, 136–37; transnational connectivity, 148

Brazil: Asunción Agreement and impact on migration, 355; age of migration, 345; assimilation policies, 352–53; emigration trends, 358; emigration to Japan, 359–62, 366–67; emigration to United States, 363–67; *Nikkeijin,* 360, 362–63

Buenos Aires, 43

Canada, 98, 99
censuses, 40–42
circular migration, 42
cities with 1 million or more foreign-born, 42–43

diasporas, 2
Dubai, 3, 5, 35, 45
Dublin: asylum seekers, 242–44, 249, 254; economic transformation, 228–30; emigration trends, 226–28; European Union immigrants, 239; *Famine* sculpture, 226–27; foreign-born statistics, 229–33; housing costs, 230n. 1; immigrant categorization, 237; immigrant impact on public services, 236; immigration trends, 245; local mobilization, 251–52; Moore Street, 233–35; racist incidents, 236; rank in Foreign Policy Globalization Index, 228; returning Irish, 237–38; student visas, 242; tourist visas, 240; work visas, 238, 240–42

entrance categories, 17–18

enumeration, 26
ethnic enterprises, 20, 213–15
ethnoburb, 36, 213

feminist migration research, 287–88
Foreign Policy's Annual Globalization
  Index, 4, 11; ranking Ireland, 11, 228

gateway. See immigrant gateway
global cities, 3–4, 128, 322. See also
  specific city names
global city status, 70, 84, 90–91, 146–47,
  177, 301, 323–24, 327–28
globalization, 1–6, 47, 128, 322

heterolocalism, 211
Hong Kong, 3

identity politics, 19
immigrant enclaves, 36
immigrant gateway: conceptualized, 31;
  connectivity, 34; cyclical nature, 16;
  defined, 2–3, 6, 22, 24–25, 31–39,
  129–30, 255; emerging, 10; entry
  points, 32; established, 8; exceptional, 12; global central business
  districts, 34; global cultural exchange,
  35–37; hyperdiversity, 15; inequalities, 288; mapping, 39–40; national
  immigration policies, 17; nodes of
  collection and dispersion, 33; sites of
  contestation, 21; spatial segregation,
  34–35; surveillance, 32; turnstiles, 37,
  200–201, 280
immigration policy, de facto, 30
immigration trends (by region): Africa,
  44, 47; Europe, 25, 27, 44–45; Latin
  America, 43–44, 46; Middle East, 45;
  Oceania, 45
International Metropolis Project, 30
Ireland: Citizenship Referendum, 246–47;
  citizenship tourism, 247; deportation
  enforcement, 248–49; Employment
  Permits Act, 247–48; immigrant-led

organizations (ILOs), 250–51; immigrants and elections, 252, 252n. 5;
  labor migration policy, 247, 253; trade
  unions, 251
Israel: aliyah (ascent), 304; citizenship,
  312; compatriots, 13, 304; foreignness, 305; foreign vs. immigrant,
  306–7n. 5; immigration trends, 301,
  303n. 2, 306–8; Jewish immigrants,
  302–4; Law of Return, 303–4, 308;
  Russian immigrants, 307–10, 314

Johannesburg: African immigrants, 260;
  circular migration, 272; collapse
  of apartheid, 256, 268–69; crime,
  277–79; European immigrants, 257,
  259; foreign-born by gender, 266;
  foreign-born statistics, 257–61, 265;
  immigrant transience, 12, 256–57,
  272–73; informal sector employment,
  267–68; irregular migration, 262,
  264; Johannesburg Metropolitan
  Police Department, 277–78; racial
  geography, 268–71; refugees, 262–
  63, 267, 271, 278; Soweto, 268–69;
  urban policy, 275–76; work permits,
  261; xenophobia, 273–74, 279–80

labor markets, 20
Lisbon, 37
London, 4, 14, 16
Los Angeles, 29

Netherlands, 154nn. 3–4; census terms,
  158–60; Integration Policy 1994,
  162; Minderhedenbeleid (Minority
  Memorandum), 162, 165; multiculturalism policy, 162–63
New York City: Caribbean immigrants, 54, 60; Chinatowns, 56, 57;
  Brooklyn immigrants, 53n. 2, 56, 59;
  Dominicans, 57; established gateway,
  3, 7–8, 51; foreign-born statistics
  (2000), 51–52, 54; hate crimes

against immigrants, 66–67, 67n. 5; housing conditions for immigrants, 58n. 3, 58–59; immigration impacts, 59–61, 63, 64; immigration trends since 1900, 51–53; location of foreign-born, 58; polyethnic enclaves, 57–63

New York Transport Workers Strike (2000), 65–66

Persian Gulf cities, 25
policies of intolerance, 29–30

refugees, 262, 264–67, 271, 278
Riyadh: female domestic workers, 294; female immigrant isolation, 295–98; foreign-born statistics, 290–91; gated communities, 288; gender-specific social spaces, 294, 299; *hajj* visas, 293, 298; immigration trends, 284, 288–91; Indonesian immigrants, 292–93; *kafala* system, 291; social segregation, 284, 298; *umma,* 295–96, 298; undocumented migrants, 293–94

São Paulo: foreign-born distribution, 357–58; foreign-born statistics, 353–56; immigration history, 348–52; internal migration; 346, 351–52; Japanese migration, 352, 356–57
Saudi Arabia: benefits to noncitizens, 291–92; immigration trends, 283–84
Saudization, 289, 291
Seoul: Cheonggyecheon Restoration, 327; cultural homogeneity, 323, 343; decentralization trends, 324, 327; diversity in Outer Seoul, 339; foreign-born statistics, 7, 329, 340–41; global city status, 323–24, 327–28, 343; immigration trends, 323–24; migrants in Outer Seoul, 338–40; population growth, 324–26; urban growth and development, 288–89

Singapore: Chinese immigrants, 192–93; Chineseness and identity issues, 194–200; Chinese transnational identities, 199–200; diaspora, 177–78; foreign-born statistics (2000), 181–83; foreign citizenship, 196–99; foreign students, 190–92; foreign workers, 184–90; global city status, 177; history of migration, 177–78n. 2, 178–81; *huaren* (Singaporean Chinese) 193; nonresident workforce, 182–84; P and Q Passes, 188–90; permanent residents, 180–82, 197; R-Passes, 185–87; Singapore Citizenship Act of 1957, 178; state policy impact on labor force, 11, 183, 185; transnational turnstiles, 200–201; work permits, 185–87; *zhongguroen* (Chinese nationals), 193–94, 199
social network theory, 346–47
sociocommerscapes, 20, 213–15
South Africa: deportations, 277; Immigration Act of 2002, 260; Refugees Act of 1997, 276; refugees, 262, 264–67, 271, 278
South African Migration Project, 260n. 1, 273
Southern African Development Community (SADC), 257, 270
South Korea: Chinese immigrants, 339–41; citizenship, 331; cosmopolitan culture, 323, 328, 343; gender distribution, 341–42; illegal migrant workers, 332, 335–36; immigration trends, 328–30; Korea's Employment Permit System, 336–37; Korea's Industrial Training System, 333–34, 337; labor migration, 332–35; restrictive immigration policies, 14, 331–32, 343
spatial assimilation, 19, 28, 212–13, 286
spatial segregation, 19
Sydney: anti-immigration, 94; Asian immigrants, 72–73; Chinese immigrants, 72; Chinese settlement, 78,

Sydney (*cont.*)
80; emergence as global city, 70, 84, 90–91; escalator effect, 9, 81–83; ethnic composition of immigrants, 71–73; foreign-born statistics, 69–73; housing prices, 89–90; immigrants in labor force, 91–92; immigration trends (2001), 68–71; internal migration, 84–87; isolated enclaves, 80–81; Long Stay Temporary Business Entrants, 76; nonpermanent migration, 75–76; outmigration, 82–84; population growth (1947–2001), 70; settlement patterns, 77–81, 95; spatial dispersal, 77; temporary labor migration, 76; United Kingdom foreign-born, 71; Vietnamese settlement, 78–79, 87; white flight, 88–89

Tel Aviv: Aid and Information Center for the Foreign Community, 315–16; Arabs 313, 319–20; foreign settlement patterns, 315, 317; foreign workers, 310–12, 315, 318; global city status, 301; immigrant statistics, 308–9; Old Central Bus Station, 315–16, 318; Palestinians, 310; Russian immigrants, 307, 314, 319–20

Tokyo, 4

Toronto: Asian immigrants, 100, 106; African immigrants, 100, 108; Caribbean immigrants, 100, 108; dispersed settlement patterns, 103, 107–8; dissimilarity index, 113–15; foreign-born statistics 2001, 28–29, 99–102; hyperdiversity, 99; immigrant employment and labor market, 9, 115–16, 117–18; immigrant enclaves, 105–6, 109–13; immigrant incomes, 121–22; immigrant unemployment rates, 120–21; labor market segmentation, 118–19; location of foreign-born, 104, 110; racial inequality, 122–25; segregation, 103–5; spatial assimilation model, 103; Toronto Region Immigrant Employment Council, 126

transnationalism, 347

transnational spaces, 287–88

United Kingdom immigration, 131–32

United States Immigration and Nationality Act, 17

United States immigration trends, 27

urban immigration policies, 18

urban-level data, 40nn. 3–4, 40–42

Vancouver, 38

Van Gogh, Theo, 150–52, 150n. 1

Vienna, 28

Washington, D.C.: African immigrants, 210–11, 212–14; Annandale Chamber of Commerce, 219–20; Asian immigrants, 209; Chinese immigrants, 210; El Salvadoran immigrants, 208; emerging gateway, 205; Ethiopians, 11, 207, 211–12, 216–17, 220–22, 225; ethnic composition, 207–9; European immigrants, 210; foreign-born statistics, 205–7; heterolocalism, 211; immigration trends since 1970, 205–8; Koreans, 11, 206, 212, 214–16, 218–20, 225; place identity, 224–25; Southeast Asian immigrants, 210; spatial assimilation model, 212–13

world-city hierarchy, 70, 177. *See also* global city status

world-city hypothesis, 5